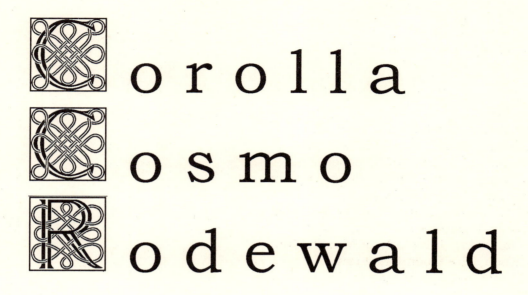

Corolla Cosmo Rodewald

Edited by Nicholas Sekunda

Cover designed by Nicholas Sekunda

Contributors:
Anthony Birley, Vindolanda Museum
John Briscoe, University of Manchester
John Davies, University of Liverpool
†John Graham, University of Pennsylvania
Nick Higham, University of Manchester
Stephen Hodkinson, University of Nottingham
Paul Holder, University of Manchester
Alastar Jackson, University of Manchester
Antony Keen, The Open University
Simon Northwood, University of Leiden
Victor Sayer
Robin Seager, University of Liverpool
Nicholas Sekunda, Gdańsk University
David Whitehead, Queens University, Belfast

Published and printed by the Foundation for the Development of Gdańsk University
for the Department of Archaeology Gdańsk University
Monograph Series Akanthina 2
Gdańsk 2007

ISBN 978-83-7531-060-3

AKANTHINA

The publishers would like to acknowledge the financial support of the C A Rodewald
Charitable Trust

CONTENTS

PREFACE

This collection of articles by colleagues, pupils and admirers of Cosmo Rodewald is intended as a gesture to honour the memory of a great man, a man who left his mark on many people he came into contact with, but a man of extreme modesty. Cosmo was such a modest and retiring person: searching for photographs of him became a major task, in which even a 1930s photograph of Cosmo hiding behind a newspaper ranks as a major find. I would like to thank the British School at Athens for permission to reproduce this photograph.

Many of Cosmo's former students work in academic, museum or archaeological posts: surely a tribute to the care Cosmo took with the students placed under his charge. I attempted to contact as many of these as possible, and I apologize to all those who would have liked to contribute but were not contacted. Many other pupils of Cosmo would have liked to contribute, if only time and the burdens of their position allowed. These include Paul Bennett, Elpida Hadjidaki, Bill Hanson and David Kennedy. I am very pleased Nick Higham was able to make a contribution dealing with the Roman Empire, in line with the recent concept that North Wales was the last part of the Roman Empire to fall to the barbarians, when it fell to the English under Edward I in 1282.

I am responsible for the statement in Victor Sayer's obituary of Cosmo for the *New College Record* 2002, 75-76 that 'His greatest sacrifice was to retire quietly to make way for a promising future student'. This was based on a misunderstanding of what took place in the mid 1970's and was in error. In fact it was David Whitehead who replaced Cosmo, not Steve Hodkinson, a former student of Cosmo's, who took up employment at Manchester later.

I would like to thank Alan Jones, of the Liverpool Philharmonic's Rodewald Society, for the family tree published in this volume which shows the connection between Cosmo and Alfred Rodewald. Alfred Rodewald was a Liverpool businessman and a friend and patron of Elgar. Alfred Rodewald founded the Rodewald Society, which, operating under the aegis of the Liverpool Philharmonic, organizes chamber music concerts. He is commemorated by the Rodewald Room in the Philharmonic Hall in Liverpool. Apart from the contributors to the biographical sections specifically named in the text, I would like to thank John Prag and Brian Pullan for their help concerning details of Cosmo's time at Manchester

It is a deep personal regret that, for a variety of reasons, I was not able to bring this volume out prior to the death of another of my teachers from my Manchester undergraduate days, John Graham, who was very anxious that it should appear before his death.

The front of this book is decorated with 'Green Bathers', painted by Keith Vaughn in 1952 and reproduced here through permission of the Whitworth Art Gallery, University of Manchester. This was Cosmo's favourite painting, and was hung in place of honour in the sitting-room above the fireplace. It will be remembered by countless former students of his who were entertained in 'Glen House'. The back is decorated with 'Charioteer' by John Golding, painted in 1960, which for many years decorated his office in the University, and will be remembered by many of his students, not least because not a few mistook it for a blackboard.

Nicholas Sekunda

Cosmo Rodewald 1915-2002

Anne Jeffery

John Ogilvie   Frank Stubbings   Oswald Dilke
Cosmo Rodewald
Arthur Beattie

Audrey Petty
Vronwy Fisher
(Reproduced with Permission of the British School at Athens)

NICHOLAS SEKUNDA, ALASTAR JACKSON

COSMO RODEWALD 1915-2002: A BRIEF BIOGRAPHY

The Rodewald family first rose to prominence in business and finance in Bremen in the eighteenth century. Members of the family had travelled to South and North America to trade, and later generations of the family settled in England and America. Cosmo's father, Carl Adolf Ferdinand, was born in Bremen in 1868 and died in London in 1953. His mother, his father's cousin Anna Fredrika, only child of Frederick Leo Rodewald of New York, was born in New Jersey in 1880 and died in Manchester in 1968. Cosmo himself was born on 17 August 1915 in New Jersey.

Following the divorce of his parents Cosmo came to settle in England together with his mother at the age of four. He went to school at Stowe. With the typically generous support of his maternal grandfather, Frederick Leo, in 1933 Cosmo entered on an academic career at Oxford as an undergraduate at New College. Although Leo was somewhat contemptuous of 'politicians and college professors', once he understood that Cosmo's ambition was to be a serious academic, he wished him well and gave him financial support as a young man. At Oxford, as elsewhere and later, he made and retained friends among leading individuals in intellectual and cultural life. Like many of his generation, growing up among the grim shadows of World War I, the Depression and the rise of fascist, racist and other dictators with imperialist ambitions, he always preferred the side of the oppressed and exploited. Although his sympathy with communism, fashionable in many circles at the time, was short lived, compassion and generosity for the less fortunate stayed with him thereafter. Cosmo finished his undergraduate studies with a First in Greats (Classics).

He went out as a student of the British School at Athens 1938-9 where he carried out research on the Greek colonies on the Black Sea coasts of Bulgaria and Rumania. His career was long interrupted by the Second World War. He performed his National Service (1940-1946) in the Non-Combatant Corps, which his principles had led him to join. Following a short term of teaching at Nottingham, Cosmo started to work for the Department of History of the University of Manchester on 25 December 1947. An appointment on Boxing Day would have been more appropriate for one who would prove such a generous benefactor of the University in later years. His long and devoted service at Manchester, his kindness and his hospitality there are noted elsewhere in this volume, as is his equally generous employment of his inherited wealth in benefactions (many anonymous) to cultural, educational and humane institutions and charities in and beyond Manchester and Great Britain.

Cosmo was distinguished by his gentlemanly patience and kindliness in trying to explain the complex political developments in his chosen period to his students. However he was best remembered by his students for his hospitality. The dinner parties Cosmo held for his students played a key role in their development as undergraduates, not to mention as human beings. These were hosted in his beautiful residence 'Glen House' on Platt Lane. Cosmo was an exotic figure to many of his colleagues in Manchester, mostly family men with two children, a mortgage and a semi-detached house in one of the leafy suburbs of Manchester. Teaching was Cosmo's greatest love but he closely followed the arts, and particularly music, in Manchester. Cosmo loved Manchester with its rich cultural heritage left over by the intellectuals and benefactors who had enriched the city during the nineteenth century.

Frederick Leo, Cosmo's grandfather already mentioned above, had amassed a fortune on the American Stock Exchange during the late nineteenth century. He had been a member of the board of the New York Stock Exchange. Foreseeing the imminent 1929 stock market crash, Leo amazed everyone by selling all his shares except for General Electric, and thereby avoided the financial disaster that ruined thousands. With his fortune intact, Leo set up a number of trusts for members of the family. Cosmo ultimately inherited this wealth in the form of the Rodewald Fund. Cosmo decided to utilize these funds to support the institutions and activities he loved. His most significant donation to the British School at Athens was the re-financing of the Macmillan Studentship. Many individuals currently working in the research areas in which the School is engaged have benefited from this generous endowment. However Cosmo preferred to donate anonymously. We shall never know how many benefited from his support. His philanthropy was not limited to the activities of the School and its members however. Many individuals and institutions engaged in the arts also received his financial support. He was particularly interested in the development of cultural life in Manchester. All this assistance, like his dedication to teaching, was of very great value, not least once government finance for universities and the cultural institutions he supported began to be reduced in the 1970s.

Cosmo's main academic interests lay in Athenian Democracy and the Peloponnesian War. He served as a regular reviewer for the *Journal of Hellenic Studies*, from 1959 to 1977, but his passion was teaching: helping his students to understand the Ancient World and in the process to become full citizens of the modern world. Cosmo genuinely cared about his students, which only started to be appreciated in the 1960s, particularly at Manchester, where the university was very much oriented towards research. Indeed the excellence of Cosmo's pastoral work played a crucial role in his belated promotion to Senior Lecturer. Promotion was a very contentious issue in the 1960s and 1970s, when the academics' professional union, the AUT, was arguing that it depended far too heavily on published research and not enough on evidence of distinction in teaching, administrative achievement, and other qualities. Cosmo's promotion was something of a problem, because for a long time he published very little.

His long years of teaching and research, despite a heavy administrative burden, eventually bore fruit in the form of his first book, *Democracy: Ideas and Realities*, published by Dent in 1974 and again in 1975. This book was designed to improve the availability of teaching aids to both students and teachers: it was one of the first collections of sources in translation to appear during the years of university expansion. In the early 1970s Manchester was perhaps the only English University in which courses in ancient history were being taken by a considerable number of students each year within a School of History. Elsewhere there was very little serious undergraduate study of ancient history outside the framework of a Classics syllabus. Cosmo's ongoing dialogue with historians, colleagues and students alike, convinced him that such a work was necessary for the development of ancient history as a separate subject of study outside the framework of Classics. Cosmo was the first academic to contribute to the History Department's own magazine, *The Clarion*, (whose motto was 'Backwards and forwards with the People'), and his contribution was entitled 'Does ancient history frustrate you?'

The appearance of this first book resulted in Cosmo's promotion to Senior Lecturer. Cosmo was also interested in numismatics. The next year saw the appearance of his last book, *Money in the Age of Tiberius*, published by Manchester University Press, which dealt with the Roman monetary crisis of AD 33. This was not, however, to be his last written work.

At least until the early 1970s Manchester was a very hierarchical university, in which professors, in theory and sometimes in practice, had absolute power within their departments, and very little formal obligation to consult their staff about the decisions they had made. In 1973 the revised charter, approved at last by the Privy Council, left ultimate authority in the hands of the professors, but established departmental boards consisting of all of the academic staff, and effectively imposed a duty to consult. Potentially, the chairman of the board could act as a kind of tribune of the people, who, if things were not handled tactfully, might become the opponent of the professors. In 1975 Cosmo was elected as chairman of the board by just one vote, partly as a fitting gesture to honour Cosmo on the eve of his retirement, but mainly because he was held in great affection and was widely respected by his colleagues: a man who could be trusted to avoid unnecessary confrontation. At the end of the year the historians held a party, to which Cosmo contributed the strawberries, having risen at some ungodly hour to buy them in the Manchester markets.

Cosmo retired early, on 30 September 1976, though during a colleague's sudden and serious illness in November and December 1978 he generously returned to fill the temporary gap in teaching. After retirement Cosmo devoted most of his time to another great love, his gardens in Manchester and in his second home in Lewes. In both these places his patience and skill as a gardener, not unlike the qualities seen in his work as an educator and philanthropist, were admired by the many who appreciated his efforts and tastes. *Cela est bien dit, répondit Candide, mais il faut cultiver notre jardin.* Less happily his eyesight declined and limited his reading, though eventually an operation brought some improvement. However, following a fall in late summer 2002 Cosmo was confined to hospital in Brighton and Lewes where his health declined. He managed to return to Manchester, though not unfortunately to his beloved Glen House. He died of pneumonia on 4 November 2002, following a second operation. During Cosmo's final years his life-long partner Victor Sayer continued to do everything possible to improve his comfort and the quality of his life.

Cosmo's donations on display in the Whitworth Art Gallery, viewed through John Milne's "Gnathos"

Cosmo and Victor on holiday in New Orleans

ALASTAR JACKSON

COSMO RODEWALD AT MANCHESTER UNIVERSITY 1947-1976

The selfless generosity that Cosmo Rodewald repeatedly displayed towards the British School at Athens among numerous other institutions was also conspicuous in many forms while he served at the University of Manchester. The traditions that produced him made him a kind of university teacher now not so common in Britain.

After service as a conscientious objector in the Non-combatant Corps from 1940-1946 he became an Assistant Lecturer in the Department of History at Manchester University in late 1947. At that time, as later, this was a leading history department, but it had been and remained until the late 1960s, dominated by powerful professors. Undergraduates were widely regarded in it, even by some whom one would have expected to think differently, as a very humble form of life. Cosmo Rodewald's view of students, formed by his own education, experience and magnanimity, was in marked contrast. He gladly recognised all his students of every sort - not only those to whom he was personal tutor - as human beings and welcome friends. This in turn won him the respect and friendship of the vast majority of his students. They appreciated his patience and clarity in explaining the complex developments in his many fields of interest: the working and rivalries of democratic Athens and of her Spartan enemies, the rise of Macedon, the age of Augustus and citizenship in ancient states. Through helping his students to understand the ancient world he helped them to develop as full citizens of the modern world. But he never indulged students or lowered his standards, least of all in the way some universities have either chosen or been forced to do after his day. Late essays were efficiently extracted by steely charm rather than by the hectoring some preferred to indulge in, and his marks were always fair.

His hospitality to students and colleagues was lavish, especially once he had moved to his large and pleasant house and garden in Rusholme. Particularly valuable were his parties for Freshers and staff each Registration Week, for they helped to break the ice that could sometimes separate students from one another and from staff. He knew well that many problems could be forestalled or, once developed, could prove soluble in alcohol aided by excellent food and friendly treatment. Devoted and skilful as a personal tutor, sagacious and tactful as a person, he could normally guide students through their good and bad times alike. His modesty, sense of justice and strong belief in the intellectual quality he found in some students and fostered in others were conspicuous and not shared by all his colleagues. The stutter that sometimes afflicted him while lecturing to large audiences sprang in part from this modesty and an element of shyness in his character, but the high quality that most students could clearly see in his teaching helped him and them to overcome this minor handicap. For Cosmo Rodewald always put into his teaching, into keeping up with his subject and (when he had time for it) into his numismatic research, work of a very high standard which some others reserved only for their research and related publication. He always, long before questionnaires for students about their teachers were ever dreamed of, gave his students full measure, and never cut his classes short (as some did) so as to spend more time on his research. Like many of the university teachers he had been taught by, he did not put his own publication and promotion as far above teaching and tutorial care as many university teachers are under pressure to do today. Likewise he performed the administrative chores that Manchester University imposed on its academic staff, very industriously. He systematically ordered countless new books for the University and Departmental libraries and helped to reform the procedures for admitting students to his department, making all stages more efficient and humane. When his professor of many years became heavily burdened with the higher administration of the University, Cosmo cheerfully performed many of the departmental chores passed on to him in addition to his own.

All this did not sour him. The reason he only greeted colleagues at the first encounter of the day and seemed to ignore them at later ones was simply a reticent wish not to distract them, and not because he had taken umbrage at some unintended offence. Young recruits to the History Department staff, reared in a more competitive and suspicious age and therefore used to making and receiving reassuringly friendly signals at every encounter, soon learned not to take alarm at this old-fashioned courtesy. Again while some of his colleagues would brag over the coffee cups about their own wealth, their splendid material possessions, their exalted contacts or their wide acquaintance with foreign languages, Cosmo never sought to compete with them even though he had all these himself, sometimes in greater measure. Nor at or above departmental level did he collaborate in unjust schemes for any individual's or group's advancement or removal or for the arbitrary domination of any faction however exalted and influential. On the contrary, he ably helped his professor to defeat the ambitions entertained by some outside the History Department to detach Ancient History staff from serious historical study and teaching and reduce them to supplying mere chronological wallpaper for other subjects. Though in recent years Ancient History at Manchester has indeed been brigaded with Classics, its academic role is in no way diminished, thanks not least to Cosmo's past defence of it as well as to the principles of present Classicists. Elected Chairman of the History Department in his last year, he always sought reasonable compromise instead of conflict, although (given its fratricidal rivalries) his defeated opponent's allies did not make his job at all easy.

Cosmo Rodewald came deepest into controversy and misunderstanding during the student troubles of 1968 to the early 1970s. Naturally he had some sympathy with the young rebels among students and staff, though not with the injustices and illegalities they perpetrated (nor with those of their more august opponents). He, like many staff, supported demands for fair student representation on the History Board and for a staff-student consultative committee. To many others this proposed committee seemed a diabolical engine of leftist tyranny aimed, so they feared, at giving Cosmo Rodewald and other supposedly terrifying radicals supreme power through student stooges. And it is true that even Cosmo once openly likened the proposed reforms and the committee to the activities of Ephialtes and to the Council of Four Hundred in ancient Athens – a comparison deeply menacing in the view of some suspicious colleagues. But reasonable reform eventually averted revolution at Manchester as elsewhere and peace broke out again. Many revolutionaries left, to ripen into despots themselves, in a not unprecedented manner, some enlightened and competent, others less so. The little committee Cosmo supported, in fact, normally promoted helpful dialogue.

Meanwhile Cosmo continued to give much help to students and postgraduates. During the course of his career he helped to train some who were very able indeed and became leading experts in, for example, Ancient Sparta, in ancient warfare and in modern popular reform movements. But he was not élitist and attended equally to all whose enthusiasm he helped to arouse whatever their academic potential.

Finally his professor retired early and the appointment of a younger, energetic and productive successor (picked largely through Cosmo's good offices on the Appointing Committee) relieved Cosmo of much of the administrative burden. Now at last he could allow himself to prove that he merited promotion to Senior Lecturer by publishing his two admirable books. *Democracy: Ideas and Realities* (1974 and 1975) was one of the first books illustrating an important theme with translated extracts from sources. Such books were then and are still very useful in a time when Greek and Latin are less and less widely taught in schools and universities. His *Money in the Age of Tiberius* (1976) ingeniously analyses a complex financial crisis of AD 33. These valuable contributions made and with his subject set fair to flourish at Manchester, he took an honourable early retirement. Unfortunately, declining eyesight prevented him from completing and publishing all his research. However his generosity continued, for example in his support for his former students' careers and in the gifts he made to other libraries from his own.

All who valued Cosmo Rodewald as teacher, educator, tutor or colleague look back on his long contribution to the History Department and to the University of Manchester with the same warm gratitude as that felt by all friends of the British School at Athens and of the many other institutions to which he proved so generous.

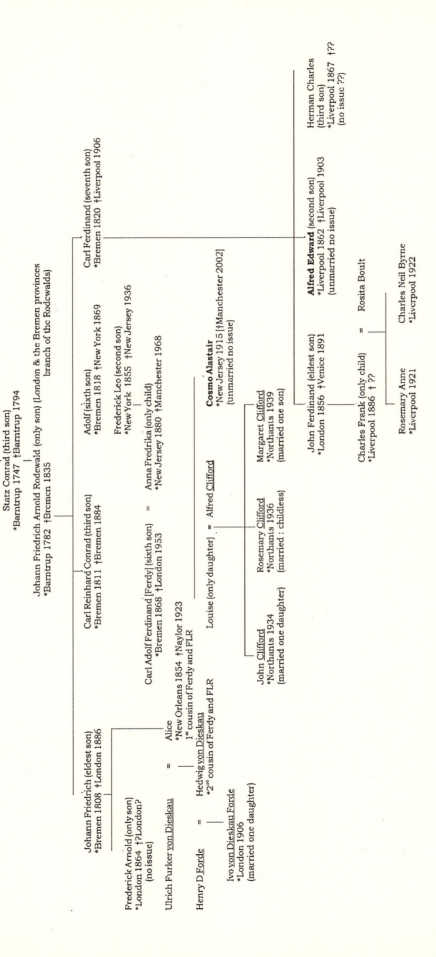

Statz Caspar Rohdewald (our earliest certain ancestor) *Selbeck (Lippe) 1659 †Barntrup (Lippe) 1719

Friederich Carl (only son) *Barntrup 1700 †Barntrup 1775

Statz Conrad (third son) *Barntrup 1747 †Barntrup 1794

Johann Friedrich Arnold Rodewald (only son) (London & the Bremen provinces branch of the Rodewalds) *Barntrup 1782 †Bremen 1835

Carl Reinhard Conrad (third son) *Bremen 1811 †Bremen 1884

Carl Ferdinand (seventh son) *Bremen 1820 †Liverpool 1906

Adolf (sixth son) *Bremen 1818 †New York 1869

Frederick Leo (second son) *New York 1855 †New Jersey 1936

Carl Adolf Ferdinand [Ferdy] (sixth son) *Bremen 1868 †London 1953 = Anna Fredrika (only child) *New Jersey 1880 †Manchester 1968

Cosmo Alastair *New Jersey 1915 [†Manchester 2002] (unmarried no issue)

Johann Friedrich (eldest son) *Bremen 1808 †London 1886

Frederick Arnold (only son) *London 1864 †?London? (no issue)

Ulrich Furker von Dieskau = Alice *New Orleans 1854 †Naylor 1923 1st cousin of Ferdy and FLR

Henry D Forde = Hedwig von Dieskau *2nd cousin of Ferdy and FLR

Ivo von Dieskau Forde *London 1906 (married one daughter)

Louise (only daughter) = Alfred Clifford

John Clifford *Northants 1934 (married one daughter)

Rosemary Clifford *Northants 1936 (married : childless)

Margaret Clifford *Northants 1939 (married one son)

John Ferdinand (eldest son) *London 1856 †Venice 1891

Alfred Edward (second son) *Liverpool 1862 †Liverpool 1903 (unmarried no issue)

Herman Charles (third son) *Liverpool 1867 †?? (no issue ??)

Charles Frank (only child) *Liverpool 1886 † ?? = Rosita Boult

Rosemary Anne *Liverpool 1921

Charles Neil Byrne *Liverpool 1922

Source: Manuscript of the late Cosmo Alastair Rodewald in the possession of his partner, Victor Sayer [AJ 18.12.04]

VICTOR SAYER, NICHOLAS SEKUNDA

COSMO RODEWALD'S PHILANTHROPY

The main purpose of this volume has been to celebrate Cosmo's contribution to academic life. Nevertheless an attempt is here made to compile an account of his charitable work, principally made in support of the arts. Cosmo's self-effacing modesty led him to despise 'conspicuous consumption', extravagance and personal display. It is likely that he would not have approved of the recognition being paid here to his charitable endeavours since he would have thought it only the most natural thing for a man in his position to do. Because he made so many contributions, often anonymously, it has been very difficult to ascertain the extent or range of his benefactors. The C.A. Rodewald Charitable Settlement continues to fund a variety of such bodies.

It has proved impossible to assemble a complete list of organizations which he helped with his charitable trust or from other funding. The main recipients of his support in the world of the Arts are, however, listed below:

The Buxton Festival Society
Welsh National Opera
Opera North
The Northern Chamber Orchestra
The Friends of the Royal Exchange Theatre, Manchester
The Hallé Concert Society
The Palace Theatre, Manchester
The Octagon Theatre Bolton
The Friends of Manchester City Art Galleries
The Penwith Society of Arts.

The Educational Bodies he supported included:

Writers and Scholars Educational Trust
New College Oxford
Koestler Award Trust
Society for the Protection of Science and Learning
The British School at Athens.

Finally he also supported organizations involved in propagating social justice, including among others:

Anti-Slavery International
Survival
Prisoners Abroad
Turning Point
Northern Refugee Centre
Minority Rights Group

The Salvation Army
Institute for the Study of Drug Dependence
Prison Reform Trust
Prisoners of Conscience Fund
Manchester Settlement
Civil Liberties Trust
Medical Foundation for the Care of Victims of Torture.

It has been possible to obtain more definite information about Cosmo's interest in, and support for, a number of specific organizations, which are detailed below.

The Department of Music at The University of Manchester

Cosmo was a regular attender at the Lindsay Evening Concerts organized by the Department of Music of the University of Manchester, and regularly supported the Department by offering small grants to enable The Lindsays to bring in extra players, such as a second viola for quintets. Professor John Casken, composer and Professor of Music at Manchester University, has written as follows:

'I first met Cosmo Rodewald shortly after I joined the Department of Music at The University of Manchester in 1992. He was a regular supporter of University Concerts, in particular those given by The Lindsays, or as they used to be known, The Lindsay String Quartet. He loved these occasions, and always chose to sit in his favoured seat towards the back of the old concert hall in the converted cinema in Denmark Road that was the home of the Manchester Music Department for many years. I remember him in those concerts, in deep concentration, entranced by the music of Mozart or Hayden, Beethoven, Tippett or Bartók, music that The Lindsays play with unmatchable beauty and intensity. Cosmo told me on more than one occasion how much he valued the range of all our concerts, and he made an especially important contribution the The Lindsay's programmes by enabling us, through his typical generosity, to engage additional players so that we could enjoy the larger chamber orchestra repertoire, such as the Brahms Clarinet Quintet, the great Schubert Quintet, or even the Octet. This gesture of Cosmo's had an enormous impact on our concerts, but it was one for which he was adamant that he neither wanted, nor sought, any kind of recognition. Even the invitations to join The Lindsays for coffee in the interval were met with a quiet "no thank you", which came not so much as a refusal, but as an expression of his natural modesty.

I also remember seeing Cosmo on a number of occasions at the Huddersfield Contemporary Music festival as a keen and interested member of the audience. To make the journey across the Pennines on those cold and wet November days says much about his interest in the contemporary arts, about his support for today's creative artists, and the range of his tastes. He was present at a performance of one of my own works at the Festival, not saying much afterwards, but showing in his face that he had listened deeply and appreciatively.

It is a source of considerable regret that Cosmo never saw the fruits of his greatest act of generosity to the University Music Department. He had arranged for a considerable bequest to be left to support Music's activities, and as the plans for our new building at the heart of the university campus progressed, we looked forward to being able to show him around our new premises. Sadly, he never saw the building finished, nor the splendid new concert hall that we named after him in recognition of his considerable generosity. I know that he admired the acoustics of the hall of the old cinema, and we were especially careful to make sure that the new hall was at least as good as the old one. I'm sure that Cosmo would have approved of the new space, its bright sound, its striking appearance, its welcoming atmosphere. It exists as a fitting tribute to the man who seemed content to know that he had helped others in the performance or enjoyment of music, content that his gift was seen but unannounced.'

The 'Cosmo Rodewald Concert Hall', along with the other new premises for Music and Drama, was officially opened on 21 October 2003. Music and Drama at Manchester had had to wait more than thirty years for these up-to-date premises which Cosmo helped to fund. Their request for a new building was almost at the head of the queue in 1973 when government cuts in public spending made it almost impossible for the University to undertake large capital projects. *This Week Next Week*, the University's magazine, says in its issue for 20 October 2003: 'The spectacular 350-seat concert hall, capable of staging full orchestral performances, is named after Cosmo Rodewald (1915-2002), a former Senior Lecturer in History who retired in 1976 and whose inherited wealth was put to many good causes, including the University'.

The Whitworth Art Gallery

Cosmo was also very interested in the Whitworth Art Gallery, Manchester University, and was a supporter of the Friends of the Gallery. Alistair Smith, who has just retired as Director of the Gallery, describes his experiences of Cosmo in the following words:

'As I write, there are on display at the Whitworth a number of works of art which belonged to Cosmo Rodewald. They were created by some artists of considerable repute – Paul Klee, Ben Nicholson and William Scott among them – and by others lesser known whose merit was nevertheless recognized by Cosmo – for example, John McLean, John Milne and Oleg Kudryashov.

In his modesty, Cosmo denied that the works which decorated his homes could aspire to the status of a 'collection', equally insisting that he was no 'collector'. He described them, in the main, as 'works by friends', acquired unsystematically, almost through whim, certainly with no thought that they might one day assume the status of 'museum objects', thereby reflecting a facet of the history of art for generations to come.

It was in the 1960s that I was first introduced to Cosmo and alerted to his quiet passion for contemporary art. That introduction took place at one of Francis Hawcroft's parties, given at his flat opposite Owens Park Student Village. Only recently graduated from the Courtauld Institute and even more recently appointed to my post as Assistant Keeper at the Whitworth, I was dazzled by these occasions. Never before had I been party to such gatherings of theatre people, musicians and artists, well-spoken and well-heeled, discoursing amusingly against the backdrop of equally civilized paintings, framed in gold on dark green tapestry. Cosmo hovered quietly on the periphery of the group, never drawing attention to himself, and it was not from himself that I learned of his collection, but from Francis.

What that 'non-collection' eventually comprised began to become apparent only on return to Manchester in 1990, after an absence of twenty years. Meeting Cosmo again, with Victor, I found him confiding that he had, in Sussex, a work by Ian McKeever ('too big for our house in Platt Lane') and by John McLean. The McKeever, a no-holds-barred contest between photography and painting masquerading as a landscape diptych, is now on display close to the entrance of the Cosmo Rodewald Concert Hall. Sweet Briar by John McLean hangs in the Pilkington Room at the Whitworth. McLean, a fellow student of mine, can no longer greet me with his habitual complaint 'Why have you not got any of my work at the Whitworth?'.

It was also in 1990, now as Director of the Whitworth and with directorial budgetary responsibilities, that I came to know of the Cosmo Rodewald Fund, dedicated to the purchase of modern art, which Cosmo had endowed, and which Victor now maintains through the aegis of the Friends of the Whitworth.

Meeting Cosmo intermittently, mainly at Friend's events and at Lindsay Concerts, I came to know that Cosmo's sight was deteriorating, and that, through this enforced visual detachment from the collection, he was hatching plans for its eventual relinquishment. In summer 2000 he wrote. Would I care to come to tea and discuss the fate of the non-collection? Many of what he described as his 'non-collection'. My colleague Mary Griffiths and I spent a couple of magical hours at the house in Platt Lane, first sipping tea in a sitting room of just the right blue to contain the range of colour around the walls. And was there colour! Keith Vaughan's Green Bathers hung in the iconic position on the fireplace wall, Terry Frost's Blue, Red, Black nearby with Brian Wynter's Earth's Riches – 'una discordanza accordatissima'.

Victor led us upstairs where already the bookshelves were emptying through Cosmo's donations to libraries. Here, perhaps most unexpected of all, unceremoniously set in a corner of the first floor over Platt Lane, was Paul Klee's Celestial Body above the Cabin, poetic, playful, humane, and, above all, for 1937, modern. Cosmo explained that, when the time came, he wanted the Whitworth to have the choice of works from the non-collection; and in due course, through Victor, this came to pass.

Victor said 'Cosmo always thought that he should use his wealth for the benefit of those less fortunate'. Cosmo's gifts to the general public, through the Whitworth and its Friends, include not only his Modern Art Fund and the works from his collection, but a financial endowment which will continue to serve the cause of modern art. However, no gallery could hope to reproduce the inspired intimacy and visual provocation of that sitting room on Platt Lane. That is for memory to preserve.'

Cosmo had previously given a Hepworth to the Whitworth on permanent loan, but on his death the Gallery benefited from a major donation. The Works of Art bequeathed to the Whitworth Art Gallery, Manchester University, by Cosmo Rodewald in 2003 comprise the following items:

Sculptures:

Henry Moore (1898-1986): *Upright Motive: maquette no. 12*; bronze with brown patina; signed and numbered 9/9; 32 cm high, 8 cm wide.

Alison Wilding: *Well*, dated 1985; leaded steel, limewood paint; 40 cm high, 29 cm wide, 14 cm deep.

John Milne (1931-1978): untitled (wall hanging); cold cast bronze with green patina; signed with initials, dated 1974 and numbered 3/6 on verso; 29cm x 22.5 cm.

John Milne (1931-1978): *Gnathos*; woodcarving – Nigerian Guarea; 61cm high, 86cm wide. The copy of *Gnathos* donated to the Whitworth Art Gallery is the original wood carving. The wood for this carving, Nigerian Guarea, was a gift from Barbara Hepworth.

Paintings, Drawings etc.

Paul Klee (1879-1940): *Gestirn über die Hütte*; watercolour on paper; inscribed and dated 1937 on section of original mount, verso; 18cm x 28cm.

Keith Vaughan (1912-1977): *Green Bathers*; oil on canvas; signed and dated 1952; 90cm x 69cm.

Marino Marini (1901-1980): *Garçon aux deux Chevaux*; pen and ink on coloured paper; 36cm x 25cm.

Ben Nicholson (1894-1982): *Rooftops*: etching; signed and dated 1962, numbered 40/50; 17cm x 27cm.

Peter Lanyon (1918-1964): *Black Oval Texas*: 1963, gouache on paper; 24cm x 35cm.

Brian Wynter (1915-1975): *Earth's Riches*: oil on canvas; signed, inscribed and dated 1958 on verso; 91cm x 61cm.

William Scott (1913-1989): *White Linen*: watercolour and gouache on paper; 50cm x 61cm.

Tony O'Malley (born 1913): *Irish Interior*: mixed media on paper; signed, inscribed and dated Dec 1962; 49cm x 75cm.

Sir Terry Frost RA (born 1915): *Blue, Red and Black*; oil on canvas; gilt and canvas frame; circa 1955; 74cm x 62 cm.

Wilhemina Barnes-Graham: *Black and White Oblongs in Ovals*: mixed media on paper; signed and dated 1962, inscribed with title and further dated on fragment of backing board verso.

Wilhemena Barnes-Graham: *Whangie*: mixed media on board; signed and dated 1979; mounted, framed and glazed; 27cm x 20cm.

John McLean (born 1939): *Sweet Briar*: oil on canvas; signed and inscribed on verso; 197cm x 146 cm.

Ian McKeever (born 1946): untitled; acrylic on photographic base; a set of two forming a diptych; 150cm x 103cm.

John Golding: untitled; watercolour on paper; signed and dated 1987; 69cm x 104cm.

Oleg Kudryaschov (born 1932); untitled; drypoint and watercolour; signed and dated 1992, number 1/1, plate no. 2266; 71cm x 104 cm.

John G. Walker (born 1939); untitled; screenprint and collage; signed and dated 1963-73, numbered 9/18; 139cm x 102cm.

The Penwith Society of Arts

The Penwith Gallery in St Ives over many years has shown work by all the town's leading artists such as Hepworth and Nicholson and others for which St Ives is world famous and which ultimately led to the building of the Tate Gallery in St Ives. Through visiting the Penwith Gallery Cosmo came into contact with many local artists whose work found its way to his home in Manchester. The sculptor John Milne, for whom Cosmo was a patron throughout his life, was an influential member of the Penwith Committee. Milne's imposing polished bronze *Gnathos*, a gift from Cosmo to the Tate, has been on prominent display at the Tate since it opened. Substantial funding came from the C.A. Rodewald First and Second Settlements, when some of the capital of the Settlements was disposed of following the death of John Milne in 1978. Further funding will be released when the Settlements are wound up in the future. The income generated from these investments is used for the maintenance and repair work on the Gallery and studios which the Society own. Cosmo loved the 'Penwith', visited St Ives regularly, and supported the Society in many ways.

New College, Oxford

New College remained in great affection in the later year's of Cosmo's life, and was the object of his charitable philanthropy. Following Cosmo's death in 2003 New College received 40% of his residual Estate, which was a sum in the region of £700,000. The Bursar, David Palfreyman, has kindly written the following words:

> 'Cosmo Rodewald, an Old Member of New College, left College a substantial and extremely generous Legacy. Mr Rodewald did not choose to restrict College in the way in which it can deploy either the capital itself or the income arising from it, but the New College Governing Body has decided that for the foreseeable future some of the income will be used to finance a part-time academic post, the Lecturer in Greek and Latin. This post is supplementary to the established teaching force for Classics and is used to assist students in progressing with their competence in Greek and Latin where they have not hitherto had adequate school preparation. The necessity for this post becomes even greater as we admit more students who have not before studied Greek, and, less commonly, Latin. The post is now known as 'The Rodewald Lecturer in the Classical Languages'.

In addition, also for the foreseeable future, the Governing Body has resolved that the income arising from the capital, which for the moment is to be held as if it were permanent endowment, should be used to ensure that College can sustain its teaching in the Humanities when, arising from difficult financial circumstances, the University imposes a delay of a couple of years in replacing its share of an academic post that has become vacant upon the retirement of the holder of the joint College/University appointment. Thus, because of Cosmo Rodewald's kindness towards the College it will be possible for us normally to proceed immediately to make a joint appointment with the College itself, using income from the Rodewald Legacy, paying the University share of the salary. It is likely, therefore, that over the years the Rodewald Legacy will be used to support academic activity in such subjects as Philosophy, History, English, Modern Languages, and, if such vacancies arise, also in Classics.

The Warden and Fellows of New College, Oxford, are extremely grateful to Cosmo Rodewald for providing such extensive financial support to College and for giving us this important flexibility in being able to sustain our continuity of teaching in these key subject areas.

The Warden and Fellows would wish to take this opportunity to thank all the contributors to this collection of essays, which makes a fitting academic memorial to Cosmo Rodewald's intellectual interests and professional endeavours over a lifetime'.

ANTONY KEEN, NICHOLAS SEKUNDA

XENOPHON THE RHETOR

The authorship of the *Athenaion Politeia*, attributed to Xenophon, has long been a subject of debate among students of antiquity. Crucial to any discussion of the authorship of the work is the date of its composition. We therefore turn to this question first.

The Date of Composition of the *Athenaion Politeia*

Gigante (1953, 51-5) cites the wide spectrum of speculation as to the date of composition more than half a century ago. Bowersock (1966, 38) has suggested that the work could be put as early as 443, if the lack of mention of the Samian Revolt of 441/0 at 3.11 necessarily entails a prior date, although Marr (1983, 46-7) has argued against any such necessity. Gomme (1940, 245) put the work at 420-414, and Fontana (1968, 31-80) at 410-406. A fourth-century date was first suggested by Bélot (1880), and more recently by Hornblower (1996, 2000), who believes the fifth-century internal references set out a dramatic date for the work, although the work is a literary exercise of the fourth century.

Despite the wide disparity of attributed dates, however, the general consensus, on the grounds of both content and literary style (see Dihle 1994, 152), is that the pamphlet cannot have been written after the end of the Peloponnesian War. Marr (1983, 45-6) argues against 2.24 entailing a date before the outbreak of the Peloponnesian War. Very few modern scholars would accept a date prior to 431. This orthodox position, supported by Gomme and Fontana as already cited above, has been advocated, to quote but a few examples, by Lewis (1969), Connor (1971), de Ste. Croix (1972, 308-9) and Hansen (1991, 5). The key to this interpretation lies in the statement given at 2.16, that 'they allow the land of Attica to be devastated' (τὴν... 'Αττικὴν γῆν περιορῶσι τεμνομένην), which implies that at least the first Peloponnesian invasion of 431 has occurred (De Ste. Croix 1972, 308-9). That the author of the *Ath. Pol.* means more than simply that the Athenians accepted these events, as implied in Pericles' speech in Thucydides 1.143.5, is demonstrated by de Ste. Croix 1972, 309, who draws attention to the uses of the present tense.

Further precision of the date of composition is less certain, though both Forrest (1970, 114) and more recently Mattingley (1997) have argued that a date after 425, when, following the decree of Thudippus (perhaps at the instigation of Cleon), the Panathenaic reassessment was very rigidly adhered to, is preferable on account of 3.5: 'I have mentioned the most important matters, except the assessment on the tribute; this happens for the most part every four years' (τὸ δὲ μέγιστον εἴρηται πλὴν αἱ τάξεις τοῦ φόρου· τοῦτο δὲ γίγνεται ὡς τὰ πολλὰ δι' ἔτους πέμπτου).

Both Hemmerdinger (1975, 74) and more recently Sommerstein (1996) have seen the remark at *Ath. Pol.* 2.18 that the Athenians do not allow the *demos* to be attacked in comedy as a reference to the threatened persecution of Aristophanes over the *Babylonians* (Ar. Ach. 377-382, 502-503, 630-631), a work which was produced in 426. Not all would agree with this argument. So much for attempts to find a *terminus post quem*.

Conversely, the work was almost certainly not written after the late summer of 424, if it is correct to see the report of the impossibility of moving troops over long distances overland (2.5) as being something that could not have been written after the expedition of Brasidas. This seems to have been pointed out first by Roscher (1842, 529; cf. Roscalla 1995, 105-6), and has afterwards been accepted by most scholars dealing with this question (Gomme 1962, 50). Gomme (1940, 224-5) and de Ste. Croix (1972, 309) both see the statement as a general rule that remained broadly true despite the occasional exception, but on the contrary the *Ath. Pol.* certainly presents the statement as if it were a fixed law that admits no exception. Others (eg. Bowersock, 1966, 33; Hemmerdinger 1975, 74) maintain the statement at 2.18 that attacks on the *demos* are not tolerated indicates that the work must have been written before the production of Aristophanes *Knights* in 424, though this is less certainly the case.

Therefore the general consensus of current opinion follows Forrest (1970), who would place the composition of the work between the winter of 425 and the late summer of 424. We agree with this dating for reasons which will become clear later on.

The False Attribution to Xenophon son of Gryllos

Diogenes Laertius (2.55), who probably wrote in the third century AD (Long & Sharples 1996) says that Xenophon's *floruit* was c. 401-400, a statement which is possibly derived from Apollodorus (cf. *FGrH* 244 F 343). Eusebius and the Suda (Ξ 47 *s.v.* Ξενοφῶν, Γρύλου) place it a year later. If one were to assume these sources meant that Xenophon was in his fortieth year around 401/0 then this would give a birthdate of 441/0 (which would still make him precocious even at the latest date for the *Ath. Pol.*). But such a calculation should not be made: Diogenes and the others have simply placed Xenophon's *floruit* at the most famous event in his life, his leadership of the Ten Thousand (cf. Xen. *An.* 3.1.25: ἀκμάζει ἡγοῦμαι). Xenophon himself says that he was quite young at this point (*An.* 3.1.25, 3.2.37), the youngest of the newly-elected generals, and by implication younger than his friend Proxenos, who was thirty (*An.* 2.6.20; see Breitenbach 1967). Athenaeus (216d) has Masurius say that Xenophon was either not born or in his infancy at the dramatic date of the *Symposium* (422). In fact the famous Xenophon son of Gryllos (*PA* 11307 = *LGPN* Ξενοφῶν 22) was probably born around 430 (Tuplin 1996). Thus Hemmerdinger (1975, 74) calculates that in 424 Xenophon would have been only seven years old.

It should be stated that this interpretation of Xenophon's own evidence has been disputed by Falappone (1979), and that a small number of scholars from Bélot (1880) to Fontana (1968, 100-102) have argued that the pamphlet was written by Xenophon son of Gryllos. Nevertheless it seems certain that the pamphlet could not have been written by the famous Xenophon, as it would have been written in the latter's childhood (eg. Anderson 1974, 41-2). Gomme (1940, 228 n. 4; cf. Bowersock 1968) sought to argue his way out of these chronological difficulties by suggesting that the *Athenaion Politeia* may have been discovered among the papers of Xenophon son of Gryllos, presumably following his death, and in this way became falsely attributed to the possessor rather than the author. This is an attractive suggestion but most unlikely. Consequntly the author is generally referred to as the 'Old Oligarch', a term seemingly first given to the author by Gilbert Murray (1898).

Given that the pamphlet cannot have been written by Xenophon son of Gryllos, a number of scholars have felt themselves free to identify the author of the pamphlet with one of any number of other individuals from the period, not called Xenophon, but whose oligarchic tendencies were well-known. It is certain that the author was an

Athenian, for when he speaks of the Athenians, he does so as 'we' (eg. Frisch 1942, 90; Leduc 1976, 52-3; Marr 1996, 39).

An admirable account of the history of the various attributions of this pamphlet is given by Marcello (1953, 55). We here give a much more attenuated version. Of all the 'non-Xenophons' proposed, the candidature of Critias has been most strongly canvassed. It was first advanced by Wachsmuth (1844, 798; cf. Gigante 1953, 56), and then supported by Böckh (1886, I 389 n. b), Müller (*FHG*), Drerup (1902, 308-14), Kalinka (1913, 20-21), Nestle (1943) and others. The argument is mainly based on the usage of the verb διαδικάζειν, 'to adjudicate', by the author of the *Athenaion Politeia* in 3.6. Pollux 8.25 tells us that Critias used this word in the sense of 'to adjudicate throughout the year' instead of in its strict technical sense (Κριτίας... ἔφη... καὶ διαδικάζειν τὸ δι' ὅλου τοῦ ἔτους δικάζειν). The verb is used in the same way in the *Ath. Pol.*, and consequently it was maintained that this must be a usage confined to Critias, and therefore that the *Ath. Pol.* must have been written by Critias. Frisch (1942, 321-22) has pointed out, however, that the verb also appears in other texts with the general meaning of 'to adjudicate', so its use in this way is not confined to Critias and the *Athenaion Politeia*. This has not prevented Canfora (1980) from more recently returning once again to the candidacy of Critias.

Apart from Critias, Thucydides the historian (Roscher 1842), Thucydides son of Melesias (Schmidt 1876, 10f. - as a preferred alternative to Xenophon son of Euripides. Canfora 1980, 17 notes that Thucydides of Melesias was advocated as he was ostracised in 443, and the work was written by an Athenian outside Athens), Alcibiades (Helbig 1861, 511 seq.), Antiphon (Lapini 1991) and Phrynichus (Müller-Strübing 1884, 71) have all been canvassed, mainly with no convincing argument in their favour other than *horror vacui*. In this context it is perhaps worth citing the words of Gomme (1940, 245) that 'to pick out a name from the *Prosopographia Attica* and give him for author, adds nothing to our understanding.'

Perhaps more sensibly, a second group of scholars have advanced the hypothesis that the author was another, earlier Xenophon. It was Schmidt (1876, 10 seq.) who first suggested that Xenophon son of Euripides of Melite, the so-called 'Xenophon the Elder', (*PA* 11313 = *LGPN* 35) may have been the author of the *Athenaion Politeia*, though he rejected this suggestion, as has already been mentioned above, in favour of Thucydides son of Melesias. Kalinka (1913, 17) also dismissed the candidacy of Xenophon son of Euripides of Melite, though it has since received support from Gelzer (1937, 103-4; cf. Frisch 1942, 104). We do not believe that the *Athenaion Politeia* was written by Xenophon son of Euripides of Melite, who died at Spartolus in 429 BC. We rather think it was written by another Athenian called Xenophon. Our starting point is, however, one which has not previously been fully brought into the argument.

The Ascription of the *Athenaion Politeia* to Xenophon the Rhetor

The ascription of the *Athenaion Politeia* actually written on the manuscript is not to Xenophon son of Gryllos, nor to Xenophon the Athenian, nor even simply to Xenophon, but rather to 'Xenophon the Rhetor'. Having noted the use of this sobriquet earlier in his work, Gomme (1940, 211, 237 n. 2) later dismissed the use of the term ῥήτωρ as being of any value as to establishing the identity of the author. He considered it as simply evidence that the work is an essay/speech rather than a narrative history. But this is surely too glib; none of the other works of Xenophon son of Gryllos have such an adscript.

At this point we return to the other suggestion of Gomme, mentioned above, that the paper had been found among the papers of Xenophon son of Gryllos following his death, and falsely ascribed to him in Antiquity. Had the pamphlet indeed been erroneously attributed to Xenophon son of Gryllos after being found amongst his papers, the ascription would have been either simply to Xenophon or to Xenophon the Athenian as it is with his other works. One might compare the works falsely attributed to Aristotle. Rather, whoever first added the ascription to the pamphlet knew that this was not the work of Xenophon son of Gryllos. Ancient writers were usually referred to by name and *polis*, and only in the case of authors sharing the same *polis* was a sobriquet added. An example of this is the pair of distinct individuals Antiphon the Orator and Antiphon the Sophist, although Gagarin (1997, 5-6) has argued for the identity of the two Antiphons.

So the appellation 'Rhetor' was most likely added in the mid- or late fourth century, when a need arose to distinguish the author from the more famous Xenophon the Athenian, the son of Gryllos. 'Rhetor' was chosen either on the basis of the work's contents, or (perhaps more likely) on the basis of a reference in some source to this Xenophon as a *rhetor* (in whatever context). *Rhetor* in its original meaning (LSJ *s.v.*) referred to people who spoke in the *ekklesia*; later it came to mean teachers of rhetoric (e.g. *OGIS* 712) or logographers. Since Xenophon son of Gryllos was neither a politician, nor a teacher, nor a logographer, the appellation 'Rhetor' is inappropriate for him, and he is never given it anywhere in ancient literature; the closest is ὁ σοφός in Plutarch (*Ages.* 20.2 [Loeb]; *Mor.* 212 b). The false grouping of this work with the *opera* of Xenophon son of Gryllos came later.

Diogenes Laertius (2.57) gives a list of works attributed to Xenophon son of Gryllos, including 'The Constitutions of the Athenians and Lacedaemonians'. He further tells us that Demetrius of Magnesia denies that the last of these works was by Xenophon. Demetrius of Magnesia was a grammarian and librarian of the first century BC (Schwartz 1901). Therefore, Diogenes' reference to him informs us that the *Athenaion Politeia* had become falsely attributed to Xenophon son of Gryllos before the first century BC.

The false association would, then, have taken place at some time between the late fourth and late second centuries. It is well-known that during this period a number of the Hellenistic monarchies had established libraries, where librarians were employed to collect, copy and collate manuscripts. The most famous of these libraries was, of course, Alexandria. Callimachus of Cyrene moved to the Museum of Alexandria under the patronage of Ptolemy Philadelphus around 280 BC. He wrote down a series of *Pinakes* ('Tables') 'of all who were eminent in any kind of literature and of their writings' on the basis of the existing, and accumulating, stocks of the Alexandrian Library. The *Pinakes* were divided by subject area and included a biography and list of works of each author, and altogether occupied some 120 'books' (Easterling & Knox 1985, 549-50). We would like to suggest that the false association was made by one of the Hellenistic librarians, such as Callimachus of Cyrene, who came across the *Athenaion Politeia* of Xenophon the Rhetor at a period when knowledge of this work and of its author had fallen into oblivion. He carelessly included it in the canon of Xenophontic works, where it lay undisturbed until Demetrius of Magnesia recognized that there was a problem.

Xenophon the Rhetor and the 'Socratic' Xenophon

On the basis of the ascription, then, we can establish the following points:

1) the author of the *Ath. Pol.* was called Xenophon;
2) he was, as usually assumed, an Athenian;
3) he was not the same as Xenophon son of Gryllos;
4) he was a regular speaker in the Assembly, a rhetorician, or a logographer (or, of course, more than one of these).

We shall now attempt to narrow down his identity further, though bearing in mind that Xenophon is a fairly common name in Attica. There are 63 occurrences of the name listed in Volume II of *LGPN*.

The sobriquet *rhetor* might well have suited Xenophon son of Euripides, who was politically active. He made a dedication on the Acropolis at some unknown date in the 450s or 440s, was Athenian *strategos* at the siege of Samos in 441/0 and 439/8, and was also general at Potideia in 430/29. However, he was killed at the Battle of the Spartolos in 429 (Davies 1971, 199-200). Thus the candidature of this Xenophon could only be accepted if an early date is accepted for the work, but we have seen that the usually accepted date for the pamphlet is 425-4.

Diogenes (2.59) comments that there have been seven Xenophons. He does not mention a 'Xenophon the Rhetor', which comes as no surprise if one accepts that common knowledge of his identity had died at some point following the middle of the fourth century BC. In fact all the Xenophons mentioned by Diogenes are either certainly later than Xenophon son of Gryllos and/or not Athenians but for two, one a mythographer, of whom nothing else is known (*PA* 11301 = *LGPN* 10, where a Hellenistic date is ascribed to this Xenophon), and the other, the last one he mentions, a poet of Old Comedy (*PCG* VII 804 = *LGPN* 53). All that is known of this Xenophon is that he was a victor at the Lenaia *c.* 400 BC (*IG* II² 2325.135). *LGPN* does not regard it as certain that he was an Athenian.

Diogenes adds the further tantalizing piece of information that 'I find in other authorities that he flourished (ἀκμάσι) along with the other Socratics around the eighty-ninth Olympiad (424-420 BC)' (εὗρον δ' ἀλλαχόθι ἀκμάσαι αὐτον περὶ τὴν ἐνάτην καὶ ὀγδοηκοστὴν Ὀλυμπιάδα σὺν τοῖς ἄλλοις Σωκρατικοῖς). Though Diogenes means this to refer to Xenophon son of Gryllos, he has already given his *floruit* as 401-400 at 2.55. Xenophon son of Gryllos was (supposedly) a disciple of Socrates (indeed note Nepos, *Ages.* 1.1 for his Socratic connections), and he might be called a 'Socratic', but the title was usually used of an individual directly concerned with sophistic inquiry, which Xenophon son of Gryllos was not. In any case the dates of 424-420 BC, as we have seen before, are clearly too early for him. One would not expect Xenophon the comic poet to be termed a Socratic, nor Xenophon the mythographer.

It therefore seems that Diogenes came across a source which discussed a Socratic named Xenophon, who flourished around 424-420 BC, a date significantly close to the suggested date of composition of the *Athenaion Politeia*. This Xenophon would seem to be the same person as 'Xenophon the Rhetor', the author, as we have suggested, of the *Athenaion Politeia*. Because knowledge of Xenophon the Rhetor had been lost by the time Diogenes wrote, he wrongly identified the 'Socratic' Xenophon as Xenophon son of Gryllos, the most obvious candidate he otherwise had available. The confusion may, indeed, have come earlier than Diogenes, and may have already been present in the source he was using. A similar confusion of the 'Socratic' Xenophon and Xenophon son of Gryllos may be reflected in the fact that the *Suda* has two entries for Xenophon, both containing biographical detail relating to Xenophon son of Gryllos. In one of these (Ξ 47) Xenophon is termed a *philosophos Sokratikos* and in the other (Ξ 48) a *Sokratous mathetes*. It may be as a result of these confused traditions that Cicero (*Tusculan Disputations* 2. 26) calls Xenophon 'a Socratic' (*Socraticum Xenophontem*).

At first glance the *floruit* date of 424-420 might imply a date of birth of *c.* 464-460, but it is more likely that the *floruit* indicates the time of Xenophon the Rhetor's most famous action, perhaps the publication of the *Athenaion Politeia*. In any case it is the opinion of a number of scholars that the author is a young man. Thus Woodhead (1970, 63-4; followed by Forrest 1975, 44-5; and Serra 1979, 8):

> 'Why he is referred to as an *Old* Oligarch I can never understand. He is very much the angry young man; his youthful blood runs hot, and he is passionate and vehement with the convictions of a youthful idealism - for we must allow that idealistic passions may burn in all their purity on the right wing as on the left'.

It has been remarked more than once that the *Athenaion Politeia* betrays many similarities with symposiastic dialogue. Kalinka (1913, 54-55), following Cobet (1858, 738-40) suggested that the pamphlet was actually part of a dialogue. This suggestion has been described as 'most peculiar' and 'perverted' by Frisch (1942, 101), but has not been quite so hastily rejected by Canfora (1979) and Lapini (1991). The work certainly seems to have been heavily influenced by the sophistic movement (Kalinka 1913, 52-5; Gomme 1940, 228; Forrest 1970, 108).

These features might well indicate a writer who frequented the sort of *symposia* at which Socrates and his circle could be found. Consequently the *Athenaion Politeia* might legitimately be labelled a 'Socratic' work, and its author a 'Socratic'. The appellation 'Rhetor' does not argue against this. Socrates had plenty of associates, such as Alcibiades, who were politically active. Furthermore, a *floruit* of 424-420 would be quite suitable for Xenophon the Rhetor if he was an associate of Socrates.

Other Literary Passages Possibly Relating to Xenophon the Rhetor

We shall now turn to examine other references to Athenians called Xenophon in the sources for this period to find whether any could plausibly be identified with Xenophon the Rhetor. An identification will be especially plausible if any of these individuals can also be identified as members of the Socratic circle. We shall pay particular attention to any traditions which have become associated with the son of Gryllos, but which seem inappropriate to him. If, as suggested, the earlier Socratic Xenophon's single surviving work had become conflated with those of the son of Gryllos, then the same is likely to be true of his biographical details. We have already demonstrated that this has apparently happened with the earlier *floruit* found in Diogenes. We shall not, however, look at the patently false traditions linked with Xenophon son of Gryllos that do not have a fifth-century context, such as that describing him as a student of Isocrates (see Photius *Bibliotheca* Codex 260 Bekker page 486b: γεγόνασι δὲ αὐτοῦ ἀκροαταὶ καὶ Ξενοφῶν ὁ Γρύλλου καὶ Θεόπομπος ὁ Χῖος καὶ Ἔφορος ὁ Κυμαῖος, οἷς καὶ ταῖς ἱστορικαῖς συγγραφαῖς προὐτρέψατο χρήσασθαι, πρὸς τὴν ἑκάστου φύσιν ἀναλόγως καὶ τὰς ὑποθέσεις τῆς ἱστορίας αὐτοῖς διανειμάμενος).

1. The most convincing piece of evidence is a tale reported by Cicero (*De inventione* 1.31.51-52), who found it in Aeschines the Socratic (fr. 8), of a conversation between Xenophon, his wife, and Pericles' mistress Aspasia. As Pomeroy (1994, 73 n. 11)

notes, a meeting between the married son of Gryllos and Aspasia is 'chronologically improbable', as that Xenophon probably did not marry until the 390s, by which time Aspasia was probably dead. Pomeroy puts the tale down to anachronistic invention. None of the sources for this story identify the Xenophon concerned however, and the equation with the son of Gryllos is an assumption of modern scholars, fuelled perhaps by the latter's references to Aspasia in his own work (*Mem.* 2.6.36; *Oec.* 3.14). Given Aspasia's connections with the Socratic circle (eg. Ath. 569f; cf. Henry 1995, 29-56), it is possible to suggest that the Xenophon here concerned was an earlier Xenophon associated with the Socratic circle in the lifetime of Aspasia, namely Xenophon the Rhetor. A further, though not particularly strong, argument against Aeschines referring to the son of Gryllos in this passage can perhaps be found in the belief that the latter drew upon Aeschines' *Aspasia*, from which this fragment almost certainly comes, for his own work (Ehlers 1966, 101-103). In that case, one may supply the biographical information not only that he was married, but unhappily so, for Marius Victorinus, in his scholion on the Cicero passage, says that Xenophon and his wife quarrelled frequently, and that Aspasia was attempting to reconcile them. In this context it might be relevant to note that some modern scholars (eg. Frisch 1942, 88; Leduc 1976, 53) have noted that that women are entirely absent from the *Athenaion Politeia*, that the author ignores them as wives and mothers, and have even suggested that the author was a misogynist. The incident is also recorded by Quintillian 5.11.27-28 and by Alcuin, *Disputatio de rhetorica et de virtutibus* 30, who substitutes a male philosopher for Aspasia.

2. The second anecdote may also be one where the identities of the Rhetor and the son of Gryllos became merged in antiquity. Diogenes (2.22) states that Socrates 'saved Xenophon, who had fallen from his horse in the battle at Delium (in 424 BC), supporting him' (Ξενοφῶντα ἀφ᾽ ἵππου πεσόντα ἐν τῇ κατὰ Δήλιον μάχῃ διέσωσεν ὑπολαβών). Another version of this story is found three centuries earlier, in Strabo (9.2.7): 'Socrates the philosopher, serving on foot, since his horse had got away from him, saw Xenophon the son of Gryllos, who had fallen from his horse; he took him up on his shoulders, and protected him for many stades' (πεσόντα ἀφ᾽ ἵππου Ξενοφῶντα ἰδὼν κείμενον τὸν Γρύλλου Σωκράτης ὁ φιλόσοφος, στρατεύων πεζός, τοῦ ἵππου γεγονότος ἐκποδών, ἀνέλαβε τοῖς ὤμοις αὐτόν, καὶ ἔσωσεν ἐπὶ πολλοὺς σταδίους). Strabo and Diogenes are clearly either using a common source, or literary works ultimately derived from the same source.

Two errors have crept into the account of Strabo. Strabo or his source have wrongly assumed that the Xenophon in question is Xenophon son of Gryllos, which is clearly chronologically impossible. Diogenes may be making the same error, but since this section comes from his discussion of Socrates, not that of Xenophon son of Gryllos, and he gives no further identification of the Xenophon concerned, we cannot be sure. Secondly, Strabo or his source has wrongly assumed that Socrates was a cavalryman: he was a hoplite, as Plato (*Symp.* 221a) makes clear. Diogenes' account of the anecdote is free from such errors, and it may be that Socrates did indeed rescue a Xenophon from the battlefield (his bravery at Delion was certainly well-known); if so, that could easily be Xenophon the Rhetor. The sentiments of the author of the *Ath. Pol.* would be entirely consonant with those of an Athenian *hippeus*, and the friendship and assistance of Socrates is easily explained if Xenophon the Rhetor was an associate of his.

There is a further complication. First, one must also consider the other story told of Socrates on the retreat from Delion, that Alcibiades came across him and escorted him off the battlefield. Brietenbach (1967, 1572-1573) suggests that there has been confusion with the story of Socrates saving Alkibiades at Poteidaia (Pl. *Symp.* 220e), which may be true, but we must nevertheless subject this story to examination. In

Plutarch's version (*Alk.* 7.6), Alcibiades comes across Socrates in the company of a few others, who could conceivably have included Xenophon the Rhetor; but in Plato's account of the incident (*Symp.* 221a-b) the only companion of Socrates on the retreat to be mentioned, apart from Alcibiades, was Laches (*cf. Lach.* 181a). Laches was perhaps a *hippeus*, although the only reference to him having money is at Ar. *Vesp.* 241, which makes reference to money Laches is supposed to have embezzled whilst in Sicily. It seems strange that Plato would not mention Xenophon, if he had been present, especially if Socrates was actually there.

It could be suggested that the story in Strabo and Diogenes originally concerned Socrates' rescue of *Laches*, for whom the name of Xenophon has later been substituted. Plato only says that Socrates accompanied Laches however, not that he saved him; Laches was, however clearly grateful for the companionship (*Lach.* 181a). Plato's literary intention may explain the difference in the accounts. He was not a historian trying to give a precise account of Socrates' actions during the retreat from Delion; his account focuses on Laches, to the exclusion of others present. Even in antiquity the accuracy of Plato's account of Socrates at Delion could be questioned (Ath. 215d-216c).

Therefore, we may still be justified in using this passage as evidence that it was thought plausible that Socrates might have saved someone called Xenophon at Delion, and hence that there was a Xenophon in Socrates' circle in the 420s, who served at Delion.

3. Philostratus (*Vit. Soph.* 1.12 [496 Olearius]) says that Xenophon son of Gryllos, whilst imprisoned in Boeotia, got himself bailed out to go and listen to Prodikos of Keos.

> Προδίκου δὲ τοῦ Κείου ὄνομα τοσοῦτον ἐπὶ σοφίᾳ ἐγένετο, ὡς καὶ τὸν Γρύλλου [Ξενοφῶντα] ἐν Βοιωτοῖς δεθέντα ἀκροᾶσθαι διαλεγομένου, καθιστάντα ἐγγυητὴν τοῦ σώματος. πρεσβεύων δὲ παρὰ Ἀθηναίους παρελθὼν ἐς τὸ βουλευτήριον ἱκανώτατος ἔδοξεν ἀνθρώπων, καίτοι δυσήκοον καὶ βαρὺ φθεγγόμενος. ἀνίχνευε δὲ οὗτος τοὺς εὐπατρίδας τῶν νέων καὶ τοὺς ἐκ τῶν βαθέων οἴκων, ὡς καὶ προξένους ἐκτῆσθαι ταύτης τῆς θήρας, χρημάτων τε γὰρ ἥττων ἐτύγχανε καὶ ἡδοναῖς ἐδεδώκει. τὴν δὲ Ἡρακλέους αἵρεσιν τὸν τοῦ Προδίκου λόγον οὗ κατ' ἀρχὰς ἐπεμνήσθην, οὐδὲ Ξενοφῶν ἀπηξίωσε μὴ οὐχὶ ἑρμηνεῦσαι. καὶ τί ἂν χαρακτηρίζοιμεν τὴν τοῦ Προδίκου γλῶτταν, Ξενοφῶντος αὐτὴν ἱκανῶς ὑπογράφοντος.

Prodikos lived in the late fifth and early fourth centuries. He seems to have still been alive at least in 399, to judge from Pl., *Apol.* 19e, and was a friend of Socrates (Pl., *Hipp. Maj.* 282c). He could therefore have been connected with either Xenophon the Rhetor or Xenophon son of Gryllos. The latter certainly knew Prodikos' work (*Mem.* 2.1.21-34), and had a close friend Proxenos who was a Boeotian (*An.* 1.1.11). There is no other evidence for Xenophon son of Gryllos ever visiting Boeotia in his early years, however, let alone being imprisoned there. Consequently, along with others (eg. Krentz 1995, 1), we are inclined to reject the tradition that Xenophon son of Gryllos was imprisoned in Boeotia.

In that case, we can either assume the anecdote preserved by Philostratus to be a complete fabrication, extrapolated from the son of Gryllos' knowledge of the works of Prodikos, or that it originally concerned a Xenophon other than the son of Gryllos; in which case Xenophon the Rhetor is the most likely candidate. Moreover, if we can deduce from Diogenes and Strabo's tale mentioned above at least that Xenophon the Rhetor served at Delion, then, although being saved by Socrates in the early stages of the retreat from the battlefield, he was later captured by the enemy, that would provide a credible context for a Xenophon to be imprisoned in Boeotia. Such an imprisonment might also provide a context for the writing of the *Athenaion Politeia*.

It was Weiske who first suggested that the author's use of αὐτόθι when speaking of Athens first suggested that the book was written outside Athens. This was objected to by Roscher and other scholars, but Frisch (1942, 92-6) concludes 'Weiske's quite natural linguistic instinct on this point is to be preferred to the later admonitions not to interpret the word in its simplest manner'. Most modern scholars (eg. Helbig 1861, 524; Nestle 1943, 233; Leduc 1976, 53; Moore 1983, 19) concur with the view that the work was written away from Athens, whilst resident in Sparta according to Hemmerdinger (1975, 74) although this is pure speculation.

De Ste. Croix (1954/5, 25) remarked that 'the Old Oligarch is surely writing for a non-Athenian audience', though he denied that the work had to be written outside Athens (1972, 308). Gelzer (1937, 976-9) then Frisch (1942, 98) noted that the treatise was addressed to 'the other Hellenes' as a warning of what might lay in store for them.

If our reconstruction of events is correct, Xenophon the Rhetor would have written the work in Boeotia immediately after his capture at the battle of Delion for a Boeotian readership. It was perhaps intended to be read by Boeotians who wanted to understand the tenacity of the Athenian democracy in warfare. The reference to the enslavement of Boeotia in 3.11 (on which passage see Bowersock 1966, 35-6) may have been included with specific reference to this audience.

The above are the literary passages most probably to be related to Xenophon the Rhetor. For completeness, we include the following possible references, but would argue that the balance of probability is against an association.

4. There is a Xenophon (*LGPN* 3) mentioned by Kratinos in his *Drapetides* (*PCG* IV p. 150 fr. 58 = Ael., *HA* 12.10), who speaks of his 'brutal [sexual] lust' and compares him with a mouse (καταπυγοσύνην μυὸς ἀστάψω Ξενοφντῶος): mice being famously lascivious (cf. Ar., *Nub.* 347; Ael., *HA* 12.10). It cannot be known whether this is a Xenophon known to us by other means. However, we have seen that the sobriquet 'Rhetor' may indicate someone prominent in Athenian politics, in which case Xenophon the Rhetor might be a possible target for a comic poet writing down to c. 423. But we cannot say on the basis of the *Athenion Politeia.* that Xenophon the Rhetor was necessarily a man with a prodigous sexual appetite, even though his purported misogyny may be of some relevance here, and Kratinos' target could as easily be, as Bergk (1858, 63) suggests, Xenophon son of Euripides, or one of the late fifth-century Xenophons known through epigraphy (see below).

5. That Xenophon's *Symposium* purports (1.1) to be an eye-witness report of a dinner-party of 422 involving Socrates is, of course, irrelevant. As a dramatic character Xenophon plays no part in the work, and indeed the writer only uses the first person once more in the work (*Symp.* 4.50: compare *Symp.* 1.8, where he speaks of what an observer *would* have noticed at the time). Xenophon son of Gryllos is here employing dramatic license (Tredennick & Waterfied 1990, 28; cf. Ath. 5.216d), and it would be perverse to assume that he is imagining himself in the *persona* of an earlier namesake, or even that the *Symposium* should be attributed to Xenophon the Rhetor. Only Falappone (1979) is prepared to believe that Xenophon son of Gryllos was present at the event concerned, to fit with her early date of birth for Xenophon.

6. Lysias, associated with the Socratic circle (Pl., *Rep.* 328b), wrote a speech (fr. 103; Thalheim 1901, 357.8-10) against a Xenophon (*PA* 11298 = *LGPN* 5), according to

Photius (*Lex.* 546, 767), who quotes a seven-word sentence (ὡς ἐπὶ καρπῶν. Θουκιδίδης ἐν γ΄·καὶ ἐν συγκωμιδῇ καρποῦ ἦσαν·καὶ Λυσίας ἐν τῷ πρὸς Ξενοφῶντα· συγκομίσας δὲ δῶρα καὶ ἀποδόμενος τὸ ἀργύριον) in his entry on Συγκομιδή, that gives no enlightenment as to the speech's general contents. Since such a speech will date *c.* 400-380, this individual may possibly be Xenophon the Rhetor, though there is no positive evidence that the Rhetor survived into the fourth century. A separate Xenophon may have been involved here (it cannot have been Xenophon son of Gryllos, who was not in Athens at the time of Lysias' speech-writing career). Moreover, when the *Etymologicum Magnum* (733.22-24) repeats Photius' entry on Συγκομιδή practically word-for-word, it makes one important change, reporting the name as Xenokrates (πρὸς Ξενοκράτην). The *Etymologicum Magnum* also changes some words in the quotation (ἀποδόμενος τὸ ἀργύριον to... ἀποδοῦς τὸν ἀγρόν), but not significantly for our purposes. Thalheim combines both traditions to... ἀποδόμενος τὸν ἀγρόν. Photius' entry is also found more-or-less *verbatim* in the *Suda* (Σ 1296 *s.v.*). It appears as if the author of the *Etymologicum Magnum* has corrected what he found in previous lexicographers; but whether he was right to do this is impossible to say (*RE s.v.* 'Xenokrates (3)' takes the view that the name should be Xenokrates).

Finally, it is hardly likely that the early fourth-century Athenian sculptor Xenophon (PA 11299 = LGPN 7; Paus. 8.30.10, 9.16.2) was also a Socratic writer.

The Epigraphic Record

This concludes our examination of the literary texts. The epigraphic record is of quite a different nature, as whilst literary evidence tends to preserve information concerning prominent individuals, epigraphic evidence is more random in its selection and survival. There are no epigraphic references which especially lend themselves to association with Xenophon the Rhetor. Most of the Xenophons found in LGPN can be eliminated on grounds of date.

Besides those obviously too late, one can probably eliminate a Χσενοφῶν from the early fifth century (LGPN 4 SEG 16.23.3 = IG I³ 1146.1) as being too early, and Xenophon of Erchia (LGPN 23 = SEG 33.932.14: perhaps a relative of the son of Gryllos?) and Xenophon of Perithoidai (LGPN 40 = IG II² 1665.2, early fourth century), and two further Xenophons who may not even be Athenians (LGPN 54 = 12342, fourth century; Ag. 21 F 145, early fourth century) as being too late

The most likely possibilities are Χσενοφῶν of Rhamnous (*LGPN* 44), named in an inscription dating to 412/0 (*IG* I³ 472.10), and a Χσενοφῶν (*PA* 11297 = *LGPN* 6) named on a funerary monument from *c.* 410 (*IG* I³ 1192.135; *Ag.* XVII 22.135). Both would fit in date (and may even be the same person), but no positive grounds exist for associating them with Xenophon the Rhetor.

Conclusion

The ascription of the *Ath. Pol.* to 'Xenophon the Rhetor' almost certainly shows the work was written by an Athenian called Xenophon, who was may have been active in politics or a rhetorician or a logographer. If the former, he presumably belonged to that category of Athenian citizens such as Theramenes and Peisandros, who held oligarchic preferences, but who nonetheless participated in the machinery of the *polis*. Like the son of Gryllos, the Rhetor was an associate of Socrates, and this is one reason why his biography has become conflated with that of Xenophon son of Gryllos.

It is therefore likely that anecdotes told of the son of Gryllos that are chronologically impossible should instead, where they have a fifth-century context, be associated with the Rhetor.

From such details we can provide the following likely biography: his *floruit* was 424-420, he was a *hippeus*, was (unhappily) married, served at Delion, where he may have had his life saved by Socrates, but was subsequently captured and imprisoned in Boeotia. It is tempting, but unprovable, to think that the work was written in exile in Boeotia. The fact that Brasidas had in the summer of 424 marched through Greece to Thrace, defying *Ath. Pol.*'s statement (2.5) that such movement was impossible, does not necessarily prevent the work being composed over the winter of 424/3, when Xenophon the Rhetor may not have been fully aware of Brasidas' achievement. In fact the Delion Campaign and Brasidas' expedition to Thrace were two simultaneous events, which are cut up and interleaved in Thucydides' narrative (Gomme 1956, 540). Our understanding of the relative chronology of these two events is not completely secure.

The most important point to arise from the establishment of Xenophon the Rhetor's identity, is the probability that he was either a politician or a professional speech-writer. This contributes to our understanding of his work. Unlike later critics of the Athenian democracy such as Plato, Xenophon the Rhetor's comments derive from his participation in the machinery of the democratic *polis*.

Endnote

This paper arose out of a discussion between the authors following a paper during the Leeds-Manchester Greek History Research Seminar in 1993, and reached more or less its present written form in the late 1990s. It was written without knowledge of the work of Rossetti 1997, which reaches very similar conclusions to those presented here, although varying in some detail. The authors thought it still worthwhile publishing this paper, however, in order to demonstrate that the attribution proposed here is not a minority opinion, and so that the argument could reach a wider audience through the English language.

Bibliography:

J.K. Anderson, *Xenophon* (London 1974).

Emile Bélot, *Xénophon, La République d'Athènes, lettre sur le gouvernement des Athéniens adressée en 378 avant J.C. par X. Au roi de Sparte Agésilas* (Paris 1880).

T. Bergk, *Commentationum de reliquiis comoediae Atticae antiquae libri duo* (Leipzig 1838).

E. Bélot, *Xénophon, La République d'Athènes, lettre sur le gouvernement des Athéniens adressée en 378 avant J.C. par X. Au roi de Sparte Agésilas* (Paris 1880).

A. Böckh, *Die Staatshaushaltung de Athener* (Berlin 1886 second ed., first ed. 1851).

G.W. Bowersock, 'Pseudo-Xenophon' *HSCP* 71 (1966) 33-55.

G.W. Bowersock in E.C. Marchant & G.W. Bowersock (eds), *Xenophon Vol. VII* (ed. Loeb, Cambridge Mass. 1968).

H.R. Brietenbach, 'Xenophon (6)' *RE* ix A 2 (1967) 1571.

L. Canfora, 'Ipotesi sull' *Athenaion Politeia* anonima' *QS* 10 (1979) 315-318.

L. Canfora, *Studi sull' Athenaion Politeia pseudosenofontea* (Memorie della Accademia delle Scienze di Torino II. Classe di Scienze Morali, Storiche e Filologiche Serie V, Volume 4, Fascicolo I, Gennaio-Marzo 1980).

C.G. Cobet, *Novae Lectiones quibus continentur observationes criticae in scriptores graecos* (Leiden 1858).

W.R. Connor, *The New Politicians of Fifth-Century Athens* (Princeton 1971).

J.K. Davies, *Athenian Propertied Families 600-300 B.C.* (Oxford 1971).

A. Dihle, *A History of Greek Literature* (London, New York 1994).

E. Drerup, *Untersuchungen zur älteren griechischen Prosaliteratur, Anfänge der rhetorischen Kunstprosa. I. Theodoros von Byzanz* (= *Jahrb. f. klass. Philologie, Supplementband* XXVII, 1902) 219-351.

Edd. P.E. Easterling & B.M.W. Knox, *The Cambridge History of Classical Literature I Greek Literature* (Cambridge 1985).

B. Ehlers, *Ein vorplatonische Deutung des sokratischen Eros: Der Dialog Aspasia des Sokratikers Aischines* (Munich 1966).

M. Falappone, 'Note di biografia senofontea' *QS* 9 (1979) 288-289.

M.J. Fontana, *L'Athenaion Politeia* (Palermo 1968).

W.G. Forrest, 'The Date of the Pseudo-Xenophontic *Athenaion Politeia*' *Klio* 52 (1970) 107-116.

W.G. Forrest, 'An Athenian generation gap' *Yale Classical Studies* 24 (1975) 37-52.

Hartvig Frisch, *The Constitution of the Athenians etc.* (Copenhagen 1942).

M. Gagarin (ed.), *Antiphon: The Speeches* (Cambridge 1997).

K.I. Gelzer, *Die Schrift vom Staat der Athener* (= *Hermes Einzelschrift Heft* 3, Berlin 1937).

M. Gigante, *La Constituzione degli Ateniesi, Studi sullo Pseudo-Senofonte* (Naples 1953).

A.W. Gomme, 'The Old Oligarch', in *Athenian Studies presented to W.S. Ferguson* (= *Harv. Stud.* Suppl. 1) (1940) 211-245, (= A.W. Gomme, *More Essays* (Oxford 1962) 38-69).

A.W. Gomme, *A Historical Commentary on Thucydides III* (Oxford 1956).

M.H. Hansen, *The Athenian Democracy in the Age of Demosthenes* (Oxford 1991).

W. Helbig, 'Alkibiades als politischer Schriftsteller' *RhM* 16 (1861) 511-531.

Bertrand Hemmerdinger, 'L'Émigré (Pseudo-Xénophon, ΑΘΗΝΑΙΩΝ ΠΟΛΙΤΕΙΑ)' *RÉG* 88 (1975) 71-80.

M.M. Henry, *Prisoner of History: Aspasia of Miletus and her Biographical Tradition* (New York, Oxford 1995) 29-56.

S. Hornblower, 'Old Oligarch', *OCD³* (1996) 1064.

S. Hornblower, 'The *Old Oligarch* (Pseudo-Xenophon's *Athenaion Politeia*) and Thucydides. A Fourth-Century Date for the *Old Oligarch?*' in edd. Pernille Flensted-Jensen, Thomas Heine Nielsen, Lene Rubenstein, *Polis & Politics. Studies in Ancient Greek History Presented to Mogens Herman Hansen on his Sixtieth Birthday, August 20, 2000* (Copenhagen 2000) 363-84.

E. Kalinka, *Die pseudoxenophontische Athenaion Politeia* (Leipzig 1913).

P. Krentz (ed.), *Xenophon: Hellenika II.3.11-IV.2.8* (Warminster 1995).

W. Lapini, 'Lo Pseudo-Senofonte e la Dialog-Hypothese', *Orpheus* 12 (1991) 18-34.

W. Lapini, 'Storie di sofisti: Antifonte de Ramnunte e la costituzione degli Ateniesi anonima', *Sandalion* 14 (1991) 21-62.

Claudine Leduc, *La Constitution d'Athènes attribuée a Xénophon* (Paris 1976).

D.M. Lewis, 'A Loeb *Constitution of the Athenians*' *CR* n.s. 19 (1969) 46.

H.S. Long & R.W. Sharples, 'Diogenes Laertius' *OCD³* (1996) 475.

G. Marcello, *La costituzione degli Ateniesi: studi sullo pseudo-Senafonte* (Naples 1953).

John Marr, 'Notes on the Pseudo-Xenophontic *Athenaion Politeia*' *Classica et Mediaevalia* 34 (1983) 45-53.

J. Marr, 'Making sense of the Old Oligarch' *Hermathena* 160 (1996), 37-43.

H. Mattingley, 'The Date and Purpose of the Pseudo-Xenophon *Constitution of Athens*' *CQ* n.s. 47 (1997) 352-357.

J.M. Moore, *Aristotle and Xenophon on Democracy and Oligarchy²* (London 1983).

H. Müller-Strübing, ''Αθηναίων πολιτεία: die attische Schrift vom Staat der Athener' (= *Philologus Suppl.* 4, Heft I, Leipzig 1884).

G. Murray, *A History of Ancient Greek Literature* (London 1897).

W. Nestle, 'Zum Rätsel der 'Ἀϑηναίων πολιτεία' Hermes 78 (1943) 232-244.

S.B. Pomeroy, *Xenophon, Oeconomicus: a Social and Historical Commentary* (Oxford 1994).

F. Roscalla, 'Περὶ δὲ τῆς Ἀϑηναίων Πολιτείας ...' QUCC n.s. 50 (1995) 105-30.

W.G.F. Roscher, *Leben, Werk, und Zeitalter des Thukydides* (Göttingen 1842).

L. Rossetti, 'Autore dell'*Athenaion Politeia* fu forse un socratico, omonimo di Senofonte Erchieo?' in edd. Marcello Gigante, Gianfranco Maddoli, *L'Athenaion Politeia dello Pseudo-Senofonte* (Perugia 1997).

G.E.M. de Ste Croix, 'The Character of the Athenian Empire' *Historia* 3 (1954/5) pp. 1-41.

G.E.M. de Ste Croix, *The Origins of the Peloponnesian War* (London 1972).

M. Schmidt, *Memoire eines Oligarchen in Athen über die Staatsmaximen des Demos* (Jena 1876).

G. Serra, *La Costituzione degli Ateniesi dello Pseudo-Senofonte* (= *Bolletino dell'Istituto di Filologia Greca, Università di Padova, Supplemento* 4, Rome 1979).

A.H. Sommerstein, 'How to avoid being a *komodoumenos*', *CQ* n.s. 46 (1996) 332.

Schwartz, 'Demetrios (80)', *RE* iv (1901) 2814-2817.

T. Thalheim, *Lysiae Orationes* (Teubner, Leipzig 1901).

H. Tredennick & R. Waterfield (tr.), *Xenophon: Conversations of Socrates* (London 1990).

C. Tuplin, 'Xenophon' *OCD*³ (1996) 1628.

E.W.G. Wachsmuth, *Hellenische Alterthmskunde aus dem Gesichtspunkte des Staats* I² (Halle 1844).

A. Geoffrey Woodhead, *Thucydides on the Nature of Power* (= *Martin Classical Lectures* 24, Cambridge Mass. 1970).

DAVID WHITEHEAD

THE REIN AND THE SPUR

rriving in the Manchester History Department in the late summer of 1975, for what turned out to be a stay of seventeen and a half years, I overlapped with Cosmo Rodewald for his final twelve months there (and ultimately became his successor). At some point during the session he agreed to look at an article I had drafted. His responses, though courteous, pulled few punches, and a couple of them have stayed with me ever since. One was a simple but devastating rhetorical question: 'so what?' I still think of this as the Rodewald test - whether or not I deem myself to have passed it - for anything I write. The other was a matter of style, which in the piece in question Cosmo described as 'Isocratean'. Of all the possible things he could have meant by this, including general long-windedness and pomposity, his actual target was a tendency he found in my expository manner to make explicit connections of thought between sentences. One could scarcely protest, to a senior colleague, that such a feature characterised much Greek prose, including some of the finest. Better to take the blow on the chin, resolve to read more Thucydides (and Tacitus), and try harder to strip out those conjunctions and particles. In the present case I expect to fail but I plead mitigation in the fact that the topic of this *opusculum* is none other, in part, than Isocrates himself.

Every student of fourth century Greek historiography[1] knows the witticism attributed to Isocrates about two of its most celebrated practitioners, both of them allegedly alumni of his Athenian academy of rhetoric. Theopompus of Chios (Professor Isocrates is said to have declared) needed reining back, Ephorus of Cyme spurring on. Michael Flower describes this judgement as 'famous', and he is right.[2] Appearing as it does to hit two birds with this one magisterial stone, it is constantly quoted by modern scholars, some of whom even know where to track it down. In Greek it occurs in the Suda entry (E 3953 Adler) on Ephorus and Theopompus, and also in one of the ancient biographies of Isocrates;[3] in Latin both Cicero[4] and Quintilian mention it.[5]

---

[1] All ancient dates are BC(E) unless otherwise indicated.

[2] M.A. Flower, *Theopompus of Chios: history and rhetoric in the fourth century BC* (Oxford 1994) 49.

[3] For both together, conveniently, see *FGrH* 70 (Ephorus) T28a and b. I shall quote each of them below.

[4] Cicero, *Brut.* 204 (ut Isocratem in acerrimo ingenio Theopompi et lenissimo Ephori traditum est, alteri se calcaria adhibere, alteri frenos); *de or.* 3.36 (quod dicebat Isocrates, doctor singularis, se calcaribus in Ephoro contra autem in Theopompo frenis uti solere); *ad Att.* 6.1.12 (Cicerones pueri amant inter se, discunt, exercentur; sed alter, ut Isocrates dixit in Ephoro et Theopompo, frenis eget, alter calcaribus).

[5] Quintilian, *Inst.Or.* 2.8.11 (an vero clarissimus ille praeceptor Isocrates, quem non magis libri bene dixisse quam discipuli bene docuisse testantur, cum de Ephoro atque Theopompo sic iudicaret, ut alteri frenis alteri calcaribus opus esse diceret, etc.); and again one-sidedly – Theopompus having already been mentioned in other terms - in 10.1.74 (Ephorus, ut Isocrati visum, calcaribus eget).

Flower's larger purpose - to challenge the orthodoxy that Theopompus and Ephorus were, in truth, pupils of Isocrates [6] - is not my concern here, but in the course of
this he notes,[7] as have others, that the rein-and-spur contrast is also found elsewhere: '[t]he credibility of the famous story that Isocrates said that Ephorus needed
the lash and Theopompus the bit is undermined by the fact that Plato is reported to
have expressed the same opinion about Aristotle and Xenocrates, and Aristotle about
Theophrastus and Callisthenes'. One way or another, then, the story does repay
another brief scrutiny. My argument will be that if we are to identify an original version (rather than simply dismiss the material *tout court* as genre-driven invention) it is
the Plato-Aristotle-Xenocrates one.

First, three putative claimants to primacy can easily be reduced to two, because
in Diogenes Laertius 5.39 the Platonic precedent is acknowledged: λέγεται δ' ἐπ' αὐτοῦ τε
καὶ Καλλισθένους τὸ ὅμοιον εἰπεῖν Ἀριστοτέλης, ὅπερ Πλάτωνα, καθὰ προείρηται, φασὶν εἰπεῖν ἐπί τε
Ξενοκράτους καὶ αὐτοῦ τούτου· φάναι γάρ, τοῦ μὲν Θεοφράστου καθ' ὑπερβολὴν ὀξύτητος πᾶν τὸ νοηθὲν
ἐξερμηνεύοντος, τοῦ δὲ νωθροῦ τὴν φύσιν ὑπάρχοντος, ὡς τῷ μὲν χαλινοῦ δέοι, τῷ δὲ κέντρου ('It is said
that Aristotle applied to him (sc. Theophrastus) and Callisthenes the same thing that
Plato, as already related, had said of Xenocrates and himself: for since Theophrastus
interpreted all his meaning with an excess of cleverness, whereas the other was congenitally sluggish, he said that the one needed a rein and the other a goad'). The
cross-reference here is to 4.6, on Xenocrates: ἦν δὲ τὴν φύσιν νωθρός, ὥστε λέγειν τὸν
Πλάτωνα συγκρίνοντα αὐτὸν Ἀριστοτέλει "τῷ μὲν μύωπος δεῖ, τῷ δὲ χαλινοῦ" καὶ "ἐφ' οἷον ἵππον οἷον
ὄνον ἀλείφω" ('He was congenitally sluggish, with the result that Plato, comparing him
with Aristotle, said "the one needs a spur, the other a rein" and "such an ass I am
training, against such a horse"').

This then (hereinafter P-X-A) is the story that - to pick up Plato's bloodstock metaphor - competes head-to-head against the rival tradition involving Isocrates, Ephorus
and Theopompus (I-E-T). How to adjudicate between them?

The mere fact that I-E-T is the more frequently found (with six instances as
against two) seems to me of no significance in itself. If I-E-T had not embedded itself
in the biographical tradition of Isocrates before Hermippus of Smyrna wrote *On the
Pupils of Isocrates* in the late third century, that was surely the situation afterwards.
Cicero will have known this work, and perhaps Quintilian did too - though in fact
nothing about Quintilian's material suggests a source anterior to Cicero. In any event
here are two rhetoricians seizing upon and perpetuating an item well-known in their
favoured genre. We can therefore set aside the Latin evidence and concentrate solely
on the Greek versions, the only ones even potentially likely to preserve anything said
by a fourth-century speaker of that language. I-E-T, in Diog. Laert. 4.6, has been
quoted already; here, abbreviated to present purposes, are the two I-E-T texts:

> Suda E3953 Adler:
> Ἔφορος Κυμαῖος καὶ Θεόπομπος Δαμασιστράτου Χῖος, ἄμφω Ἰσοκράτους μαθηταί, ἀπ'
> ἐναντίων τό τε ἦθος καὶ τοὺς λόγους ὁρμώμενοι. [...] ὁ γοῦν Ἰσοκράτης τὸν μὲν ἔφη χαλινοῦ
> δεῖσθαι, τὸν δὲ Ἔφορον κέντρου. [...] ('Ephorus of Cyme and Theopompus, son of
> Damasistratus, of Chios, both pupils of Isocrates, starting from contrary
> positions as regards both their character and their language. [...] At any rate
> Isocrates said that the one needed a rein, but Ephorus a goad').

---

[6] M.A. Flower, *Theopompus of Chios: history and rhetoric in the fourth century BC* (Oxford 1994)
42-62.
[7] *Op. cit.* p. 49.

Vita Isocratis III p. 257, 98 Westermann:
περὶ δὲ Θεοπόμπου καὶ Ἐφόρου φέρεταί τι τοιοῦτον αὐτοῦ καὶ ἀστεῖον. [...] "ἔχω τινὰς δύο μαθητάς, ὧν ὁ μὲν δεῖται μάστιγος, ὁ δὲ χαλινοῦ" ('Concerning Theopompus and Ephorus some witticism of his like this is on record. [...] "I have two pupils, of whom the one needs a whip, the other a rein"').

Here, in both P-X-A and I-E-T, is a teacher seeking to encapsulate the contrast between two of his pupils by resort to an equine metaphor. That is to state the obvious. But equally obvious, I cannot help thinking, is a question which ought to be posed but which, to the best of my knowledge, has not been: how far do Isocrates and Plato do this elsewhere? The answer turns out to be: very differently in each case - such that, as indicated already, the superior claim of P-X-A looks strong.

Isocrates (to take him first) shows very little unforced interest in horses. One must make the proviso 'unforced' in order to take account of his early forensic speech *On the Team of Horses* (Περὶ τοῦ ζεύγους), no. 16 in the standard numeration. There the factual background to the lawsuit in which his client, the younger Alcibiades, was involved in the early 390s made some reference to matters equine unavoidable. However, once Isocrates had left the grubby and uncongenial profession of logography behind him and was speaking in his own voice this is not a subject that he chooses to take up in more than half a dozen brief instances.[8] And as regards the equine/equestrian world as an illustration of human behaviour, the closest he comes to this - which even so is not very close - is in a passage of *On the Antidosis*. One of the blind spots of critics of philosophy, he says there (15.211), is that 'even if in relation to horses and dogs and most other animals they see individuals possessing certain skills by which they make them braver or gentler or more intelligent, they do not suppose that in relation to human nature the kind of education has been discovered which could improve men in the respects in which we improve the beasts'. Besides not being a precise example of expressing human characteristics in animal terms, it may again reflect Isocrates' response to an already-existing point or fact, rather than the generation of one of his own.

Contrast Plato. Above and beyond all the occasions when the nature of his subject-matter makes mention of horses mandatory, they seem to be in the forefront of his mind anyway, ready to hand for illustrative purposes. Witness *Phaedo* 96d-e ('I had been content to think, when I saw a tall man standing beside a short one, that he was taller by a head; and similarly with one horse and another'); *Republic* 352d-e (horse as example of something which has a function) and 601c (horse-harness as example of what a painter can paint without understanding); and the high ἵππος - content of the *Cratylus* (e.g. 385a, 393bff). Horses, or occasionally foals, supply brief analogies and paradigms[9] in such passages as *Euthyphro* 13a (οἷον...ἵππους) and 13b (ὥσπερ... οἱ ἵπποι), *Republic* 413d (ὥσπερ τοὺς πώλους), *Theaetetus* 184d (ὥσπερ ἐν δουρείοις ἵπποις), and *Laws* 666e (οἷον ἀθρόους πώλους), 701c (οἷόνπερ ἵππον) and 708d (καθάπερ ἵππων ζεῦγος). And the particular matter of controlling and restraining with a *chalinos* - which can variously mean bridle, bit or rein: see LS-J *s.v.* - features in passages such as *Laches* 185d, *Republic* 496b, and *Laws* 701c (already cited) and 808e.

Of this last group of passages, *Republic* 496b and *Laws* 808e are especially noteworthy for their application of the *chalinos* not to equine but to human kind: a particular individual in the first case; a generalization (about young children) in the second. But for reiterated horse/human parallelism nothing betters the central section of the *Apology*. Socrates recalls how he had invited Callias Hipponicou to recon-

---

[8] See 1.27 (but the *To Demonicus* is not securely Isocratean), 2.15, 6.55, 7.45, 15.211, 15.298.
[9] And the charioteer analogy in *Phaedrus* 253Cff is of course anything but brief.

sider the way he had educated his two sons by imagining them a pair of foals or calves (20a-b). The prosecutor Meletus is rhetorically asked to admit the absurdity of a single corrupter of youth by contemplating the same thing in horse-training (25a-c). 'Is there anyone who does not believe in horses but believes in horses' activities?' (27b) To believe in the children of gods but not the gods themselves 'would be as foolish as believing in the children of horses and asses - mules - but not in horses and asses' (27d-e). And then the climax (30e, in Hugh Tredennick's translation): 'If you put me to death, you will not easily find anyone to take my place. It is literally true (even if it sounds rather comical) that God has specially appointed me to this city, as though it were a large thoroughbred horse which because of its great size is inclined to be lazy and needs the stimulation of some stinging fly (νωθεστέρῳ καὶ δεομένῳ ἐγείρεσθαι ὑπὸ μύωπός τινος)'.

The city of Athens itself is thus νώθρος, as Plato thought of Xenocrates (and later Aristotle of Callisthenes); but an even more striking word is μύωψ. Here in the *Apology* it clearly does mean a fly, as the passage goes on to make certain; and Socrates as the pestering, stinging gadfly or horsefly (*tabanus*) is the image we all know and accept. But the other principal meaning of the word is the one in P-X-A, quoted earlier: τῷ μὲν μύωπος δεῖ, τῷ δὲ χαλινοῦ. In the second half, the restraint half, of this contrast χαλινός is the noun used not only there but also in both versions of I-E-T, but its opposite is different in each of the three cases: κέντρον,[10] μάστιξ, μύωψ. A *mastix* is a plainly a whip; the other two words refer to the sting delivered by spurs. J.K. Anderson has suggested that these equestrian accessories arrived in Athens in the later fifth century.[11] Be that as it may, *kentron* (already in common use for hand-held goads, not to mention other meanings) was to become the standard term for them. The alternative - in this sense - μύωψ is much rarer in the classical period but does occur in Xenophon (*On Horsemanship* 8.5)[12] and Theophrastus (*Characters* 21.8: worn by the *mikrophilotimos*). As to Plato, in *Apology* 30e we see him using the word in its 'fly' meaning. So perhaps, thanks to Diogenes Laertius, it is permissible to suggest that he employed it again when formulating the difference between two of his pupils - only the duller of whom, the man who needed the sting of the μύωψ, would ever sit in his shoes.[13]

---

[10] See also in this respect the apparent echo (couched in general terms) in [Longinus], *On the Sublime* 2.2.

[11] J.K. Anderson, *Ancient Greek Horsemanship* (Berkeley & Los Angeles 1961) 88.

[12] See also, more generally, section 9 of this work on dealing with a horse that is either too spirited or else (in a brief tailpiece) too lazy..

[13] See D. Whitehead, 'Xenocrates the metic', *RhM* 124 (1981) 223-244, the preface of which acknowledges the help of Cosmo Rodewald. As to the present piece, it has passed muster with Craig Cooper, to whom my thanks and the customary exemption from any blame.

STEPHEN HODKINSON

THE EPISODE
OF SPHODRIAS AS A SOURCE FOR SPARTAN SOCIAL HISTORY

t is a pleasure to contribute to this volume in memory and honour of Cosmo Rodewald. It was Cosmo who first introduced me, as a student of history, to the fascination and significance of ancient Greece. He gave me my first opportunity to give a university lecture to a group of my peers during my very first year as an undergraduate student! And it was he who encouraged and guided the first steps of my research on Sparta, which has been the focal point of my academic career. In recognition of the multiplicity of these academic debts, I have chosen in this essay to examine an account of a historical episode which is of significance both at the cutting-edge of Spartan research and as a teaching aid through which students may better understand the character of her society in the classical period.

It was in 1974, as a final-year undergraduate taking Cosmo Rodewald's Special Subject on 'Athens and Sparta, 413-386 BC' - more precisely, whilst researching its associated thesis - that I first encountered the historical episode, as narrated in Xenophon's *Hellenika*, that forms the subject of this article.[1] My thesis was (ambitiously) entitled 'Kings, society and foreign policy: the character of government in classical Sparta'; and it was characteristic of Cosmo's enlightened approach to student learning that he encouraged me to spread my wings beyond the Special Subject's nominal chronological limits and extend its primary focus on inter-state relations into a broader examination of the socio-political context of Sparta's foreign policy.[2] It was my resultant wider reading of Xenophon and study of the reign of King Agesilaos II that brought me to the subject of this paper: the significant and revealing episode surrounding the misdeeds and subsequent trial and acquittal of the Spartan commander Sphodrias.[3]

The episode in Xenophon's narration[4]

In winter 379/378 BC King Kleombrotos I (king of the Agiad royal house), while campaigning against Thebes following its recent liberation from Spartan control, installed one of his followers Sphodrias as harmost (governor) in the neighbouring polis of Thespiai. In summer 378, after Kleombrotos' return home, Sphodrias was bribed by

---

[1] Xen., *Hell.* 5.4.20-34.

[2] It was also characteristic both of his approach and of a now long-departed mode of teaching administration that I was permitted to submit, without penalty, a thesis of some 40,000 words, notwithstanding an official recommendation of a mere 15-20,000!

[3] My attention was especially drawn to the episode by the perceptive remarks in Ste Croix's seminal chapter on Sparta in his then recently-published *The Origins of the Peloponnesian War* (Ste Croix 1972, 134-5).

[4] My paper will focus almost exclusively on Xenophon's narration of the episode in his *Hellenika* as our sole account by a contemporary source who knew several, if not all, of the persons involved. (All references without indication of author or title are to this work.) The most substantial subsequent account, that in Plutarch's *Agesilaos* 24-5, is an intelligent and rational, but secondary, re-working of Xenophon's account (Shipley 1997, 286-99).

the Thebans, according to Xenophon's account, to launch an unexpected and unprovoked attack on Athenian territory. He made his attack at the very time that Spartan ambassadors were visiting Athens for diplomatic negotiations, and indeed staying at the home of Kallias, a prominent Athenian citizen. The attack misfired and Sphodrias' forces returned to Thespiai; but the Spartan ambassadors were put under arrest and released only when they convinced the Athenians that the Spartan authorities were not implicated in Sphodrias' attack and would shortly put him to death.[5]

We can follow the remainder of the episode through Xenophon's own account.[6]

[24] And in fact the ephors did recall Sphodrias and impeached him on a capital charge. Sphodrias, however, was too frightened and did not obey. Nevertheless, in spite of the fact that he failed to appear at the trial, he was acquitted. And it seemed to many people that this was the most unjust verdict given in Lakedaimon. The reason why it was given was as follows.

[25] Sphodrias had a son Kleonymos, who had just grown out of the age of boyhood and was the best looking and most highly regarded of his peers. And it happened that Archidamos, the son of Agesilaos [king of the Eurypontid royal house], was in love with him. Now the friends of Kleombrotos, who were comrades (*hetairoi*) of Sphodrias, were inclined to acquit him; but they were afraid of Agesilaos and his friends and also of those who stood in the middle, since it did seem that he had done a dreadful deed.

[26] Therefore, Sphodrias spoke to Kleonymos as follows: 'My son, it is within your power to save your father by asking Archidamos to make Agesilaos favourable to me at my trial.'

[27] When he heard this, Kleonymos summoned up the courage to go to Archidamos and to ask him for his sake to become the saviour of his father. Archidamos, on his side, seeing Kleonymos weeping, wept with him as he stood beside him; but when he heard his request, he replied: 'Kleonymos, I must tell you that I cannot even look my father in the face. If I want to get something done in the *polis*, I go with my request to anyone rather than my father. But all the same, since you are asking me, you can be sure that I shall make every effort to get this done.'

[28] He then left the mess (*philition*), went to his home and retired to rest. He got up at dawn and watched to be sure that he did not miss his father when he went out. But when he did see him going out, he first of all gave way to any of the citizens who happened to be there and wanting to speak to Agesilaos, then to any foreigner (*xenos*), and then again he even gave way to any of the servants with requests to make. Finally, when Agesilaos came back from the [River] Eurotas and went indoors again, he went away without even having approached him. And on the following day he acted in exactly the same way.

---

[5] 5.4.15-23.
[6] 5.4.24-34. For convenience of reference, I have indicated the section numbers in the translation.

[29] Agesilaos suspected why he was following him about, but asked him no questions and let it be. As for Archidamos, he was, naturally enough, longing to see Kleonymos, but did not see how he could go to him until he had talked with his father about his request. And the friends of Sphodrias, since they did not see Archidamos coming to visit, whereas formerly they saw him come often, were greatly afraid that he had been reprimanded by Agesilaos.

[30] Finally, however, Archidamos did pluck up the courage to approach Agesilaos and to say, 'Father, Kleonymos tells me to beg you to save his father; and I, too, beg you to do this, if it is possible.' He replied, 'So far as you are concerned, I forgive you. But I don't see how I myself could be forgiven by the *polis* if I failed to declare guilty a man who has made money for himself to the harm of the *polis*.'

[31] Now at the time Archidamos made no reply to this; but, submitting to the justice of it, went away. Later, however, whether on his own initiative or at the suggestion of someone else, he went to him and said: 'Father, if Sphodrias had done nothing wrong, I know that you would have acquitted him. Now, as it is, even if he has done something wrong, let him for our sakes be forgiven by you.' He replied: 'Well and good, if this should be honourable for us, it shall be so.' When he heard this, Archidamos went away in great despondency.

[32] Now one of the friends of Sphodrias, during a conversation with Etymokles, said, 'I suppose that all of you friends (*philoi*) of Agesilaos will put Sphodrias to death.' Etymokles replied, 'By Zeus, then we shall not be doing the same as Agesilaos, for he is saying the same thing to everyone with whom he discusses the matter: that it is impossible that Sphodrias has not done wrong; but, on the other hand, it is a hard thing to put to death a man who as a boy (*pais*), youth (*paidiskos*) and young man (*hēbōn*) has consistently performed with honour in every way. Sparta has need of such soldiers.'

[33] When he heard this, he went and told Kleonymos. He was delighted and went at once to Archidamos and said: 'Now we know that you really care for us. And be sure, Archidamos, that we shall try, too, to take care that you will never feel ashamed of our friendship.' And he did not prove false to his word, but while he lived he acted in every way that is honourable in Sparta; and at Leuktra, fighting in front of his king with Deinon the *polemarchos*, he died after falling three times, first of his citizens and in the midst of the enemy. Although this grieved Archidamos extremely, he had kept his promise: he did not shame him, but rather brought him honour. It was in this way, then, that Sphodrias escaped.

[34] And among the Athenians those who favoured the Boiotians pointed out to the people that the Lakedaimonians, so far from punishing him, had actually commended Sphodrias for intriguing against Athens. As a result the Athenians built gates for Peiraieus, fitted out ships, and gave help to the Boiotians with all zeal.

Historical and societal implications

As the end of this account implies, the acquittal of Sphodrias had significant implications for Greek inter-state relations. Xenophon contrasts the Athenians' attitude before and after Sphodrias' raid. Before the raid they were so alarmed at Sparta's deployment of military forces in central Greece that they convicted their two generals who had recently collaborated in the liberation of Thebes,[7] and were negotiating with Spartan ambassadors. Sphodrias' acquittal, he claims, led the Athenians to throw their weight decisively behind the Boiotians and against Sparta. Scholars have not been slow to point out the deficiencies in Xenophon's analysis, especially his complete omission of the foundation of the Second Athenian Confederacy, which was created during the same summer, possibly *before* Sphodrias' raid, and which included Theban membership. There is no doubt that the year 378 witnessed a decisive shift in Athenian policy towards active hostility to Sparta; but the significance of the episode of Sphodrias in causing that shift has been a matter of debate. Recent scholarship has provided extensive discussion of these controversial issues.[8]

It is the implications of the episode for our understanding of Sparta's internal affairs, however, on which I wish to focus. Here too there are serious deficiencies in Xenophon's account, especially in his narration of the legal process.[9] The precise charge against Sphodrias is never specified. There is no account of any formal hearing: the story apparently ends before he was formally acquitted. We are told that he absented himself from his trial (*krisis*); but it is left unclear whether his disobedience to the ephors' summons extended to refusing even to return to Sparta.[10] Even his absence from the trial is puzzling, given that it was public knowledge beforehand that he would be acquitted.[11] As Vivienne Gray rightly cautions, 'Xenophon is not writing a political analysis... His desire [is] to focus on the morality of the situation.' Yet, as she also observes, 'there is a great deal of valuable incidental information about Spartan life and politics in the story.'[12] This information is invaluable for the historian; and even the moralising elements, as represented by a man who knew Sparta well, can offer important insights into her system of values.

Certainly, several of the episode's implications for the character of Spartan politics have been thoroughly explored in recent studies. First, Xenophon's direct statement that the body due to try Sphodrias included two blocks of men who could be relied upon to follow the dictates, respectively, of Kings Agesilaos and Kleombrotos, along with his clear implication that these blocks were sufficiently large that when combined together they outnumbered the independent group of persons 'in the middle', have been deployed as a powerful piece of evidence by scholars who argue that Spartan decision-making was typically controlled by a small minority of citizens and by those who believe that her politics normally revolved around conflicts between solid factions,

---

[7] 5.4.19.

[8] Cf. McDonald 1972; Cawkwell 1973; Rice 1975; Kallet-Marx 1985; Cartledge 1987, 136-8; 299-301; Hamilton 1991, 167-74.

[9] See especially the trenchant critique of Shipley 1997, 296-9.

[10] This is assumed by Shipley 1997, 296; but, if so, it is hard to see how he could have spoken to his son, since it seems unlikely (as we shall see below) that Kleonymos' strictly-controlled way of life as a *paidiskos* would have permitted travel abroad.

[11] Is it possible that Xenophon has elided two stages in the formal process: an initial court hearing at which Sphodrias did not appear, followed by an adjournment to a final hearing at which his punishment was to be decided; and that the protracted informal events narrated by Xenophon stretched over a long period from before the initial hearing into the period before the final one?

[12] Gray 1989, 62.

two of which centred on the two kings.[13] Extra weight has been added to these arguments by the probability that the judges largely under the control of the kings consisted mainly of members of the *Gerousia* (the Council of Elders), the most influential collective body in Spartan society.[14] Secondly, studies of these general aspects of Spartan political structure have also exploited the episode for its insights into the specific state of internal politics in the 370s BC, especially the political relationship between the two kings. The acquittal of Sphodrias had a significant impact in enabling Agesilaos and Archidamos to place Kleombrotos and members of his close circle in their personal debt, a fact which contributed to Agesilaos' continued dominance over Spartan politics up to 371, when Kleombrotos, Sphodrias and Kleonymos all met their deaths at the battle of Leuktra, executing an anti-Theban policy which was very much Agesilaos' own.

Less systematic attention, however, has been given in recent work to the episode's revelation and illustration of a range of other phenomena of Spartan social life. The multiplicity and significance of these themes put the episode of Sphodrias on a par in evidential value with the other significant episode which Xenophon takes pains to relate in his *Hellenika*, the conspiracy of Kinadon, c.398 BC.[15] Yet whilst at least two recent articles have been devoted to the insights of Kinadon's conspiracy,[16] there have been no comparable discrete studies of the acquittal of Sphodrias. In my attempt to remedy this comparative neglect, I will examine the passage for the insights it sheds into the phenomena of bribery, personal relations with foreigners, informal influence, servile labour, the upbringing and its age grades, the modalities of pederasty and of father-son relationships and, finally, the *hippeis* and the Spartan 'beautiful death'.

Bribery

The episode commences with Sphodrias' suspected acceptance of a Theban bribe to launch his attack on Athens. Xenophon's reference to Sphodrias' openness to bribery is his sole explicit reference to the bribery of Spartiates in any of his works;[17] but it ties in with a long series of similar incidents narrated by a range of classical writers from Herodotus to Theopompos, backed up by general statements by Aristotle about the endemic susceptibility of Spartiate officials to the taking of bribes.[18] So, however, does the manner in which Xenophon reports the incident: the Thebans are said to have persuaded Sphodrias, 'giving money, so it was suspected' (5.4.20: χρήματα δόντες, ὡς ὑπωπτεύετο). Although the cumulative weight of evidence for Spartan susceptibility to bribes is impressive, the inevitable secrecy surrounding transactions such as the negotiations between Sphodrias and the Thebans means that these suspected cases of

---

[13] For the first view, see esp. Ste Croix 1972, 134-5; Cartledge 1987, 136-8; 156-9. For the second, Hamilton 1991, 171, developing ideas originally put forward in Hamilton 1970 & 1979.
[14] Discussion of the judicial role of the Gerousia, Ste Croix 1972, 349-50; MacDowell 1986, 127-29; Cartledge 1987, 133-8.
[15] 3.3.4-11.
[16] David 1979; Lazenby 1997.
[17] King Pausanias in 403, desiring to overturn Lysander's policy in Athens, was able to lead out the army, 'having persuaded (πείσας) three of the ephors' (2.4.29). The verb πείσας is formally ambiguous: it could signify persuasion either by money or simply by words (Harvey 1985, 78-9; Noethlichs 1987, 157 n.151).
[18] Noethlichs 1987; Arist., *Pol.* 1270b8-13; 1271a3-5; 13-18: discussed in Hodkinson 2000, 359-61.

bribery must necessarily remain in the realm of allegation.[19] A man's enemies, of course, tended to assume the worst - and so too in this episode, when Agesilaos assumes without question that Sphodrias was 'a man who made money to the harm of the *polis*'.[20] The change of tone in Xenophon's account, from his own cautious reporting of the suspicions to the unambiguous assertion he puts into the mouth of Agesilaos, is a skilful representation of the political realities of rumour and allegation inextricably wound up in such events.

Personal relations with foreigners

Certain aspects of the subsequent development of the episode illustrate an important reason why the receipt of bribes featured as such a common, but (for the modern historian) problematic, allegation. As we have noted, when Sphodrias launched his attack, a Spartan diplomatic mission was already present in Athens. During their stay the ambassadors were accommodated at the house of the prominent Athenian, Kallias. Xenophon informs us that Kallias held the position of Sparta's *proxenos*, the Athenian chosen by the Spartans to act as their external representative and intermediary in their diplomatic and other dealings with Athens. This was not the first time that Kallias and his lineage had acted in concert with the Spartans. In a speech during a visit as ambassador to Sparta in 371 BC, Kallias asserted that his ancestors had acted as the Spartans' *proxenoi* as far back as his great-grandfather (in the late sixth century) and that he himself had successfully concluded peace agreements on two previous visits to Sparta.[21] Recent general studies have given us a good understanding of the normal socio-economic context of *proxenia* in Greek society. *Proxenoi* were frequently men who already had close personal relations of guest-friendship (*xenia*) with leading citizens from the foreign *polis* whose interests they represented.[22] Relationships of *xenia* typically involved the mutual provision of personal services, both intangible favours and material resources, including money and valuables.[23] Similar material exchanges must frequently have occurred when a man acted as *proxenos*. In the episode under discussion Kallias offered his personal material resources in accommodating, and doubtless entertaining, the Spartan ambassadors. It would be surprising if this act of personal hospitality did not also involve exchanges of gifts between host and guests. In a world in which political negotiations and personal relationships were closely inter-linked and in which transfers of material resources were embedded within the very fabric of such elite interactions, accusations of bribery were an almost inevitable response by third parties attempting to explain unexpected changes of behaviour. We do not know the nature of the contact between Sphodrias and the leading Thebans who persuaded him to attack Attica; but, whether it was conducted clandestinely through intermediaries or secret meetings or through more open encounters, his unexpected action was bound to elicit the suspicion that he had been bribed.

It is worth considering the particular case of Kallias and the Spartan ambassadors a little further. Xenophon gives the ambassadors' names: Etymokles, Aristolochos and Okyllos. Aristolochos is otherwise unknown to us; but we can say more about Etymokles and Okyllos. Both men re-appear together as fellow ambassadors (two out of

---

[19] Other motivations are possible. Diodorus (15.29.5) claims that Sphodrias acted on the prompting of King Kleombrotos.

[20] 5.4.30.

[21] 6.3.4.

[22] Herman 1987, 138-42; Mitchell 1997, 33-5.

[23] Herman 1987, 58-61, 73-115; Mitchell 1997, 18-21.

five men selected) in Athens eight years later in winter 370/69 BC[24] - a good illustration of Sparta's regular practice of ensuring continuity in her foreign negotiations with
particular states by re-selecting men who had formerly served as ambassadors.[25] The
personal connections established during previous visits could be of critical importance
in oiling the wheels of inter-state diplomacy. What then can we say about the personal
relationship between Kallias and our Spartan ambassadors? Here a little speculation
is necessary. A mere 18 months before Etymokles' and Okyllos' second visit to Athens
in 370/69, Kallias had - as we have seen - visited Sparta as ambassador. Xenophon's
account is uninformative about arrangements for his hospitality, as indeed about
which Athenian hosted the Spartan ambassadors in 370/69 BC. However, Kallias'
claim that he had twice previously successfully negotiated peace agreements in Sparta
on the conclusion of wars implies the existence of some longstanding close personal
relationships with leading Spartiates. It is not over-fanciful to suggest that one of
these leading Spartiates was his guest of 378, Etymokles. The two men were near-
contemporaries. Kallias was born around 450 BC.[26] If Etymokles was, as normally
assumed, a member of the *Gerousia* in 378 BC, then he must have been born some-
time - possibly several years - before 438 BC. The agreements to which Kallias referred in his speech are probably the swearing of oaths in Sparta in 386 following the
imposition of the King's Peace and the peace treaty of 375.[27] As a friend of King Agesilaos, it is probable that Etymokles was very much involved in both sets of negotiations, a mere eight years before and three years after his visit to Athens as a respected
Elder in 378.

Sphodrias and Etymokles are, of course, not the only Spartans who have friendly
contact with foreigners in the course of the episode. The implications of the longstanding friendship of Kallias' lineage with leading Spartiates are reinforced by Xenophon's
inclusion of foreigners among the groups of people wanting to speak to King Agesilaos;
Xenophon implies that they were sufficiently numerous or regular a category of royal
suitors as to merit specific mention. This scene forms one piece in a range of evidence
from other sources that Spartiates were thoroughly implicated in relations of *xenia*
(pl. *xeniai*) with leading men from other states. Relationships involving Spartiate
partners constitute almost a quarter (23 out of just over 100) of the cases in Gabriel
Herman's catalogue of *xeniai* in the archaic and classical periods. Similarly, on a
shorter timescale, a Spartan connection appears in as many as 20 out of 90 cases in
his list of networks of *xeniai* during the Peloponnesian war.[28] These abundant instances indicate that leading Spartiates stood at the centre of a network of foreign
contacts which gives a real meaning to the part-title of Irad Malkin's book, 'the Spartan Mediterranean'.[29] Many of the foreigners approaching Agesilaos in summer 378
may well have come from cities within the Spartan alliance, known in modern times
as the Peloponnesian league. Recent research has emphasised how Sparta's control
over its alliance rested on *xeniai* between the oligarchs in its constituent cities and
leading Spartiates, especially members of the two royal houses.[30] Agesilaos, in particular, is known to have inherited or established close ties with multiple Peloponnesian
states.[31]

---

[24] 6.5.33
[25] Mosley 1973, 50-4.
[26] Davies 1971, 263.
[27] Cawkwell 1976, 276 n.25.
[28] Herman 1987, 166-75, 180-4.
[29] Malkin 1994.
[30] Tuplin 1977; Cartledge 1987, 243-6; Hodkinson 2000, 346-8.
[31] Xen., *Ages.* 2.21-3, 27; *Hell.* 4.1.29-40; 5.2.3, 3.13; 6.5.4.

Informal influence

The list of Agesilaos' suitors was of course not confined to foreigners. The scene described in our episode is a remarkable account of a morning in the life of a powerful king. The 66-year-old Agesilaos emerges from his house - apparently not long after dawn - to walk down to the Eurotas,[32] and is quickly surrounded by a host of citizens, foreigners and servants, all wishing to talk with him. They are apparently so numerous that by the time they have finished Agesilaos is ready to return to his house.[33] Quite apart from his nervousness, Archidamos has little opportunity to approach his father; and the same occurs on the following - and presumably subsequent - day(s), until he does 'finally' approach his father. Xenophon is reticent about the precise nature of Agesilaos' conversations with his fellow citizens. They are described simply as wanting to 'converse with' him (διαλέγεσθαι): in contrast to the servants, who are specifically said to come to him with a request or need (δεομένῳ).[34] However, he gives a more transparent account in a passage of the *Agesilaos*, comparing Agesilaos' approach with that of the Persian king:

> ... the one [the Persian king] prided himself on being difficult of approach; the other [Agesilaos] was glad to make himself accessible to all. And the one affected tardiness in negotiation; the other was best pleased when he could send his suitors away quickly with their requests granted (ὧν δέοιντο).[35]

There could be no clearer indication that the scene narrated in the *Hellenika* should be interpreted as representing a powerful king dispensing personal patronage as widely as possible to his citizens.

Indeed, the importance of Agesilaos' informal influence in citizen affairs is highlighted throughout the entire episode. On the surface the prosecution of Sphodrias follows a formal procedure. The ephors exercise their official powers, as detailed by Xenophon in his *Polity of the Lakedaimonians*,[36] depriving him of his office and bringing a capital charge against him to be tried by a formally constituted tribunal. But Sphodrias' request to his son assumes that, despite his disobedience of their summons, the outcome of the formal process will depend upon the personal influence of Agesilaos. This assumption is shared by everyone in the episode: by Kleonymos and Archidamos, who put the plea to Agesilaos; by Agesilaos himself; by the friends of Sphodrias, who fear that Agesilaos has rebuffed the request. Above all, it is shared by the friends of Agesilaos like Etymokles, who have been listening attentively to Agesilaos' views and for whom the idea of acting differently from the king is unthinkable.[37]

It may be open to question whether Spartan politics was always dominated by coherent factions surrounding the kings. Not all kings were powerful or influential figures, especially in the fifth century;[38] and there is a strong argument that the situa-

---

[32] On Agesilaos' probable age, Cartledge 1987, 20-1.

[33] Cf. Xenophon's use of τέλος to characterise Agesilaos' return home.

[34] Is this perhaps due to his not wishing to describe Spartiate and helot behaviour in identical fashion?

[35] *Ages.* 9.2. Note that Xenophon here applies to all requests the same verb used of the servants' requests in the *Hellenika*.

[36] *Lak. Pol.* 8.4.

[37] My argument stands whether or not one accepts the argument of Gray (1981, 327-8) that Xenophon intimates through his dialogue that Agesilaos intended to influence his friends to vote to acquit Sphodrias by leading them to a mistaken inference about how he himself would vote.

[38] Cf. the telling remarks of Lewis 1977, 43-8

tion in 378 represents a relatively new phenomenon deriving from the development of relatively fluid patron-client ties into more solid patronal groups during the last years of the Peloponnesian war and the early fourth century.[39] Nevertheless, it is clear that, whatever the achievements (or lack of them) of his predecessors, Agesilaos was able to build up a considerable and firm body of personal support among leading Spartiates.

We have some insight into the means by which he forged such personal bonds with members of the *Gerousia*. According to Plutarch, he used to send a cloak and an ox as a mark of honour to each newly-elected member.[40] However, this was clearly just part of a longer process of obtaining their support; and the evidence of Agesilaos' openness to talk to all citizens during his morning 'audiences' by the Eurotas suggests that his patronage was not restricted to the elite circles of the *Gerousia*. Plutarch's comment that the ephors imposed a fine on him for making public citizens his private property, though possibly invented, captures the essence of his policy.[41]

These suggestions are indeed corroborated by a variety of other evidence for the king's patronal methods which provides broader context for the incidents narrated in our episode.[42] In his encomium of the king in his *Agesilaos* Xenophon lists the wide range of men personally indebted to him:

> By his relatives he was described as 'attached to his family', by his close associates as 'unhesitatingly devoted', by those who served him as 'ever mindful', by those wronged or treated unjustly as 'a champion', and by those who endured dangers with him as 'a saviour second only to the gods'.[43]

The assiduous care which Agesilaos took to cement firm bonds of friendship with his relatives and to use them as his agents in positions of responsibility is well attested. He appointed his brother-in-law Peisandros admiral (*nauarchos*) in 394 and obtained a range of military commands for his half-brother Teleutias, the son of Agesilaos' mother by her second husband. Indeed, he rescued his mother's kinsfolk from poverty by giving them half the additional property he had acquired in middle age as inheritance from his own half-brother King Agis II.[44] Although both Peisandros and Teleutias died prematurely in battle, Agesilaos' broader policy of support for his relatives may be directly relevant to his control of votes at the trial of Sphodrias, since Herodotus' statement that, in the absence of one of the kings from the *Gerousia*, his vote was cast by his nearest kinsman among the Elders implies that the *Gerousia* often included relatives of the kings.

The 'close associates' mentioned in this passage surely included Agesilaos' friends (*philoi*) within the *Gerousia* who voted for Sphodrias' acquittal. This group of men is mentioned under various names elsewhere in Xenophon's encomium of the king: for example, the *hetairoi*, for whom he showed considerable zeal, and 'his own people', for whom he spent his own goods.[45] The importance of these men's support is illustrated by an episode just one year previously, in 379, when Agesilaos was close to gaining the surrender of the city of Phleious after a long siege. The Phleiasians attempted to bypass his control by sending an embassy to surrender their city into the hands of the

---

[39] Cartledge 1987, 139-59.

[40] Plut., *Ages.* 4.3; *Mor.* 482c-d.

[41] *Ages.* 4.2.

[42] Cf. the excellent discussion of Cartledge 1987, 143-59.

[43] *Ages.* 11.13.

[44] Appointment of Peisandros: Xen., *Hell.* 3.4.29. List of the commands of Teleutias in Poralla 1985, no.689. Donation to his mother's kin: Xen., *Ages.* 4.5; cf. Plut., *Ages.* 4.1.

[45] *Ages.* 6.4; 11.8.

authorities in Sparta. Agesilaos, however, 'sent to his friends at home and arranged that the decision about Phleious should be left to him'.[46]

The remaining categories of his beneficiaries ('those who served him', those 'wronged or treated unjustly', and 'those who endured dangers with him') appear to refer mainly to ordinary Spartan citizens whom Plutarch claimed had become his 'private property'. Our understanding of the nature of personal relationships between Agesilaos and such ordinary citizens is imprecise; but the limited evidence permits some suggestions. The last category clearly refers to those who served under Agesilaos on campaign: where, as in Sparta, he gained a reputation for his accessibility to his fellow-soldiers.[47] The second category indicates an area of Spartan life - including but not necessarily limited to formal judicial proceedings - which may have prompted many of the king's petitioners to seek his help. The righting of wrongs may also be implied by Xenophon's comment in the *Agesilaos* that 'he rejoiced to see the avaricious poor and to enrich the upright'.[48] The second part of this quotation also hints at another area of potential assistance: material patronage. Agesilaos' reign was a period in which many citizen families were becoming increasingly impoverished, with the danger of losing their citizen rights through non-payment of their mess dues.[49] According to Xenophon, Agesilaos was a man 'who delighted to give away his own for the sake of others' and of whom 'many acknowledged that they had received many benefits from him'.[50] Requests for subsistence help were therefore probably another significant reason why many citizens approached the king on those early mornings in 378.

The range of evidence discussed above makes it possible to reconstruct the outlines of Agesilaos' use of patronage and informal influence. The comparative lack of evidence, however, should not blind us to the hints in our episode that the exercise of informal influence was not limited to a powerful king. When first asked to approach his father, Archidamos had initially demurred: 'Kleonymos, I must tell you that I cannot even look my father in the face. If I want to get something done in the city, I go with my request to anyone rather than my father.'[51] Other men evidently exercised such personal influence that even the son of a king might need their assistance. Sphodrias, too, had comrades within the *Gerousia*, who were willing to vote for his acquittal. In this case their influence was insufficient against the might of Agesilaos; but on other matters it was doubtless more effective.

Servile labour in Sparta

The final category of Agesilaos' suitors was a group described as τῶν θεραπόντων, the *therapontes*, 'servants': perhaps largely his own servants, whose number was probably quite large. Xenophon's choice of term is interesting, describing them by their function or role rather than by their status. It is noteworthy, in particular, that he does not refer to them as 'helots', Sparta's predominant servile labour force. This is consistent with Xenophon's general practice when referring to servile persons attached to Spartiate households or individuals in Sparta itself. There are several examples in his *Polity of the Lakedaimonians*. He uses the generic slave term *douloi* to describe both the female labour force that made the clothing of Spartiate households and the male

---

[46] Xen., *Hell.* 5.3.24
[47] Xen., *Ages.* 5.7.
[48] Ibid. 11.3.
[49] Cf. Arist., *Pol.* 1270a34-b6.
[50] Xen., *Ages.* 4.1.
[51] 5.4.27.

servile personnel in a Spartan army camp.[52] When describing the Spartiates' arrangements for communal use of private property, he uses another generic servile term (*oiketai*) to describe the arrangements for the communal use of *human* property; and he uses the same term when describing the impossibility of large amounts of Sparta's bulky currency being brought into the household without the knowledge of its inhabitants.[53] Xenophon does use the term 'helot(s)' on seven occasions in the *Hellenika*; but the contexts are either geographical locations outside Sparta itself (for example, the countryside of Lakonia or Messenia or outside Spartan territory) or generic references to the helots as a population group.[54] His use of non-specific terms when referring to servile persons *inside* Sparta seems, therefore, to be purposeful. It probably reflects a genuine historical diversity of servile statuses and official terminology. A sprinkling of passages suggests that, alongside their helots, Spartiates possessed modest numbers of chattel-slaves.[55] Several sources also refer to a category of servile Lakonians called *mothônes* who were brought up alongside the free children.[56] It has been plausibly argued that these *mothônes* were helot children reared as personal attendants of Spartiate boys after being born within the household to female helot servants.[57] Hence, in addition to different types of servile statuses, there may also have been a variety of nomenclature for different types of helots.

Also worthy of note is the manner in which Agesilaos relates to his 'servants' in public, giving each an opportunity for a personal request. On this point Xenophon is one of several sources who indicate the close and enduring character of the personal relationship between Spartiate households and their servants. Male servants accompanied their masters as batmen on campaign and probably also on their daily round of activities;[58] sometimes, as we have seen, this service originated in boyhood. Female servants wet-nursed and cared for Spartiate children, and in one episode are depicted as sharing the intimate sexual secrets of the wife of a Spartan king.[59] Some had sexual intercourse with their Spartiate masters: their sons were partly integrated into the institutions of Spartiate life and were given their own separate term: the *nothoi* ('bastards'). These men make an appearance in Xenophon's *Hellenika* just three years before our episode as part of the forces which King Agesipolis took against Olynthos in 381: Xenophon describes them as 'men of very good appearance and not without experience of the life of honour in the polis ($\tau\tilde{\omega}\nu$ $\dot{\epsilon}\nu$ $\tau\tilde{\eta}$ $\pi\delta\lambda\epsilon\iota$ $\varkappa\alpha\lambda\tilde{\omega}\nu$ $o\dot{\upsilon}\varkappa$ $\check{\alpha}\pi\epsilon\iota\varrho\sigma\iota$).[60] The Greek term translated as 'life of honour' (*ta kala*) is the same term as that by which Agesilaos characterises Sphodrias' successful performance as a citizen youth.[61] Of course not all persons of servile origin will have gained such benefits: close relationships between Spartiates and their household servants must often have involved a great deal of exploitation, degradation and brutality. Nevertheless, the degree to which servile members were integrated into the life of Spartiate households is symbolised by their incorporation into certain household rituals. For example, on the second day of the annual

---

[52] Xen., *Lak. Pol.* 1.4; 12.4.

[53] Ibid. 6.3; 7.5.

[54] 1.2.18; 3.3.6, 8; 5.12; 6.5.28; 7.1.12; 2.2.

[55] The evidence is discussed by MacDowell 1986, 37-9; Hodkinson 1997, 47-8; 2000, 336.

[56] Harpokration, s.v. *mothôn*; Schol. Aristop. *Wealth* 279; Schol. Aristop. *Knights* 634; Hesychios, s.v. *mothônas*. Full texts in Lotze 1962, 427.

[57] Cantarelli 1890, 472; Bruni 1979, 21-24; Ducat 1990, 166-8; Hodkinson 1997, 51 n.12; cf. *Etym. Magn.*, s.v. *mothôn*.

[58] Hdt. 7.229; Thuc. 4.8, 16; Kritias 88B37 (Diels-Kranz); Xen., *Hell.* 4.5.14; 8.39.

[59] Hdt. 6.61; Plut., *Lyk.* 16.2-3; *Alk.* 1.2; *Ages.* 3.1.

[60] 5.3.9.

[61] Cf. also *Lak. Pol.* 3.3.

festival of the Hyakinthia citizens included 'their personal slaves' (τοὺς δούλους τοὺς ἰδίους) in the entertainment to dinner which they offered to all their acquaintances.[62]

Sparta's servile groups, and especially the helots, have been the subject of fierce recent scholarly debate. Were Spartiate-helot relations marked by a 'class struggle', with the Spartans fearing the helots as a human volcano constantly liable to erupt in revolt?[63] Or were the helots mainly compliant and subservient to Spartiate rule?[64] On the basis of the passages from his *Polity of the Lakedaimonians* mentioned above, the evidence of Xenophon has been adduced in support of the opinion that - in contrast to the views of Thucydides and Aristotle, who stress the magnitude of the helot threat - the helots 'may not have seriously troubled the consciousness of the average Spartiate'.[65] This opinion is not fully supported by the evidence of the *Hellenika*. Of the seven explicit references to helots in the *Hellenika*, four refer to helot trouble, real or potential: one to helot revolt, another to helot flight, yet another to an order to arrest certain helots, whilst a fourth involves a (perhaps unfounded) claim that they would join a planned conspiracy.[66] The other three references, however, are all to helots actively supporting Spartan military efforts: serving as rowers in Spartan ships, even acting as harmosts, and volunteering to defend Sparta from enemy invasion.[67] The passage in our episode certainly adds weight to these images of unproblematic relations. The servants who approach Agesilaos know their place: they wait until after the citizens and also any foreigners; but their position as petitioners in public audience to the king appears to be accepted.

The upbringing and its age grades

The episode also contains considerable insights into Sparta's official social institutions. We can start with the Spartiate public upbringing and with the reported words of Agesilaos in justifying Sphodrias' acquittal:

> '... it is a hard thing to put to death a man who as a boy (*pais*), youth (*paidiskos*) and young man (*hêbôn*) has consistently performed with honour in every way. Sparta has need of such soldiers (τὴν γὰρ Σπάρτην τοιούτων δεῖσθαι στρατιωτῶν).'

The last part of this passage is sometimes interpreted as a reference to the Spartans' need of military manpower due to the growing problem of *oliganthrôpia*, the decline of their citizen numbers.[68] The phrase 'such soldiers', however, more plausibly signifies men who had performed as well in the upbringing as had Sphodrias. The passage, indeed, appears to be clear testimony to the significance of the upbringing in a Spartiate's career. Sphodrias' successful performance in his younger years was still remembered and could be deemed to count for something, even several years later when he had been appointed to a military command.[69] The implication is also that his performance in the upbringing may have played an important role in his rise to high

---

[62] Polykrates, *ap.* Athen. 139f.

[63] Ste Croix 1972, 89-94; Cartledge 1987, 160-79.

[64] Talbert 1989.

[65] Whitby 1994, 92.

[66] 7.2.2; 1.2.18; 3.3.8; 3.3.6.

[67] 7.1.12; 3.5.12; 6.5.28.

[68] E.g. Cartledge 1981, 29; 1987, 158.

[69] Sphodrias must have been at least around 40, since his son Kleonymos was probably age 14-15 (see below).

command. Not that it was sufficient: Sphodrias had achieved his harmostship at Thespiai only through his appointment by King Kleombrotos. However, his outstanding performance when young may have been a significant factor in drawing him to the attention of the king and to the members of the *Gerousia* who appear as his *hetairoi* in our episode.

The passage is also important testimony to the structure of the classical upbringing. It provides one of only two full statements of the number and names of the age grades through which every young Spartiate had to pass: *pais, paidiskos, hêbôn*. The only other full statement comes in chapters 2-4 of his *Polity of the Lakedaimonians*, which discuss the three age grades in sequence and mention the same names for the grades, this time in their plural form: *paides, paidiskoi* and *hêbôntes*.[70] These passages are of considerable importance in showing that the structure of the Spartan upbringing in the classical period differed markedly from its structure in the Hellenistic and Roman periods, as attested in various later sources.[71] The classical upbringing as a whole covered an extended period of the young Spartiate's life; whereas, as Nigel Kennell has recently shown, the upbringing of the hellenistic and Roman periods covered only his years from age fourteen or sixteen, respectively, to age twenty.[72]

Xenophon does not indicate the precise duration of the classical upbringing. Other evidence indicates that the grade of the *paides* commenced at age seven and that the grade of the *hêbôntes* lasted from age 20 to 29 inclusive.[73] What is less certain is the age of transition between the grades of the *paides* and the *paidiskoi*. This uncertainty is of particular relevance to our episode because Xenophon tells us that Kleonymos had just grown out of the age of boyhood (ἡλικίαν τε ἔχων τὴν ἄρτι ἐκ παίδων). The best clue is Xenophon's own indication in the chapter of his *Polity* dealing with the *paidiskoi* that his comments relate to the period 'when they pass out of *paides* to enter into adolescence (εἰς τὸ μειρακιοῦσθαι), in other words around age 14-15.[74] This age is compatible with two known facts about Kleonymos: first, that he fought and died in the battle of Leuktra seven years later in 371 BC, when at the age of 21-22 he would have been just above the minimum age of 20 for service in the army; secondly, that he already has a lover in the shape of Archidamos since, according to Plutarch, it was at the age of 12 that Spartan boys acquired lovers (*erastai*) from among the reputable young men (*neoi*).[75]

The modalities of pederasty

Indeed, it is to the pederastic relationship between Archidamos and Kleonymos that we can now turn. It is of course one of the key features of the episode: the relationship which creates the vital link between Sphodrias and his adversaries in the camp of Agesilaos through which the accused general could legitimately channel his plea for mercy. I mentioned earlier that Agesilaos' granting of this request put Sphodrias and his associates in permanent debt to Agesilaos; and Xenophon rightly stresses how it

---

[70] Cf. esp. *Lak. Pol.* 2.14; 3.1; 3.5; 4.1. In the *Lak. Pol.*, however, the name of the second grade is slightly obscured by the fact that Xenophon reserves reference to the name until the end of the relevant chapter.

[71] Kennell 1995, 35-9, 117. The sources are cited by MacDowell 1986, 159-61.

[72] See the table in Kennell 1995, 39. It is unclear whether or not within the broad age grades the classical upbringing also had specific year-groups akin to those of the post-classical upbringing.

[73] Plut. *Lyk.* 16.4; 25.1; Kennell 1995, 117-18.

[74] Hippokrates, *De Hebdomadibus* 5 (éd. Littré, VIII, p.636); cf. Kennell 32 & 179 n.13.

[75] Plut., *Lyk.* 17.1.

also put Kleonymos and Sphodrias in similar debt to Archidamos: 'we, too, shall try to take care that you will never feel ashamed of our friendship.' Paul Cartledge's discussions of the episode have rightly highlighted the key role that pederastic relationships among leading Spartiates could potentially play in high-level Spartan politics, especially in the reign of Agesilaos.[76] Agesilaos himself had long experience of the potential political benefits of the close relationship between lover (*erastês*) and beloved (*erômenos* or *paidika*). His own acquisition of the kingship had been aided by the support of his own *erastês* Lysander during the succession dispute following the death of his half-brother, Agis II.[77] Xenophon, moreover, attests the role that discussion of *paidika* played in Agesilaos' conversations with the previous king of the Agiad royal house, Agesipolis I.[78] It is likely, therefore, that Agesilaos had played a role in encouraging the creation of the relationship between his own son and an up-and-coming boy from a family closely associated with his new rival, King Kleombrotos.

Before we consider Xenophon's account of the relationship, it is worth considering one aspect that he does not explicitly mention: the age differential between Kleonymos and Archidamos. The role of pederasty within Greek society in general involved the socialisation of an adolescent boy by a young unmarried man normally in his 20s.[79] Kleonymos' age clearly conforms to this norm, and there are several indications that Archidamos' age did too. First, there is a general indication in the form of Plutarch's statement that the new *erastai* came from the *neoi*, which normally refers to men in their 20s. Since *erômenoi* received their lovers at 12 years old, there will therefore have been a minimum of eight years' age difference between lover and beloved. Then there are several particular indications regarding Archidamos himself. Xenophon's passing indication that Kleonymos approached him when he was in the mess (*philition*) indicates that he was over age 20, since that was when a young Spartiate's full mess membership commenced.[80] This is confirmed by the fact that he was of a sufficient age to command an army seven years later in 371 BC,[81] which surely means that he was at least age 30. He would thus have been at least 23 at the time of our episode. This is his minimum possible age: however, it is unlikely that he was many years older, since in 366 BC he was still sufficiently young that in his *Archidamos* Isokrates could plausibly depict him as having to excuse himself for coming forward to speak in spite of his youth.[82] Given the probability that Kleonymos was 14-15 years old at the time of our episode, this all fits well with the minimum eight years' age differential suggested by the generic evidence of Plutarch.

Despite the existence of other evidence, some of it discussed above, our text has rightly been called 'the *locus classicus* of Spartan pederasty'.[83] Although it is apparent that pederasty was a significant phenomenon in Spartan society, the relationship between Archidamos and Kleonymos is one of only two specific cases of pederastic relationships in the surviving evidence; and it is the only one recorded by a contempo-

---

[76] 1981, 29; 1987, 158.
[77] Their pederastic relationship is attested by Plut. *Ages.* 2.1; *Lys.* 22.3. On the succession dispute, the primary source is Xen., *Hell.* 3.3.1-4.
[78] *Hell.* 5.3.20.
[79] Buffière 1980, esp. 605-17
[80] Although Archidamos, as heir to the Eurypontid throne, was not a normal youth, there is no reason to think that the age when he joined a mess will have differed from that of other youths.
[81] Xen., *Hell.* 6.4.18.
[82] Isokrates, *Archidamos* 1.
[83] Cartledge 1981, 29.

rary source.[84] Above all, this text provides our only surviving account of the personal interaction between two lovers.

Their first interaction comes when Kleonymos approaches Archidamos to ask him to intercede with Agesilaos. Note that Xenophon emphasises that this was no straightforward task: Kleonymos is said to have to summon up courage (ἐτόλμησεν) to go to Archidamos with his request. By the time of our episode their relationship had been going on for 2-3 years, since Kleonymos was 14-15 years old. But Kleonymos was still very young: he had only recently come out of the lowest age grade of the *paides*. It is also relevant that he had now entered the age grade of the *paidiskoi*. In his *Polity* Xenophon indicates that youths in this age grade were expected to behave with extreme modesty, keeping their hands under their cloaks, walking in silence, with their eyes fixed on the ground.[85] In other words, Kleonymos had been asked by his father to behave in a precocious manner completely contrary to the behaviour officially demanded of him.

Kleonymos' difficulty was exacerbated by the location of their conversation, which took place, as we have seen, in the mess. Xenophon's *Polity* emphasises that 'when they [the *paidiskoi*] attend the mess (*philition*), you have to be content if you can even get an answer to a question.' [86] Kleonymos therefore had to initiate an approach to Archidamos in a social context in which a *paidiskos*' expected behaviour was to be so reticent that he often might not speak even when spoken to. There was also further pressure upon Kleonymos because his presence at the mess was not by right. The attendance of a *paidiskos* at the mess was part of a long process of scrutiny, whereby the adult members were able to assess his suitability for full membership. When he reached the age of 20, the existing members would vote whether to admit him permanently, in a ballot in which a single negative vote would mean rejection.[87] It is probable that Kleonymos had ambitions to join the mess at which he made his request, since it seems likely that a youth was normally introduced into the mess of his *erastês*, as we know happened in fourth-century Crete.[88] Since membership of a mess was a criterion for the possession of Spartiate citizenship,[89] any inappropriate behaviour on his part which alienated just one of the existing members might jeopardise his entire future. That said, there is some obscurity in Xenophon's text about the precise timing and conditions of Kleonymos' request within the mess meeting. His description implies that Kleonymos simply approached Archidamos and immediately made his request; but it also implies that the request took place at or after the end of the meal, since the text appears to indicate that straight after their conversation Archidamos left the mess and went home.[90] It is unclear whether Xenophon envisaged Kleonymos as simply making a brief visit to the mess at the end of the meal, or as attending throughout the entire meal and making his approach to Archidamos towards the end, perhaps even in a private moment as the other guests were departing.

Xenophon depicts the tenor of the ensuing conversation in such a way as to reveal the deep emotional bond between Archidamos and his beloved - in marked contrast to the apparent lack of emotional commitment between Archidamos and his father. Kleonymos cries even before he makes his request, and Archidamos weeps with him in

---

[84] The other known specific relationship, that between Lysander and Agesilaos, is specifically recorded as a *pederastic* relationship only by Plutarch. Although Xenophon devotes considerable attention to the relationship between the two men, he never designates it as pederastic.

[85] Xen., *Lak. Pol.* 3.4-5.

[86] *Lak. Pol.* 3.5.

[87] Plut., *Lyk.* 12.4-6.

[88] Ephorus, *FGrH* 70F149, ap. Strabo, *Geography* 483c.

[89] Arist., *Pol.* 1271a35-7.

[90] Taking Xenophon's τότε in the sense of 'next'.

sympathy. Kleonymos begs Archidamos to save Sphodrias 'for his sake' (αὐτῷ). Despite expressing his deep reservations, Archidamos undertakes to assist for the sake of his beloved: 'since you are asking me (ἐπεὶ σὺ κελεύεις), you can be sure that I shall make every effort to get this done for you (σοι)'. As the episode develops, the text continues to highlight the intensity of the relationship. After an unknown number of days have passed Archidamos is keen to see his beloved: 'naturally enough', adds Xenophon in a personal commentary. He feels unable to do so, however, until he has spoken to Agesilaos. At this point Xenophon switches to representing the perceptions of Sphodrias' friends, who have become aware of the change in Archidamos' behaviour. He is no longer coming to see Kleonymos, whereas previously he had visited frequently – another indication of their closeness, and also of the unusual character of Kleonymos' approach *to* Archidamos. Finally, at the end of the episode the relationship's intensity is confirmed as Xenophon emphasises the extreme grief which Archidamos felt on his beloved's death.

Another aspect of the pederastic relationship apparent in the episode is its openness, conducted in public with the knowledge of mutual friends and acquaintances. This impression too is confirmed by the episode's conclusion. Kleonymos assures Archidamos that he and his father would ensure that Archidamos would never feel shame at their friendship; and Xenophon comments that indeed Kleonymos' death at the battle of Leuktra did not shame Archidamos, but rather brought him honour. The notions expressed here tie in with evidence from other sources that these feelings of honour and shame were matters not merely of internal emotion but of public reputation. In his discussion of the *paidiskoi* in the *Polity of the Lakedaimonians* Xenophon indicates that the Spartan lawgiver Lykourgos 'arranged for them to be supervised not only by the men publicly appointed but also by those personally connected with them (τοὺς κηδομένους ἑκάστων), so that they might not, by flinching, lose all their standing in the *polis*'.[91] These persons (*hoi kēdomenes*) with a supervisory role most probably included the youths' *erastai* alongside their kinsfolk, in precisely the same way that these two parties shared responsibility for supplying the household needs of young men under 30 who were not yet permitted to enter the *agora*.[92] Official expectations that *erastai* should perform this supervisory role would provide a plausible context for the assertions of later sources that *erastai* shared the good or bad reputation of their boys and were punished for their boys' wrongdoing.[93] In recent scholarship there has been debate over whether the practice of pederasty was 'institutionalised' within the Spartiate public upbringing.[94] Whilst it is true that none of the sources say or imply that pederasty was mandatory for every young man or boy, the evidence of our episode suggests that it was thoroughly integrated into the fabric of Spartiate life.

The modalities of father-son relationships

Though mediated through relations of pederasty, it is clear that family affairs loom large in our episode. The story begins with Sphodrias asking his son for help. On the surface, the request is represented in straightforward terms, with Sphodrias as the senior party speaking directly to his son, without any of the reticence or aloofness

---

[91] *Lak. Pol.* 3.3.

[92] Plut., *Lyk.* 25.1. The term *kēdemones* often bore the sense of kin (Cartledge 1987, 144), but the verb *kēdomai* can also refer to the affection of a lover, as in Plato, S*ymp.* 210c (MacDowell 1986, 64).

[93] Plut., *Lyk.* 18.4; Aelian, *VH* 3.10.

[94] The argument for 'institutionalisation' was put by Cartledge 1981, 22, but challenged by MacDowell 1986, 64; cf. also Fisher 1989, 46 n.37.

shown later between Archidamos and Agesilaos. In fact, strictly, Sphodrias does not actually ask Kleonymos to save his life; he merely states that it is within his son's power to do so. However, that observation in itself contains a reversal of normal roles of influence. As we have just seen, it would normally be Sphodrias' role, as father, to work alongside Archidamos, as *erastês*, in supervising Kleonymos' progress during his critical period as a *paidiskos*. Yet, as Sphodrias' words indicate, it is now within Kleonymos' power to save his father by using his own influence with Archidamos. Despite this role reversal, the bond between father and son remains firm. Note the inclusive tone of Kleonymos' expression of thanks to Archidamos at the end of the episode:

> 'Now *we know* (ἴσμεν) that you really care *for us* (ἡμῶν). And be sure, Archidamos, that *we shall try* (ἡμεῖς πειρασόμεθα), too, to take care that you will never feel ashamed of *our friendship* (τῇ ἡμετέρᾳ φιλίᾳ).' [my italics]

Kleonymos' repeated use of plural rather than singular pronouns, verbs and adjectives consistently links his father and himself together in a coherent family unit.

The encounters between Archidamos and Agesilaos stand in marked contrast to the apparent informality of that between Sphodrias and Kleonymos. Here the junior party has to approach his father; and, as when Kleonymos had to approach his *erastês*, Archidamos is represented as having to pluck up his courage to do so. Also, as in the case of Kleonymos' approach, he has to do so in a public setting. Unlike Kleonymos, however, he is not a *paidiskos*, but a young man in his 20s: of an age when young Spartiates were expected to behave no longer demurely but in a bold and competitive fashion.[95] Yet, unlike Kleonymos, Archidamos states that he cannot even look his father in the face: he goes to anyone else for assistance; and he is represented as avoiding approaching Agesilaos on at least two separate days.

Archidamos' reticence is matched by a corresponding aloofness on the part of Agesilaos. He suspects why his son is following him about, but takes no initiative to speak to him; and when Archidamos does make his request, he responds judgementally (Ἀλλὰ σοὶ μὲν ἔγωγε συγγνώμην ἔχω) in terms of pardon and forgiveness, as if his son had committed some wrong.[96] Subsequently, his reply to Archidamos' second approach is so non-committal that Archidamos mistakenly assumes that it is a negative response. Finally, when Agesilaos has decided to acquit Sphodrias, Xenophon leads us to believe that he does not communicate it directly to his son, since it is Kleonymos who goes to see Archidamos about the news. (Given the prior stress upon Archidamos' desire to see his beloved, the reader is surely being led to expect that Archidamos would have gone to Kleonymos with the news, had he already known.) Once again, the state of their relationship is reflected in their own words, as they appear in Archidamos' second approach to Agesilaos:

> 'Now, as it is, even if he has done something wrong, let him *for our sakes* (ἡμῶν) be forgiven *by you* (ὑπὸ σοῦ).' He [Agesilaos] replied: 'Well and good, if this should be honourable *for us* (ἡμῖν), it shall be so.' [my italics]

Although Agesilaos' reply expresses an inclusive family unit, Archidamos' appeal 'for *our* sakes' appears to refer not to his father and himself, but to himself and Kleonymos, thus contrasting their unity as a couple with his father as an isolated individual.

---

95 Xen., *Lak. Pol.* 4.1-6.

96 Of course, the representation of his judgement on Archidamos is connected to the idea of his own judgement by the polis if he were to acquit Sphodrias; but, nevertheless, his use of the terminology is still revealing.

Xenophon's narration of the reserved formality between father and son is a puzzle. It could represent a veiled commentary on the real personal relationship between Agesilaos and Archidamos. In certain respects, however, the nature of their relationship in this episode reflects certain structural features of the lifestyle of Spartan kings, in contrast with that of ordinary citizens. We have seen that ordinary Spartiate families were given a close role in supervising and assisting the progress of their sons through their critical years as *paidiskoi*. It is often claimed that the influence of Spartiate families over their sons was largely undermined by the public nature of the upbringing, by the role of the *erastês*, and by the general authority which all fathers possessed over all boys. However, as Jean Ducat has recently argued, this is to underplay the significant role retained by the family, often in cooperation with these outside influences.[97] For example, Xenophon's statement that 'if a boy tells his father when he has been whipped by another man, it is a disgrace if he does not give his son another whipping' implies a father's regular contact with his son and responsibility for his development.[98] As we have already seen, this supervision and assistance continued in the age grades of the *paidiskoi* and *hêbôntes* in collaboration with the *erastês*. As heir to the throne, however, Archidamos was exempt from the public upbringing and from having to pass its tests to achieve Spartiate citizenship.[99] We are sadly ignorant about the upbringing of a royal heir, but, structurally, there was no equivalent need for a supporting role of father for son. It is also possible that the public position and profile of both king and heir acted as a hindrance to more private contacts.[100] Despite the fact that, unlike ordinary Spartiate boys, a royal heir did not have to reside away from his family from age 7 to 30, there is apparently no opportunity in Xenophon's account of this episode for Archidamos to speak to his father in the privacy of the family home.

The *hippeis* and the Spartan 'beautiful death'

As we have seen, on hearing of his father's prospective acquittal, Kleonymos promises that he and his father would ensure that Archidamos would never feel ashamed of their friendship. Xenophon's subsequent comment on the fulfilment of that promise embraces both Kleonymos' life in Sparta and his death seven years later at the battle of Leuktra. Although Kleonymos' promise had covered both his father and himself, Xenophon focuses solely upon the honourable behaviour of the younger man, despite the fact that Sphodrias too had died nobly at Leuktra.[101] If Kleonymos was 14-15 at the time of our episode, Xenophon's comment on his honourable actions in Sparta during the remaining seven years of life will relate to the remainder of his time as a *paidiskos* and his brief period as a *hêbôn* from age 20. The words by which Xenophon describes his actions (ἐποίει ὅσα καλὰ) echo the very words (πάντα τὰ καλὰ ποιῶν) that Agesilaos had used to describe Sphodrias' successful achievements in the upbringing. They also tie in with his following comments on Kleonymos' death at Leuktra. There

---

[97] Ducat 1999, 45-6.
[98] *Lak. Pol.* 6.2.
[99] Plut., *Ages.* 1.2.
[100] Plutarch, *Ages.* 25.5, claims that Agesilaos was very fond of his children and narrates an episode in which he was espied by a friend playing horse with children. This, however, was when his children were very young, and it perhaps speaks volumes for the formality expected of a king that Agesilaos felt it necessary to ask his friend not to tell anyone before he himself became a father.
[101] *Hell.* 6.4.14.

we learn that Kleonymos had died fighting 'in front of his king' (πρὸ τοῦ βασιλέως).[102] The implication is that he had been so successful in the upbringing that as a *hêbôn* he had gained selection to the elite corps of 300 *hippeis*, who among other things formed the king's hoplite lifeguard.[103]

In fact, our passage contributes a small but significant piece of evidence for the functioning of this elite group within the Spartan army in the early fourth century. The surviving manuscripts of Xenophon's account of Leuktra mention a unit of Spartan soldiers called the *hippoi* (horsemen) who were fighting in the right wing of the phalanx alongside the aides of the *polemarchos*. Both the location of this unit within the hoplite phalanx and the fact that the cavalry had already been routed earlier in the battle provides good reason for amending the text's *hippoi* to the elite corps of *hippeis*.[104] The presence of the *hippeis* in the battle poses an issue about how they were deployed within the army. Since there were only 700 Spartiates present at the battle in total, it is implausible that the *hippeis* fought as a separate unit: if all 300 were present, the four Lakedaimonian regiments (*morai*) at the battle would each have contained only 100 Spartiates out of their complement of 500-600 men.[105] It is more plausible to believe that the *hippeis* were incorporated in some way within the structure of the *morai*: either within all the *morai* or, at the very least, within the *mora* associated with the king. Xenophon's information that Kleonymos died 'fighting in front of his king with Deinon the *polemarchos*' provides a clear piece of supporting evidence for this interpretation, indicating that the corps of *hippeis* who formed the king's lifeguard formed a unit within one of the regular Lakedaimonian *morai* commanded by its officer, the *polemarchos*. This information is repeated in different form in Xenophon's account of the battle itself:

> But when Deinon the *polemarchos* and Sphodrias from among the king's tent-companions and Kleonymos his son had died, the *hippeis* and the so-called aides of the *polemarchos* and the others fell back...[106]

Here Xenophon provides a precise account of the composition of the *mora* associated with the king: Deinon the *polemarchos* with his aides and the ordinary soldiers of the *mora*; the king and his small number of tent-companions, including Sphodrias (Kleombrotos himself is not named because at this point in the battle he had already been carried off the field); and the *hippeis*, including Kleonymos.[107]

It is, however, the manner of Kleonymos' death that most interests Xenophon. Kleonymos receives no mention in Nicole Loraux's classic article on the Spartan 'beautiful death.'[108] Yet Xenophon's account of his death is a perfect exemplification of Spartan

---

[102] Here we should give full value to the word πρὸ: Kleonymos was fighting, not just 'for' or 'in defence of' his king, as in the Penguin Classics or Loeb translations, but physically in front of King Kleombrotos. In his subsequent account of the battle (6.4.13-14), Xenophon is at pains to point out that, when Kleombrotos was struck down, his men were able to carry him out of the battle whilst still alive because those fighting πρὸ αὐτοῦ held the advantage at the time. Here πρὸ clearly means 'in front of' and the soldiers in question must include Kleonymos, who is mentioned in person in the next sentence alongside Deinon the *polemarchos*, as in our episode. We should therefore give πρὸ the same sense in our passage.

[103] The selection process is described in Xen. *Lak. Pol.* 4.3. See, generally, Figueira 2006.

[104] Cf. Anderson 1970, 247; Lazenby 1985, 10-11; Figueira 2006, 58. The passage in question is at 6.4.14; the rout of the cavalry is described earlier at 6.3.13.

[105] For the numbers of Spartiates at the battle, *Hell.* 6.4.15.

[106] 6.4.14.

[107] I leave aside the debate as to whether the *hippeis* constituted the *agêma* of the first *mora* mentioned by Xenophon as being led by the king (*Lak. Pol.* 13.6; cf. 11.9).

[108] Loraux 1977.

military ideology as promulgated by the canonical Spartan poet, Tyrtaios. The poems of Tyrtaios were recited to Spartan soldiers on campaign,[109] and would have been well known to Kleonymos and other Spartiates - and quite probably to Xenophon too.[110] His representation of Kleonymos' death 'after falling three times, first of his citizens and in the midst of the enemy' forms a close match to Tyrtaios' praise of the man who stood fast fighting in close quarters with the enemy, his valorisation of the warrior who died for his homeland, his exhortation to the young men not to hide behind their elders; and above all, his assertion of the beauty of the young man who dies fighting in the front ranks.[111] But we should also remember the short-term historical context. The defeat at Leuktra had serious socio-political consequences inside Sparta. Xenophon himself narrates the sharply differentiated reactions following news of the defeat: 'one could see those whose relatives had been killed going about in public with bright and cheerful faces, while of those whose relatives had been reported as living you would have seen but few, and these few walking about gloomy and downcast.'[112] Plutarch records that large numbers of survivors of the battle were regarded as cowards and were brought to trial.[113] Each of Xenophon's three phrases about Kleonymos' death emphasises his difference from the cowards. He was struck down and rose twice before succumbing; he was foremost in the Spartans' ranks; and, above all, while he lived the Spartans had been winning the battle, penetrating the enemy's ranks - a point Xenophon makes explicitly in his account of the battle.[114] Xenophon's concluding statement that Kleonymos did not shame him but brought him honour is more than simply an instance of Greek thinking in terms of polarity: there were hundreds of relatives and *erastai* who had felt shamed by their young men's behaviour at Leuktra.

****

At the start of this essay I noted the deficiencies in Xenophon's account of this episode. As Shipley has rightly said, as an account of a legal case his narration is in several respects 'incomplete and superficial'.[115] Yet the fact that Xenophon is writing a moral tale rather than a political analysis does not mean that his account, however incomplete or superficial, is politically innocent or socially unaware. The moral elements in the episode - Sphodrias' misdeed, Kleonymos' courage, Archidamos' struggle between love for his beloved and reticence towards his father, Agesilaos' dilemma between the demands of justice and of family self-interest, and Kleonymos' final repayment of his lover's favour - are all narrated against a backdrop of authentic and realistic Spartan values and with a keen awareness of the wider historical and social context. Xenophon's references to these values and contexts may often be implicit and allusive, and they are rarely impartial or objective. But embedded within his text there

---

[109] Lykourgos, *Against Leokrates* 107.

[110] Compare Tyrtaios fr.11.11-13 (Gerber): 'Those who dare to stand fast at one another's side and to advance towards the front ranks in hand-to-hand conflict, they die in fewer numbers...' with Xen., *Lak. Pol.* 9.1-2: '... they actually lose a smaller proportion of their men than those who prefer to retire from the danger zone... escape from premature death more generally goes with valour than with cowardice'.

[111] Tyrtaios fr. 11.21-4; 10.1-2, 15-27, 30 (Gerber).

[112] 6.4.16.

[113] *Ages.* 30.2-4. They were acquitted by Agesilaos, who had been appointed as lawgiver and announced that the laws should sleep for a day.

[114] The insistence that he was fighting in the midst of the enemy's ranks would also provide an excuse for any wounds in the back which might otherwise be taken as a sign of flight.

[115] 1987, 296.

lie rich seams of information and political intelligence which the modern interpreter can mine and exploit to advance our understanding both of the character and functioning of classical Sparta and of the agenda of the writer who constitutes our primary contemporary source. If this essay has gone some way to developing those understandings, it is in no small part due to the inspiration of Cosmo Rodewald's teaching and the example of his precise and painstaking historical scholarship.

Bibliography

J.K. Anderson, *Military Theory and Practice in the Age of Xenophon* (Berkeley and Los Angeles 1970).

G.B. Bruni, 'Mothakes, neodamôdeis, Brasideioi' in *Schiavitù, Manomissione e Classi Dipendenti nel Mondo Antico*, Pubbl. Ist. di Storia Antica, Univ. di Padova 13 (1979) 21-31.

F. Buffière, *Eros Adolescent: La pédérastie dans la Grèce antique* (Paris 1980).

L. Cantarelli, 'I mothakes spartani' *RFIC* 18 (1890) 465-484.

P. Cartledge, 'The politics of Spartan pederasty' *PCPhS* n.s. 27 (1981) 17-36.

P. Cartledge, 'Sparta and Samos: a special relationship?' *CQ* n.s. 32 (1982) 243-65.

P. Cartledge, *Agesilaos and the Crisis of Sparta* (London 1987).

G.L. Cawkwell, 'The foundation of the second Athenian confederacy' *CQ* n.s. 23 (1973) 47-60.

G.L. Cawkwell, 'The imperialism of Thrasybulus' *CQ* n.s. 26 (1976) 270-7.

E. David, 'The conspiracy of Cinadon' *Athenaeum* n.s. 57 (1979) 239-59.

J.K. Davies, *Athenian Propertied Families 600-300 B.C.* (Oxford 1971).

J. Ducat, *Les Hilotes* (*BCH* Supplément XX, Paris 1990).

J. Ducat, 'Perspectives on Spartan education in the classical period' in edd. S. Hodkinson and A. Powell, *Sparta: New Perspectives* (London 1999) 43-66.

T.J. Figueira, 'The Spartan *hippeis*' in edd. S. Hodkinson & A. Powell, *Sparta and War* (Swansea 2006) 57-84.

N.R.E. Fisher, 'Drink, *hybris* and the promotion of harmony in Sparta' in ed. A. Powell, *Classical Sparta: Techniques behind her success* (London 1989) 26-50.

V. Gray, 'Dialogue in Xenophon's *Hellenica*' *CQ* n.s. 31 (1981) 321-34.

V. Gray, *The Character of Xenophon's* Hellenica (London 1989).

C.D. Hamilton, 'Spartan politics and policy, 405-401 B.C.' *AJPh* 91 (1970) 294-314.

C.D. Hamilton, *Sparta's Bitter Victories: Politics and diplomacy in the Corinthian war* (Ithaca and London 1979).

C.D. Hamilton, *Agesilaos and the Failure of the Spartan Hegemony* (Ithaca and London 1991).

F.D. Harvey, '*Dona ferentes*: some aspects of bribery in Greek politics' in edd. P.A. Cartledge and F.D. Harvey, *Crux. Essays presented to G.E.M. de Ste. Croix on his 75th birthday* (= *History of Political Thought* 6.1/2) (Exeter and London 1985) 76-117.

G. Herman, *Ritualised Friendship and the Greek City* (Cambridge 1987).

S. Hodkinson, 'Servile and free dependants of the classical Spartan *oikos*' in edd. M. Moggi and G. Cordiano, *Schiavi e Dipendenti nell'ambito dell'Oikos e della Familia* (Pisa 1997) 45-71.

S. Hodkinson, *Property and Wealth in Classical Sparta* (London 2000).

R.M. Kallet-Marx, 'Athens, Thebes and the foundation of the second Athenian League' *ClAnt* 4 (1985) 127-51.

N.M. Kennell, *The Gymnasium of Virtue: Education and culture in ancient Sparta* (Chapel Hill and London 1995).

D.M. Lewis, *Sparta and Persia* (Leiden 1977).

J.F. Lazenby, *The Spartan Army* (Warminster 1985).

J.F. Lazenby, 'The conspiracy of Kinadon reconsidered' *Athenaeum* n.s. 85 (1997) 437-47.

N. Loraux, 'La belle mort spartiate' *Ktema* 2 (1977) 105-120; translated as 'The Spartans' "Beautiful Death"', in N. Loraux, *The Experiences of Tiresias: The feminine and the Greek man* (Princeton) 77-91.

D. Lotze, 'ΜΟΘΑΚΕΣ' *Historia* 11 (1962) 427-35.

A. McDonald, 'A note on the raid of Sphodrias' *Historia* 21 (1972) 38-44.

D.M. MacDowell, *Spartan Law* (Edinburgh 1986).

I. Malkin, *Myth and Territory in the Spartan Mediterranean* (Cambridge 1994).

L.G. Mitchell, *Greeks Bearing Gifts: The public use of private relationships in the Greek world, 435-323 BC* (Cambridge 1997).

D.J. Mosley, *Envoys and Diplomacy in Ancient Greece* (*Historia* Einzelschriften 22, Wiesbaden 1973).

K.L. Noethlichs, 'Bestechung, Bestechlichkeit und die Rolle des Geldes in der spartanischen Aussen- und Innenpolitik vom 7. bis 2. Jh. v. Chr.' *Historia* 36 (1987) 129-70.

P. Poralla, *A Prosopography of Lacedaemonians from the Earliest Times to the Death of Alexander the Great (X-323 B.C.)* (2nd edn., revised by A.S. Bradford, of the original 1914 edn., Chicago 1985).

D.G. Rice, 'Xenophon, Diodorus and the years 379/78 B.C.: Reconstruction and reappraisal' *Yale Classical Studies* 24 (1975) 95-130.

G.E.M. de Ste Croix, *The Origins of the Peloponnesian War* (London 1972).

D.R. Shipley, *Plutarch's Life of Agesilaos: Response to sources in the presentation of character* (Oxford 1997).

R.J.A. Talbert, 'The role of the helots in the class struggle at Sparta' *Historia* 38 (1989) 22-40.

C.J. Tuplin, 'Kyniskos of Mantinea' *Liverpool Classical Monthly* 2 (1977) 5-10.

M. Whitby, 'Two shadows: images of Spartans and helots', in edd. A. Powell and S. Hodkinson, *The Shadow of Sparta* (London 1994) 87-126.

JOHN GRAHAM

PLATO'S ANACHRONISMS

n his fundamental paper of 1873 E. Zeller found anachronisms in the following Platonic dialogues:

Menexenus (Socrates and Aspasia are still alive in 386). However, Zeller did not attribute this anachronism to Plato, because, true to his time, he held the *Menexenus* to be spurious.

Alcibiades I (After years of silence, Socrates addresses his first words to Alcibiades, when all his other lovers have ceased to be lovers; 103a). This too, however, was seen by Zeller as unplatonic, because he took the dialogue to be spurious. Doubts about the authenticity *of Alcibiades* I and II are still entertained today (Rutherford 1995, 3); but it has been argued recently by Denyer (2001, 14-26) that they are genuine.

Symposium (Aristophanes is made to refer at 193a to the Spartan *dioikismos of* Mantinea, which took place in 385/4, even though the dramatic date of the dialogue is established as 416 by Agathon's dramatic victory). Attempts have been made to save Plato from anachronism here, by attributing the reference to Sparta's treatment of Arcadia after their victory at Mantinea in 418. These attempts were shown to fail by Dover (1988, 86-92). Dover's main argument, from the meaning of the verb διοικίζειν, had already been used by Field (1930, 73-4). There is a second anachronism, if the passage 178e-179b refers to the Sacred Band of Thebes, as seems very possible (Rutherford 1995, 185-6), for the Sacred Band was founded in 378.

Meno (The mention at 90a of the acceptance of a large bribe by Ismenias of Thebes in 395). Attempts have been made to escape the anachronism, on the grounds that the transmitted name of the donor of the bribe, Polycrates, is different from that of the historical agent of the Great King, Timocrates (Xen. *Hell.* 3.5.1: see Dover 1988, 90 n.l6), but the essential name is surely Ismenias.

Gorgias (Although the dramatic date of the dialogue is clearly at the time of, or immediately subsequent to, the well known visit of Gorgias in 427, the violent deeds of Archelaus in seizing the throne of Macedon in 414 are mentioned at 470d-471d, 479a and 525d, and Socrates' own famous behaviour in 406, at the trial of the generals at Arginusae, is clearly referred to at 473e-474a).

Protagoras (The dramatic date is clearly before the outbreak of the Peloponnesian War, yet Callias did not own his splendid house until the death of his father Hipponicus shortly before 422/1; see Athen. *Deipn.* 5.218b. The mention at 327d of Pherecrates' *Agrioi,* which was produced in 420 (Athen. *Deipn.* 5.218d) is equally anachronistic).

Parmenides (see below).

Laws (The visit of Epimenides the Cretan to Athens is dated to ten years before the Persian Wars at 642d, almost a century later than the traditional date for Epimenides' visit). Zeller excused Plato of making this glaring anachronism by assuming it was the work of the editor, who brought out the work, when Plato had left it unfinished at his death.

To Zeller's list we now have to add the *Phaedrus*. For the dramatic date of the dialogue the years 415-404 are excluded, because Phaedrus was then in exile for his part in the profanation of the Mysteries. Because Plato conveniently provides Phaedrus' patronymic and demotic at 244a, the identification with the Φαίδρο τō Πυθοκέος Μυρρινοσίο of the lists of confiscated property *(IG* i³ 422.229-230, 426.102) is quite certain. The period 420-415 has been suggested by Rutherford (1995, 250), who is aware of the problem of finding a dramatic date, but we then have trouble with Lysias and his brother Polemarchus, who only returned from Thurii to Athens in 411, after the Athenian defeat in Sicily of 413. The sources for this (Dion. Hal. *Lys.* 1; Ps.Plut. *Lives of the Ten Orators*, 3. 83 5e; *Suda* s.v. Lysias; Photius, *Bibl.* (Budé ed.) 8.53) all state that Lysias was expelled from Thurii for *attikismos*. It would have been possible for Socrates and Phaedrus to walk out into the countryside after peace was established in 404, when Phaedrus could have returned from exile, but he was no longer a naive, enthusiastic boy (παῖς) or stripling (μειραίσκος) by that time. For these terms see 237b. That they applied to Phaedrus is shown by the passage 243e (see Rutherford 1995, 246-7). In any case, the time available is very short, since Polemarchus is still alive (257b), and he was murdered by the Thirty in February 403, to follow the chronology of Krentz (1982, 152). Dover (1968, 33, 42) offered another argument against this late dramatic date: Sophocles and Euripides seem to be alive at 268c, whereas both were dead before the end of the war. Finally, Lysias is famous for his speeches, and was called (derogatorily) a *logographos* (257c), yet it is very unlikely that Lysias wrote speeches for money before the family fortune was lost at the time of the Thirty. One speech in the corpus, 20, seems to be of earlier date than 403, but the authenticity of that speech is dubious (see W. R. M. Lamb, Loeb edition of Lysias, 452-3). It is an unavoidable conclusion that no plausible dramatic date for the *Phaedrus* can be found, which does not require the acceptance of striking anachronisms.

It would be necessary also to add the *Euthydemus,* if we follow those who identify the unnamed opponent of 304e-306c with Isocrates. The identification is regularly made (eg. Dušanić 1999, 1-16; Rutherford 1995, 112, 118-20), but since he is not named, explicit anachronism is avoided here.

These examples are sufficient for Zeller's conclusions: that Plato committed anachronisms; that these anachronisms, since they are visible to us, must have been even more unmistakable to Plato and his first readers; that if we, with our imperfect knowledge, can detect these anachronisms, there may be others, which we cannot now see, but which would have been obvious to Plato and his contemporaries; and that Plato introduced anachronisms intentionally.

Zeller's paper is rarely cited in our epigonous times, which may be the reason for some confusion in the ideas of modern scholars. It is cited by Rutherford (1995, 7 n. 12), but does not figure in his bibliography. It is also referred to by Tsitsiridis (1998, 23) in a good, brief, statement about Plato's anachronisms. In his bibliographical note (23 n.4) the most recent work cited is dated 1905. While Rutherford (1995, 249) can write of 'Plato's well-known penchant for anachronisms', C. Kahn (1996, 35) states that 'Plato's dialogues are relatively free of anachronism'. While Kahn (1996, 32) writes of Plato's 'well-defined fictive dates', A. Laird (2001, 13 n. 5) says that 'the dramatic dates in Plato can rarely be fixed with certainty'. Everyone recognizes the gross anachronism of the *Menexenus,* but F.H. Sandbach (1985, 497) found the work 'most puzzling'. There have also been many attempts to explain away individual anachronisms, which prompted Dover (1988, 90 n. 16) to write 'no one should feel happy about how much has to be explained away if we are to construct a Plato who eschews all anachronism'.

Reluctance to accept Plato's anachronisms is surprising, since some were recognized in extant ancient authors, as Aelius Aristides (ed. Lentz and Behr) 3.577-580 and Athen. *Deipn.* 5.217c-218e, 11.505f. It is also surprising, because it is widely perceived that Plato's dialogues are fiction (Sandbach 1985; Kahn 1996, 2-3, 34-5; Kingsley 1999, 45-6). Momigliano (1971, 102 cf. 46-7) wrote that 'Plato cared for historical truth no more than did Isocrates'.

Two aspects of this subject will now be examined. The first is very simple and straightforward: the putative date and the *dramatis personae* of a Platonic dialogue should never be used in the search for true, historical, chronology. The method is not legitimate. Yet it has been, and is, often so used, and I give three examples.

In the first two the dramatic date of the *Republic* is so used. When Zeller wrote in 1873, he was able to state that the greatest experts on Plato's writings were in such disagreement that the range of dates proposed for the occasion of the discussion ran from 445 or earlier to 410. By summarily dismissing all the evidence about the life of Lysias, Zeller felt able to argue that everything in Plato himself could be accommodated by a low dramatic date, 409 or 408.

The occasion of the dialogue is Socrates' visit to the Piraeus to take part in the rites of Bendis, a Thracian goddess, whose cult had been introduced in the Piraeus. The easiest and most natural interpretation of Plato's words is that this was the first occasion when her cult was celebrated. That is the interpretation of H.W. Parke (1977, 150), whose words I cite:

> "The *Republic* of Plato commences with Socrates describing how he and Plato's brother, Adeimantus, the son of Ariston, had 'gone down to the Peiraeus the previous day to pray to the goddess and at the same time wishing to see in what way they kept the festival since they were holding it for the first time. And indeed the procession of the local people seemed to me to be fine and not less suitable seemed the procession that the Thracians arranged. So we said our prayers and saw the sights and were setting off to return to Athens', when they were intercepted by Polemarchus whose father Cephalus, an old man, was a prosperous manufacturer, living as a resident alien (*metoikos*) in the Peiraeus. Socrates and Adeimantus were invited to return and have dinner with Cephalus, as they had not yet seen a unique part of the ceremonies. It is introduced by this description in the dialogue:
> 'Do you not know', said he, 'that there will be a torch race on horses in the evening in honour of the goddess'? 'On horses', said I, 'that is a novelty. Do they hold torches and pass them to each other while racing on horseback - or what do you mean'? 'Just that', said Polemarchus. 'Also besides they will hold an all-night festival which is worth seeing. We shall rise from the table after dinner and see the all-night festival'."

The cult of Bendis was introduced before 429/8, when Bendis appears in the accounts of the Treasurers of the Other Gods (*IG* i³.383.143; cf. 369.68). The name is partly restored in both places, but the restoration is certain. The whole matter is well handled by Pečirka (1966, 122-30). This *terminus ante quem*, the evidence for which was not known to Zeller, makes it impossible for Plato's brothers, Adeimantus and Glaucon, to have taken part in the discussion of the *Republic*.

There have been attempts to escape from this conclusion, as, for instance, by R. Parker (1996, 170-75). He assumes that the dramatic date of the *Republic* is established as *c.* 410, and argues that Plato refers, not to the first celebration of the cult of

Bendis, but to the first celebration after the rites had been revised. The basis for this argument is a very incomplete inscription, *IG* i³ 136, which prescribed arrangements for the cult of Bendis. This inscription is not dated, but has been tentatively placed in 413/2. Both the date of the inscription and the precise nature of its provisions are quite uncertain. It cannot provide a sufficient basis for Parker's argument, in which it is remarkable that he assumes, without evidence or argument, that the dramatic date for the *Republic is c.* 410. We may conclude that it is better to assume that Plato meant what he said, when he described the occasion as the first celebration of the cult of Bendis.

If, in addition to the cult of Bendis, we bring in the information that we possess about Lysias, and we should, more impossibilities are found. Lysias' father Cephalus died before 444/3, and Lysias and his brother Polemarchus were away from Athens from that date till 411 (see below). It is clear that the *dramatis personae of the Republic* could never have been together for the discussion related by Plato.

Yet Dover (1968, 28-46) used presumed dramatic dates of the *Republic* and the *Phaedrus* as arguments for the rejection of dates in the *Life* of Lysias. We have four sources for that *Life:* Dion. Hal. *Lysias 1;* Ps. Plut. *Lives of the Ten Orators,* 3; *Suda, s.v.* Lysias; Photius, *Bibl.* (Budé edition) 8.52-3. In both form and content these accounts are closely connected. In the best treatment known to me, U. Schindel (1967) stressed the central position of the pseudo-Plutarchian *Life,* which gives all the facts in Dionysius of Halicarnassus and the closely similar statement of the *Suda,* but also additional material, and is fuller in detail than Photius. Schindel showed that the author used good sources, and noted that the work is entirely free from romantic anecdotes. It is important also to remember that Lysias was a very prominent figure of the Classical period, from whom there was an unbroken tradition down to at least the High Roman Empire. Casual dismissal of the facts and the dates of the *Life* is quite unjustifiable, and one has only to read F. Blass' comprehensive discussion (1887, 339-45) to see that, as soon as we leave those precise facts and dates, we enter a bog of uncertain conjecture. Modern scholars have felt able to dismiss the dates of the *Life,* because Lysias' own statement that his father Cephalus was invited to Athens by Pericles, and lived there as a metic for thirty years (12.4), is thought to be irreconcilable with the statement of the *Life* that Cephalus was dead before Lysias and Polemarchus joined in the colonization of Thurii in 444/3. It is assumed that Pericles' invitation could only have been made after he became dominant politically in *c.*460, and suggested that Lysias went to Thurii at some time after the foundation of the colony. But Pericles was of the most distinguished ancestry and already prominent in 472, when he was *choregos* of the *Persae,* and the wording of our sources makes it certain that Lysias participated in the foundation of Thurii. Schindel argued strongly and well for the high date of Cephalus' arrival in Athens, even if some of his detailed conjectures were bold. In view of this, it is astonishing that Dover felt able to prefer the putative dramatic dates of the *Republic* and the *Phaedrus* to the precise factual information of the *Life.* Dover also used the conjectured age of Neaera, but his arguments for that conjecture are in the highest degree forced and speculative. We have seen the lack of historicity in those dramatic dates.

My second example is more recent. In a paper advocating a low date for the Old Oligarch, H. B. Mattingly (1997, 354 and n. 13) uses the introduction of the festival of Bendis as an analogy for his interpretation of the arrangements for the festival of the Hephaistia. Neither the Hephaistia nor the rest of his argument about the date of the Old Oligarch concern us here, but his statements about Bendis are relevant to this paper. He writes in his text '... a new festival is being created, like that for Bendis in 413/2', and in his note 'Bendis' festival was certainly instituted in 413/2; see Plato, *Republic* I. 327- 328A'. We have already seen that the cult of Bendis was introduced before 429/8. The fact that Mattingly considered a reference to the beginning of the *Republic* sufficient evidence for his statements is very striking. With no word about the problem of finding a dramatic date for the *Republic,* he uses it as a historical source for a fact and a date.

It might be thought that, even if historians fall into the error of using Plato's dialogues as sources for true history and chronology, philosophers would know better; but not so. The test case here is the date of Parmenides.

We have an acme date for Parmenides, ἤκμαζε δὲ (Παρμενίδης) κατὰ τὴν ἐνάτην καὶ ἑξηκοστὴν ὀλυμπιάδα, i.e. 504-500 (Diog. Laert. 9.23). This date is Apollodoran, as was shown conclusively by F. Jacoby (1902, 227-32 = *FGrH* 244 F341), who gave it as his frg. 26 of Apollodorus' *Chronica*. Because the colony at Elea was not founded till c. 540, Jacoby thought we should choose the last year of the Olympiad, 500, which implies that Parmenides' date of birth was 540. Apart from Apollodorus' date, there are a number of synchronisms in late authors, all of which Jacoby (1902, 233-4) showed to be worthless. As far as our historical sources go, therefore, only the Apollodoran date comes into consideration.

In the *Parmenides,* however, Plato makes an old Parmenides of about 65 years hold a discussion with a very young (σφόδρα νέον) Socrates (127b-c). Plato also referred to the meeting in the *Theaetetus* (183e) and *Sophist* (217c). We know that Socrates was born in 469, so the earliest possible date of the discussion reported in the *Parmenides* must be c. 450. At that time, according to Apollodorus, Parmenides would have been about 90, and a meeting with Socrates in Athens quite impossible. Plato's indication of Parmenides' age gives a date of birth of c. 515, which is quite irreconcilable with that of Apollodorus. The anachronism was already pointed out by Athenaeus *(Deipn.* 11.505f).

Zeller took this to be an example of Platonic anachronism, motivated by Plato's desire to explore the relationship between Eleatic ideas and his own philosophy. To put that in his normal dialogue form, he created a fictitious meeting between Socrates and Parmenides, which required a significant lowering of the date of Parmenides. Many other students of ancient philosophy, however, have preferred the date indicated by Plato. In his book, which was published in 1902, Jacoby was already able to give a numerous list of those who, in his opinion, misused the Platonic dialogue, and concludes (1902, 233-4) 'in this whole question one observes a wonderful inconsistency of the learned critics'.

In modern times the Platonic date was preferred by G. S. Kirk and J. E. Raven in their influential book (1957, 263-4), a passage not changed by M. Schofield in his revised edition (1983, 240), and H. Erbse (1998, 17-18) has written recently that this dating is generally accepted. But this is to fall into methodological error. The Platonic date is in no way comparable to that of Apollodorus. The latter is history, the former fiction. We do not have two historical dates to choose from. We have one, that of Apollodorus.

That date is obviously calculated. As Jacoby pointed out, Parmenides' acme is forty years after that of Xenophanes, and forty years before that of his pupil Zeno. Scholars have also noticed that Parmenides' date of birth coincides with the foundation date of Elea. It is on such arguments that many have felt justified in rejecting Apollodorus' date (see, e.g., Kirk, Raven, Scholfield1983). But we cannot know what evidence and indications were available to him. His date cannot be taken as accurate to the year, but if we reject it, we have no ancient date for Parmenides, and are thrown back onto conjecture alone.

While the first aspect of Plato's anachronisms examined here is very simple and straightforward, the second, Plato's motive, does not admit of certain conclusions.

Zeller thought that Plato was not a historian but a poet, and if it suited his artistic aims, had no compunction about introducing anachronisms. That explanation works well in the case of the *Parmenides,* as we have just seen. It also works for the *Protagoras,* since it is obviously appropriate to hold the gathering of the great Sophists at the house of Callias, whom Plato (*Ap.* 20a; *Cra.* 391b) and Xenophon (*Symp.*1.5) depict as notorious for his expenditure on Sophists. Plato may also have had good reasons for bringing together the people in the *Republic,* and it obviously suited his purposes in the *Phaedrus* to have Socrates and a young Phaedrus walk out into an idyllic countryside, and show the weaknesses of a famous orator, Lysias.

Motives of a similar kind have been suggested for the gross anachronism of the *Menexenus.* L.J. Coventry (1989, 4) thought that: 1) it enables Plato to explore the inconsistencies of Athenian policy, notably in relations with *barbaroi;* 2) it provided an extreme example of the rhetoricians' habit of preparing speeches long before they are to be delivered; and 3), Plato could therefore emphasize rhetoricians' indifference to truth. Whether or not one regards these explanations as convincing, they offer an example where an anachronism is thought to serve Plato's artistic or philosophical aims.

There are anachronisms, however, which seem to carry no compositional advantage and appear gratuitous. Examples would be the anachronisms in the *Symposium, Meno, Gorgias* and *Laws.* Though E. R. Dodds (1959, 241-2) had some subtle ideas about Plato's possible motives for introducing Archelaus of Macedon into the *Gorgias.* One explanation that would account for all the anachronisms is that Plato purposely introduced them, in order to warn the reader that his dialogues are not accounts of historical occasions, but his own free compositions. It might be objected to this explanation that, in that case, we should expect more anachronisms, but here we have to remember that, as Zeller saw, there may well be more anachronisms in Plato's work than we, with our imperfect knowledge, can now detect.

As Kahn (1996, 34-5) rightly notes, while Xenophon's Socratic works are patently fictional, Plato's 'are so convincing that the reader feels as if he or she had been present at an actual conversation'. Yet, as C. Gill (1993, 66-8) pointed out, Plato was unlike Thucydides in giving no formal indication of the fictionality of his dialogues. Thucydides' statement about the speeches in his work (1.22.1) may be opaque, but it undoubtedly warns the reader that they are at least in part his own compositions.

Some of the ways in which Plato presents his dialogues have been seen as warnings that they are not historically true. Rutherford (1995, 71) notes that when dialogues are narrated by people other than Socrates, they are often set far in the past. He points to the 'intricate "layered" structure' of the *Symposium.* Apollodorus is asked by a friend to describe the occasion, and he states that he only knows it from Aristodemus, who was present. The long distance from the actual time of the event is emphasized (173a); Aristodemus admits that his account is selective (178a; 180c); and that he became drowsy towards the end (223c-d). Rutherford (1995, 181) sees all these indications as casting some doubt on the authenticity of the narrative. The *Parmenides* is related at third hand and by a man who has become mainly interested in horses (126-127a). Sandbach (1985, 483) suggested that that was to show in a humorous way that the dialogue was not historical truth.

If these ideas are right, we see that Plato, even if he did not provide, as Thucydides did, an explicit statement, found ways of implying that his dialogues are not historically accurate accounts of actual occasions. The insertion of anachronisms would have implied that very strikingly, as would have been obvious to his first readers.

My thanks are due to my friends, Don Lateiner, Martin Ostwald, David Rankin and Martina Stemich, who kindly read this paper in draft and made helpful suggestions for its improvement.

Bibliography.

F. Blass, *Die attische Beredsamkeit I* (second edition, Leipzig 1887).

L.J. Coventry, 'Philosophy and rhetoric in the *Menexenus*' *JHS* 109 (1989) 1-15.

ed. N. Denyer, *Plato, Alcibiades* (Cambridge 2001).

K.J. Dover, *The Greeks and their Legacy* (Oxford 1988) 86-101 (republishing id., 'The Date of Plato's *Symposium*' *Phronesis* 10 (1965) 2-20).

K. J. Dover, *Lysias and the Corpus Lysiacum* (Berkeley 1968).

S. Dušanić, 'Isocrates, the Chian intellectuals, and the political context of the *Euthydemus*' *JHS* 119 (1999) 1-16

H. Erbse, 'Parmenides und Sokrates bei Platon. Ein literatur-geschichtlicher Versuch' *Hermes* 126 (1998) 15-30.

G. C. Field, *Plato and his Contemporaries* (London 1930).

C. Gill, 'Plato on falsehood and fiction' in edd. C. Gill and T. P. Wiseman, *Lies and Fiction in the Ancient World* (Exeter 1993) 38-87.

F. Jacobi, *Apollodors Chronik* (Berlin 1902).

C. Kahn, *Plato and the Socratic Dialogue* (Cambridge 1996).

P. Kingsley, *In the Dark Places of Wisdom* (Shaftesbury, Boston, Melbourne 1999).

G. S. Kirk and J. E. Raven, *The Presocratic Philosophers* (Cambridge 1957).

G. S. Kirk and J. E. Raven *The Presocratic Philosophers* (second edition rev. M. Schofield, Cambridge 1983).

P. Krentz, *The Thirty at Athens* (Ithaca and London 1982).

A. Laird, 'Ringing the changes on Gyges: philosophy and the formation of fiction in Plato's *Republic*' *JHS* 121 (2001) 12-29.

H.B. Mattingley, 'The date and purpose of the Pseudo-Xenophon Constitution of Athens' *CQ 47* (1997) 352-7.

A. Momigliano, *The Development of Greek Biography* (Cambridge, Mass., 1971).

H.W. Parke, *Festivals of the Athenians* (London, 1977).

R. Parker, *Athenian Religion: a History* (Oxford 1996).

J. Pečirka, *The Formula for the Grant of Enktesis in Attic Inscriptions* (Prague 1966).

R. B. Rutherford, *The Art of Plato* (London 1995).

F.H. Sandbach, 'Plato and the Socratic work of Xenophon', in *The Cambridge History of Classical Literature* I, ed. P. E. Easterling and B. M. W. Knox (Cambridge 1985) 478-497.

U. Schindel, 'Untersuchungen zur Biographic des Redners Lysias' *RhM* 110 (1967) 32-52.

S. Tsitsiridis, *Plato's Menexenus* (Stuttgart and Leipzig 1998).

E. Zeller, 'Über die Anachronismen in den platonischen Gesprächen' *Abhand. königl. Akad. Wiss. Zu Berlin, Phil-hist. Kl,* 1873, 79-99 (= *Eduard Zellers Kleine Schriften* I (Berlin 1910) 115-35).

JOHN DAVIES

THE PHOKIAN HIEROSYLIA AT DELPHI: QUANTITIES AND CONSEQUENCES

t the end of his narrative of the Third Sacred War Diodoros gives a detailed account of the losses which the sanctuary at Delphi had sustained as a result of the Phokians' conversion into coin of much of the bullion which had been incorporated in the dedications. The estimate was initially made (it seems) by the Phokians themselves when Onomarchos, Phayllos and their financial administrator Philon (16.56.3-5) became the focus of an internal enquiry,[1] though Diodoros' narrative slides imperceptibly from an internal Phokian wartime witch-hunt to the post-war outcome in reporting that the sum total was over 10,000 T(alents) (16.56.6). Conspicuously and suspiciously round figure though that is, commentators have largely tended to accept it as a reasonable approximation.[2] That acceptance has derived partly from a fragmentary fourth-century inscription (Reinach 1928) which has been interpreted as preserving part of the accounting and might therefore confirm that the calculation was made in detail, but mainly from the way in which the indemnity was imposed upon the Phokians, since it clearly implied that the total sum to be recouped was known.[3] Moreover, Diodoros' reference to the dedications made by Kroisos of Lydia (16.56.6) picks up He-rodotos' description of them (1.50-1) accurately enough to suggest that at least some attempt at precision was made at the time (cf. the reckonings made by McQueen 1995, 129-30). However, the first part of this paper argues that a much lower figure, of 4000 to 5000 T, should replace the transmitted figure of 10,000 T. The second part attempts to assess the economic impact of the re-entry of the Delphian bullion into monetary circulation, in the light of contemporary interpretations but also in the context of two other substantial concurrent additions to the Greek money supply. The third part seeks to show that Phokian behaviour was much less innovative than the literary tradition would have us believe.

Acknowledgements
This paper was first presented at seminars in Oxford and Liverpool in October and November 2003. For helpful comments and additions I am very grateful to my Oxford respondent Jez Stanley, to other seminar participants, and to Manuela Mari. Its topic is not so remote from Cosmo Rodewald's main scholarly preoccupations as might appear, for like his book of 1976 it deals directly with money, while its sub-text, the tension between behavioural norms and economic realities, echoes the title of his 1974 book and is intended to illustrate its theme. In any case, it is not just our shared professional niche, or today's close collegiality between ancient historians in Liverpool and Manchester, which make it a particular pleasure to contribute to this volume, but also my membership of the Rodewald Society, the Liverpool-based group which sponsors chamber music concerts in the city. Its name commemorates Cosmo's great-uncle, the Liverpool-based merchant and musician Alfred Edward Rodewald (1862-1903), who was a friend and early patron of Elgar. That a rehearsal room (well known to me in another capacity) in the Philharmonic Hall also commemorates his name reflects a warm recognition of the family's contribution to the city's cultural life. I am most grateful to Mr Alan Jones, of the Royal Liverpool Philharmonic Society, for helpful information.

[1] Thus 16.56.3, with McQueen 1995, 128-9 for a suggested date (winter 347/6) and political context.
[2] References in Sanchez 2001, 138 n.78 and Mari 2002, 127; add McQueen 1995, 129-30, but note also Lewis's cautiously distancing tone (Lewis 1989, 234 = 1997, 379).
[3] Diod. 16.57.1; 60.1-2, with Sanchez 2001, 139.

I

The first step in assessing the credentials of the 10,000 T figure is to consider the inscription. First published by Reinach in 1928, it has now been revisited and (with another fragment) republished by Lefèvre with the deepest scepticism (*CID* IV Appendice, no. A, pp. 385-7). The texts run:

Inv.4549:
    vac. A *vac.*
    - - ΜΑΤΑΤΑΠΡ̣ - -
    - ΓΡΑΨΑΙΕ -
4 - ΤΩΝΠΟΛ -
    - ΗΧΩΡΑΕ -
    - ΜΗΘΗΙΔ -
    - [*vac.*] ΑΛΥΑΚΤΟ̣ -
8 - ΙΕ̣ΠΤΑ *v.* ΑΠ -
    - ΕΔΑΙΜΟΝΙΩ -
    - ΑΛΚΟΥΣΜΑΓ -
    - ΥΝΕΝΤΗΙΧ̣ -
12- ΙΟΥΑ -
    - Ι Ι -
    - Ρ -

Inv. 6722:
    traces
    ΟΙΝ - -
    ΑΣΤ -
4 ΩΝΟ -
    ΚΤΙΟ -
    Ι̣.ΕΟ -
    .ΤΗΛΗ̣ -
    vac.

Since, to be fair, the letters ΑΛΥΑΚΤΟ[-] on Inv. 4549 line 7, which look like a reference to Alyattes of Lydia (cf. Hdt. 1.25.2: **Appendix 1**, item 3) and were the original peg for Reinach's interpretation, are still there and are still suggestive, I am not myself so sure as Lefèvre that Reinach's approach, though indeed adventurous, was misguided; when Theopompos reports that 60 T of the plundered monies went to the Athenian general Chares (*FGrH* 115 F 249), the Wortlaut in Athenaios (12.43, 532d-e), which suggests that the fragment came from a tabulated list of beneficiaries, indicates that lists were indeed made. Similarly, the ethnic ΛΑΚ]ΕΔΑΙΜΟΝΙΩ[Ν (or –Ι)] in Inv. 4549, line 9, is at least not out of place. However, even if Reinach was right, and even if his wild calculations of an 80-letter line are acceptable, these two miserable scraps will not go far to validate Diodoros' text. It will be wisest to take that possible prop off-stage.

We ought to be on stronger ground with references in literary texts to what was stolen. Reinach reported (1928, 41) that he could identify 26 ransacked objects, mostly of gold, but then tiresomely failed to show his working by presenting his list. An attempt to fill the gap is set out in **Appendix I**. The list which emerges is both reassuring and alarming: reassuring in that the number of objects is not much larger than Reinach's, but alarming in that it is a long way from reaching 10,000 T. Even if we ignore the problem of whether the literary tradition is reckoning in the Aiginetan talent or the much lighter Euboiic talent, even if we count into the total not just the items explicitly identified as ending in the melting-pot but also the other gold and silver items, even if we give 'white gold' a high (up to 75%) gold content, even if we convert gold into silver at 13:1,[4] and even if we accept Diodoros' figure for item 12, the items for which we have plausible figures yield the equivalent of 4173.5 T in silver. The question is how far beyond that approximate figure we should push the total. On the one hand we may be sure that much was lost of which the literary record pre-

---

[4] McQueen 1995, 130; but the table in Lewis 1968,108 shows how the ratio had already slipped to near 12:1 by the 350s.

serves no trace. Indeed, as the list makes clear, there were other dedications, especially those of Kroisos, which were likely targets, while to the plundered dedications must be added Onomarchos' appropriation of the god's own funds (Diod. 16.56.5). All the same, the chances are that we have got a record of the major items, as the use of Herodotos by Diodoros' source strongly suggests, while the jewellery cited by Theopompos for its shock-horror impact had value as dividends for womenfolk and favourites rather than as convertible assets. Likewise, the evidence of the contemporary building accounts (Davies 1998) hardly suggests that the shrine was flush with money in 356: on the contrary, though money was trickling in from Amphiktyonic percepts (the First and Second Obols), and though Delphi City had made a credit allocation available, it was a case of spending what they received rather than working their way through a cash mountain. All in all, it is hard to believe that the overall total of misappropriated monies and objects will have much exceeded the equivalent of 5000 T of silver at an absolute maximum.

A third ground of doubt over the reliability of the transmitted figure comprises the evidence for the numbers of soldiers likely to have been in Phokian pay. Though Diodoros repeatedly refers to 'large numbers of soldiers' (16.24.2), 'large numbers of mercenaries' (25.1), 'large numbers of mercenaries' (28.1), 'a huge mercenary force' (30.1), 'a large mercenary force' (30.1), 'a strong force of men' (30.2), 'an army of some size' (30.3), 'a considerable number of mercenaries' (32.4), and 'many mercenaries and a considerable number of allies' (37.2), the few figures which he gives are much less formidable than his clichés might suggest: 5000 for the initial invasion of Lokroi (25.1), over 10,000 for a later invasion (30.3), 7000 for the initial unsuccessful response to Lykophron's request (35.1), the entire army with Onomarchos for his defeat of Philip in 353 (35.2), 20,000 foot and 5000 cavalry for the Battle of Crocus Field in early summer 352 (35.4), and a mixed bag of Spartans, Achaians, Athenians, and Pheraians amounting to 10,400 in all at Thermopylai later that summer (37.3). Demosthenes' figures of 10,000+ foot and 1000 cavalry (Dem. 18.230), though undated and dangerously round, may reflect that campaign. Crocus Field apart, the Phokian commanders seem rarely to have had more than 10,000 men at their disposal, and often fewer: for one engagement, the Boiotians and Achaians with 14,500 men between them are said to have been far superior in numbers (31.3), while the slaughter of 6000 unfortunates after Crocus Field and the capture of 3000, if accurately reported (35.6), will at least have cut the wages bill substantially. True, we are told (twice, indeed, because of the doublet) both that at the outset Philomelos offered 1½ times normal pay (25.1 = 30.1) and that after Crocus Field Phayllos offered double pay (36.1). Yet, even if, on the assumption that normal pay was 4 obols per diem,[5] that implied a daily rate initially of 6, later 8 ob., then even an army of 10,000 employed for 300 days p.a. would not have generated an annual wages bill of more than 500 T, later 750 T – figures which not even the attested scale of activity before 352, let alone the subsequent low-key stalemate, can plausibly sustain over the *dekaetia*. In any case, as Williams points out (1972, 46), by no means all the men under Phokian command will have been mercenaries,[6] so that his estimate of *ca.* 3840 T for the final

[5] See Griffith 1933, 297 ff.; Gomme & Sandbach 1973, 496-7; Pritchett 1971/1974,3-29. Loomis's slightly higher figures (Loomis 1997, 32-61) focus primarily on Athens, but Central Greece may not normally have needed premium rates. The calculations in the text differ from those of Williams (1972, 53-4).
[6] Numbers for pre-war Phokian military manpower are irritatingly elusive. The figure of 600 *aristoi* at the Chalk Battle (Hdt. 8.27.3) plainly cannot reflect full military strength, for Herodotos does not describe the contingent of 1000 hoplites at Thermopylai in 480 (Hdt. 7.203.1 and 217.2) as *pandemei*, as he does that of the Opountian Lokrians: in 479, beside 1000 hoplites under Harmokydes at Plataiai in 479 (Hdt. 9.17.2; 31.5), other non-Medizing Phokians

total of expenditure on mercenaries, though based on an average figure of 8000 men which perhaps underestimates the likely scale of oscillation,[7] has a good chance of being realistic.

Even so, it is not these figures which undermine the Diodoran narrative so much as the coins themselves. Fortunately, it is generally agreed that those minted by the Phokian commanders in 356-346 can be identified as those which carry a frontal ox-head on the obverse and an Apollo facing right on the reverse (Period V in the classification of Williams 1972), contrasting thereby with previous series which show Artemis. Williams's catalogue divides them into six sections, distributed thus:

Section	denomination	obverse dies	specimens	specimens per obverse die
A, 356-4	½-drachmas	9	46	5
	obols	2	3	1.5
B, 356-4	½-drachmas	2	7	3.5
C, 354-46	½-drachmas	18	35	2
	obols	11	12	1
D, 354-46	½-drachmas	7	76	11
	obols	5	6	1
E, 354-46	½-drachmas	3	3	1
F, 354-46	drachmas	2	4	2

The predominant denomination, the half-drachma, shows 164 specimens representing 39 obverse dies.[8] Though there has been a long-standing debate about the likely rate of survival of Greek coins, there is now some (though far from complete) agreement that the higher the ratio of surviving specimens per obverse die, the likelier it is that all the obverse dies which were used for the particular series are exemplified by surviving coins. To cite the most recent discussion, 'these calculations need some care below a ratio of 3:1, are potentially dangerous below a ratio of 2:1 and must be avoided if the ratio falls below 1.5:1'.[9] The present case is therefore non-problematic, for while the meagre obol issues show a dangerously low ratio, for well-known reasons stemming from the lower survival rate of low-value issues,[10] the ratio for the half-drachma issues is well over 4, thereby offering some confidence that most of the obverse dies used by the Phokian moneyers at Delphi are exemplified by surviving coins.

Yet the more confidence is thus offered, the more subversive the consequences are, for the next objective must be to seek to determine what initial weight of bullion is represented by the Period V issues. The argument turns here on the outcome of a second debate among numismatists, this time that of establishing (a) the theoretical possibility of an average value for the number of coins struck from each obverse die,

---

were acting as guerrillas round Parnassos (9.31.5). That the Spartans looked to Phokis (as to Boiotia and Lokris) for cavalry rather than infantry in 431 (Thuc. 2.9.3) presumably reflects Spartan need as much as the nature of Phokian society (though McInerney 1999, 191 draws a more confident inference), while a peltast force had appeared by 371 (Xen. *Hell.* 6.4.9, with McInerney 1999, 197).

[7] Williams 1972, 53-4, following Parke 1933, 140.

[8] Williams's figures will no doubt need revision in the light of new finds and hoards, but the pattern is already so clear that new evidence is unlikely to subvert it. De Callataÿ 2003 does not cover Phokis.

[9] De Callataÿ 2005, 75, with an outline of the debate on 73-79.

[10] Kim 2001, 12-13.

and (b) the likely range of such an average value. Again, exposition can be cut short by referring to the most recent discussion, which concludes that the figure of 20,000 specimens per obverse die is a reasonable working assumption.[11] That this is a soft figure, open to being doubled or halved, does not matter, for the calculations make their impact in any event. If each of 39 dies struck 20,000 half-drachma specimens, the total minted was 780,000 specimens. At an average weight of 2.75 g. (thus Williams 1972, 61), they will have weighed 2,145,000 g., i.e. 2145 kg. or 2.14 tonnes of silver. Translated into talents, that figure corresponds to 56.7 Aiginetan T of 37.80 kg. or 82.9 Attic-Euboic T of 25.86 kg. Between such sums and the possible 4173.5 T (silver equivalent) of the embezzled dedications or the possible 3840 T of the mercenaries' wage bill, let alone between them and the 10,000 T of the Diodoran tradition, stands a gulf so wide as to be absurd – and the more doubt is cast on the assumption of 20,000 specimens per obverse die, the wider that gulf becomes.

The challenge is to save the phenomena. It is perhaps best to start with the figures for the dedications and the wages bill, for having been reached independently it is encouraging that they are at least within distant sight of each other. The figure for the wages bill, moreover, is comfortably compatible with those for other large-scale but shorter military operations, such as the 1400+ T spent by Athens on suppressing the Samos revolt in 441-439 (*IG* i³ 363), the 2000+ T spent on the Poteidaia campaign (Thuc. 2.70.2), or the 2000++ T spent by Syracuse on resisting the Athenian attack in 415-13 (Thuc. 7.48.5). Given that compatibility, it will not be unreasonable to think of 4000+ T as something like the real figure for the Phokian spend, so that it is the rogue figures, in Diodoros and from the AR coinage, which need explanation.

Oddly enough, the Diodoran figure is easier to account for. Just as Theban domination of the Amphiktyony had ensured before 356 that the Phokians were fined 'many talents' for cultivating Sacred Land, even though the Phokians claimed (disingenuously, perhaps, in the light of 16.23.3) that 'only an extremely small portion of the land had been cultivated' (Diod. 16.23.5, tr. McQueen), so too it had ensured in the 370s not merely that Sparta was saddled with an unpayable 500 T as penalty for the seizure of the Kadmeia (Diod. 16.29.2: no specific figure at 16.23.2), but also that because of failure to pay the figure was doubled to 1000 T.[12] If we assume that the 10,000 T figure does correctly report the fine eventually imposed on the Phokians, that precedent suggests that the actual total of misspent resources was set at 5000 T and was followed by a genuinely historical but unattested decision by the Amphiktyones in 346, to exact double the value of the losses. That is not an unreasonable assumption, if we allow either for a long tail of objects known at the time to have been melted down but not known to our surviving tradition, and/or for a degree of overvaluation, unscrupulous or otherwise, and/or for a possible computation of interest due to the god, and/or for a heavy dose of vindictiveness on the part of the post-war Amphiktyones. None of these suppositions creates major difficulty.

II

It is therefore the figure for the AR coinage which is seriously out of kilter with the rest - vastly more so, indeed, than Williams envisaged when he emphasised that 'the sur-

---

[11] De Callataÿ 2005, 75-79.

[12] Diod. 16.29.2-3; Lefèvre 1998, 242; Sanchez 2001:483 n.104. The account in [Dem.] 59.97--8 of Pausanias being fined 1000 T for inscribing his name on the tripod of Plataiai transmits a wildly exaggerated figure (contrast the historical figure of 50 T levied on the Athenians in 340/39 for a roughly comparable offence, Aisch. 3.116) but could well be, as Sanchez implies, a further echo of the Spartan fine.

viving Phokian silver has been underestimated' (1972, 53). To try to rescue it by adding the trivial obol and drachma issues onto the balance will obviously be futile, as will the assumption that far more were minted but were recalled after 346 as looted sacred property. Some indeed were, to be transformed into the statue of Apollo which the Amphiktyones erected 'from the sin of the Phokians towards the god',[13] but that will have been only a token, for no one such statue could have accommodated the sheer weight and bulk of the embezzled silver. In fact, for two further reasons the search for a solution has to be far more radical. The first is, as noted above, that the predominant coin in Period V was the half-drachm of 2.75 g. Not only will such a coin have represented at best a day's wage for a mercenary (and not even that after the wage increases) and therefore have been wholly impractical as a medium of payment for long-term employment, but also the Apollo head on its reverse, openly proclaiming its origin, will have revealed it as a minor coinage (of suspect origins, moreover, insofar as coin-changers cared about such matters) well outside the mainstream of fourth-century coined silver as represented by Korinthian Pegasi or Athenian tetra-drachms. Any search for what the mercenaries actually received should be looking for pegasi or owls, whether genuine, imitation, or counterfeit.

The second reason is that much of the bullion which the Phokian commanders melted down was in gold, not silver. Simply in terms of weight, the reported gold content of the major relevant items amounted to just over 325 T,[14] i.e. (at 12:1) the equivalent of 3900 T of silver, so that the fate of this gold, and the route by which it was converted into mercenaries' wages, need to be identified. The well-known problem which such a quest poses is that while Diodoros asserts that both Onomarchos and Phayllos struck gold coins as well as silver,[15] no such Phokian gold coin has ever been identified. Williams was surely right to suggest that instead the gold was 'dispersed for large-scale bribery and exchanged either for acceptable silver coinage from outside, such as Athenian tetradrachms, Corinthian staters, or Lokrian didrachms... or for silver bullion which the Phokians themselves could turn into silver coins'. However, as we have just seen, on quantitative grounds his subsequent argument that 'there was no real need for a gold coinage' is likely to have been seriously astray.[16]

In any case, the principal question remains: where did the gold go? Diodoros gives us no answer beyond the alleged gold coinage itself, but two more satisfactory answers are available, one direct, the second indirect. The first, direct, answer is to endorse and to support Williams's surmise that it was 'exchanged for acceptable silver coinage from outside'. True, his conjecture that the Arethusa/Aias issues of Eastern Lokris were one such issue meets the fatal objection that the series seems to have begun *ca.* 380,[17] while there is no immediately obvious horizon in the production of Korinthian staters until the changes associated with the support given to Timoleon in and after 344.[18] Athens, however, is a different matter. Given her accessibility, given the existence of the Laureion silver mines, and given her tacit support for the Phokians throughout the war, it would be natural to look in that direction in any case, but indi-

---

[13] Paus. 10.15.7; Jacquemin 1999, 47 and 309 no. **017**. In any case recent re-calculations suggest that the proceeds from the Phokian indemnity payments amounted only to some 61 T (Marchetti 1999, against Kinns 1983). The replacement of the gold *perirrhanterion* gifted by Kroisos can be followed from 334/3 onwards in *CID* II.
[14] **Appendix 1**, items 2 (30 T), 4 (10 T), 5 (170 T), 6 (6½ T), 7 (8 ⅔ T), 12 (23½ T), 15 (8 T), 22 (16 T), and 25-28 (50 T): total just over 325 T weight of gold.
[15] Diod. 16.33.2; 36.1; 56.5; 61.3.
[16] Williams 1972, 56.
[17] Williams 1972, 53 n.2; Kraay 1976, 122-3.
[18] Kraay 1976, 85-88. No firm date can be given to a small issue of gold trihemiobols (Ravel 1935, 1-6; Kraay 1976, 86 n.2).

rect evidence makes it overwhelmingly probable that Delphian gold was exchanged for Athenian tetradrachms. Admittedly, since the frightful task of cataloguing fourth-century Athenian tetradrachms remains a mirage, the coins themselves do not yet provide direct quantitative information, but the mine-leases, together with the expansion and elaboration of shafts, furnaces and washeries,[19] are unequivocal. They show a steady increase in the annual number of mine-lease transactions, from the 17 recorded in 367/6 (*Agora* XIX, **P5**) through the fragmentary but substantial records of the 350s (**P6-P12**) to the gigantic lists of the 340s (**P13-26**) and beyond. Not, of course, that such expansion was being driven purely, or even mainly, by the arrival of gold-bearing Phokian emissaries, for Xenophon's *Poroi* of *ca.* 355, with its advocacy of public investment in mining via a slave workforce (4.11-52), may already be reflecting what it urges, a greater awareness of the possibilities which Laureion offered. All the same, and although the estimates of silver bullion yield which have been made on the basis of the leases, at *ca.* 1000 T. annually, are probably over-optimistic except perhaps for the late 340s and 330s,[20] we can be reasonably confident that the bullion supply from Laureion could have comfortably met the Phokian commanders' needs for coin.

Of course this direct answer to the question 'Where did the gold go?' fuels the need for an indirect answer, since the emergence of some 325 T of gold must have had a major impact. Here we are fortunate, for evidence of such an impact emerges from the more complex tradition begun by Theopompos' pamphlet *On the treasures plundered from Delphi*[21] and by the essay *On the tyrants in Sicily* of Phainias of Eresos. Both must have been written within a generation or so after 346, and were followed a century or so later by Anaxandridas' work with the same title as Theopompos', by Polemon's rejoinder, and by at least two other works of the second century BC, Hagesandros' *Hypomnemata* and Alketas' *On the dedications at Delphi*.[22] In itself this tradition clearly morphed into an anecdotal-antiquarian debate on the basis of monuments and dedications, but it formed the basis of a genuine interpretative insight which comes from a surprising source, Athenaios' Book 6. At 6.13, 228c, Ulpian changes the subject abruptly away from fish and fishmongers in order to pose the questions whether 'we have evidence to show that the ancients used silver vessels at their dinners and whether *pinax* [here in the sense of 'salver'] is a Greek word'. At the cost of inserting excessive detail, but with the dividend of providing up-to-date references,[23] the entire subsequent exposition deserves detailed summary.

After a digression on *teganon* 'saucepan' (6.14) comes (6.15, 229b) a citation from Alexis' *Phygas*, F 259, and the statement (from Juba, *FGrH* 275 F 87) that 'until Makedonian times diners used pottery utensils', with references to Kleopatra VII[24] and the *Hypomnemata* of Ptolemy VIII (*FGrH* 234 F 7). There follow (6.16, 229e) references to silver *pinakes* in Aristophanes' *Ploutos* (812-15), Plato's *Presbeis* (F 127) and Sophron's *Mimes* (F 29), in turn followed (6.17, 230a) by a caustic sketch in Philip-

[19] References most conveniently in Goette 2001, 209-19 and 397 nos. 168-182.

[20] Isager & Hansen 1975, 44-5. De Callataÿ 2003 does not offer estimates for Athenian emissions.

[21] *FGrH* 115 F 247-249 - if it was a separate book (thus Flower 1994, 36-7) and not part of the *Philippika*. For the problem cf. Davies 2000, 558 n. 14, and for the biographical tradition Shrimpton 1991, 3-15 and Flower 1994, 11-25.

[22] Respectively Phainias F 11-13 Wehrli², Anaxandridas *FGrH* 404 F 2, Polemon *FHG* III 123-4 F 28, Hagesandros *FHG* IV 412-22, and Alketas *FGrH* 405, with discussions by Jacquemin 1999, 264 and Mari 2002, 87 n2.

[23] All references to the fragments of mime and comedy are to Kassel-Austin.

[24] For the evidence which this passage provides of her lavish use of Eastern Sigillata see now Lund 2005.

pides' *Argyriou aphanismos* (F 9) of rich metics flaunting silver vessels, by a vignette in Alexis' *Agonis/Hippiskos* (F 2) of a young lover trying to impress his mistress similarly, and by a malicious aside of Athenaios himself in the mouth of Aimilianos (6.17, 230c-d, with 231b) about a 'fellow citizen of ours' who was at pains to distinguish 'the winter silver service' from the 'summer silver service'.[25] Then come citations from Nikostratos' *Basileis*, F 8, Antiphanes' *Lemniai*, F 143, Sopatros' *Orestes* F 14 and *Phake* F 18, and a fragment of Theopompos (*FGrH* 115 F 252) recounting how his fellow-citizen Theokritos came to use silver and gold vessels when he used to have to use chipped pottery. Further citations (6.18, 321a) come from Diphilos' *Zographos*, F 43, Philemon's *Iatros*, F 35, Menandros' *Heautontimoroumenos*, F 78, and *Hymnis,* F 366, and Lysias' speech *Against Kleon on the gold tripod*, F 56 Thalheim (148a Sauppe).

Pontianos then takes up the discourse (6.19, 231b), illustrating his claim that gold and silver used to be very rare in Greece by citing Douris' report, *FGrH* 76 F 37a, of Philip always keeping a gold cup under his pillow, Herodoros' rationalising explanation of the golden sheep of Atreus (*FGrH* 31 F 57) and Anaximenes, *FGrH* 72 F 3, on how the fame of the bracelet of Eriphyle derived from gold and silver being scarce. In contrast, he continues, after the Phokian capture of Delphi all such things became abundant. Whereas even rich people used to use bronze goblets, a passage of Herodotos (2.151) being very tendentiously called in aid, the crucial Wende is reemphasised: after the Phokian sack of Delphi gold and silver shone forth among the Greeks, and then with Alexander's conquest, in the words of Pindar, 'widespread wealth arose' (*P.* 5.1). At this point (6.20, 231e) Athenaios clearly has resort to the monumental-antiquarian tradition, using Phainias' lengthy F 11 Wehrli and Theopompos, *FGrH* 115 F 193, in order to prove that the first silver and gold dedications at Delphi were those of Gyges and Kroisos, followed by those of Gelon and Hieron: the Spartans, says Theopompos, had had to go to Kroisos to procure gold for the statue of Apollo at Amyklai, just as Hieron's agents managed to locate as a gold supply only the stockpile assembled by Architeles of Korinth, while Phainias gilds the story further (6.21, 232c) by citing Trojan-War period inscriptions on bronze dedications. In his final section (6.22, 232d) Athenaios cites Ephoros' gossip-column account (*FGrH* 70 F 96) of how the Phokian generals' womenfolk appropriated the *kosmos* of Eriphyle dedicated by Alkmaion and the necklace of Helen dedicated by Menelaos, only for one of the women to run off with an Epeirote toyboy while the other plotted her husband's death. Thereafter (6.23, 233b) the discourse veers off to report the hostility of Plato, Lykourgos and Zenon towards silver and gold and to pick up, after a lacuna and some non-relevant material, (6.24, 233f) Poseidonios' report (*FGrH* 87 F 48) that the Spartans, being forbidden to import gold and silver, deposited it with the Arkadians instead, while it had previously been deposited with Apollo at Delphi; its public importation by Lysandros and Gylippos had horrendous consequences.

There is clearly a real story here, articulated soon after the event by Theopompos, taken up by Phainias and others, and capable of being illustrated in remorseless but invaluable detail.[26] Of course, it cannot be taken straight, for it is simplistic, tendentious, chronologically telescoped, and buttressed by some very dubious evidence: it needs to be tested. On the one hand, confirmatory detail is forthcoming. If, for example, Athenaios' citations are re-sorted into approximate chronological order, he has one (late?) fifth-century example (Sophron), and three (Aristophanes, Plato comicus, and Lysias) from before 380, but the bulk of them does indeed date from after the

---

[25] Arnott 1996, 61-2 argues conclusively that this example was Athenaios' own, not a paraphrase of Alexis.

[26] It is regrettable that no paper in Braund and Wilkins 2000 focuses explicitly on it. Note also Theopompos' comment on contemporary extravagance (*FGrH* 115 F 36).

350s. Likewise, the general case that gold and silver dedications at Delphi were set up either by Anatolian kings or, if by Greeks, in the fifth and fourth centuries BC seems to be justified, while the sketch of the growth of use of silver for plate in Archaic and Classical Greece made by Strong 1966 clearly confirms the general accuracy of Athenaios' account. Indeed, the well-known fact that Greek-made silver vessels are largely found in the Balkans and South Russia, but barely at all in Greece itself, strongly suggests that the bullion went out as coin in direct or indirect payment for corn or iron[27] and was then converted into plate by itinerant or local craftsmen - a picture amply confirmed by the Rogozen hoard.[28]

However, the decisive test is whether the step-change after the 340s in the supply of gold and silver which the *logos* asserts (a) was real, and (b) was due directly to the Phokians' release of the accumulated Delphian treasures. That it was real can scarcely be doubted: whether it can wholly be attributed to Phokian action is another matter, for two other major processes of accretion to the money supply available to Greece in general were taking place in the same period. The first, already noticed, derives from the intensification of exploitation of the Laureion mines from the 350s to the 320s. The second was the massive increase in regal Macedonian coinage under Philip II, conventionally linked to Diodoros' notice (16.8.6-7) of Philip's re-activation of the gold mines at Krenides/Philippoi after 356 and attested by the 2598 surviving specimens catalogued by Le Rider.[29] Hence, even if we try to isolate and leave aside, as a separate and later step-change, the even more violent increase in the money supply brought about after 330 by Alexander's re-activation as coin of the gigantic Achaimenid accumulations of specie,[30] no fewer than three mid-century processes come into question. Their relative importance is hard to assess, especially when we have no reliable and datable figures for Athenian production.

However, two indirect indicators are available, namely the shift in the gold:silver ratio and the likely order of magnitude of Philip's production of gold and silver coin. The first is informative precisely because no one power except the barely monetised Persian Empire was in a position to enforce a bimetallic currency system,[31] so that the relative values of the two metals might change, and were known to be liable to do so.[32] However, with gold generally in use in Athens for ceremonial crowns, at least spasmodically in use in Greece for coin, and more so in Phoenicia and Punic North Africa,[33] enough evidence of their relative values in the fifth and fourth centuries has survived to allow a fairly coherent picture to be drawn down to 355/4. On Lewis's calculations, a ratio which had stood at 15:1 before the Archidamian War had slid below 14:1 by 415 and perhaps below 11:1 by 402, only to recover to over 13:1 by the 370s and to slide again down to just over 12:1 by 355.[34] Thereafter, however, rapid change ensued. Solid ground is provided by Alexander, issuing silver on the Athenian standard and gold staters which are explicitly said in late fourth-century sources to

---

[27] The *syngraphe* reproduced in Dem. 35.10-13 offers explicit evidence for such a practice.

[28] Fol et al. 1986; Cook 1989; Archibald 1998, 260-281. In general Strong 1966.

[29] Le Rider 1977; totals for each series and group most conveniently accessible via the table in Le Rider 1996, 70.

[30] 50,000 T taken over by Alexander at Sousa in 331 (Curtius 5.2.11 and Arrian, *Anab.* 3.16.7, with Bosworth *ad loc.*; 120,000 T acquired at Persepolis (Diod. 17.71.1, Curtius 5.6.9 and Arrian, *Anab.* 3.18.10, with Bosworth *ad loc.*). The hyperbolic comparison with the Delphian monies, reported by Diod. 16.56.7, has rhetorical force only.

[31] Bellinger 1963, 29, citing Reinach 1893.

[32] Xen. *Poroi* 4.10.

[33] Cf. Jenkins & Lewis 1963; Kraay & Hirmer n.d., 300-301.

[34] Thompson 1963, 121-141; Lewis 1968. The reference for Lewis's no. 43, of 348/7, should be 'ii.1441.8-9'.

reflect a 10:1 ratio,[35] but the intervening period is hard to follow. A Syracusan gold issue of *ca.* 340 is interpreted as still reflecting a 12:1 ratio,[36] but entries in the Delphian accounts for spring 335[37] and 324/3[38] indicate ratios oscillating between 10:1 and *ca.* 11:1.[39] Given that the massive silver production of Laureion of the mid-century should if anything have reduced the relative value of silver, a major counter-weight in the form of an enhanced gold supply has to be identified. The conventional view is that the Philippeioi provided it,[40] but Philip's huge production of silver coinage should have affected the ratio too, while matters are further complicated by the debate over the chronology of Philip's issues which was stimulated by the publication of Le Rider 1977.[41]

   With all appropriate caution, the best route may again lie through tentative quan-tification on the basis of obverse dies.[42] For Series A and B of the silver tetradrachms, Le Rider identified 427 obverse dies. At 20,000 specimens per obverse die, and at an average weight of 14.3 g., the silver used was 122,122 kg. The gold staters show 249 obverse dies. Again at 20,000, and at a rough average weight of 8.60 g., the gold used was 42,828 kg (1672 T Attic/Euboean, 1133 T Aiginetan). Such a ratio of relative production, conjecturally 122:42 by weight (say 3:1), though obviously not commen-surable with ratios by value, gives some idea of the likely impact of Philip's gold coin-age, and that impact would remain considerable even if the multiplier for gold coins were reduced to 10,000, yielding 21,414 kg.[43] It would have to be drastically reduced, well below the threshold of plausibility, before the impact of the 325 T of gold from Delphi began to be comparable. In consequence, Athenaios' story has to be interpreted as a serious distortion of historical fact. Insofar as it goes back to Theopompos, who had seen the consequences of Macedon's new-found wealth at first hand, it is hard to acquit him of eliding the economic facts in favour of a focus on behaviour. That the release of the bullion from Delphi had rapid and unfortunate effects on behaviour in Central Greece, a coin-poor region[44] with no bullion resources of its own,[45] is wholly understandable, but its release will have had far less effect on the money supply than did the new bullion emanating from Laureion and from Macedon.

---

[35] (a) In 306/5 80T of *argyrion Alexandreion* and 18,000 *chrysoi* are valued at 140 T (*IG* ii² 1492.101-3). Hence the *chrysoi* are equivalent to 60 T, so 300 *chrysoi* = 1 T, hence 1 *chrysous* = 10 dr. (b) The 10:1 ratio is explicit in Menandros, *Parakatatheke*, F 289 *ap.* Pollux 9.76, and (c) in Polemarchos *ap.* Hesychios *s.v. chrysous*, with Thompson 1963, 123 after Reinach 1893.

[36] Kraay & Hirmer n.d., no.133 (Plate 47 & p.293); Le Rider 1977, 440.

[37] 'To the *naopoioi* for cypress wood, 150 *Philippeioi* of gold, each at 7 staters' (*CID* II **76**, II 9-11, more safely dated (archon Dion) than Bellinger feared [1963, 31 n.126]).

[38] '190 Darics reckoned at 7 staters; another 30 darics reckoned at 7 and drachma' (*CID* II 102, IIA 6-9 and IIB 2-3) (archon Theon).

[39] For the problems presented by these entries cf. Bogaert 1968, 108-111; Le Rider 1977, 433, 439, and 441; Melville-Jones 1979; Bousquet 1985, 225-233 (= Bousquet 1988, 115-123).

[40] Bellinger 1963, 31; Le Rider 1977, 439-441; Mørkholm 1991, 4-5 and 43.

[41] Survey and summary in Le Rider 1996, 13-20, with especial attention (*ib.* 33-47) to the arguments of Price 1979.

[42] Figures for obverse dies are taken from Le Rider 1996, 70, with n. 11 above for the justifica-tion of a 20,000 multiplier against Le Rider's cautious and sceptical choice of much lower figures of 1000-15,000 (1996, 76-77).

[43] Le Rider's own calculations (1996, 76-77) address only the possible parameters of annual gold production.

[44] Cf. Kraay 1976, 110 (Boiotia), 120 (Phokis, following Williams 1972), and 121-3 (other states of Sterea Hellas).

[45] Treister 1996, 21-34 and 182-9 (but his Ill. 1 omits Damastion).

III

Such a conclusion invites the same sceptical eye to be turned towards the Diodoran narrative, with its moralising portrait of *hierosylia* reaping its due reward. For the purist, or naïve, view one turns to Pausanias. At the end of his description of Polygnotos' painting in the Knidian Lesche at Delphi, he comments (10.28.6) that

> 'people were still strongly devoted to reverence of gods, as the Athenians made clear, when they took the shrine of Olympian Zeus in Syracuse without touching any of the dedications and leaving the Syracusan priest as guard over them.[46] So did the Median Datis, both by the speeches he made to the Delians and by his act, when having found an image of Apollo in a Phoenician ship he returned it to the Tanagraioi for [Boiotian] Delion.[47] In this way everybody then held the divine in honour, and it was for a reason of such a kind that Polygnotos depicted what happened to one who pillaged sacred things.'

Reality was otherwise, as the widespread laws against, and punishments for, *hierosylia* make clear.[48] Even the question of when legitimate (or semi-legitimate) borrowing became pillaging was not straightforward. An earlier paper (Davies 2001) on the topic outlined how shrines and sanctuaries, along with the polities which controlled them and the public opinion which lay in the background, codified the ways in which goods and resources deemed to be the property of divine entities could properly be used. Some such objects, such as (say) the women's clothes dedicated to Artemis Brauronia or the crockery used for ritual meals at Isthmia and then ceremonially   broken, were valueless and not re-usable, but others were potentially productive assets which could yield rent (in produce or coin) or straightforward monetary interest if god and man were content that such uses were proper.[49] The extreme practice, widely adopted in fifth- and fourth-century Athens, was to melt down dedications and convert the bullion into units of uniform size, weight, and value (Athene's Golden *Nikai* are the classic case), so that the bullion could be quickly recycled (or turned into coin) for urgent needs, especially military. The main argument in my earlier paper was that some such recycling, or 'borrowing', passes without any adverse comment, whether by contemporary society or by the narrating source, while other examples aroused 'doubt, disapproval, and even ferocious (though sanctimonious) condemnation' (Davies 2001, 125). The explanation which I offered for the discrepancy was that initiatives for such borrowings came from maritime powers, for whom the costs of   naval warfare had generated a much more 'detached and manipulative' attitude towards temple treasures. Though doubts have been expressed,[50] other evidence for the high-handed use of

---

[46] This is an unctuously slanted version of the incident in autumn 415 recorded by Thuc. 6.70.4–71.1, Diod. 13.6.4-6, and Plut. *Nikias* 16.7-8, where Thucydides makes no allusion to the dedications and Plutarch asserts that Nikias held the Athenians back and allowed the Syracusans to set guard 'thinking that if the soldiers plundered the treasures, the commonwealth would not be assisted while he would get the blame for the impiety'. A like calculation 80 years previously is recorded of Hippokrates of Gela by Diod. 10.28.1-2, as Gomme notes (*HCT* IV 346).

[47] Cf. Hdt. 6.97.2 and 6.118.1-3.

[48] Cf. Parker 1983, 170-1.

[49] To the examples set out in Davies 2001 should be added a deme decree of Eleusis of 332/1, which enjoins that the revenues from a quarry which was the property of Herakles should not be used for any other purpose than the festival of Herakles (*SEG* XXVIII 103, lines 36-9).

[50] By von Reden 2002:148; but note Austin in *CAH*² VI 557-8.

temple treasures, whether by borrowing or sequestration or straight theft, both confirms that interpretation and allows its extension.

A fuller review of the evidence[51] may therefore be helpful. The first two known cases, indeed, show the sequestration gambit declined, for the Ionians, while seeking to finance a navy, declined to follow Hekataios' advice to the Ionians to use the dedications which Kroisos gave to Apollo at Branchidai, while in 493 or 492 Hippokrates of Gela is said to have punished the Syracusans who were removing treasures (including the 'golden cloak') from the sanctuary of Olympian Zeus outside Syracuse, and ostentatiously refrained from pillaging it himself.[52] Likewise, though there was pillage during the Graeco-Persian Wars, it was principally a matter of revenge, not of appropriation to meet urgent expense.[53] For decades thereafter, such appropriation was categorised as 'borrowing', in an open and formalised way at Athens even if we have no idea how the consent of Apollo and/or Athene had been obtained for the transactions visible during the Samian revolt and subsequently, and even if the monies thus borrowed were never fully returned to Athene.[54] By 432/1 the Korinthians were prepared to follow suit, with their suggestion that the *chremata* at Delphi and Olympia could be borrowed in order to finance a fleet,[55] though whether any licit use was thus made is left very unclear in the terms of the truce of 423 (Thuc. 4.118.3).

Thereafter, however, all pretence of 'borrowing' seems to have been abandoned. True, the first datable and plainly illicit sequestration of sacred goods since the Graeco-Persian Wars was by a non-Greek in wartime, viz. Himilco's sack of the temples of Demeter and Kore in Achradina outside Syracuse in summer 395,[56] but Himilco's opponent Dionysios I of Syracuse had probably already flouted the tabu by initiating what became a massive and continuing sequence of misappropriation of silver and gold objects from sanctuaries. It falls into three groups: (a) within Syracuse during the 390s, (b) in S. Italy in the 380s, and allegedly (c) in mainland Greece.[57] Those in group (a), largely undated because significantly absent from Diodoros' summary of Philistos' account, include the enforced donations of women's jewellery to Demeter, which Dionysios then sequestered as a 'loan',[58] the sale by subterfuge of the dedications from the sanctuary of Asklepios in Syracuse, which Dionysios then had compulsorily returned while retaining the proceeds,[59] the looting of all the shrines in Syracuse, including the cloak and adornments worth 85 gold T from the statue of Zeus, and the golden curls of hair from an Apollo statue (no value stated),[60] the theft

---

[51] Already largely assembled by Parker 1983, 170-6 and Pritchett 1991, 160-8.

[52] Respectively Hdt. 5.36.3-4 and Diod. 10.28.1-2, with Dunbabin 1948, 400.

[53] For Herodotos the destruction of the shrine of Kybele at Sardis was accidental (6. 101-102), but as noted by Jacquemin (1999, 239) the revenge-motif attributed to Xerxes (Hdt. 7.8 β.2-3) and exemplified at Eretria (7.101.3) indicates that that was not the Persian view, even if Dareios is subsequently made to say (Aisch. *Pers*. 805-28) that the defeat at Plataiai was punishment for the Persian sack of sanctuaries.

[54] Cf. *imprimis* Kallet-Marx 1993; summary in Blamire 2001.

[55] Thuc. 1.121.3; 1.143.1; Migeotte 1984, 89 no. 22.

[56] Diod. 14.63.1-3, with 70.4, 76.3-4, and 77.4: Lewis, *CAH* VI² 143-4.

[57] The most detailed treatment is that of Stroheker 1958, 161-166, but his exposition is synchronic and (unlike that of Pritchett 1991, 163-5) knits together the use of sacred and of secular resources (so also Caven 1990:160-6). The essay of Bullock 1929-30 wholly lacks source-references.

[58] [Ar.] *Oik*. 2.20a, 1349a; Stroheker 1958, 164 (suggested date 400-396) and 246 n. 135, with further references.

[59] Polyain. 5.2.19.

[60] Ael. *VH*. 1.20; Cic. *De nat. deorum* 3.84, siting the act at Olympia rather than Syracuse in error (Pritchett 1991, 164-5); Clem. Al. *Protrept*. 4.52.2, attributing the act to the younger Dionysios in error.

of a table used in the Agathos Daimon cult,[61] and the theft of cups hung as thank-offerings onto cult images.[62] Group (b) includes, after his capture of Kroton c.382 or c.378,[63] the possession of a himation dedicated to Hera Lakinia by Alkisthenes of Sybaris, which Athenaios reports him as selling to the Carthaginians for 120 T,[64] plunder from the temple of Persephone at Lokroi,[65] and, much more spectacularly and profitably, the sack of the temple of Eileithuia/Leukothea at Caere/Pyrgoi in Etruria c.384/3, yielding 1000+ T from the sanctuary and 500+ T from booty.[66] Group (c) is more dubious, for the allegation that Dionysios pillaged Olympia and the Asklepieion at Epidauros is either a misquote from memory or a caricature, while the allegation that he intended to pillage Delphi has met with little credit.[67]

All the same, it was undoubtedly Dionysios with his characteristic insouciance, and not the Phokian generals, who broke the mould, for even before their depredations began the practice had been copied by Iphikrates in 373,[68] taken onto the mainland by 370 if Xenophon's cagey hint (*Hell.* 6.4.30) that Iason had eyes on the sacred moneys during the run-up to the Pythian Games of 370 has any foundation, into Asia Minor during the Satraps' Revolt,[69] and taken into Peloponnese during the 360s, both at Sikyon[70] and (very uneasily, it is true) in Arkadia.[71] Plainly, just as

---

[61] The tradition is contradictory: gold and dedicated to Asklepios (Athen. 15.593e), or silver and dedicated to Apollo (Ael. *VH.* 1.20), or silver tables from all the shrines ([Ar.] *Oik.* 2.41, 1353b20-2; Cic. *De nat. deorum* 3.84).

[62] [Ar.] *Oik.* 2.41, 1353b22-4; Val. Max. 1.1.*ext*.3; Stroheker 1958, 246 n.139.

[63] Livy 24.3.8; Dion. Hal. *AR* 20.7.3; Justin 20.5.1-3; not mentioned by Diod. at 15.15-17).

[64] Athen. 12.58, 541a-b, citing Polemon F 85 (*FHG* III 141) and [Ar.], *Mir. Ausc.* 96, 838a 15-25, with a detailed description of the cloak and its sale: Val. Max. 1.1. *ext.* 3. Though the aleatoric chronology precludes certainty (Stroheker 1958, 114; Lewis, *CAH* VI² 149; Purcell, *CAH* VI² 387, with further references in n. 19), the simplest assumption is that the object formed part of the indemnity of 1000 T paid to the Carthaginians by Dionysios after the battle of Kronion (Plato, *Ep.* VII 332c and 333a; Diod. 15.17.5; *aliter* Pritchett 1991, 164 and 196, citing Grote).

[65] Thus Cic. *De natura deorum* 3.83 and Val. Max. 1.1. *ext.* 3, but the statement is surprising in view of his close relationship with the city, while Diodoros 27.4 notes how Pyrrhos had despoiled the shrine even before Pleminius did so in 205 but says nothing of Dionysios.

[66] Diod. 15.14.3-4, with Strabo 5.2.8, C226, for Eileithuia. Polyainos 5.2.21 names the goddess as Leukothea, reports him as taking 500 T from the shrine, and states that '1000 T of gold and much more of silver' had been looted by his soldiers and sailors, all of which Dionysios sequestered in two stages. Much the same story is offered by [Ar.] *Oik.* 2.20i, 1349b33 ff, without the figures, and very briefly by Ael. *VH* 1.20 (Dionysios looted all the monies of Apollo and Leukothea), while Philo *De providentia* 2.6 reports a general figure of 1200 T without localisation. Cf. Stroheker 1958, 127-8; Caven 1990, 191 and 261 n. 6; Lewis *CAH* VI² 148.

[67] Respectively Cic. *De nat. deorum* 3.83 and Val. Max. 1.1. *ext.* 3; Diod. 15.13.1-2; but Caven 1990, 149 and 259 n. 34 argues that Dodona, not Delphi, was his objective.

[68] Iphikrates as Athenian general near Kerkyra captured ships transporting gold and ivory statues from Dionysios to Olympia and Delphi. When he sought advice the Athenians instructed him 'not to enquire too closely into what concerned the gods but to ensure that his soldiers were properly fed', so Iphikrates sold the objects off, triggering an angry letter (whether real or confected) from Dionysios to Athens (Diod. 16.57.2-3: Pritchett 1991, 162-3).

[69] Datames is reported to have hijacked all the 'hollow silver' from the shrines of a city in order to pay his men, first taking the bullion to Amisos to have it coined ([Ar.] *Oik.* 2.24a, 1350b 16-30).

[70] Euphron supported his coup d'état by using public and sacred moneys to pay mercenaries (Xen. *Hell.* 7.1.46 and 7.3.8).

[71] The use by the Arkadians of the sacred moneys of Olympia to pay their *eparitoi* soldiers encountered strong opposition from the Mantineans, yielding a brief civil war till the practice was discontinued (Xen. *Hell.* 7.4.33-34; Diod. 15.83.1; Pritchett 1991, 167-8).

Athens in the fifth century had used Athene's resources in order to pay the mercenaries they employed at sea, so now the need to recruit and pay competent profes-
sionals for warfare on land was forcing ambitious men to stifle such scruples as they
still retained.

Indeed, they could be argued to have done Greek society a major favour. That is
not to belittle the tragedy of the loss of major works of art at Delphi and elsewhere or
the pitiful visual impoverishment of the sanctuaries which resulted. It is however to
balance such regret, or even the sense of outrage about Phokian depredations which
Diodoros transmits from Ephoros-Demophilos, against the positive economic effects of
thus recycling into the active economy such huge mothballed accumulations of
bullion. The main direct, though temporary, effect will have been to dampen down
social tensions. Given the areas of conspicuous poverty from which mercenaries
largely came, the abundance of their supply,[72] and the likely patterns of diffusion via
mercenaries' pockets, such monies will have helped to alleviate the pressures noted by
Isokrates both before and after the Third Sacred War:[73] even in Diodoros' morality tale
in 16.61-64 about the subsequent fate of Phayllos and the mercenaries the element of
desperation is unmistakable. The Delphian proceeds may even have helped to fuel the
inflation which is perceptible in the relevant period,[74] though the contributions of
Laureion and Macedon will have had a much greater effect. Indeed, Delphi's part in
adding to the money supply is likely to have had the most significant long-term
impact, by helping to lubricate all transactions with an economic content (whether
fiscal, or located within a price-setting market, or functioning as part of 'social reci-
procity' is immaterial). Whether that impact can be assessed quantitatively, rather
than just qualitatively, has to be matter for a later occasion.

---

[72] Cartledge 1987, 314-30.
[73] Isok. 4. *Paneg.* 167-9; 5. *Philippos* 122.
[74] Loomis 1998, 240-250.

Appendix I: Dedications attested or inferred to have been pillaged by Phokians

26 items were known to Reinach 1928, 41, who guessed maybe 70-80 items in all. The list below, based on my own initial list of 26 items, compiled in autumn 2003, has been revised and extended in the light of Typaldou-Fakiris' discussion (2004, 291-6). Numbers in **bold** refer to the catalogue of monumental offerings in Jaquemin 1999, 307-372. In what follows, Au(rum) = gold, Ag (argentum) = silver, EL = Electrum (for which see item 5 below). Au weights have been converted to Ag at 13:1.

A Major early items.

1. (Throne of Midas King of Phrygia, recorded by Hdt. 1.14.3 as being in the Korinthian treasury. Its silver or gold content, if any, is unknown, nor is it listed as a victim of the Phokians.)

2. Many silver and gold offerings were made by Gyges King of Lydia in the second quarter of the seventh century, most notably six gold *krateres* weighing 30 T, standing in the Korinthian treasury (Hdt. 1.14.1-3; Strabo 9.3.8, C421) (Jacquemin 1999, 340 no. **346**, not citing Herodotos and dating to the early sixth century). Their meltdown is inferred, not stated. There is no means of telling whether the *krateres* were really Au or (perhaps more likely) EL. If they were all-Au, then 30 T Au = **390 T Ag**; if EL, then ((say) 225 T Au =) 286 T Ag + 15 T Ag = **294 T Ag.**

3. Large silver *krater* on a base of forged iron, work of Glaukos of Chios, dedicated in the early sixth century by Alyattes King of Lydia (Hdt. 1.25.2); no weight recorded. The base (Jacquemin 1999, 340 no. **342**) is cited by Plut. *Mor.* 436a, Paus. 10.16.1-2, and Athen. 5.45, 210b-c (citing Hegesandros, *FHG* 4. 421 F 45) as surviving in the second century AD. The *krater* itself may have been melted down by the Phokians, but no explicit statement survives.

B King Kroisos' dedications.

4-6. Lion monument (Jacquemin 1999, 340 no. **343**) comprising:

4. 4 pure gold ingots, each weighing 2½ T, dedicated by Kroisos of Lydia (Hdt. 1.50.2).
(10 T Au =) **130T Ag.**

5. 113 'white gold' ingots, each weighing 2 T, dedicated by Kroisos (Hdt. 1.50.2), so 226 T EL in all. Diod. 16.56.6 less precisely reports items 4 & 5 together as 120 gold ingots, each of 2 T, all melted down by Phayllos. The bullion value of these ingots, by far the most important single item on this list, is problematic. The gold content of electrum coins varies widely, from 35% to 65-70%, but the natural alloy has an Au:Ag ratio of *ca.* 3:1 (Kraay 1976, 9-11; Healy 1978, 201-3; *Neue Pauly* s.v. Elektron. Treister 1996 is silent on the substance). In order not to err on the side of underestimating, that latter ratio is used here. Hence 226 T EL is deemed to comprise 170 T Au + 56 T Ag, i.e. a silver equivalent of (2120 + 56 =) **2176 T Ag.**

6. Lion of pure gold, initially weighing 10 T but reduced to 6 ½ T after the fire of 548, dedicated by Kroisos (Hdt. 1.50.3).   (6½ T AV=) **85 T Ag.**

7. Gold *krater*, weighing 8 T 42 mnai, dedicated by Kroisos (Hdt. 1.51.2).
                                                            (8 2/3 T AV=) **113 T Ag.**

8. Silver *krater*, no weight stated, capacity 600 amphorai, work of Theodoros of Samos, dedicated by Kroisos (Hdt. 1.51.2, with Griffith 1988 and Blackman & Sawyer 2000).

9. Four silver *pithoi*, no weight stated, dedicated by Kroisos (Hdt. 1.51.3).

10. One silver and one gold *perirrhanterion*, no weight stated, dedicated by Kroisos (Hdt. 1.51.3).

11. 360 (?) round silver basins [presumably *phialai mesomphaloi*], dedicated by Kroisos (Hdt. 1.51.5). Herodotos gives no number or weights, while Diod. 16.56.6 provides the number 360, weight 2 mnai each, and lists them as melted down by Phayllos.
                                                            12 T Ag.

12. Gold statue of Kroisos' 'baking-woman' (more plausibly of Kybele with a tympanon, cf. Harvey 1995), 3 cubits high, no weight stated, dedicated by Kroisos (Hdt. 1.51.5; Plut. Mor. 401e) (Jacquemin 1999, 340 no.**344**). Melted down by Phayllos (Diod. 16.56.6). McQueen 1995, 130 refers to her the figure of 30 T Au cited by Diod. 16.56.6 for 'a lion [presumably item 6] and a woman of gold', but it is inconceivable that a half-life-size statue even of gold could have weighed (30-6½ =) 23½T. If the figure has any basis, then   (23½T Au =) **305.5 T Ag.**

13. Necklace and girdles of his wife, dedicated by Kroisos. Materials not stated (Hdt. 1.51.5).

14. Large golden shield, given to (Athene) Pronoia [sic] by Kroisos of Lydia (Hdt. 1.92.1), said by the Delphians in Pausanias' time (10.8.7) to have been robbed by Philomelos. Jacquemin 1999:73 no. **289** (citing Theopompos F 192 in error for 193.)

C   Other items explicitly said to have been melted down by the Phokians.

15. Gold *krater* dedicated by Romans after capture of Veii in 395 (Diod. 14.93; Livy 5.28), weighing 8 T (Plut. *Camillus* 8), destroyed by Onomarchos (App. *Ital.* F 8.2-3).
         Not cited by Jacquemin 1999.   (8 T AV =) **104 T Ag.**

16. Four golden tiaras, dedicated by the Sybaritai, given by Onomarchos to the son of Pythodoros of Sikyon (Theopompos, *FGrH* 115 F 248 ap. Athen. 13.605a-b; more vaguely Strabo 9.3.8, C421).

17. Silver drinking-cup 'of Phokians' (so perhaps not strictly a dedication) given by Phayllos to the flute-girl Bromias (Theopompos *l.c.*).

18. A <golden crown> of ivy, 'of Peparethians', also given to Bromias (Theopompos *l.c.*, with Casaubon's supplement).

19. \<Golden\> crown of laurel, dedication of Ephesians, given by Onomarchos to Lykolas of Trichoneia (Theopompos *l.c.*, with Meineke's supplement).

20. Offering of Pleisthenes, material not stated, given by Onomarchos to Damippos of Amphipolis (Theopompos *l.c.*).

21. Golden crown of laurel, dedicated by Lampsakenoi, given by Philomelos to Pharsalia of Thessaly (Theopompos *l.c.*).

(Nos 16-21 are clearly listed by Theopompos so as to illustrate the Phokian leaders' favouritism to women and boys, not their conversion of bullion into coin.)

22. Gold of the Tripod on top of the Serpent Column commemorating Plataiai (Jacquemin 1999, 336 no. **310**), 'not left in the same state' by the Phokian leaders (Paus. 10.13.10). Typaldou-Fakiris 2004, 293-4, citing Amandry 1987, 89 for its location close to Gelon's commemoration of Himera (no. 24 below) and inferring that rivalry would have engendered monuments of comparable cost, ascribes to it the same bullion content, 16 T. On that (fragile) assumption, (16 T AV =) **208 T Ag**.

23. Necklace of Eriphyle, and necklace of Helen, given to their wives by the Phokian generals (Athen. 6.22, 232d ff.).

24. A gift of the Spinetai is implied by Strabo 9.3.8, C421 to have been among the plundered dedications.

D Offerings of the Sicilian tyrants.

25. Gold tripod and statue of Nike, commemorating the victory over the Carthaginians at Himera, dedicated by Gelon tyrant of Syracuse (*SIG* 34A = ML 28; Athen. 6.20, 231f; Diod. 11.26.7, reporting it as weighing 16 T). Jacquemin 1999, 353 no. **446**.

26. Gold tripod and statue of Nike dedicated by Hieron tyrant of Syracuse (Athen. 6.20, 231f-232a-b, from Theopompos *FGrH* 115 F 193): Jacquemin 1999, 353 no. **447**. Typaldou-Fakiris 2004, 294 assumes that it too contained some 16T of gold.

27-28. An epigram attributed to Simonides (*Anth. Pal.* VI 214 = Simonides 141B, 106D, XXXIV Page) reports the two other sons of Deinomenes, Polyzelos and Thrasyboulos, as also dedicating golden tripods at Delphi, the total weight of the four being 50T 100 *litrai* (lines 3-4): Bacchylides' reference to golden tripods in his 468 ode for Hieron (3.17-21) is some guarantee of the tradition, though the challenge of assigning the right dedicant to the right base is far from solved (doxography in Molyneux 1992, 220-224). Using the gap between a Sicilian talent of 32.73 kg and an Attic talent of *c.* 26 kg, an ingenious reconciliation with Diodoros's figure has been offered (Reinach 1903), but the reliability of the transmitted text is variously assessed (contrast the optimism of Cavaignac 1923 and Typaldou-Fakiris 2004, 294 with the caution of Page). If it is acceptable and credible, then items 24-27 will collectively have weighed (50 T AV =) **650 T Ar.**

E   Other offerings of gold which may have fallen victim.

29. A stick of celery in gold, dedicated by the Selinountioi, no longer there in Plutarch's time (*Pyth. Orac.* 12, *Mor.* 399F) was claimed by Reinach 1928, 41 without positive evidence as a casualty of the Phokians.

30. Axe of gold, dedicated by Tenedioi (*ibid.*), likewise listed by Reinach.

31. Statue in gold of King Alexandros Philhellen of Makedon (Hdt. 8.121.2; [Dem.] 12.21; Jacquemin 1999, 340 no. **347**).

32. Three gold stars, dedicated by Aiginetai at Delphi in commemoration of Salamis (Hdt. 8.122; Jacquemin 1999, 332 no. **277**).

33-35. 'Golden summers' dedicated by the Apolloniatai of Illyria (Plut. *Mor.* 401F), the Metapontinoi (Strabo 6.1.15, 264C) and the Myrinaioi (Plut. *Mor.* 401F), respectively Jacquemin 1999, 313 no. **065**, 342 no. **365**, 343 no. **371**.

[36. However, the golden stars of the Dioskouroi dedicated by Lysandros to commemorate Aigospotamoi are said by Plutarch (*Mor.* 397F; *Lysandros* 18.1) to have vanished before Leuktra and should not have been listed by Typaldou-Fakiris 2004, 295 as possible victims.]

If the higher figure is used for item 2, if the fragile inference for the weight of item 20 is accepted, if the evidence of the epigram for items 24-27 is accepted, and if all the items reported as 'gold' were really gold rather than electrum or gold leaf (the latter possibility is canvassed by Jacquemin 1999:167), the grand total from transmitted figures is **4173.5 T Ag.**

Bibliography

T. Alfieri Tonini, 'Problemi di fonti nei libri XVI e XVII di Diodoro' in edd. Galvagno and Molè Ventura 1991, 65-75.

P. Amandry, 'Trépieds de Delphes et de Péloponèse' *BCH* 111 (1987) 79-131.

Z.H. Archibald, *The Odrysian kingdom of Thrace: Orpheus unmasked* (Oxford 1998).

edd. Z.H. Archibald, J.K. Davies, V. Gabrielsen, *Making, moving and managing: the new world of ancient economies* (Oxford 2005).

edd. M. Austin, J. Harries, and C.J. Smith, *Modus operandi. Essays in honour of Geoffrey Rickman* (*BICS* Supplement 71, London 1998).

A.R. Bellinger, *Essays on the coinage of Alexander the Great* (American Numismatic Society, Numismatic Studies 11, New York 1963).

D.R. Blackman and J. Sawyer, 'Croesus' craters at Delphi' *OJA* 19 (2000) 319-21.

A. Blamire, 'Athenian finance, 454-404 B.C.' *Hesperia* 70 (2001) 99-126.

A. Boeckh, *Die Staatshaushaltung der Athener* I³-II³ (Berlin 1886, repr. Berlin, 1967).

R. Bogaert, *Banques et banquiers dans les cites grecques* (Leyde 1968).

J. Bousquet, 'Notes sur divers comptes', *BCH* 109 (1985) 221-253 [reprinted in Bousquet 1988, 111-143].

J. Bousquet, *Études sur les comptes de Delphes* (Paris 1988).

D. Braund and J. Wilkins, *Athenaeus and his world* (Exeter 2000).

J. Buckler, 'Thebes, Delphoi, and the outbreak of the Third Sacred War' in edd. P. Roesch and G. Argoud, *La Béotie antique* (Paris 1985) 237-46.

J. Buckler, *Philip II and the Sacred War* (*Mnemosyne* Suppl. 109, Leiden 1989).

C.J. Bullock, 'Dionysius of Syracuse – financier' *CJ* 25 (1929-30) 260-76.

P. Cartledge, *Agesilaos and the crisis of Sparta* (London 1987).

E. Cavaignac, 'Sur les offrandes des Deinomenides' *BCH* 47 (1923) 423-29.

B. Caven, *Dionysius I: Warlord of Sicily* (New Haven and London 1990).

E.E. Cohen, *Athenian economy and society: a banking perspective* (Princeton 1992).

ed. B.F. Cook, *The Rogozen treasure. Papers of the Anglo-Bulgarian conference, 12 March 1987* (London 1989).

J.K. Davies, 'Finance, administration, and Realpolitik: the case of fourth-century Delphi' in Austin et al. 1998, 1-14.

J.K. Davies, 'Athenaeus' use of public documents' in Braund & Wilkins 2000, 203-217 with 558-9.

J.K. Davies, 'Temples, credit, and the circulation of money' in Meadows & Shipton 2001, 117-128.

F. De Callataÿ, *Recueil quantitative des emissions monétaires archaïques et classiques.* (Wetteren: Numismatique romaine, 2003).

F. De Callataÿ, 'A quantitative survey of Hellenistic coinages: what has been recently achieved' in edd. Archibald et al. 2005, 73-91.

T.J. Dunbabin, *The Western Greeks* (Oxford 1948).

M.A. Flower, *Theopompus of Chios. History and rhetoric in the fourth century B.C.* (Oxford 1994).

edd. A. Fol, B. Nikolov and R.F. Hoddinott, *The new Thracian treasure from Rogozen, Bulgaria* (London 1986).

edd. E. Galvagno and C. Molè Ventura, *Mito storia tradizione. Diodoro Siculo e la storiografia classica* (Catania 1991).

A.W. Gomme and F.H. Sandbach, *Menander: A Commentary* (Oxford 1973).

G.T. Griffith, *The mercenaries of the Hellenistic world* (Oxford 1933).

J.G. Griffith, 'Two passages in Herodotus and the bronze crater from the royal tomb at Vix-sur-Seine (Chatillonais)', in ib., *Festinat senex* (Oxford 1988) 5-21.

N.G.L. Hammond, 'Diodorus' account of the Sacred War' *JHS* 57 (1937) 44-77.

D. Harvey, 'Lydian specialities, Croesus' golden baking-woman, and dogs' dinners' in edd. Wilkins et al., 1995, 273-285 at 278-81.

J.F. Healy, *Mining and metallurgy in the Greek and Roman world* (London 1978).

S. Hornblower, *The Greek world 479-323 BC* (3rd ed. London 2002).

S. Isager and M.H. Hansen (tr. J.S. Rosenmeier), *Aspects of Athenian society in the fourth century B.C.* (Odense 1975).

A. Jacquemin, *Offrandes monumentales a Delphes* (BÉFAR 304) Athens and Paris 1999).

G.K. Jenkins and R.B. Lewis, *Carthaginian gold and electrum coins* (Royal Numismatic Society, Special Publications 2, London 1963).

L. Kallet-Marx, *Money, expense, and naval power in Thucydides' History 1—5.24.* (Berkeley, Los Angeles, London 1993).

H.S. Kim, 'Archaic coinage as evidence for the use of money' (in Meadows & Shipton 2001, 7-21).

P. Kinns, 'The Amphictionic coinage reconsidered' *NC* 143 (1983) 1-22.

C.M. Kraay, *Archaic and Classical Greek coins* (London 1976).

C.M. Kraay and M. Hirmer, *Greek coins* (London and New York, n.d. 1966?).

F. Lefebvre, *L'Amphictionie pyléo-delphique: histoire et institutions* (BEFAR 298, Athens and Paris 1998).

F. Lefèvre, *Corpus des Inscriptions de Delphes,* IV: *Documents Amphictioniques* (Athens and Paris 2002).

G. Le Rider, *Le monnayage d'argent et d'or frappé en Macédoine de 359 à 294* (Paris 1977).

G. Le Rider, *Monnayage et finances de Philippe II. Un état de la question* (*Meletemata* 23, Athens 1996).

D.M. Lewis, 'New evidence for the gold-silver ratio', in edd. C.M. Kraay and G.K. Jenkins, *Essays in Greek coinage presented to Stanley Robinson* (Oxford 1968) 105-110.

D.M. Lewis, 'Persian gold in Greek international relations' *REA* 91 (1989) 227-34, [reprinted in Lewis 1997, 369-379].

D.M. Lewis (ed. P.J. Rhodes), *Selected papers in Greek and Near Eastern history* (Cambridge 1997).

W.T. Loomis, *Wages, welfare costs and inflation in Classical Athens* (Ann Arbour 1998).

J. Lund, 'The making, moving and managing of Eastern Sigillata A' in edd. Archibald *et al.* 2005, 229-249.

P. Marchetti, 'Autour de la frappe du nouvel amphictionique' *RBN* 145 (1999) 99-113.

M. Mari, *Al di là dell'Olimpo. Macedoni e grandi santuari della Grecia dall'età arcaica al primo ellenismo* (*Meletemata* 34, Athens 2002).

edd. A. Meadows and K. Shipton, *Money and its uses in the ancient Greek world* (Oxford 2001).

M.M. Markle III, 'Diodorus' sources for the Sacred War' in ed. I. Worthington, *Ventures into Greek history* (Oxford 1994) 43-69.

J. McInerney, *The folds of Parnassos. Land and ethnicity in ancient Phokis* (Austin 1999).

E.I. McQueen, *Diodorus Siculus: The reign of Philip II. The Greek and Macedonian narrative from Book XVI* (London 1995).

J.R. Melville-Jones, 'Darics in Delphi' *RBNum* 125 (1979) 25-36.

L. Migeotte, *L'emprunt public dans les cites grecques* (Québec and Paris 1984).

J.H. Molyneaux, *Simonides: a historical study* (Wauconda IL 1992).

O. Mørkholm, (edd. P. Grierson and U. Westermark), *Early Hellenistic coinage, from the accession of Alexander to the Peace of Apamea (336-186 B.C.)* (Cambridge 1991).

H.W. Parke, 'The Pythais of 355 BC and the Third Sacred War' *JHS* 59 (1939) 80-3.

M.J. Price, 'The coinage of Philip II' *NC* 129 (1979) 230-241.

W.K. Pritchett, *Ancient Greek military practices* I (*University of California publications: Classical Studies* 7, Berkeley, Los Angeles and London 1971) [Re-issued in 1974 as *The Greek state at war* I].

W.K. Pritchett, *The Greek state at war* V (Berkeley, Los Angeles, London 1991).

O. Ravel, 'Rare and unpublished coins of Corinthian types' *NC*[5] 15 (1935) 1-15.

Th. Reinach, 'De la valeur proportionelle de l'or et de l'argent dans l'antiquité grecque' *RN* 1893 (1893) 1-26 and 141-166.[non vidi]

Th. Reinach, 'Le rapport de l'or à l'argent dans les comptes de Delphes' *RN* 1902. [non vidi]

Th. Reinach, 'Les trépieds de Gélon et de ses frères' *RÉG* 16 (1903) 18-24.

S. Reinach, 'Une inscription historique de Delphes' *RevArch*[5] 28 (1928) 34-46.

P. Sánchez, *L'Amphictionie des Pyles et de Delphes. Recherches sur son role historique, des origins au IIe siècle de notre ère.* (*Historia,* Einzelschrift 148, Stuttgart 2001)..

G.S. Shrimpton, *Theopompus the historian* (Montreal, Kingston, London, Buffalo, 1991).

M. Sordi, *Diodori Siculi Bibliothecae Liber XVI* (Firenze 1969).

K.F. Stroheker, *Dionysios I. Gestalt und Geschichte des Tyrannen von Syrakus* (Wiesbaden 1958).

D.E. Strong, *Greek and Roman gold and silver plate* (London 1966).

W.E. Thompson, *The Athenian gold and bronze coinages of the Dekeleian War* (Ann Arbor: University Microfilms 64-2282, Diss. Phil., Princeton 1963).

M. Yu. Treister, *The role of metals in ancient Greek history* (Leiden, New York, Köln, 1996).

C. Typaldou-Fakiris, *Villes fortifiées de Phocide et la IIIe guerre sacrée 356-346 av. J.-C.* (Université de Provence 2004).

S. Von Reden, 'Money in the ancient economy: A survey of recent research' *Klio* 84 (2002) 141-174.

edd. J. Wilkins, J. Harvey and M. Dobson, *Food in antiquity* (Exeter 1995).

R.T. Williams, *The silver coinage of the Phokians* (Royal Numismatic Society, Special Publications 7, London 1972).

SIMON NORTHWOOD

QUINTUS FABIUS PICTOR: WAS HE AN ANNALIST?

Was Quintus Fabius Pictor an annalist? In so far as all historians of Rome *ab urbe condita* are commonly termed annalists, he certainly was. But of course the question implies a more precise definition of the term 'annalist'. Then the problem becomes more complex, encompassing a variety of fundamental questions about the origin and development of historical writing at Rome. If I cannot here offer a confident answer, I hope nevertheless to present a discussion of the relevant material which does justice to the complexities of the problem and clarifies at least some of the issues. In particular, in addition to analysis of the fragments and testimonia, I hope to have something to say about the role of Greek historiographical models, the *annales maximi*, Fabius' use of Greek, and his intended audience and purpose.

I

It is well known that there is no word in Latin for 'annalist'. The closest expression is *auctor annalium*. But there is a problem of definition, for we need to know whether *annales* corresponds to our 'annals'. That the ancients were not in possession of a single un-disputed meaning of the term is shown in a well known passage of Aulus Gellius (*NA* 5.18.1-7).[1] Here we learn that Verrius Flaccus in *de significatu uerborum* reported a definition according to which *annales* were a narrative of non-contemporary history, in contrast to *historia*, which concerned contemporary events.[2] Gellius himself prefers a second definition, and supports it with a quotation from Sempronius Asellio (fr.2P). This second definition is that *annales*, like our 'annals' or 'chronicles', were year by year accounts lacking description of causation, while *historia* (or in Asel-

Acknowledgements

This paper was presented at the University of Nottingham in July 1998 at a meeting organized by the group editing *The Fragmentary Roman Historians*, and again at the Ancient History Seminar at the University of Oxford in November 2003. I am grateful to the audiences on both occasions, and particularly to Prof. T.P. Wiseman for his correspondence after the Nottingham meeting. All dates are BC unless indicated otherwise.

[1] 'Historiam' ab 'annalibus' quidam differre eo putant, quod, cum utrumque sit rerum gestarum narratio, earum tamen proprie rerum sit 'historia', quibus rebus gerendis interfuerit is, qui narret; eamque esse opinionem quorundam Verrius Flaccus refert in libro de significatu uerborum quarto. Ac se quidem dubitare super ea re dicit, posse autem uideri putat nonnihil esse rationis in ea opinione, quod ἱστορία Graece significet rerum cognitionem praesentium. Sed nos audire soliti sumus annales omnino id esse, quod historiae sint, historias non omnino esse id, quod annales sint: sicuti, quod est homo, id necessario animal est; quod est animal, non id necesse est hominem esse. Ita 'historias' quidem esse aiunt rerum gestarum uel expositionem uel demonstrationem uel quo alio nomine id dicendum est, 'annales' uero esse, cum res gestae plurium annorum obseruato cuiusque anni ordine deinceps componuntur. Cum uero non per annos, sed per dies singulos res gestae scribuntur, ea historia Graeco uocabulo ἐφημερίς dicitur... I do not wish to get into the problem of how far the whole passage relies on Verrius Flaccus. However, I should point out that it is not clear that Verrius Flaccus preferred the version attributed to him directly by Gellius.

[2] Cf. Servius *Aen.* 1.373; Isidore *Etym.* 1.44.1-5; Lucan 5.384.

lio *res gestae*) was not so ordered and the concern was rather for analysis of historical causation. It is natural to think that this was the longstanding definition out of which grew the idea of *historia* as contemporary history, *annales* as non-contemporary. Such a development would have been governed by the fact that the nature of source material and the common practice of ancient historians meant that *historia* in the sense of causal explanation of *res gestae* was only really applicable to contemporary or near-contemporary history. Therefore the later definition based on the author's chronological relationship to his material could develop out of and coexist happily with the earlier definition based on nature of exposition.[3]

This is a natural explanation, but it may not be correct; indeed I am sure that the matter is more complicated than this. The problem is whether *annales* as a term for an historical work ever, even during the early period of historical writing at Rome, had the technical definition of an account with a particular chronological framework. The adjective *annalis* is described in *TLL* as *ad annum pertinens*, but the relationship to a year is variable: it can mean something occurring annually, or something confined to or lasting for a year (therefore it is context and common sense which determine that *feriae annales* are festivals which occur annually rather than festivals which last for a year).[4] *Libri annales* could therefore conceivably be a variety of different types of work: books compiled annually; books presented annually; books about individual years; books about years in general; books about past years. Here I am simply making the point that the adjective *annalis* does not allow us to assume that *annales* inevitably implied a year by year chronological account of the past, even if the first *libri annales* were those of the *pontifex maximus*, and so called because they were books that resulted from annual compilation and were presented in the form of an annual chronicle. When Romans required an expression to describe works of history it would have been quite natural to use *libri annales* even if the histories did not share the annalistic form of the *annales maximi*. We all know that in later Latin there was no distinction in use between *annales* and *historiae*, and that in Livy *annales* means nothing more specific than 'history'; but it may well be that much earlier, and perhaps even from the start, *annales* did not necessarily imply a year by year record of the past.[5] The point is well made if we recall that Ennius called his work *Annales* but surely cannot have based his narrative around a complete rendition of the consular *fasti*.[6] For him *annales* was appropriate for a non-annalistic verse history of Rome and was probably already a common Latin term for any historical account. So, had he written in Latin, Fabius could have called his history *annales* without any implication for its narrative form.

My purpose in prefacing this discussion of Fabius with an analysis of the meaning of *annales* is to point out that, when we ask the question, 'Was Fabius an annalist?', we are asking a modern question, one not necessarily equivalent to, 'Did Fabius write *annales*?' The answer to that question would be unequivocally affirmative. Whether

---

[3] Cf. Jacoby 1949, 86-7: 'Since a pragmatic explanation is truly possible for events of the time of the historian alone ... it becomes clear why Roman testimonies define Historia as the history of the time of the writer, limiting the concept annals to earlier times...'.

[4] Annual event: *clauus annalis* (Paul. Fest. 49L); *feriae annales* (Varro *Ling.* 2.26). Period of a year: *annale genus temporis* (Varro *Rust.* 1.27.1); *annale tempus*. Note also *lex annalis* (Cicero *Phil.* 5.47; *De orat.* 2.261; cf. Livy 40.44.1).

[5] My comments in this paragraph owe much to Verbrugghe 1989.

[6] The title is first attested in Lucilius 343 and is doubted neither by Skutsch 1984, 6-7, nor Jocelyn 1972, 1008. But note Verbrugghe 1989, 196: 'such usage... may not be a reference to a specific title, but could simply be an extension of the generic use of the word *annalis* as a reference to a history of Rome... even one written in verse'. For evidence of annalistic presentation in the later books see 290 Sk. (Book 8, Second Punic War); 304-5 Sk. (Book 9, 204BC); 324 Sk. (Book 9, 200BC); 329 Sk. (Book 10, 198BC).

Fabius was an annalist in our terms remains a relevant question, for even if *auctor annalium* never corresponded to our word 'annalist', we still know that some of the historians of the second century wrote what we would call 'annals' and that their authors were therefore 'annalists'. (This much is apparent from Asellio fr.1-2P.) It seems reasonable therefore to ask if Fabius Pictor can be counted among them.

I must pause again before considering the fragments themselves, in order to define 'annalist' in our own terms. In its fullest sense and in the Roman context an annalist is one who offers a yearly record of state affairs in which each year is treated according to a fixed pattern of elections, expiation of prodigies, allotments of provinces etc., and who regularly reports certain types of non-annual occurrence, e.g. grain scarcities, pestilences, triumphs etc. This is a definition which corresponds to the narrative we find in the later surviving books of Livy, but of course it is too severe for his first decade, in which the fixed pattern is merely a recording of events within the framework of a list of annual magistrates.[7] Therefore we should allow some variation in our expectations when we come to accounts of the early republic. So when we ask if Fabius was an annalist, we are asking whether and to what extent his work corresponded to the pattern we see in Livy; in fact we are asking whether the last writer *ab urbe condita* wrote according to a model more or less established by his furthest predecessor. In what follows I shall begin primarily with Fabius' treatment of the early republic, partly for reasons of space, and partly because it is this area of Fabius' work which has attracted most controversy. Few, for example, conceive of the later part of Fabius' narrative not being annalistic; but plenty have thought differently about his account of the early republic.[8]

II

It comes as no surprise that the fragments do not admit a definite answer to the question. There are at most thirty-six fragments (including those apparently from a work in Latin) collected by H. Peter and F. Jacoby in their separate editions; many of these concern the regal or pre-regal period, and those that do not could equally well stand in a non-annalistic as in an annalistic account. But two fragments have on occasion been used as evidence for or against an annalistic form. First fr.6P (Latin Fabius = *FGrH*. 809 33J)[9]:

> quapropter tum primum ex plebe alter consul factus est duouicesimo anno postquam Romam Galli ceperunt. (Aulus Gellius *NA* 5.4.3)

> So then for the first time one of the consuls was chosen from among the plebeians, in the twenty-second year after the Gauls captured Rome.

This fragment has often been put forward as evidence that Fabius dated events by means of intervals, and therefore did not organize his narrative according to a complete sequence of consuls. The problem with this conclusion is that interval dating

---

[7] Cf. Rich 1996.

[8] A full consul list was not absolutely required by Momigliano 1966, 60. He saw Orosius 4.13.5-7 and Eutropius 3.5 (fr. 23P = fr. 19J) reporting Fabius on 225 as evidence of consular dating. It is not clear if Momigliano thought an incomplete list possible only for the early republic. Gelzer 1954, 346-7 = 1964, 109, suspected that consuls did not appear as eponyms but arose naturally within the narrative, as they do in Polybius.

[9] I assume, for the sake of argument, that the Latin work attributed to Fabius is simply a translation of the original *Graeci annales*.

and a consul list are not mutually exclusive. Even Livy could give interval dates, mostly AUC, for major events.[10] Moreover, a consul list requires such devices if any serious chronological point is to be made. We must therefore consider this fragment inconclusive. If it does suggest anything positive, it is that Fabius felt he had the means to date the consuls of 366 relative to the sack, and this implies that he at least had access to a consul list.

The second fragment is fr.19P/16J, concerning 294 BC:

> Fabius ambo consules in Samnio et ad Luceriam res gessisse scribit, tra-ductumque in Etruriam exercitum (sed ab utro consule non adiecit) et ad Luceriam utrimque multos occisos, inque ea pugna Iouis Statoris aedam uotam, ut Romulus ante uouerat. Sed fanum tantum, id est locus templo effatus, fuerat. Ceterum hoc demum anno ut aedem etiam fieri senatus iuberet bis eiusdem uoti damnata re publica in religionem uenit.
> (Livy 10.37).

> Fabius writes that both consuls campaigned in Samnium and near Luceria, that the army was taken across to Etruria (by which consul he does not say), that both sides suffered heavy losses near Luceria and that during the battle the temple was vowed to Jupiter the Stayer, as Romulus had vowed before. He says, though, that only the sanctuary, that is, the site conse-crated for the temple, had been marked out, but that this year the Senate at last took action under pressure of its religious duty, seeing that the state had been put under obligation twice by the same vow, and gave orders for the temple to be built. (trans. Radice).

This fragment was claimed by F. Bömer as a typical annalistic entry. Such a claim was rejected out of hand by M. Gelzer, and it is true that Bömer offered no decisive reason why it had to come from a fully annalistic account, merely drawing attention to its general appearance and Livy's remark *huius anni parum constans memoria est*.[11] But the best evidence that this fragment is indeed from an annalistic account has been overlooked. This is the sequence of events: i) the campaign in Samnium and at Luceria; ii) the campaign in Etruria; iii) the report of losses at Luceria, and the vowing of the temple. This sequence suggests an annalistic form in which the consecration of temples is treated separately from the narrative of military affairs, and in which the vowing of the temple is recorded separately from the battle of Luceria. Of course this evidence cannot be pressed too far, for we do not know to what extent the sequence in the fragment is genuinely Fabian or due instead to editing by Livy. And even if the sequence is genuine, it suggests an annalistic character for this year, but does not necessarily prove that Fabius gave a full year by year account of the mid-early republic. [12]

This exhausts the number of fragments traditionally brought to bear on the present problem. There is a possibility to introduce a further fragment, however, which is not specifically attributed to Fabius but which may well come from him. This

---

[10] See Briscoe's note on Livy 31.1.4.

[11] Bömer 1953/4, 201. Gelzer 1964, 106, responded that the events at Luceria and in Etruria could naturally arise even in the κεφαλαιωδῶς section of Fabius, implying they would be relevant for a Greek readership.

[12] Frier 1999², 269: 'The superficial resemblance of this paraphrase to the notices in a chroni-cle is perhaps illusory; Livy only summarizes Pictor. But Pictor's failure to specify the name of the consul and the sequence of the operations is probably a more significant sign of his use of the chronicle'.

is Livy 2.18 on the first dictatorship, attributed to *ueterrimi auctores*. Now we know that Livy considered Fabius to be *scriptorum antiquissimus* (1.44.2) and *longe antiquissimus auctor* (2.40.10), and there is a suspicion that when he refers to *antiquissimi auctores* (8.30.7) he really means Fabius, and Fabius alone (note how this reference is immediately followed by a fragment from Fabius: §9). By analogy the *ueterrimi auctores* at 2.18 may well also be Fabius:

> in hac tantarum exspectatione rerum sollicita ciuitate dictatoris primum creandi mention orta. Sed nec quo anno, nec quibus consulibus, quia ex factione Tarquiniana essent – id quo denim traditur – parum creditum sit, nec quis primum dictator creatus est, satis constat. Apud ueterrimos tamen auctores T.Largium dictatorem primum, Sp.Cassium magistrum equitum creatos inuenio, consules legere; ita lex iubebat de dictatore creando lata. Eo magis adducor ut credam Largium, qui consularis erat, potius quam M.' Valerium Marci filium Volesi nepotem, qui nondum consul fuerat, moderatorem et magistrum consulibus appositum.

> These grave apprehensions having occasioned a general anxiety, the appointment of a dictator was suggested, for the first time. But there is no general agreement as to the year, or which consuls were distrusted as being of the Tarquinian faction – for this is included in the tradition – or who it was that was first named dictator. In the oldest writers, I find it said that Titus Largius was the first to be made dictator, and that Spurius Cassius was master of the horse. They chose men of consular rank, for so the law prescribed which had been passed to regulate the selection of a dictator. I am therefore the more disposed to believe that Largius, a consular, rather than Manius Valerius the son of Marcus and grandson of Volesus, a man who had not yet held the consulship, was assigned to be the director and superior of consuls. (trans. Foster).

It is possible that this confusion arose because the first dictatorship appeared initially in a non-annalistic account. Livy mentions the dictatorship here in 501, Dionysius three years later in 498 (M.' Valerius appears in 494 in both authors: Livy 2.30.5; DH *AR* 6.39.2). Both 501 and 498 are years in which Larcius was consul, so it is natural to think that confusion arose as to which of his consulships was honoured with a dictatorship. It is possible that this was because the ultimate source did not make the matter clear, i.e. that the event was not fixed in a year by year narrative organized by consuls.[13] I do not want to stretch the point too far: it is still possible that Fabius was clear on the matter and that others, for reasons now lost, wilfully contradicted him. But I offer the interpretation as a possibility, and as an example of the scrutiny which has to be applied to the various fragments in order to make any advance. Unfortunately, even the sort of scrutiny offered here, however interesting and instructive, does not lead to any firm conclusions.

III

The paucity of fragments of Fabius and their impenetrability for the purposes of the investigation in hand has led to considerable discussion of the testimonia, and also

---

[13] Cf. the general remarks of Hanell 1956, 168-9, noting that Livy never refers to Fabius in order to settle disputes, and that this suggests he did not present a full list of eponyms. Instead he dated by intervals, possibly adding eponymous dates for special events.

discussion of those parts of Polybius which can reasonably be assumed to derive from Fabius. The most important testimonium is that of Dionysius of Halicarnassus (*AR* 1.6.2), who tells us that Fabius and his contemporary, Cincius Alimentus, wrote in detail (ἀκριβῶς) on contemporary events but ran through in summary fashion (κεφαλαιωδῶς) the early events after the foundation (κτίσις). The essential problem lies in defining 'ktisis'.[14] Three interpretations can be found in the scholarly literature: i) ktisis = foundation by Romulus;[15] ii) ktisis = regal period;[16] iii) ktisis = period up to Decemvirate. The first of these is the most natural reading; those who maintain the second reading point to the fullness apparent in the surviving fragments of Fabius on the regal period, and also the fragments of Polybius 6 (they might also appeal to the remains of Ennius on the regal period, assuming Ennius is following Fabius); the third position, argued by D. Timpe, is based on analogy with ktisis literature, which regularly went far beyond foundations and included subsequent constitutional developments.[17] Timpe appeals also to the fullness in the fragments concerning the very early republic (e.g. fr.16P/13bJ = *ludi maximi*; fr.17P/14J = Coriolanus), and to a comparison with Cato, who is commonly thought to have extended his account of the regal period to include the early republic up to the Decemvirate.

The second and third interpretations outlined above should almost certainly be rejected in favour of the natural reading. First, anyone who has done any detailed work on the fragments of the early Roman historians, poets, and antiquarians knows that the pattern of distribution of the fragments does not accurately represent the economies of the works concerned. This is easily demonstrable in the cases where survival of book numbers allows us to analyze the data: Ennius, Piso, Cn. Gellius, even Varro's *de uita populi romani*.[18] So it is dangerous to base any firm conclusions on the pattern of the fragments, as do Gelzer and Gabba.[19] Second, Dionysius himself clearly implies a 'ktisis' ending with the foundation by Romulus.

Dionysius says that his second book (ending with the death of Remus and the ritual marking out of the city) onwards will be περὶ δὲ τῶν πράξεων ἃς μετὰ τὸν οἰκισμὸν εὐθέως ἀπεδείξαντο (concerning the deeds they performed **immediately after the founding of the city**) and again that readers μαθοῦσί γε δὴ παρὰ τῆς ἱστορίας ὅτι μυρίας ἤνεγκεν ἀνδρῶν ἀρετὰς εὐθὺς ἐξ ἀρχῆς μετὰ τὸν οἰκισμόν (shall have learned from my history that Rome from the very beginning, **immediately after its foundation** produced infinite examples of virtue). His period, immediately after the foundation by Romulus, must surely be meant to correspond to the period covered only κεφαλαιωδῶς by Fabius

---

[14] There is general agreement that the contemporary section of the narrative is conceived as the period from the First Punic War onwards.

[15] Implicit in A. Drummond's discussion in his review of Gabba (1967) in *JRS* 60 (1970) 201. Cornell 1980, 20-1; Petzold 1993, 163-5, whose arguments are similar to those presented here; Poucet 1976, 214; Verbrugghe 1980, 2167 n. 14; U.W.Scholz, *DNP*, 4. 374 (1998).

[16] Gelzer 1964, 105; Gabba 1967, 135; Forsythe 1994, 43-4.

[17] Timpe 1972, 932-40.

[18] Even where we know treatments of the early republic to have been more extensive than that of the kings, quotations from the latter still predominate. Piso is quoted sixteen times from Book 1 but only eight times from Book 2 (H. Peter, *HRR*). From Cn. Gellius' three regal books we have eighteen fragments, but only seven from the next twelve, which narrated the republic up to 389 (H. Peter, *HRR*). Ennius (Skutsch) is cited ninety four times from his three volume regal period but only thirty-two times from the subsequent three volumes, which deal with the period up to 265. In Varro's *de uita populi Romani* (B. Riposati, 1972) we have fifty-five fragments from Book 1 (the regal period) but only twenty-five from Book 2 (the early republic to 265 BC). Only in the case of one author, Hemina, can we be sure that treatment of the kings exceeded treatment of the early republic: Book 2 included part of the regal period (fr.11P) and the early republic up to at least 281 (fr.21P): Northwood 1994, 18-19.

[19] n.16 above.

and Cincius. Those who think that Dionysius' remarks refer to the period up to the Decemvirate are guilty of asking what 'ktisis' might have meant to Fabius, rather than what it meant to Dionysius, on whose account we rely.

Having established the period treated κεφαλαιωδῶς, it is important to determine, if possible, what is meant by this term. First, fullness of narrative is a relative thing, and Dionysius judges Fabius and Cincius inadequate by his own standard, a standard by which even Livy might be considered κεφαλαιωδῶς. Second, this characterisation covers a wide variety of authors (Hieronymus, Timaeus, Antigonus, Polybius, Silenus, Fabius, Cincius) who relative to each other probably offered accounts of early Rome very different in scale: few would doubt that Fabius and perhaps even Polybius gave substantially more on early Rome than Hieronymus and Timaeus. Moreover, we still do not know that κεφαλαιωδῶς necessarily excludes an annalistic form, nor that the 'hour glass' shape of Fabius' work excludes the possibility of a full list of consuls.[20] Timpe thinks that the expression is similar to *capitulatim*, the word used by Nepos to describe the later 'historical' books of Cato's *Origines*. Hence it is claimed that Fabius, while relying on Roman material of dry and 'annalistic' cha-racter, wrote his account of the early republic under headings, i.e. according to topics or themes, and did not offer a complete chronological account from beginning to end.[21] There is in fact little evidence that κεφαλαιωδῶς should be taken to mean *capitulatim*. But the point is sometimes maintained using Polybius as evidence. At Polybius 1.6 we hear that after the sack of Rome the Romans fought first Latins, then (in sequence) Etruscans, Celts, and Samnites. At 2.18-20, starting from the sack, Polybius records the intermittent incursions of the Gauls and dates them by intervals (relative to each other) until events reach a conclusion with final defeat for the Gauls in 283.[22] Then at 2.21-23 we get the settlement of Picenum in 232 and the sequence of events leading to the battle of Telamon in 225. Fabius, probably correctly, is generally considered to be Polybius' source, but these passages seem to me to fall a long way short of proving a *capitulatim* treatment by Fabius. The whole section on the Gauls from the sack to 225 can hardly have stood as a single topic in Fabius, for it extends beyond the κεφαλαιωδῶς section and into the ἀκριβῶς, and would have required a separate record of the First Punic War. The full excursus 390-225 is much more likely the creation of Polybius himself. It remains possible, however, that the account from the sack to 283 corresponds to a single topical section in Fabius, other topics being the Latins, the Etruscans, and the Samnites, as outlined by Polybius at 1.6. But this I still doubt. The military events involving these peoples, including the Gauls, were so interconnected that any narrative built around such a scheme would involve repetition and confusion on a large scale.[23] We cannot be sure that these events were treated annalistically, but I think

---

[20] *contra* Gelzer 1964, 105-6. Gelzer makes much of κεφαλαιωδῶς being the word used by Thucydides to describe his (non-annalistic) *pentekontaetia* and Dionysius's reference to Latin authors as ταῖς Ἑλληνικαῖς χρονογραφίαις ἐοικυῖαι (1.7.3 cf. 1.8.3). He thinks both exclude annalistic treatment by Fabius. Neither observation is compelling: κεφαλαιωδῶς need not be interpreted so mechanically, and Dionysius' comments on the Latin authors need not imply a contrast with the Romans writing in Greek. Fabius and Cincius are grouped with their Greek predecessors on account of the language in which they wrote and their lack of coverage of Dionysius' subject matter, not on account of their narrative arrangement; so the fact that the Latin historians are labelled as 'like the Greek chronological histories' does not exclude Fabius and Cincius from also being similar to them.

[21] Timpe 1972, 949-52; cf. Gelzer 1934, 49-50 = 1964, 96-7.

[22] For an interval date in the Latin Fabius see above, fr. 6P/33J.

[23] We could of course say that Fabius was indeed repetitive and confused, but the treatment of the Gauls in Polybius does not suggest so. Timpe 1972, 952, underestimates the problems of a narrative organised by topics: 'sie entfernte sich von der annalistischen Jahresfolge nicht so weit, daß sie grosse kompositionelle Probleme mit sich gebracht hätte'.

we can be reasonably confident that they were treated chronologically within a single narrative.[24]

IV

We have now pretty much exhausted the fragments and testimonia. Another approach to understanding the form of Fabius' work is through the models he is likely to have followed. There was a variety available: annalistic local histories, accounts of individual wars organized under various chronological schemes, universal history, 'ktisis' literature, and *Sikelika*, to name the most prominent. Greek historiography would not have forced upon Fabius an annalistic framework, though those who think his work to have been annalistic naturally suggest a link with the Atthides, the local histories of Athens.[25] But we do not know if Fabius ever read an Atthis. We can be reasonably confident, however, that he read 'ktisis' literature (according to Plutarch *Rom.* 3 he read Diocles of Peparethus), and similarly confident that he had read Timaeus and Philinus; indeed the influence of Timaeus can be detected in the fragments: Fabius' concern with national customs, religious ceremonies, anecdotal details, and his Olympiad dating all required Timaeus as a model.[26] The idea of presenting a work which connected contemporary history and early legends could have come from either Atthides or the Sicilian historians, but since we know for sure only that he read the latter, this route seems more plausible. It is this influence which is often held to account for the general shape of Fabius' work, particularly his scanty treatment of the early republic and overwhelming interest in legendary times and contemporary events. But would the outcome have really been so different had he relied wholly on Roman sources? Did Fabius have to jettison local material in order to cohere with the Greek view of Rome? The answers are negative: the pre-literary Roman view of her legendary past had already been influenced by Greek contact, and there will have been much more information both oral and documentary on the periods closer to Fabius' own lifetime than on the early republic. Neither the shape nor content of Fabius' narrative necessarily involved conscious capitulation to externally imposed historiographical models.

Fabius' dependence on Greek predecessors has been expressed most categorically by G.P.Verbrugghe: 'Pictor... wrote a Greek work indistinguishable in form and content from previous Greek histories written on the same subject', and 'Pictor and Cincius... had narrated the history of Rome no differently from any other authors who wrote in Greek'.[27] These must surely be overstatements of the case. When Dionysius describes the accounts of Hieronymus, Timaeus, Antigonus, Polybius, Silenus, Fabius, and Cincius as κεφαλαιωδῶς, he does not mean they are all written at the same level **relative to each other**, simply that they are all inadequate **compared to him**. The scale of Fabius' narrative must have exceeded that of Timaeus etc. (If the Tauromenium Dipinto summarizes Fabius' first book, we see that it covered the ori-

---

[24] But cf. Walbank 1945, 17 'It is quite likely that Fabius treated such topics as the Gallic Wars *en bloc*... Polybius too wrote normally by Olympiad years, but on occasion allows himself the liberty of combining related events from a series of years within a single passage. Gelzer is not therefore justified in setting up a rigid *either... or* on this question, as if the fact that Fabius occasionally treated events outside the year-by-year chronology rules out any annalistic scheme at all.'

[25] Jacoby 1949, 60-64, 283-6, thought Fabius wrote annalistically.

[26] Momigliano 1966, 62; Momigliano 1990, 100-1.

[27] Verbrugghe 1980, 2167, 2171. Less starkly in Fornara 1983. For a balanced view of Greek and Roman influences see Dillery 2002, 8-9, 15, 22.

gins up to (and including?) the rule of Romulus, a substantial treatment which must have been significantly grander than any previous account.)[28] Fabius may have owed much to Greek predecessors, but he was not uncritical of them. For example, he accepted Olympiad dating from Timaeus, but not his date of 814 for the foundation of Rome. As we shall see, Fabius included a significant amount of material which would not or could not have been used by the Greek historians. That he included in his work much material which was oriented to a Roman audience is clear from the fragments. Fabius' version of Romulus and Remus may have been influenced (through Diocles) by Greek tragedy and Homer, but it contained also legal details which must have been Roman in origin.[29] The fragment concerning Fabius Rullianus (fr.18P/15J), the master of horse who burned military spoils in order to deprive the dictator, L.Papirius Cursor, of glory is probably typical of much material – fully comprehensible only to a Roman audience. As a Roman senator Fabius must have presented material which was driven by the concerns and outlook of his peers, including both family traditions and the views of the senatorial elite as a whole.[30] Moreover, if we conceive of Fabius writing and even publishing during the Second Punic War, we could imagine his account of the past upholding Roman morale in a time of crisis.

Those who want to argue for a brief and episodic Fabian version of the early republic have a further argument, viz. that only this (and not an annalistic account) would match the purpose and intended audience of his work. Fabius' adoption of historiography and above all his decision to write in Greek are said to have arisen from his desire to use history as a tool of contemporary foreign policy which would explain and justify Rome's record, particularly in response to negative views of Rome already circulating in the Greek world. In order to achieve his purpose he had not only to write in Greek but also to adopt a literary form that would not repel Greek readers. They after all would find meaningless an account based around the consul list.[31] There are, however, alternative views.

One is that Fabius chose to write in Greek because of the relatively undeveloped state of Latin prose. This is possible but not certain. Technical treatises were first appearing in Latin (e.g. Sex. Aelius Paetus Catus' [cos. 198] *tripertita*, a commentary on the Twelve Tables), there was a basic prose tradition in the *laudationes funebrae*, and (for what it is worth) Livius Andronicus was producing verse in Latin, and Naevius was producing original epic. So it may be possible that Fabius could have said what he wanted in Latin.[32] (There is of course an element of *petitio principii* here, since whether he could have used Latin depends partly on our conception of the sort

---

[28] Frier 1979, 230, 251-2, 322, assumes the Dipinto summarizes Fabius' first book; *contra*: ed. Suerbaum 2002, 362. If Frier is correct, Fabius' account will have been more expansive than that of Livy, who fits the entire regal period into one book, and closer to that of Dionysius. It would be useful for our purposes if Frier were right, but the matter is very unclear.

[29] Tragic influence on Fabius' account of Romulus and Remus is summarised usefully in Dillery 2002, 20-1; for Roman features in the account see Frier 1979, 265-8.

[30] Momigliano 1966, 63. Note Fabius' inclusion of Heracles' arrival in Italy (Tauromenium Dipinto): the descent of the Fabii from Hercules may have gone back to Pictor's time: cf. Fabius Maximus' removal of the statue of Hercules from Tarentum to the Capitol and the erection of his own statue next to it (Plutarch *Fab. Max.* 22.6; Strabo 6.278; Pliny *HN* 34.40).

[31] Thus Gelzer 1964, 96.

[32] See Momigliano 1966, 57; 1990, 91. Zimmermann 1933, 248-51, argues the case most forcefully, but his claim that Fabius wrote in both Latin and Greek is to be rejected. A longstanding view of the underdevelopment of Latin prose can be seen in edd. Schanz, Hosius 1927, 170, where the prose of the late third and early second centuries is considered to have been inflexible and unable to reach the stylistic level required for history; a social aversion is also adduced: Latin had been used by foreigners of low birth. Suerbaum 2002, 358, suggests progress in Latin verse had not been matched in prose.

of history he was writing). A more promising alternative might be the argument that, even if he could have written in Latin, Fabius' choice of Greek does not imply a specific posture other than the desire to be read widely (he could reach both Romans and Greeks) and to be treated seriously as an historian. Every work of history known to him was in Greek. These were the works on which he relied as both models and in part as sources, and to which he owed any understanding of the literary requirements of history. Just as in later times opera would for so long be written in Italian, history had to be written in Greek. In the words of Momigliano: 'We should not be far from the truth if we said that Fabius wrote history in Greek because everybody else was doing so'.[33]

In truth we can never know the motivations behind Fabius' enterprise. It may be that he was initially driven by anger at the anti-Roman perspectives of Philinus, who had written on the First Punic War, and perhaps others writing positively about Hannibal. But this is not a sufficient explanation for the work he finally produced. If it had been conceived simply as a response to anti-Roman historiography, it would have assumed a very different shape. The work of Philinus, for example, covering the First Punic War (possibly with an introduction on the legendary period), did not require a full history of Rome in order to be refuted. The history which Fabius produced must have involved many programmes, only one of which was the defence of Rome's reputation against such hostile historians. When Fabius dealt with events covered by anti-Roman historians, he was certainly biased; but (as Momigliano and Hanell have stressed) he was not wholly indiscriminate.[34] C.W. Fornara puts it nicely when he says, 'Fabius's account of the wars was a patriotic history of a "pious and just set of engagements..." because this was the Romans' view of their world. The concept was not manufactured for foreign consumption.'[35] And F.W. Walbank remarks (following Vogt) that it was hardly likely that the process of creating a literary history of Rome for the first time was simultaneously a work of propaganda.[36] It is difficult therefore to maintain that Fabius eschewed the annalistic form because it ill suited his propagandist purpose: that is to focus too narrowly on one aspect of his work at the expense of other equally significant elements.

V

Fabius' sources for internal affairs would obviously have included the family traditions of the nobility, but the source which is most often seen as a guarantee that Fabius wrote annalistically is the *annales maximi*. There is not the space here to delve fully into the complexities and problems of these documents, but it is appropriate to discuss one major piece of evidence for Fabius' use of them. This is the well known fragment of Cato's *Origines* Book 4 in which Cato declared that he did not consider it appropriate to record celestial prodigies or times when grain was dear (fr.77P: *non lubet scribere, quod in tabula apud pontificem maximum est, quotiens annona cara, quotiens lunae aut solis lumine caligo aut quid obstiterit*). This comment has often been seen as an attack on Fabius' use of the *annales maximi* (by implication, but not necessarily, in an annalistic account) and as a justification for Cato's omission of the

---

[33] Momigliano 1990, 99. Gruen 1984, 254-5, is the strongest proponent of the idea that Fabius' choice of language was not determined by propagandist aims; cf. Usher 1969, 131-2. The position adopted here is a modified version of Northwood 1994, 12-14.

[34] Momigliano 1966, 64-7; 1990, 103-4. Hanell 1956, 175, emphasizes that Fabius' account of the kings and early republic was not a vehicle for propaganda.

[35] Fornara 1983, 41.

[36] Walbank 1945, 17.

early republic before the First Punic War. This view goes back, I think, to Korne-mann.[37] It is a perfectly acceptable interpretation, maybe even the right one; but others are possible. It may be, for example, that Cato's comment looks forward and not back, in which case it would be a justification for the difference between the cha-racter of his rendition of the Punic Wars and that of Fabius.[38] Another interpretation has recently been offered by G. Forsythe, who holds that Cato's target was not Fabius but Ennius.[39] I should prefer, however, to think that in a work of history Cato would be attacking another prose historian. It is true that many of the sorts of material usually connected with the chronicle were to be found in Ennius' *Annales*,[40] and that he could certainly have imitated directly the style of the *annales maximi* (the pontiff's whitened board was still in use in his time); but it seems more likely that he found his actual material in an earlier historian than that he consulted the *annales maximi* for himself.

If we believe that Cato's comment was indeed directed at Fabius, it does not ne-cessarily follow that his use of the pontifical records means that he presented an annalistic account. We have already noted that Ennius' *Annales* seem to have con-tained such material but can hardly have been fully annalistic in character. All we can assume is that Fabius used pontifical material to an extent which made Cato's attack credible.

VI

If I have done nothing else, I hope to have shown the intractability of the evidence for the arrangement of Fabius' history. There is, however, a final approach to the problem, which needs to be discussed. This approach appeals not only to the frag-ments and testimonia but also to the character of the other authors writing *ab urbe condita*. Fabius is classified by default: if another author can convincingly be identi-fied as the first true annalist, or if the primary source for annalistic histories can be shown to post-date Fabius, then Fabius cannot have been an annalist. This approach has a long pedigree. Gelzer used it as an additional tool in his analysis of Fabius: not only could he claim accurately to characterize Fabius by means of the fragments, *testimonia*, and traces of Fabius in Polybius, but he could also describe and explain the later growth of annalistic historiography. Ultimately he was to connect this growth with the publication of the *annales maximi* towards the end of the second century, a work which he considered the target of Asellio's attack on *annales*.[41] More fundamen-

---

[37] Petzold 1993, 168-9, and Timpe 1972, 953 (cf. Gelzer 1964, 99; 1964, 105-6), think Cato's remarks do account for his omission of the Zwischenzeit, which would have had to be filled by reference to pontifical records, but are not also directed against Fabius. But note Walbank 1945, 17: 'This assertion [sc. of Cato's] is hard to understand as a mere definition of Cato's position (as the first *Latin* historian) relative to the pontifical material, and would seem to be directed to Fabius'. Bömer 1953/4, 198. Kornemann 1911, 256.

[38] Thus Kierdorf 1980, 206, 221; this is implied also in Frier 1999², 87.

[39] Forsythe 1994, 46, 48, 69-70: Cato's comments refer to early **and** middle republic but are directed towards Ennius, since Fabius did not have an annalistic account. Also Rüpke 1995, 200 n.82.

[40] Examples listed in Jocelyn 1972, 1008-9: transfers of *imperium*, *prodigia* and their expiation, food crises, new religious rites and institutions, *uota* and *dedicationes*, adjustments to the ca-lendar, establishment of colonies, censors' quinquennial lustrations, funerals of statesmen, the sending and receipt of embassies, treaties, assignment of *prouinciae*, declarations of war, mili-tary levies. Ennius was also influenced stylistically, replicating their bald style in an otherwise ornate narrative.

[41] Gelzer 1964, 95; 1964, 110.

tally he saw annalistic historiography as a response to a change of audience and expectation, specifically the replacement of a Greek audience with a Roman one dominated by priests and senators.

Gelzer's argument has been restated and reformulated by K.-E. Petzold.[42] With regard to the *annales maximi* Petzold retains the longstanding view that the cessation of the public display of *tabulae* in the pontificate of P. Mucius Scaevola (Cicero *De orat.* 2.52) coincided with the publication of the complete record of the *tabulae* in an eighty volume edited edition (Serv. Dan. *Aen.* 1.373). The connection between Scaevola and the eighty book edition has been challenged strongly (and in my view convincingly) by B.W. Frier, who sees it as an Augustan work.[43] Petzold considers it the work of Scaevola himself, produced perhaps with the help of his brother P. Licinius Crassus Dives Mucianus (*pontifex maximus* 132-30 BC) and other *pontifices et scribae*. He argues that such an enterprise is precisely what we might expect of Scaevola, a man whom we know to have written ten books on the *ius ciuile*, and whose son Quintus wrote a further eighteen on the same subject. But in fact Petzold presents a paradox: Scaevola was a famous public figure and antiquarian, yet we have no direct attribution to him of any edition of the *annales maximi*, a work which would have been the crowning achievement of any such scholar and which would have stood as the basis for all subsequent histories of Rome. It passes belief that we should know of Scaevola's scholarly credentials without knowing too of his production of an eighty book edition of the *annales maximi*. Furthermore, in common with most others who have defended a late second century date for the edition of the *annales maximi*, Petzold fails to engage with Frier's argument that the fragments of the eighty book edition (one from Aulus Gellius and three from the *origo gentis Romanae*) are at the earliest triumviral in date.[44] Although Frier's view of the *annales maximi* is extremely problematic, it seems to me that critics have failed seriously to damage it.

A late date for the publication of the *annales maximi* removes one of Gelzer's arguments against Fabius being an annalist: even later works generally accepted as annalistic would then predate the *annales maximi*, and the published *annales maximi* would therefore not be responsible for the annalistic form in Roman historiography. T.P. Wiseman, however, has argued that annalistic history was delayed for further reasons. For him Fabius was not an annalist because annalistic writing could not exist before the independent construction of consular *fasti* by antiquarians such as M. Fulvius Nobilior (*cos.* 189; *cens.* 179) and C. Sempronius Tuditanus (*cos.* 129).[45]

---

[42] Petzold 1993, 151-61 (cf. Momigliano 1990, 95-7). Very similar arguments (with similar weaknesses) are put forward apparently independently by Forsythe 1994, 55-69, adding N. Fabius Pictor as one of Scaevola's potential colleagues, and Hemina and Junius Gracchanus as further examples of burgeoning antiquarian religiosity. He thinks the *annales maximi* may have been compiled but not published.

[43] Frier 1999², esp. chapter 9.

[44] Frier 1999², chapters 2-3. The failure to deal with this important part of Frier's argument, be it right or wrong, is worrying. Cornell 1986, 71-2 rightly says 'that fact (sc. Scaevola's cessation of recording events on the *tabulae*) might seem to be evidence, not of Scaevola's enthusiasm for the chronicle, but rather of his indifference to it', but then claims that the eighty book edition comprised simply the chronicle as compiled up to the time of Scaevola. Another issue generally dealt with inadequately is Servius Danielis' use of *ueteres*. Ogilvie 1981, 200, argued that Serv. Dan.'s reference to the compilers of the *annales maximi* as *ueteres* excluded them from being later than republican; I cannot comment specifically on Servius (Ogilvie in fact cited no specific evidence), but the references in the index to *GL* 3 (s.v. *ueterum* and *antiquorum*) show that Priscian regularly included Augustan authors among the *ueteres*. The same applies to Nonius: Mazzacane 1985, 192-3.

[45] Wiseman 1979, c.2, esp. 12-16; Rawson 1976, 704-5, was similarly tempted. My critique of Wiseman and Fornara is a revised version of Northwood 1994, 33-8.

Nor is he alone, for a similar argument has been put forward by J. Rüpke.⁴⁶ The thesis is, however, problematic. It is not clear to me why there could not have been a relatively secure set of *fasti* already in existence at the end of the third century. Nor does there seem to be any sound evidence for the sort of antiquarian efforts on which the argument depends. The *fasti* of M. Fulvius Nobilior, set up in the temple of Hercules Musarum, may have been simply a calendar with no consul list attached.⁴⁷ And even if there was such a list, which I do not discount entirely, there is no guarantee (or indeed evidence at all) that it was the first of its kind. Indeed, if there was anything novel about Fulvius' effort it was surely his addition of a commentary on the origins of the calendar: it is this after all that attracts the interest of the sources. Nor is it clear that Tuditanus' *libri magistratuum* were sparsely annotated consular *fasti*.⁴⁸ For the clinching argument, however, we must return to Polybius' account of Rome, almost universally thought to derive from Fabius: how could the chronologically detailed account of the Gallic wars have been constructed if a functional consul list had not already been available to Fabius? Our conclusion must be that if the development of annalistic history was delayed, it was not for want of the necessary raw materials.⁴⁹

Wiseman has a further argument, viz. that Piso was the first to title his work *annales* and was therefore the first true Roman annalist.⁵⁰ This relies on a number of fragments of Piso: from Cicero (Piso fr.40P), Dionysius of Halicarnassus (fr.14, 15, 25P), Varro (fr.6, 9, 41P), Pliny (fr.13P – fr.10P might also be relevant), Aulus Gellius (fr. 19, 27P), and Priscian (fr.18P), all of whom quote Piso's work as *annales*. The citations in Varro, Aulus Gellius, Pliny, and Priscian are in fact inadmissable (these

---

⁴⁶ Rüpke 1995, 184-202. I am surprised that Rüpke does not cite Wiseman.
⁴⁷ Wiseman 1979, 17, does not disguise the possibility that Nobilior's *fasti* had no consul list. The evidence is Macrobius *Sat.* 1.12.16 (the general context is his discussion of the Roman year, months, modifications by Numa, and intercalation in 1.12-13): *nam Fuluius Nobilior in fastis quos in aede Herculis Musarum posuit Romulum dicit, postquam populum in maiores iunioresque diuisit ut altera pars consilio altera armis rempublicam tueretur, in honorem utriusque parties hunc Maium sequentem Iunium mensem uocasse.* Later at 1.13.21 we have: *Fulvius autem id egisse M'.Acilium consulem dicit ab urbe condita anno quingentesimo sexagesimo secundo, initio mox bello Aetolico.* (This can hardly be right; probably Acilius' *lex de intercalando* resulted from the 'realisation of an extraordinary degree of dislocation of the calendar': Briscoe 1981, 19). Neither Macrobius nor citations elsewhere (Varro, *Ling.* 6.33 [probably not S. Fulvius Flaccus, the orator mentioned at Cic. *Brut.* 81]; Censorinus *DN* 22.9 cf. 20.2-4; Charis. *Gramm.* 1.175 Barwick; Lydus *Ost.* 16a) compel belief in a consular list). It is also unclear whether we are dealing with an inscription (thus De Sanctis 1953, 258 n. 577) or a written volume (thus Boyancé 1955, 174). Belief in a consul list (suggested by De Sanctis) relies on analogy with later *fasti* where a consul list and calendar were combined (most notably the *Fasti Antiates Maiores*, which are connected with Fulvius on account of their chronological starting point and the appearance there of no temple foundation dates later than that of Hercules Musarum itself): see Rüpke 1995, 199-200, for recent exposition of the theory, suggesting Ennius as the first beneficiary of the consul list. Rüpke 1995, 189-91, argues that there was actually no need for a consul list until the *lex Villia annalis* of 180, and that the consul list was less a chronological device than a tool for regulating elite competition. This leaves much to be desired: what then was the Roman chronological system, and if consul dating was not used for chronological purposes, why do we not hear of any alternative system?
⁴⁸ The *libri magistratuum* by Tuditanus (fr.7P: Book 3 Decemvirate; fr.8P: *commentarii* Book 13).
⁴⁹ In his correspondence after the Nottingham meeting at which this paper was first presented Professor Wiseman wrote that Fabius probably did have a consul list available to him from at least 356.
⁵⁰ Wiseman 1979, 12-13; similar conclusion in Forsythe 1994, 42, but different arguments.

authors refer regularly to authors earlier than Piso as authors of *annales*).[51] But the quotations in Dionysius do seem genuinely to reflect a title. Wiseman (quite reasonably) renders the following as *annales*: Dionysius of Halicarnassus *AR* 4.15.5: ἐν τῇ πρώτῃ τῶν ἐνιαυσίων ἀναγραφῶν ; 4.7.5: ἐν ταῖς ἐνιαυσίοις πραγματείαις ; 12.9.3: ἐν ταῖς ἐνιαυσίοις ἀναγραφαῖς. But can even these references be taken to mean that he was the first Roman to write annalistic history? He may have been the first to title his work *annales*, but this is not the same as being responsible for the creation of the annalistic form.[52] Writing in Greek, the earliest Roman historians could hardly have called their work *annales*.[53]

Wiseman argues that historians before Piso titled their works with the Greek equivalents of *res gestae* or *res romanae* rather than *annales*. There are indeed two instances where citing sources, Nonius and Aulius Gellius, refer to Fabius and Postumius Albinus in this way, and the expressions used probably translate the Greek Ῥωμαίων Πράξεις and Ῥωμαικά.[54] But can we believe that these Greek titles are evidence for the structure of the histories they described? There is no evidence that they necessarily reflected arrangement when they were used in Greek historiography. Did the title Ἑλληνικά define the structure of the works of Xenophon, Theopompus, or Callisthenes, or Μακεδονικά that of Duris, Περσικά of Baton, Αἰγυπταικά of Manetho, or Βαβυλωνιακά of Berossus? It seems unlikely that if he used the title Ῥωμαικά Fabius was making a special point about the nature of his narrative.

Πράξεις too cannot be pressed. It is commonly used by Polybius to refer to a narrative of events (e.g. 8.2.3 τὰς Σικελικὰς ἤ τὰς Ἰβερικὰς πράξεις), but it can also describe the history of a particular nation (2.37.4 τὰς Ἑλληνικὰς πράξεις and τὰς Περσικὰς πράξεις are contrasted with Polybius' own Universal treatment). Antipater of Magnesia wrote τὰς Ἑλληνικὰς Πράξεις (*FGrH* 69 T1), but more often πράξεις appears in the context of the deeds of an individual, e.g. Antipater's Περδίκκου Πράξεις Ἰλλυρικάς (*FGrH*. 114 T1), Callisthenes' Ἀλεξάνδρου Πράξεις (*FGrH* 124 F14), and Straton's Φιλίππου καὶ Περσέως Πράξεις (*FGrH* 168 T1).[55] Here again one cannot think that the use of this expression by

---

[51] Cicero refers to Piso *in annalibus* but in like manner to Fabius *in Fabi Pictori Graecis annalibus* (fr3P). Varro has Piso *in annalibus* (fr.6, 9, 41P) and also Cato *in libro originum* (fr.43, 52P): we cannot assume he would not have referred to other earlier authors *in annalibus*. Aulus Gellius could refer to Hemina (fr.8P) and the Latin Fabius (fr.6P) just as he does to Piso. Pliny quotes Fabius (fr.24, 27P) and Hemina (fr.37P) as authors of *annales* (it is well known that Pliny *HN* 13.84 refers to Piso as author of *commentarii* and to Hemina as *uetustissimus auctor annalium*, a contrast which could of course be turned in Wiseman's favour). In the later authors (as Wiseman admits) *historiae* and *annales* had become synonymous. This is best seen in Priscian's references to Claudius Quadrigarius as writer of both *annales* (fr.39, 56, 74P) and *historiae* (fr.49P), and in Nonius' references to Hemina's *annales* (fr.17, 21, 24, 28, 33, 36P) and *historiae* (fr.9, 10, 16, 34, 35P). Some loss of distinction is already apparent in Aulus Gellius who refers to Valerius Antias' *annales* (fr.60P) and *historiae* (fr.1, 21, 62P). See also Goodyear 1972, 1. 85-7 for a similar loss of precise meaning in Tacitus.

[52] Briscoe 1981b, 50, points out that Livy 9.44.4, discussing Piso's omission of two successive pairs of consuls, does not seem to be written in the context of Piso being the first annalist.

[53] Daly 1943, 20-38, wondered if the historians of the republic regularly gave their works formal titles. Horsfall 1981, 105-6, is more inclined to think that they did. It seems to me that in the case of Fabius et al. it would depend on whether the Greek histories with which they were familiar had formal titles (cf. Daly 1943, 30). On this I do not feel able to comment.

[54] For Ῥωμαικά see Dionysius *AR* 7.71.7 (Fabius Pictor); for Ῥωμαίων Πράξεις see Diodorus 7.5.4 (Fabius Pictor); for *res gestae* see Nonius 834L (Latin Fabius); for *res romanae* see Aulus Gellius *NA* 11.8.2 (Postumius Albinus). Balsdon 1953, 161, suggests Περί τῆς Ῥωμῆς as another possible title used by the earliest Roman historians.

[55] It is not absolutely clear that all such references are formal titles, but this does not affect the argument.

Roman historians is at all meaningful. *Res romanae* and *res gestae* seem therefore to have been translations of standard Greek titles of works of history which the first Roman historians, writing in Greek, had naturally adopted but which had no implications for the formal arrangement of their works. That the translations into Latin may have subsequently developed some technical meaning is of course irrelevant.

C.W. Fornara has also claimed to identify the first Latin annalist. For him it is Cassius Hemina. He argues that Hemina's fragments, unlike those of the earlier Roman historians writing in Greek, show the first signs of material appropriate to local history on an annalistic model ('horography').[56] The content is much more diffuse and parochial and seems very much like a collection of annalistic entries: the first intercalation (fr.18P); demolition work by the censors (fr.23P); the arrival of the first Greek doctor in Rome (fr.26P); a musical exhibition in honour of *mater matuta* (fr.27P); the corruption of vestal virgins in 216 (fr.32P); and the *ludi saeculares* (fr.39P). The same can be argued for Piso, whose fragments are characterized by the record of numerous firsts: the first grant of a *corona aurea* (fr.21P); the first appearance of elephants in a triumph at Rome (fr.30P); the first triumph on the Alban mount (fr.31P); the introduction of luxury items in the triumph of 187 (fr.34P). Again these look very much like annalistic entries, to which could be added the removal of statues by censors (fr.37P); the fig tree prodigy (fr.38P); and once again the *ludi saeculares* (fr.39P).

There is certainly a different tone in the fragments of Hemina and Piso. Perhaps this grew from an increased interest in internal history and 'a moment... of eager antiquarian interest – just before... the more special studies of those specialised grammarians and antiquarians... split the two genres of annals and antiquarian investigation'.[57] But it would be premature to see here the very origin, and not simply a development, of annalistic history at Rome. Those who might wish to support Fornara would need to explain why this new antiquarian history chose to appear in annalistic form if that was not already an established historiographical genre.

VIII

I have attempted to show the weaknesses of the arguments often used by those who would deny Fabius was an annalist. This does not mean I am committed to a belief that Fabius indeed wrote annalistically. I should rather stress the level of doubt in a matter often treated with excessive confidence; and I have suggested ways in which the testimonia and fragments might be interpreted either way (and have been in the literature). In fact the dichotomy annalist/non-annalist is a stark one, perhaps too stark. Within an annalistic structure one could write histories of very different character, from dry factual reports to the most literary efforts of Greek historiography. By the same token, a non-annalistic structure need not imply sophistication. So if Fabius did not write annalistically, this would not necessarily imply a lack of continuity between the early Roman historiography in Greek and its later fully annalistic form in Latin.[58] Nor would it exclude Fabius' work from having a character very different from that of his Greek predecessors. For example, one could imagine (again without commitment) a Fabian narrative (on the early republic at least) which occasionally omitted consuls or groups of consuls and yet included under the remainder sometimes a developed episode, sometimes a simple report of a battle, temple foundation, or famine. Such a narrative would not be annalistic. But it would in terms of content and out-

---

56 Fornara 1983, 25 (for fr. 37P read fr. 39P). For his discussion of Roman 'horography' see 38-42.
57 Rawson 1976, 689.
58 Cf. Walbank 1945, 18.

look be the start of a continuous tradition culminating in Livy's *ab urbe condita*. And, as we have seen, it would still be *annales*.

Bibliography.

J.P.V.D. Balsdon, 'Some questions about historical writing in the second century B.C.' *CQ* 3 (1953).

F. Bömer, 'Thematik und Krise der römischen Geschichtsschreibung im 2. Jahrhundert v. Chr.' *Historia* 2 (1953/4) 189-209.

P. Boyancé, 'Fulvius Nobilior et la dieu ineffable' *Revue de Philologie* 29 (1955) 172-92.

J. Briscoe, *A Commentary on Livy XXXIV-XXXVII* (Oxford 1981).

J. Briscoe, *CR* 31 (1981b) 49-50 (review of Wiseman 1979).

T. Cornell, 'Alcune Reflessioni sulla formazione della tradizione storiographica su Roma arcaica' in *Roma arcaica e le recenti scoperte archeologiche: giornato di studio in onore di U.Coli* (Circolano Toscano di Diritto Romano e Storia del Diritto, Milan 1980) 19-34.

T.J. Cornell, 'The formation of the historical tradition of early Rome' in edd. I.S.Moxon, J.D.Smart, A.J.Woodman, *Past Perspectives* (Cambridge 1986).

W.A. Daly, 'The Entitulature of Pre-Ciceronian Writings' in *Classical Studies in Honour of W.A.Oldfather* (Urbana 1943) 20-38.

G. De Sanctis, *Storia dei Romani*, IV 2.1 (Turin 1953).

J. Dillery, 'Quintus Fabius Pictor and Greco-Roman Historiography at Rome' in J.F. Miller, C. Damon, K.S. Myers (ed.), *Vertis in Usum. Studies in Honor of Edward Courtney* (Munich 2002) 1-23.

C.W. Fornara, *The Nature of History in Ancient Greece and Rome*, (Berkeley, Los Angeles, London 1983).

G.Forsythe, *The Historian L.Calpurnius Piso Frugi and the Roman Annalistic Tradition* (Lanham, New York, London 1994).

B.W. Frier, *Libri Annales Pontificum Maximorum: The Origins of the Annalistic Tradition* (*Papers and Monographs of the American Academy in Rome* XXVII: Rome 1979, 1999[2]).

E. Gabba, 'Considerazione sulla tradizione letteraria sulle origini della republica' in *Entretiens sur l'antiquité classique XIII: Les Origines de la Republique Romaine* (Fondation Hardt: Vandoeuvres-Genève 1967).

M. Gelzer, 'Der Anfang römischer Geschichtsschreibung' *Hermes* 69 (1934) 46-55 [= 1964, 93-103].

M. Gelzer, 'Nochmals über den Anfang der römischen Geschichtsschreibung' *Hermes* 82 (1954) 342-8 [= 1964, 104-10].

M. Gelzer, *Kleine Schriften* III (Wiesbaden 1964).

E.S. Gruen, *The Hellenistic World and the Coming of Rome* (California 1984).

K. Hanell, 'Zur Problematik der älteren römischen Geschichtsschreibung' *Entretiens sur l'antiquité classique IV: Histoire et Historiens dans l'antiquité* (Fondation Hardt, Vandoeuvres-Genève 1956).

F.R.D. Goodyear, *The Annals of Tacitus* (Cambridge 1972).

N. Horsfall, 'Some Problems of Titulature in Roman Literary History' *BICS* 28 (1981) 103-14.

F. Jacoby, *Atthis: The Local Chronicle of Ancient Athens* (Oxford 1949).

H.D. Jocelyn, 'The poems of Quintus Ennius' *ANRW* I.2 (1972) 987-1026.

W. Kierdorf, 'Catos ‹Origines› und die Anfänge der römischen Geschichts-schreibung' *Chiron* 10 (1980) 205-24.

E. Kornemann, 'Die älteste Form der Pontifikalannalen' *Klio* 11 (1911) 245-57.

R. Mazzacane, 'Nonio ed i veteres' *Studi Noniani* 10 (1985) 189-211.

A.D. Momigliano, *Terzo Contributo* 1 (Rome, 1966) 55-68 = 'Linee per una Valutazione di Fabio Pittore' *RAL* 7.15 (1960) 310-20.

A.D. Momigliano, *The Classical Foundations of Modern Historiography* (Sather Classical Lectures 54, Berkeley 1990).

S.J. Northwood, *Three Studies in Roman Historiography and Source Criticism* (University of Manchester MPhil. Thesis, Manchester 1994).

R.M. Ogilvie, (reviev of Frier) *JRS* 71 (1981) 199-200.

K.-E. Petzold, 'Zur Geschichte der römischen Annalistik' in ed. W.Schuller, *Livius: Aspekte seines Werkes* (Konstanz 1993) 151-188.

J. Poucet, 'Fabius Pictor et Denys d'Halicarnasse: "Les Enfances de Romulus et de Remus"' *Historia* 25 (1976) 201-216.

E. Rawson, 'The First Latin Annalists' *Latomus* 35 (1976) 689-717.

J.W. Rich, 'Structuring Roman History: The Consular Year and the Roman Historical Tradition' *Histos* (October 1996) http://www.dur.ac.uk/Classics/histos/rich1.html#t*
J. Rüpke, 'Fasti: Quellen oder Produkte römischer Geschichtsschreibung?' *Klio* 77 (1995) 184-202.

edd. M.Schanz, C.Hosius, *Geschichte der römischen Literatur* 1[4] (Munich, 1927).

O. Skutsch, *Ennius* (Oxford, 1984).

ed. W.Suerbaum, *Die archaische Literatur* (= edd. R.Herzog, P.L.Schmidt, *Handbuch der lateinischen Literatur der Antike* 1, Munich 2002).

D. Timpe, 'Fabius Pictor und die Anfänge der Römischen Historiographie' *ANRW* 1.2 (1972) 932-40.

S. Usher, *The Historians of Greece and Rome* (London 1969).

G.P. Verbrugghe, 'Three Notes on Fabius Pictor and his History' in ΦΙΛΙΑΣ ΧΑΡΙΝ. *Miscellanea di studi classici in onore di Eugenio Manni* VI (Rome 1980) 2157-2173.

G.P. Verbrugghe, 'On the meaning of Annales, On the meaning of Annalist' *Philologus* 133 (1989) 192-229.

F.W. Walbank, 'Polybius, Philinus and The First Punic War' *CQ* 39 (1945) 1-18.

T.P. Wiseman, *Clio's Cosmetics: Three Studies in Greco-Roman Literature* (Leicester 1979).

R.C.W. Zimmermann, 'Zu Fabius Pictor' *Klio* 26 (1933) 248-66.

JOHN BRISCOE

POLYBIUS, LIVY, AND THE DISASTER IN THE MACEDONIAN ROYAL HOUSE

The last three books of Livy's fourth decade are each dominated by a single episode. In book 38 the account of the trials of the Scipios (38.50.4-60) occupies about 10.66 pages[1] out of just under 64, in book 39 the suppression of the Bacchanalia (39.8-19) 11 pages out of 55. In book 40, the dominance of the quarrel between Perseus and Demetrius, the two sons of Philip V of Macedon, the assassination of Demetrius, and the last days of Philip is even more marked, occupying, in three separate passages (40.3-16.3, 20.3-24, 54-58), 22.5 pages out of 55. The story in fact begins in book 39, with Demetrius' mission to Rome to defend his father against the accusations made by embassies from both mainland Greeks and Eumenes of Pergamum (39.46.6-48.1) and the reactions in Macedon when Demetrius returned (39.53).

There is no doubt that Livy's account is essentially derived from Polybius; much of the latter's narrative is lost,[2] but sufficient survives (Pol. 23.1-3, 7, 10-11) to enable us to see that Livy has made significant alterations to what he found in Polybius. My purpose here is to discuss these alterations, and in particular the arguments put forward by Lanciotti in *Materiali e discussioni per l'analisi dei testi classici* 10-11 (1983), 215-54.[3] This is the second part of an article entitled 'Il tiranno maledetto. Il modello dell' 'exsecratio' nel racconto storico'; the first part (*Materiali e discussioni* 7 (1982), 103-21) discusses the theme of cursing which runs through Livy's account, culminating in Philip's cursing of Perseus on his deathbed (40.56.9). Lanciotti's approach, like that of many of the authors of articles in *Materiali e discussioni* (the journal is edited by Gian Biagio Conte), is narratological - Livy is frequently referred to as 'il narratore' - and it is clear that he is not a historian (note the criticism of historians on pp. 228-30). I too, however, am not concerned here with establishing what actually happened in Macedon in the years 183-179 BC.

The two most striking aspects of Livy's account are these.

(i) Polybius, after describing how Demetrius had read out to the senate the aide-memoire which he had been given by Philip concerning the charges made against him, says that the senate replied that it accepted all that Demetrius had said, and would send ambassadors to inform Philip that he had obtained this indulgence because of Demetrius (Pol. 23.2). Polybius goes on to write that the senate's attitude buoyed up Demetrius, but pained Philip and Perseus (Pol. 23.3.6). Polybius then says that T. Quinctius Flamininus (consul in 198, and the victorious Roman commander in the Second Macedonian War) summoned Demetrius and engaged him in secret conversation. He inveigled Demetrius with the promise that Rome would before long secure for him the throne of Macedon.

---

[1] I make these calculations from the old Teubner editions (M. Müller's revision of Weissenborn's 1851 edition (1891) for book 38, that of Heraeus (1908) for books 39 and 40). They are not possible on the basis of my edition (1991), because of the varying amount of text from page to page.

[2] Only the first five books of Polybius survive in their entirety. For the rest we depend, for the most part, on excerpts made in the tenth century AD for the Byzantine emperor Constantine VII Porphyrogenitus; the excerptor not infrequently compressed what Polybius had written, particularly, but not exclusively, at the beginning and end of extracts.

[3] Note the bibliography at 228 n. 27; add Hammond *ap*. Hammond, Walbank 1988, 471-2, 490.

Furthermore, Flamininus provoked Philip by writing to urge him to send Demetrius to Rome again with as many and as serviceable friends as possible (Pol. 23.3.7-9). Livy (39.48.1) softens what Polybius says at 23.3.6 with a statement that the senate's actions were designed to increase Demetrius' reputation, but in fact produced first hostility towards him and then his destruction. Most seriously of all, Livy then totally omits Flamininus' conversation with Demetrius and his letter to Philip. He does, however, put mention of the letter into the mouth of Perseus at 40.11.1.

(ii) At 23.10.1-11 Polybius, departing for once from his normal principles (cf. especially Pol. 2.56), prefaces his account of the fatal quarrel in the Antigonid house with a passage in which he portrays τύχη ('fortune') as haunting Philip with furies and avenging spirits to punish him for his earlier misdeeds; these furies and spirits implanted in him the idea that essential preliminaries to waging war on Rome were the transplantation of populations and the elimination of the children of those he had executed earlier. The theme is continued at 23.10.12 and 16, where the quarrel between Perseus and Demetrius is described as a τρίτον δρᾶμα ('third drama') deliberately put on stage by τύχη. Livy (40.3.5, 5.1) refers to the cursing of Philip arising from the forced mi-grations and the episode in which Theoxena, daughter and widow, respectively, of two of those executed, together with her second husband, Poris, her son by her first marriage and the children of her late sister Archo,[4] committed suicide to avoid capture by Mace-donian sailors (40.4), and speaks of Philip's mind being sick (40.5.14 *aegra mens*, 6.4 *si mens sana esset*), but does not take up the rest of Polybius' tragic language.[5]

For Lanciotti these changes are not isolated and unconnected with each other, but are part of a sustained reworking of Polybius, which has the effect of distancing Rome from responsibility for the disaster which overtook the Antigonids, making the fatal quarrel between Perseus and Demetrius begin only after the deportations and murders, not immediately after Demetrius' return from Rome, as in Polybius, and making the disaster a result of the curses of the Macedonians, not of the actions of τύχη.

Central to Lanciotti's case is his attempt to show that Walbank[6] was wrong in regarding Polybius 23.10 as having been compressed by the excerptor and holding that Livy can be used to reconstruct the original text. Walbank argued that after 23.10.11 Polybius had the story of Theoxena and the equivalent of what stands in Livy at 40.5.1 - the tragedy of Theoxena leading to Macedonians cursing the royal house, and these curses causing Philip to order the assassination of Demetrius; Polybius 23.10.16 (from the excerpts *de sententiis*; 23.10.1-15 are from the *de uirtutibus et uitiis*) is another version of what is said at 23.10.12. At 23.10.14-15 Polybius says that the anger of the gods caused by Philip's earlier crimes will be clear ἐκ τῶν ἑξῆς ῥηθησομένων ('from what will be said next'), which Walbank takes to refer to 'the development of the quarrel between Philip's sons, related in Livy xl.5.1-6 (*sic*; he meant 16).3'.[7]

Lanciotti's rebuttal of this is based on the fact that in MS. Tours, Bibliothèque municipale 880 (P), the sole witness for the excerpts *de uirtutibus et uitiis*, the phrase just quoted is followed by ζήτει ἐν τῷ περὶ παραδόξων ('look in the section on wonders'), a set of excerpts which does not survive. Lanciotti argued that the equivalent of 40.4.5-16.3 cannot have provided material for the excerpts περὶ παραδόξων, and hence cannot have stood in the lacuna after 23.10.15; rather, what is lost is the story of Theoxena, the

---

[4] Archo's first husband had also been killed (Livy 40.4.2); she then married Poris, who, after Archo's death, married Theoxena.

[5] Benecke, *CAH* VIII 254 implausibly thought that Polybius was influenced by an existing play or historical novel on the matter; cf. Wiseman, 1998, 4, 52-3, Walsh, 1996, 14-15. See Walbank, 1985, 210-23 (=*JRS* 58 (1938), 55-68), Walbank 1979, 229.

[6] 1979, 232-3; 1985, 214-19.

[7] 1979, 233.

unusual nature of which could have led to its inclusion.[8] It follows that there is no compression in Polybius 23.10.12 and that Livy 40.5.1, the causal connection between the tragedy of Theoxena and the assassination of Demetrius, was entirely due to Livy. Polybius 23.10.16 is, then, not another version of 23.10.12, but the introduction to the quarrel, following the story of Theoxena.

The principal objection to Lanciotti's view is that it is hard to see how the story of Theoxena in itself could have been regarded by Polybius as making clear the anger of the gods at Philip's previous misdeeds. And while I would not deny that the story could have qualified as a παράδοξον, the description of the purification of the Macedonian army (Livy 40.6.1-6) could equally well have done so.[9]

There are good reasons for thinking that Pol. 23.10.16 preserves the original language of Polybius: as both Walbank (ad loc.) and Lanciotti (1983, 239) observe, τῆς τύχης ὥσπερ ἐπίτηδες ἀναβιβαζούσης ἐπὶ σκηνήν ('with fortune, as it were, deliberately putting on stage') occurs also at Pol. 29.19.2 and, with slight variation, at 11.5.8. Polybius was certainly capable of repeating himself,[10] but the most plausible conclusion is that Walbank was right, and that 23.10.16 gives the words of Polybius' himself, while in 23.10.12, as Walbank said, 'the words τρίτον... δρᾶμα may be the excerptor's but they reflect the tone of the narrative'.[11]

I now return to Livy book 39. For Lanciotti (1983, 249-50) the suppression of Flamininus' conversation with Demetrius means that for Polybius the motivation of Demetrius is illegitimate and injurious to Rome's good name, while for Livy it is legitimate because it is the Macedonians themselves who are responsible for his ambitions (Livy 39.53.1-4). First of all, it should be noted that Lanciotti seems to regard Flamininus as acting on the authority of the senate:[12] it is, in fact, perfectly clear that Polybius regarded Flamininus as acting on his own initiative (similarly at 40.11.1 Livy makes Perseus refer only to Flamininus, not to the senate as a whole). Secondly, once Livy had removed Flamininus' role, what Livy says at 39.53.1-4 is a perfectly reasonable interpretation of Polybius 23.7. The senate had said that it was accepting Philip's defence as a mark of its goodwill towards Demetrius, and as a result of this Perseus was afraid that he would not succeed his father. It was quite natural for Livy to portray the Macedonians as a whole, regarding Demetrius as responsible for preventing war (Pol. 23.7.2-3), as hoping and anticipating (Livy 39.53.2 spe haud dubia) that Demetrius would become king; it is not either a 'fantasma' (Lanciotti 1983, 227) or 'soltanto loro speranza o desiderio' (Lanciotti 1983, 249-50). That is not, of course, to say that 'the Macedonians', Philip and Perseus apart, really had these thoughts.[13]

Lanciotti's view that Polybius saw the quarrel as beginning immediately after Demetrius' return from Rome, Livy only after the tragedy of Theoxena, imputes too much to Polybius and too little to Livy. Crucial here (Lanciotti 1983, 247) is the genitive absolute at 23.10.13 τῶν μὲν νεανίσκων ἀλλήλοις ἐπιβουλευόντων,[14] which Lanciotti takes as an indication that mutual plotting had been taking place previously. First of all, it is possible that these words too are those of the excerptor, not of Polybius himself, who may have said that with both Perseus and Demetrius accusing the other of plotting against

---

[8] Cf. Lanciotti 1983, 245 n. 66.

[9] It is, of course, not necessary to hold that the whole of the equivalent of Livy 40.5-16.3 was included in the περὶ παραδόξων.

[10] Not, of course, in so short a space as appears from our texts, if the story of Theoxena in fact stood after 23.10.15.

[11] 1979, 232. He should have included κατὰ τὸν αὐτὸν καιρὸν ἐπεισήγαγεν, since ἐπεισήγαγεν is equivalent to ἀναβιβαζούσης at 23.10.16.

[12] Cf. Lanciotti 1983, 247 'per conto di esso, da T. Quinzio Flaminino'.

[13] Cf. Walbank 1979, 224.

[14] To avoid begging the question, I refrain from offering a translation.

him, Philip was placed in a position where he had to decide either that Demetrius had indeed plotted to murder Perseus or that Perseus had plotted to secure the execution of Demetrius on a false charge (cf. Livy 40.8.7). Alternatively, ἐπιβουλευόντων may mean 'intrigue' rather than 'plot', and refer to actions of Perseus and Demetrius designed to get the better of each other, not to plots to secure the death of the other and his own succession.

Lanciotti (1983, 249) also sees significance in Polybius' statement (23.7.7; the text breaks off at this point), omitted by Livy, that Perseus tried to corrupt the φίλοι (literally 'friends', but it here has the common Hellenistic meaning of 'courtiers') of Demetrius. But what Perseus is doing, clearly, is to attempt to detach Demetrius' φίλοι from him or persuade them to spy on Demetrius (see below). It is quite a different matter from his later attempt (Livy 40.5.3) to gain the support of Philip's φίλοι for his designs against Demetrius, and it is wrong to see significance in Livy's failure to mention it.

As Lanciotti himself notes (1983, 225), Livy by no means portrays Demetrius as a total innocent,[15] taking no action against Perseus. They both treat the mock battle as a real one (40.6.6), each has spies and traitors in the other's house (40.7.7); Livy makes Demetrius say that 'perhaps' he ought not to hope for the kingdom or argue about it.[16] And Demetrius returned from Rome 'puffed up' by the favours shown to him (39.53.8; cf. Lanciotti 1983, 223 n. 20). One can go further: Livy makes Philip say that the words and facial expressions of his sons had indicated their mutual hostility (40.8.8-9) and that both had entered on their inheritance while he was still alive (40.8.17); Persus says that for long he and Demetrius had been on bad terms (40.9.8). As Lanciotti says, none of this amounts to concrete initiatives on the part of Demetrius: but Philip could reasonably say that he had seen the storm coming (40.8.8), and it is wrong to regard Livy as marking a very clear distinction between what had preceded and what is described in 40.5 ff.

My conclusion is that all the other characteristics of Livy's narrative are the result of the two major alterations he made to Polybius' account, and that these alterations are readily explicable in their own terms. Lanciotti seems to be unaware that the first is only one of a number of places where Livy suppresses criticisms of Flamininus or remarks which appear to place him in a bad light.[17] Livy could not believe that Flamininus had attempted to divide the Macedonian royal house against itself and perhaps thought - and perhaps rightly - that Polybius was biassed against him. As to τύχη and furies, Livy probably thought that Polybius' picture was too extreme, and, in any case, this Greek conception of τύχη was quite alien to a Roman.[18]

Endnote

Some of the material in this paper will appear, as part of the note on Livy 39.48.1, in my forthcoming *Commentary on Livy Books 38-40* (Oxford ?2007). An earlier version was read to a seminar at the Department of Classical Studies, Duke University, Durham NC, in October 2005.

---

[15] For his naivety cf. 40.5.8, 7.5, 12.17, 20.5, 23.1.

[16] Though Livy may be making Demetrius hint that Perseus' trumped-up accusations make him unfit to be king.

[17] Cf. Briscoe 1973, 22-3 n. 4.

[18] Cf. Lanciotti 1983, 251.

Bibliography.

J. Briscoe, *Commentary on Livy Books xxxi-xxxiii* (Oxford 1973).

N.G.L. Hammond, F.W. Walbank, *A History of Macedonia, Volume III 336-167 B.C.* (Oxford 1988).

S. Lanciotti 'Il tiranno maledetto. Il modello dell' 'exsecratio' nel racconto storico II' *Materiali e discussioni per l'analisi dei testi classici* 10-11 (1983) 215-54.

T.P. Wiseman, *Roman Drama and Roman History* (Exeter 1998).

F.W. Walbank, *Selected Papers: Studies in Greek and Roman History and Historiography* (Cambridge 1985).

F.W. Walbank, *A Historical Commentary on Polybius, Volume III, Commentary on Books XIX-XL* (Oxford 1979).

P.G. Walsh, *Livy, Book XL* (Warminster 1996).

ANTHONY BIRLEY

SEJANUS: HIS FALL

Terentius. For whom the morning saw so great and high,
Thus low and little, 'fore the'even, doth lie.
(Ben Jonson, *Sejanus His Fall*, Act V, scene ix, 912-913)

In 1603 the King's Men - with eight actors, among them William Shakespeare - gave the first performance, probably at the court of James I, of a play by Ben Jonson, *Sejanus His Fall*. It was repeated the next year at the Globe Theatre, but was not a great success with 'the multitude'. Unlike Shakespeare, Jonson was well-versed in Latin and Greek, and 'drew upon some of the best sixteenth-century classical scholarship', including Justus Lipsius.[1] Up to a quarter of the play is directly based on the ancient sources, principally Tacitus, Suetonius, Cassius Dio and Juvenal. This did not go down well with the theatre-goers, who had had enough of the classics at school.[2] Besides, both main characters, Sejanus and Tiberius, are thoroughly unattractive anti-heroes. Those who are portrayed positively, such as Arruntius and Terentius, hardly have a large enough role to compensate. Besides this, whereas Shakespeare's Roman plays, particularly *Julius Caesar* and *Antony and Cleopatra*, treat figures that have always been household names, most of Jonson's good two dozen characters in *Sejanus* could hardly ring a bell with audiences then (or now). The poet naturally took liberties with his sources, conflated characters and adapted, indeed telescoped, the chronology. He followed the Tacitean portrayal of Sejanus as a deep-dyed villain, who seduced Livilla, had her husband, Tiberius' son Drusus, poisoned in

Acknowledgements
The translations of sources are my own, except for Tacitus, *Annals*; for this I have used, with kind permission of Hackett Publishing Co., Inc., the splendid new version by Woodman 2004, of which I have anglicized the spelling in some cases. It hardly needs to be added that I have been unable to consult all the vast modern literature. For assistance in obtaining some items I am grateful to Paul Holder, Michael Schellenberg and Tony Woodman. I am happy to offer this paper in tribute to the memory of Cosmo Rodewald, whose monograph, *Money in the Age of Tiberius* (Manchester 1976), dealt with this period, albeit in a much more sober fashion. When I came to Manchester in 1974, I had the great benefit of Cosmo as a colleague and friend for a few years, and recall giving a seminar in 1974 or 1975, which he attended, mainly about the Aventine election - never prepared for publication, and the manuscript has been lost in the course of several removals, likewise that of a juvenile paper on Sejanus, never published, written in 1960. My interest in Sejanus was sparked mainly by the teaching of the incomparable C.E. Stevens (Tom Brown to his friends) and of Ronald Syme.

[1] Syme 1960, 9f.=Syme 1979-91, I 474f., praised the fine scholarship of Jonson, a former pupil of William Camden (after whom Syme's Chair at Oxford was named), who supposedly despised the translation of his contemporary, Richard Greneway: 'Jonson needed no such aids, and he could allow himself the luxury of contempt.' But Ayres 1990, 14-16, detects mistakes in Jonson's renderings of Tacitus shared with Greneway, whose version of the *Annals* (1598) he must after all have used.
[2] See the introduction in Ayres 1990, 9-10 ('Date, and place in Jonson's career'); 10-16 ('Sources, influences, characterization'); 28-37 ('Jonson's way with Roman history' - also discussing his *Catiline*); 37-40 ('Stage history').

23, went on to dispose of other members of the imperial family and their supporters, and finally plotted to deal with Germanicus' youngest son Caligula and to overthrow Tiberius, only to be forestalled by the superior craft of Tiberius - whose preparations to dump Sejanus by the agency of Macro begin, however, on the eve of the emperor's withdrawal from Rome (Act III, scene 3).

Jonson was called before the Privy Council 'for his Sejanus'. A plausible reason has been suggested: 'The trial of Ralegh took place only weeks before the probable time of the first production of *Sejanus*.' Act I begins with C. Silius and Titius Sabinus, victims of Sejanus in 24 and 27-8 respectively, discussing the grim situation at Rome. 'The principal characteristics that Jonson gives his Silius... [in the trial, Act III, scene 1, were] all well-known ingredients of Ralegh's unrestrained individualism.' The prominence given to Silius probably alarmed the government, although, in the event, Jonson escaped punishment and the play appeared in print, with some changes, in 1605.[3]

If, like Jonson, one accepts Tacitus' account, not to mention the viewpoint of other sources, such as the Tiberian author Valerius Maximus (9.11.*ext*.4, an obvious *addendum* to his section on *dicta improba aut facta scelerata*), with his passionate denunciation of the unnamed but clearly identifiable treacherous parricide, or indeed contemporary inscriptions, Sejanus' fall is not a problem. This demonic figure was responsible for a multitude of crimes, many not revealed until after his death; he had finally conspired against Tiberius, who was forewarned and, through the agency of Macro, managed to forestall him. It is true that even Tacitus expresses doubt here and there about the tradition that he followed.[4] Of course, that part of the *Annals* that covered much of 29, all of 30, and the first nine and half months of 31 is missing.[5] All the same, one wonders whether even Tacitus would have been able to find out, or to infer, why - and exactly when - Tiberius turned against his friend.[6] The lost part of the *Annals* may well have been the source of Juvenal's sixty lines on Sejanus (10.54-113) in his satire on the vanity of human wishes.[7] After the plebs had smashed up and melted down the favourite's statues and dragged his remains with the hook, some asked: 'But on what charge did he fall? Who was the informer - and with what evidence, with what witnesses did he prove it?' The answer was: 'None of these things; a wordy and inflated letter came from Capreae.' 'That's all right then, I shan't enquire further.''*sed quo cecidit sub crimine? quisnam/ delator quibus indicibus, quo teste probavit?'/ 'nil horum; verbosa et grandis epistula venit/ a Capreis.'* '*bene habet, nil plus*

---

[3] Ayres 1990, 16-22 ('*Sejanus* and the Privy Council').

[4] As noted by Syme 1958, 752: 'Tacitus knew that the craft and influence of Seianus were liable to be magnified (IV.11.2; 57.1). As for the death of Drusus Caesar, he dismissed one atrocious legend (IV.10 f.).' But he adds: Tacitus 'did not try to subvert the whole tradition'. That was left to certain modern scholars (see below).

[5] Book 5 begins with the year 29, of which Tacitus' account continues until 5.5. Thereafter, although there is nothing in the manuscript to indicate a gap, what follows, 5.6-11, is manifestly from book 6, and deals with the aftermath of Sejanus' fall, down to the end of the year 31. The reason for the lacuna may be chance. Still, it is tempting to suspect the hand of a Christian scribe, enraged by what Tacitus wrote about events in Jerusalem in the year 30, or perhaps, rather, enraged to find that Tacitus had not written anything at all about them.

[6] Note the comment by Yavetz 1999, 145: 'Mir scheint, das Rätsel dieser Affäre könnte auch dann nicht gelöst werden, wenn wir über den verlorenen Teil des fünften Buches von Tacitus' Annalen verfügen würden. Fragen offen zu lassen und Zweifel zu erhalten würde der Darstellung des Tacitus entgegengekommen sein, so daß er die Probleme kaum aufgelöst, vielmehr die Ungewißheiten mit seiner Darstellungskunst getarnt hätte.' Syme 1958, 255, had taken a similar view: 'There are many obscurities. Too much to hope that all would be dispelled by the Tacitean narrative.'

[7] R. Syme, 'Juvenal, Pliny, Tacitus', *AJP* 100 (1979) 250-278, at 267=Syme 1979-91, III 1135-1157, at 1148: 'Juvenal, it is not too much to claim, betrays awareness of Tacitus' account'.

interrogo' (10.69-72).[8] But what he adds shows that (so at least it was thought) it might have been Tiberius who was overthrown: the plebs 'as always, follows Fortune, and hates those who have been condemned. The same *populus* - if the Nortian [Etruscan goddess of Fortune] had favoured the Etruscan [Sejanus], if the protected old *princeps* had been overthrown - would have called Sejanus "Augustus", at this very same hour.'...*sequitur fortunam, ut semper, et odit/ damnatos. idem populus, si Nortia Tusco/ favisset, si oppressa foret secura senectus/ principis, hac ipsa Seianum diceret hora/Augustum...* (10.73-77). (Shortly afterwards comes perhaps Juvenal's most quoted famous remark: the once sovereign people now only had two concerns, *panem et circenses*, 10.81). Nonetheless, Cassius Dio, who provides the only surviving full historian's account of the year 31, does not mention a conspiracy by Sejanus. The point made in 1926 by Hermann Dessau remains valid: 'Wir wissen nicht, aus welchem Anlaß und in welchem Augenblick Tiberius' abgöttische Verehrung für den Günstling sich in bitteren Haß kehrte; und es wußte es keiner'.[9] But modern scholars, many sceptical about a conspiracy by Sejanus, continue to make conjectures. Another one (only a slight variant on some previous efforts) is offered here.

The family of Sejanus and his rise

First, some details on Sejanus' family, his rise to predominance and the supposed series of crimes that made it possible. Tacitus supplies the only real evidence for Sejanus' early career, at the opening of Book 4 of the *Annals*.:

> 'Tiberius was experiencing his ninth year [23] with the state calm and his household flourishing (Germanicus' death he reckoned among the successes), when suddenly fortune started to turn disruptive and the man himself savage - or to present control to savages. The beginning and reason lay with Aelius Sejanus, prefect of the praetorian cohorts, about whose powerfulness I recalled above; now I shall expound his origin, behaviour, and the act by which he moved to seize mastery. 2. Begotten at Vulsinii, his father being Seius Strabo (a Roman equestrian), in his early youth he was a regular follower of C. Caesar (grandson of Divine Augustus) and rumoured to have offered the sale of illicit sex to the rich and prodigal Apicius; later, by various means, he shackled Tiberius to such an extent that the latter, dark as he was towards others, was rendered uniquely unguarded and unprotected in respect of Sejanus himself - this not so much by artfulness (indeed it was by the same means that he was vanquished) as by the anger of the gods against the Roman cause, for whose extermination he alike thrived and fell. 3. His body was enduring of toil, his mind daring. Always self-concealing, he was an accuser of others. Sycophancy coexisted with haughtiness. Outwardly he had a calm reserve, internally a lust for acquiring supremacy, and for that reason there was sometimes lavishing and luxuriousness, but more often industry and vigilance - no less harmful when they are moulded towards the procurement of kingship.'

> *nonus Tiberio annus erat compositae rei publicae, florentis domus (nam Germanici mortem inter prospera ducebat), cum repente turbare fortuna coepit, saevire ipse aut saevientibus vires praebere. initium et causa penes Aelium*

---

[8] Cf. Syme 1960, 10=Syme 1979-91, I 475: 'Jonson [in Act V, sc. ix] essays the "verbosa et grandis epistula" on hints from Juvenal, Suetonius, and Dio'.
[9] Dessau 1926, 72.

Seianum, cohortibus praetoriis praefectum, cuius de potentia supra memoravi: nunc originem mores et quo facinore dominationem raptum ierit, expediam. 2. genitus Vulsinis patre Seio Strabone equite Romano, et prima iuventa C. Caesarem, divi Augusti nepotem, sectatus, non sine rumore Apicio diviti et prodigo stuprum veno dedisse, mox Tiberium variis artibus devinxit, adeo ut obscurum adversus alios sibi uni incautum intectumque efficeret, non tam sollertia (quippe isdem artibus victus est) quam deum ira in rem Romanam, cuius pari exitio viguit ceciditque. 3. corpus illi laborum tolerans, animus audax; sui obtegens, in alios criminator; iuxta adulatio et superbia; palam compositus pudor, intus summa apiscendi libido, eiusque causa modo largitio et luxus, saepius industria et vigilantia, haud minus noxiae, quotiens parando regno finguntur (Ann. 4.1-3).[10]

His service in the entourage of Augustus' adopted son Gaius, no doubt with the rank of *tribunus militum*, was clearly during the latter's eastern expedition, between 1 BC and AD 4. Another military tribune, Velleius Paterculus, was also of the company, as he recalled (2.101.2-3). When Tiberius, languishing on Rhodes in self-imposed exile since 6 BC, had to go to Samos to pay his respects to Gaius Caesar, several of the young man's *comites*, notably M. Lollius, treated Tiberius badly (Suet. *Tib.* 12.2-13.2). Sejanus, it may be assumed, had the foresight to show him respect. Dio also has the story that Sejanus had 'once been παιδικά of Marcus Gavius Apicius' (57.19.5, from Xiphilinus and the *Exc. Val.*); he adds that Apicius was 'the most extravagant of all mankind'. The allegation may refer to this period in the east.[11] A connection with the notorious epicure might be suggested by the name of Sejanus' wife, Apicata (Tac. *Ann.* 4.3, 4.11; Dio 58.11.6). This may be coincidence.[12] But an indirect later link deserves mention: as a notice in the *Suda* records, the younger Q. Junius Blaesus, when holding office as (suffect) consul, in 26, was invited to dinner, with his consular colleague L. Antistius Vetus, by Apicius; Blaesus brought with him the Ciceronian scholar Asconius Pedianus, whose patron was he was.[13] Blaesus was Sejanus' first cousin: his father, of the same names, *cos. suff.* 10, was Sejanus' maternal uncle, as Tacitus mentions on two occasions (*Ann.* 3.35.2, 3.72.4). The elder Blaesus must be the consular *avunculus* referred to by Velleius in a much-debated passage: *Seianum Aelium, principe equestris ordinis patre natum, materno vero genere clarissimas veteresque et insignes honoribus complexum familias, habentem consularis fratres, consobrinos, avunculum* (2.127.3).

Sejanus' mother, it is natural to assume from the statements of Velleius and Tacitus, must have been a sister of the elder Blaesus, hence a Junia. But a complication arose. In 1904 Cichorius identified a prefect of Egypt, whose name is missing

---

[10] The Sallustian language, recalling *Cat.* 4.5-5.8, 10.1, on Catiline, and *Jug.* 41.2, has often been noted; also the similarity, but with a different emphasis, to the language of Velleius on Sejanus, esp. at 2.127.3-4, cited below. See Woodman 1977, 251-3, and the commentary on *Tacitus. Annals Book IV*, by R.H. Martin and A.J. Woodman (Cambridge 1989) 77-87, with further references.

[11] The numerous sources on M. Gavius Apicius are cited in *PIR²* G 91; see also, on Gaius Caesar in the east, R. Syme, *Anatolica. Studies in Strabo* (Oxford 1995) 317-334, esp. 322 and n. 35, where it is assumed that Apicius was one of Gaius Caesar's *comites*.

[12] Thus e.g. A. Stein, in the entry for Sejanus, *PIR²* A 255: 'Apicii, *cuius filia videtur Apicata Seiani*'. But the similarity of name may be a coincidence: the rare Apicatus was a *gentilicium* rather than a *cognomen*, W. Schulze, *Zur Geschichte der lateinischen Eigennamen* (Berlin ²1933) 292. Cf. *AE* 1961.9: T. Apicatus Sabinus, quaestor in Cyprus under Augustus - perhaps a kinsman of Apicata?

[13] *Suda*, s.v. Ἀπίκιος Μᾶρκος. For Q. Blaesus jr. see *PIR²* J 739 (assigning his consulship to 26 not 28, as previously supposed).

from an inscription at Volsinii, the home town (*genitus Vulsiniis*), as Sejanus' father Seius Strabo - who, after commanding the Guard, jointly with Sejanus from soon after the beginning of Tiberius' reign, had been transferred to that province: *[...] praefectus Aegypt[i, et] Terentia A. f. mater eiu[s, et] Cosconia Lentulii Malug[inensis f.] Gallitta uxor eius, ae[dificiis] emptis et ad solum de[iectis] balneum cum omn[i ornatu Volsiniensi]bus ded[erunt ob publ]ica co[mmoda]* (*CIL* XI 7283=*ILS* 8996).[14] The prefect's mother, Terentia A.f., was taken to be a sister of Maecenas' wife and of the notorious (Terentius) Varro Murena (long identified as the *cos. ord.* 23 BC), who conspired against Augustus;[15] and his wife, Cosconia Gallitta, daughter of Lentulus Maluginensis, to be Sejanus' mother. Kinship with the Terentii Varrones and the patrician Cornelii Lentuli seemed to fit Velleius' *materno vero genere clarissimas veteresque et insignes honoribus complexum familias*. Cichorius long held the field, with the necessary variant that Cosconia must have been half-sister to Blaesus.[16] Identification of the consular brothers (perhaps adoptive) and cousins seemed unproblematic if Sejanus' maternal grandfather was a Lentulus. The prolific Lentuli provided numerous consuls in the early principate. One consular brother of Sejanus, L. Seius Tubero (*cos. suff.* 18), could be identified without difficulty, assumed to be an Aelius Tubero adopted by Sejanus' father.

Cichorius was eventually challenged, notably by Sumner: the prefect on the Volsinii stone, he argued, was a later one, in office under Nero, C. Caecina Tuscus.[17] Sumner won adherents,[18] but his theory was ultimately shown to be untenable. Further suggestions, by Sumner and others, found more favour. Syme reviewed the whole business in his usual sovereign fashion in the 1980s, adding the hypothesis that Seius Strabo was married first to Sejanus' mother, a Junia - who had herself been previously married, to an Aelius Tubero - then to Cosconia Gallitta. Among other refinements, Syme reinstated the old view, going back to Borghesi, that the Aelius who had adopted Sejanus was Aelius Gallus, prefect of Egypt in 24 BC (although it is not quite certain that his *praenomen* was L.). As he pointed out, Aelius Gallus 'may well derive from an old senatorial family'.[19]

A slight oddity, that the daughter of Lentulus Maluginensis was not called Cornelia but Cosconia, has now been better explained by Kajava: surely Lentulus had himself been adopted, by a Cosconius, but retained his patrician *cognomina* (a procedure for which there are precedents).[20] There would be in any case problems in making Cosconia the mother of Sejanus, if her father was the *cos. suff.* 10 and *flamen Dialis*: Sejanus must have been born at the very latest *c.* 18 BC if he went east with C. Caesar; the Lentulus who was consul in 10 must surely, as a patrician, have been born not many years before Sejanus. Better to suppose that Cosconia was sister of the *cos. suff.* 10, and Sejanus' stepmother. However this may be, any who wish to eliminate the Lentuli from Sejanus' kin should note that the consular colleague of Lentulus in 10 was none other than Sejanus' uncle Blaesus. Links between consular colleagues can be found often enough.

---

[14] C. Cichorius, 'Zur Familiengeschichte Seians', *Hermes* 39 (1904) 461-471.

[15] For difficulties about the conspirator, probably not after all the same as the consul, who evidently died before entering office, and the 'crisis' of 23 BC, cf. A.R. Birley, 'Q. Lucretius Vespillo (cos. ord. 19)', *Chiron* 30 (2000) 711-748, at 729-733.

[16] Note e.g. Syme 1939, 358, 384; *PIR²* A 255 (A. Stein); C 1993 f. (E. Groag), suggesting that Cosconia was half-sister of Blaesus.

[17] Sumner 1965.

[18] E.g. Bird 1969, 61 f.

[19] Syme 1986, chapter XXII, 'Kinsmen of Seianus', 300-312, with stemma XXIII; he rejects Caecina Tuscus at 303 f.; for Aelius Gallus, 308 f.; also id., *History in Ovid* (Oxford 1978) 101 f.

[20] M. Kajava, 'Sull' origine di Cosconia Gallitta', *Helmantica* 45 (1991) 243-250.

This is really enough about Sejanus' relatives.[21] But another idea about the Volsinii inscription deserves mention: that the prefect married to Cosconia Gallitta was Aelius Gallus, in office in Egypt in 24 BC, and the postulated adoptive parent of Sejanus.[22] Only further finds are likely to solve these questions. It is enough to note that Sejanus had distinguished close relatives on the mother's side (one or more consular brothers may really have been step-brothers). He had two sons and a daughter, whose names are registered in the *Fasti Ostienses*: the elder son was called Strabo, the younger Capito Aelianus, the daughter Junilla.[23] Strabo was clearly named after his paternal grandfather, but may well have been called Gallus as well, after his presumed grandfather by adoption, if he is the Aelius Gallus who sought refuge with Pomponius Secundus after Sejanus' fall (Tac. *Ann.* 5 [really from 6].8.2; cf. below on Pomponius). If so, his full names were no doubt L. Aelius Gallus Strabo.[24] Capito Aelianus had presumably been adopted, probably either by C. Ateius Capito (*cos. suff.* 5), the 'eminent and subservient jurist', who died in 22 (Tac. *Ann.* 3.75), or, less likely - because he seems to have had a son of his own, *cos. ord.* in 59-C. Fonteius Capito (*cos. ord.* 12).[25] The daughter, presumably Aelia Junilla, had a *cognomen* taken from the *gentilicium* of her mother.

Seius Strabo was already Prefect of the Guard when Augustus died: he swore allegiance to Tiberius in that capacity, with the *praefectus annonae* C. Turranius, immediately after the consuls (Tac. *Ann.* 1.7.2). How long he had been in office is not clear. Macrobius has a story about a man called Strabo accompanying Augustus on a visit to a house once lived in by Cato Uticensis, and, to flatter the *princeps*, making an adverse comment on Cato's perversity. Augustus gently put him right: *venit [sc. Augustus] forte in domum qua Cato habitaverat, dein Strabone in adulationem Caesaris male existimante de pervicacia Catonis ait 'quisquis praesentem statum commutari non volet et civis et vir bonus est' satis serio et Catonem laudavit et sibi, nequis adfectare res novas consuluit* (*Sat.* 2.4.18). Surely this was the Guard Prefect.[26] Sejanus, who had probably served under Tiberius from AD 4 onwards in several campaigns, was made his father's colleague by Tiberius in 14. Strabo was then sent to Egypt, as Dio mentions (57.19.6), perhaps not until the next year.[27] This left Sejanus as sole prefect until his death.

---

[21] One may also consult with profit M.-Th. Raepsaet-Charlier, *Prosopographie des femmes de l'ordre sénatorial (Ier-IIe siècles)* (Louvain 1987), esp. nos. 295, Cosconia Gallitta; 465, (Iunia); and her stemmata X and XXIII.

[22] S. Demougin, *Prosopographie des chevaliers romains julio-claudiens* (Rome 1992) 236.

[23] Vidman 1972, 42.

[24] Proposed by Sumner 1965, 141; approved by Syme 1986, 308.

[25] For Ateius as likely adoptive father, see Syme 1986, 307 f., and numerous further mentions of this jurist, contrasted by Tacitus with the 'unimpeachable' and independent minded Antistius Labeo. It should be noted that, like some others, Syme takes the entry in Vidman 1972 recording the boy's execution in 31, [...]*Dec. Capito Aelianus*, to give him a *praenomen*, i.e. *Dec(imus) Capito Aelianus*. Surely not: *Dec.* gives the date, see below at n. 72. For the Fonteii see *PIR²* F 462-471, esp. 470-1.

[26] As proposed by Cichorius 1922, 'VII. Aus dem Kreise des Augustus. Augustus und Strabo', 292-3.

[27] That Dio meant 'sent to Egypt (as prefect)' is generally accepted, e.g. in *PIR²* A 255; B.E. Thomasson, *Laterculi Praesidum* (Gothenburg 1984) 343 no. 13; and indeed everywhere else, except by Hennig 1975, 7 ff. The scepticism of this excellent scholar seems excessive; he also doubts the emendation, *Sei* for *eius*, by O. Hirschfeld, *Kleine Schriften* (Berlin 1913) 793 [a note first published in *Hermes* 8 (1874) 473 f.] of Pliny, *NH* 36. 197: 'Tiberius sent back an obsidian statue of Menelaus', *repertam in hereditate Sei, qui praefuerat Aegypto*. Seius Strabo presumably succeeded M. Magius Maximus, attested in Egypt in AD 11/12 and 14/15 (perhaps in his second term of office): *PIR²* M 89. Strabo may have died there soon after he arrived, since

In the official version Sejanus seduced Livilla (Livia Julia), the wife of Drusus Caesar, sister of Germanicus, and had Drusus poisoned, in 23 - as was only revealed eight years later, by Apicata, the wife that Sejanus had divorced. He attacked a series of persons close to Agrippina, Germanicus' widow, as a preliminary to having her and her eldest son Nero exiled and her second son, Drusus imprisoned; and in 31, when the exiled Nero died, from supposed suicide, he was planning to dispose of the third and youngest, Caligula. It was he that had brought about Tiberius' withdrawal from Rome in 26, then in 27 to Capri, the better to carry out his other evil designs. As to what he was aiming for, Tacitus is clear, 'to seize mastery' (*nunc... quo facinore dominationem raptum ierit, expediam*) or 'the procurement of kingship' (*parando regno*) (*Ann.* 4.1). His bid to marry Drusus' widow in 25 was initially rejected by Tiberius, but by the end he could be described as 'Tiberius' son-in-law'. The sources are not clear about which 'princess' he had married or was betrothed to at the time of his fall; but he is said to have seduced not only Livilla, but her daughter Julia, wife of Nero Caesar, and a great many other women. He disposed of offices and was courted by all.[28]

Eventually, Tiberius' eyes were opened, in one version by a letter from his sister-in-law Antonia, warning him that Sejanus was conspiring against him. This is reported by Josephus (*AJ* 18.179-182) and Dio (65[66].14.1). But Dio mentions the letter only very briefly, at least in Xiphilinus' epitome, and not in the context of his account of the year 31, for which his full text (from 58.5.1-16.7) is available - and where he has nothing to say about a conspiracy against Tiberius or indeed why Tiberius turned against Sejanus. Suetonius (*Tib.* 61.1) reports what seems to have been Tiberius' own explanation, in his memoirs, for his drastic change of mind: 'he punished Sejanus, because he learned that he was raging against the children of Germanicus, his own son', *Seianum se punisse, quod comperisset furere adversus liberos Germanici filii sui*. Perhaps Antonia later claimed to have informed him.[29] This should be compared with a remark a little earlier in the *vita*: referring to the deaths of Tiberius' friends, including, *cum plurimorum clade Aelium Seianum*, the biographer adds *quem ad summam potentiam non tam benivolentia provexerat, quam ut esset cuius ministerio ac fraudibus liberos Germanici circumveniret, nepotemque suum ex Druso filio ad successionem imperii confirmaret* (*Tib.* 55). In other words, Sejanus was only the instrument 'to encompass the sons of Germanicus and ensure the succession of his grandson by his son Drusus', not the evil genius.

Still, the ancient literary sources are pretty uniformly hostile to Sejanus. There is a single exception, so it appears: Velleius Paterculus. Velleius dedicated his history to one of the consuls of 30, M. Vinicius, when Sejanus still seemed all powerful. Towards the end of his work he produces what has traditionally been taken as a eulogy; modern interpreters have argued that the language suggests reservations or even veiled hostility.[30] It is a lengthy passage, requiring extended quotation:

C. Galerius, husband of Seneca's aunt Helvia, died *c.* 32 after sixteen years as prefect, Sen. *Cons. ad Helv.* 19.6: *PIR²* G 25; Thomasson 343 no. 14.

[28] He was even supposed by H. Willenbücher, *Tiberius und die Verschwörung des Seian* (Gütersloh 1896) XII, to have had a hand in the death of Germanicus (*non vidi*; cited by Hennig 1975, 2: 'seinem Gift war Germanicus erlegen'); the ancient sources, and even Ben Jonson and R. Graves in his *I, Claudius* (London 1934 and numerous reprints), know nothing of this.

[29] J. Nicols, 'Antonia and Sejanus', *Historia* 24 (1975) 48-58, shows convincingly that Antonia's part was probably magnified by Josephus, or by the sources that he used, because of the role of the future king of Judaea, Agrippa I. On the story in Suetonius see further below at n. 77.

[30] On Velleius see especially G.V. Sumner, 'The truth about Velleius Paterculus: prolegomena', *HSCP* 74 (1970), 257-297; A.J. Woodman, 'Velleius Paterculus', in T.A. Dorey, ed., *Empire and Aftermath: Silver Latin* II (London 1975) 1-25; id., 'Questions of date, genre, and style in Velleius: some literary answers', *CQ* 35 (1975) 272-306; Woodman 1977, *passim*; R. Syme, 'Mendacity in Velleius', *AJP* 99 (1978) 45-63, repr. in Syme 1979-91, III 1090-1104; Schmitzer

2.127.1. 'It is seldom that eminent men do not use great assistants to guide their fortune, as the two Scipios used the two Laelii, whom they made equal to themselves in everything, as the Divine Augustus used M. Agrippa and, next to him, Statilius Taurus, in whose cases the newness of their family did not bar them from being elevated to multiple consulships and triumphs and numerous priesthoods. For, indeed, great undertakings need great assistants, 2. and it is in the interest of the republic that what is necessary for its service should be eminent in rank and that usefulness should be fortified by authority. 3. Following these examples, Tiberius Caesar has had and still has Sejanus Aelius as incomparable assistant for all matters in the burdens of the principate. He was born to a father who was the foremost man in the equestrian order and indeed, on his mother's side is connected to senatorial and ancient families, distinguished with public office, and has brothers, cousins and an uncle who have been consuls. He himself indeed has the greatest capacity for hard work and loyalty, also the bodily strength to match his mental energy. 4. He is a man of old-fashioned strictness and of the most joyous cheerfulness, active while being very like those who are at leisure. He claims nothing for himself and thereby acquires everything, and he always estimates himself lower than do others. In his expression and in his way of life he is tranquil, his mind is sleeplessly alert. 128.1. In the appreciation of this man's virtues the opinions of the state have long since been competing with those of the *princeps*; nor indeed is this a new manner of thinking by the senate and people of Rome, that what is best is the most noble.

127.1. *raro eminentes viri non magnis adiutoribus ad gubernandam fortunam suam usi sunt, ut duo Scipiones duo Laeliis, quos per omnia aequaverunt sibi, ut divus Augustus M. Agrippa et proxime ab eo Statilio Tauro, quibus novitas familiae haut obstitit quominus ad multiplicis consulatus triumphosque et complura eveherentur sacerdotiia. etenim magna negotia magnis adiutoribus egent, 2. interestque rei publicae quod usu necessarium est, dignitate eminere utilitatemque auctoritate muniri. 3. sub his exemplis Ti. Caesar Seianum Aelium, principe equestris ordinis patre genitum, materno vero genere clarissimas veteresque et insignes honoribus complexum familias, habentem consularis fratres, consobrinos, avunculum, ipsum vero laboris ac fidei capacissimum, sufficiente etiam vigori animi compage corporis, singularem principalium onerum adiutorem in omnia habuit atque habet, 4. virum priscae severitatis, laetissimae hilaritatis, actu otiosis simillimum, nihil sibi vindicantem eoque adsequentem omnia, semperque infra aliorum aestimationes se metientem, vultu vitaque tranquillum, animo exsomnem. 128.1 in huius virtutum aestimatione iam pridem iudicia civitatis cum iudiciis principis certant; neque novus hic mos senatus populique Romani est putandi, quod optimum sit, esse nobilissimum.*[31]

2000. Sumner, Woodman and Schmitzer all take the view (in varying degree) that Velleius was very far from being a fervent admirer of Sejanus and may even have been hostile to him. Syme defends the traditional view, which he had expressed earlier on numerous occasions. He repeated it in a later work, Syme 1986, 435 f., although conceding there: 'That Velleius was an open and decided adherent of Sejanus evades ascertainment'.

[31] Schmitzer 2000, 280 comments: 'Die Seian-Charakteristik ist durch die Beschränkung auf nur zwei Kapitel so auffällig auf eng begrenzten Raum beschränkt, daß sogar vermutet wurde [he cites here Koestermann 1955, 371 f., and H.J. Steffen, 'Die Regierung des Tiberius in der

Velleius goes on (2.128.2-3) to list precedents for the rise of deserving *novi homines*, going back to 'before the Punic war three hundred years ago': Ti. Coruncanius (*cos.* 280 BC, *pontifex maximus* 254), Sp. Carvilius (*cos.* 293 BC, *II* 272, also censor, as Velleius alone records), M. Cato (*cos.* 195 BC, the famous censor), (L.) Mummius Achaicus (*cos.* 146 BC), C. Marius (*cos. VII* 86 BC), M. Tullius (Cicero, *cos.* 63 BC), (C.) Asinius Pollio (*cos.* 40 BC), with brief comments on each.[32] Then, he concludes,

> 128.4, 'This natural following of precedent has led Caesar to put Sejanus to the test, and, indeed, has led Sejanus to help to support the *princeps'* burdens, and it has moved the senate and people of Rome to call upon those qualities, that they have understood by experience to be the best, to protect their own security.'

> *haec naturalis exempli imitatio ad experiendum Seianum Caesarem, ad iuvanda vero onera principis Seianum propulit senatumque et populum Romanum eo perduxit, ut, quod usu optimum intellegit, id in tutelam securitatis suae libenter advocet.*[33]

Some modern views

It will be necessary to return to Velleius later. But first a sample of the numerous modern discussions may be offered.[34] Doubts about Sejanus' villainy arose in the nineteenth century. In 1880 J.P. Pistner evidently argued that Sejanus was the innocent victim of a campaign of defamation by ancient historical writers and their modern interpreters. He saw him as Tiberius' totally selfless assistant, who attracted universal

---

Darstellung des Velleius' (unpublished Kiel dissertation of 1954; *non vidi*), 81 f.], sie sei in das bereits weitestgehend fertiggestellte Werk zu einem recht späten Zeitpunkt unter dem Druck der politischen Verhältnisse eingefügt worden.' Certainly, the passage may be 'a late insertion in a work already largely completed'—although this is doubted by B. Manuwald, 'Herrscher und Historiker. Zur Darstellung des Kaisers Tiberius in der antiken Geschichtsschreibung', in H. Hecker (ed.), *Der Herrscher. Leitbild und Abbild im Mittelalter und Renaissance* (Düsseldorf 1990) 19-41, at 25 n. 23. But it is odd to describe it as 'restricted to only two chapters': no other figure, apart from the emperor himself, receives so much space in the Tiberian narative as does Sejanus.

[32] Syme 1956, repr. in Syme 1979-91, I 305-314, at 261-5=310-313, has a perceptive explanation for the choice of Carvilius as one of the exemplary *novi homines*: his son or grand-nephew, *cos.* 234 and 228 BC, proposed (unsuccessfully) adlecting new senators from the Latin towns (Livy 23.22.9). More interesting still, the consul of 293 BC built a shrine to Fors Fortuna, near the one built by Servius Tullius (Livy 10.46.14). Servius Tullius and his image of Fortuna were precious to Sejanus, cf. below. Hennig 1975, 74-76, discussing Syme's argument, is unduly sceptical about the relevance of Carvilius to Sejanus. (One may also note that Carvilius was supposedly the first Roman to divorce his wife, as Syme mentions, 261 f.=311. Still, by this time Sejanus hardly needed to appeal to this precedent when he divorced Apicata.)

[33] See above all the very full discussion by Woodman 1977, 245-263. It is impossible to comment in detail here, but one or two items are examined below. I follow Woodman 254 f., in accepting Bothe's emendation, reading *priscae severitatis, laetissimae hilaritatis* rather than *severitatis laetissimae, hilaritatis priscae* at 2.127.4. *laetissimae hilaritatis* is difficult to translate: 'most joyous cheerfulness' sounds rather absurd, it has to be confessed.

[34] This is only a rather arbitrary selection, and such a summary cannot of course do justice to the works cited. A valuable conspectus is offered by Hennig 1975 on items published up to the early 1970s.

hatred by carrying out the measures ordered by the emperor.[35] A few years later Furneaux, in his commentary on the *Annals*, expressed doubt about Sejanus' guilt on the main charges, but nonetheless concluded that 'if the generally unscrupulous and ambitious character of Seianus be assumed; every act in the drama as described, from the concentration of the guards to the final plot, appear to follow obviously from what had preceded it; to be suggested by an adequate motive; to be the natural step to take at that particular stage. If therefore the familiar story of his career is left to stand, it would seem to be one of those cases in which a history, by its thorough coherency and intrinsic probability, appear to prove itself.'[36]

Marsh's monograph of 1931 on Tiberius was to hold the field for some forty years. He accepted the truth of most of the charges against Sejanus, such as the seduction of Livilla and the murder of Drusus, responsibility for prosecutions against 'the Julian party', intrigues 'to increase dissensions in the imperial family' and to undermine Agrippina and her sons. He was content to accept Antonia's letter as the trigger which led Tiberius to prepare the favourite's overthrow. But he rejected 'the view commonly accepted by modern historians that Sejanus was engaged in a conspiracy to depose and murder Tiberius in order to seize the throne', as he explained in an appendix. Although he conceded that Sejanus might have discussed a possible coup with his associates in the months before his fall, he insisted that he had no sufficient motive for a real conspiracy.[37] In the *Cambridge Ancient History* a few years later Charlesworth took a cautious line: 'and then something happened, or rather two things; the suspicions of Tiberius were aroused and Sejanus lost patience'. Caligula was brought to Capri, '[b]ut for some months Tiberius took no overt action, not so much through fear as through agonizing doubt'. When Tiberius blocked Sejanus' attempt to have L. Arruntius convicted (between 1 July and 1 October 31),[38] Sejanus' eyes were opened and he planned something, but was betrayed by Satrius Secundus (*coniurationis index*, 6.47.2, cf. 6.8.5).[39]

Twenty years on, Koestermann, preparing his commentary on the *Annals*, offered a new attempt to explain the fall, because he was convinced that 'ein wichtiger Gesichtspunkt bisher außeracht gelassen worden ist', namely the evidence of Dio, especially Dio's comparison of Sejanus with the all-powerful prefect of Severus, Plautianus (58.14.1). The latter, Dio stressed, was framed by his son-in-law Caracalla (76.3.1-6.3; Herodian, 3.11.1-12.12, reproduced the official version, that Plautianus had plotted against Severus). Sejanus, likewise, had probably not really conspired against Tiberius, at most he had made 'alle Vorkehrungen für den Fall X'.[40]

In his great monograph on Tacitus, published in 1958, Syme judged that 'the only plot that can safely be assumed is the plot devised and executed by Tiberius Caesar'. He devoted an appendix to the subject, asking the question: 'Was there a conspiracy of Seianus? Many scholars believe in it. A few are sceptical. The proper questions have

[35] J.P. Pistner, *L. Aelius Seianus* (Programm der königlichen-Bayerischen Studien-Anstalt Landshut für das Studienjahr 1879/1880). *Non vidi*: I rely on the summary by Hennig 2 f.

[36] H. Furneaux, *P. Cornelii Taciti Annalium ab excessu divi Augusti libri. The Annals of Tacitus* (Oxford 1883) 129; the passage quoted is unchanged in the second edition (1896) 150 f.

[37] F.B. Marsh, *The Reign of Tiberius* (Oxford 1931) 162-199, 304-310.

[38] Dio 58.8.3, not naming Arruntius, combined with *Dig.* 48.2.12, citing the decree of the senate that followed, passed *ex sententia Lentuli dicta Sulla et Trione consulibus*. For Sulla and Trio as consuls see below. Cf. *PIR*[2] A 1130; Syme 1986, 268, with further references.

[39] M.P. Charlesworth, *CAH* X (1934) 635-640.

[40] Koestermann 1955. Koestermann's view that Dio used Tacitus' *Annals* has not found support: cf. Syme 1958, Appendix 36, 'Tacitus and Dio', 688-692, at 690: 'At the best Tacitus was only a subsidiary source for Dio'; also 753, on the parallel with Plautianus stressed by Koestermann.

not always been asked: when precisely did it take shape, with what purpose, and with what allies?' Nonetheless, he was prepared to concede that 'the imperial minister, towards the end, may have started to plan some counterstroke, whatever be the 'novissimum consilium' to which M. Terentius is made to allude [*Ann.* 6.8.3].'[41]

Syme and all previous writers, it must be noted, could not use the new evidence about the man who carried out the overthrow of Sejanus, and succeeded him as Guard Prefect, Macro. An inscription from Alba Fucens, evidently his home town, first published in 1957, revealed that he had been *praefectus vigilum* before becoming Guard Prefect; it also corrected one of his names - he was called Q. Naevius Q. f. Fab. Cordus Sutorius [not Sertorius, as Dio 58.9.2] Macro.[42]

A few years after Syme, Boddington tried a new tack, in a paper still often consulted: 'According to Tiberius, Sejanus fell because he was a traitor; and the Emperor's word has generally been accepted. But not by everybody. Cassius Dio believed Tiberius was the conspirator, Sejanus the victim, and his view has recently come back into favour.' She finds 'signs that the fall of Sejanus was ultimately due to a group of powerful politicians, who refused to tolerate his eminence and compelled Tiberius to overthrow him... If Sejanus hoped to be the next Princeps, the elimination of Gaius was a natural aim, though it might be achieved more safely after Tiberius was dead. But if he hoped to be regent for Gaius, as seems more likely, he would have every reason for keeping him alive. Perhaps, when his power was crumbling, he made a desperate and treasonable bid to save it; and such a *novissium consilium* would have been aimed at Gaius as well as Tiberius. But this is not what Josephus says.' After discussing various possibilities, she conjectures that 'the likeliest cause is a secret revolt by powerful members of the governing oligarchy.' Tiberius was still unaware of Sejanus' intrigues in 31, when he revealed his plans for the succession of Gaius, under the regency of Sejanus. Then came the crisis. 'The very men on whom Tiberius most relied refused to support him, and insisted that he drop Sejanus. Sejanus probably prepared a counter-stroke.'[43]

A few years later, in a lengthy article, after discussing Sejanus' career and his supporters, and reviewing various theories, Bird concluded: 'There are several signs that a plot of some kind did take place... most probably this was a counter measure planned by Sejanus and some of his adherents, such as P. Vitellius... when the minister sensed that his position was beginning to crumble.'[44]

In a new biography of Tiberius, published in 1972, Seager asked the familiar question: 'Why did Tiberius destroy the man he had raised above all others, the one man he had trusted in his loneliness and fear? And was there a conspiracy of Seianus, and if so what was its object: did Seianus' ambitions at the last vault too high and the patience that had served him so well desert him, was there a last desperate effort at self-preservation when he realized too late that his master was planning his downfall, or was the plot nothing but an invention of Tiberius' guile or a figment of Tiberius' imagination? Yet it is impossible to believe that Sejanus would ever of his own accord have murdered Tiberius. His position depended on Tiberius'

---

[41] Syme 1958, esp. 404-6 and Appendix 65, 'The conspiracy of Seianus', 752-4; the quotations are from pp. 406 and 753.

[42] *AE* 1957.250, Alba Fucens, first published by F. de Visscher, *Rendiconti...dei Lincei* 1957, 39-49, also discussed by him in several other places: I have only consulted his posthumously published 'Macro, Préfet des Vigiles et ses cohortes contre la tyrannie de Séjan', *Mélanges d'archéologie et d'histoire offerts à André Piganiol* (Paris 1966) 761-768; some theories there advanced are unconvincing. On Macro as *praefectus vigilum* and his successor Graecinius Laco see further below.

[43] A. Boddington, 'Sejanus. Whose conspiracy?', *AJP* 84 (1963) 1-16.

[44] Bird 1969, 88-9.

favour as much as it had ever done, and his only hope of ultimate power was still as the guardian of Tiberius Gemellus, appointed by Tiberius himself... If then the story of a plot against Tiberius is not pure fiction, it can only have been a desperate measure undertaken not as part of a rational plan but as a last hope of survival when Seianus found out that Tiberius had turned against him. A plot against Gaius on the other hand is much more likely... If Antonia succeeded in turning him against Seianus, she is most likely to have done so by convincing him that he had been duped by the man he thought his friend.' He adds that Dio's narrative 'contains the fundamental truth that at some point Tiberius became convinced that Sejanus, far from being his faithful servant, was using him for his own ends... If Antonia succeeded in turning him against Seianus, she is most likely to have done so by convincing him that he had been duped by the man he thought his friend.'[45]

Reviewing Seager's book, Syme reiterated his own previous position: 'Sejanus was destroyed for high treason. Two questions arise. First, was there a conspiracy of Sejanus? Such was the official version, as was to be expected in Rome of the Caesars. At the most (as S[eager] concedes) Sejanus may have been improvising some tardy countermeasures when he suspected that the toils might be closing around him. In fact, the only plot that can be understood and narrated is the conspiracy engineered by Tiberius Caesar. Sejanus was circumvented by arts the equal of his own. It is enough to suppose that the Emperor, aroused from his lethargy, realized at last the direction in which his policies were conveying him, logically and inexorably: his own supersession. As he once observed in sarcasm to a repentant spendthrift: "You have taken a long time to wake up".'[46]

Shortly afterwards Hennig's monograph on Sejanus appeared. He argues that Tacitus presented a picture of Sejanus, derived from his sources, that was only created after his fall. The limited amount about him before 23 shows that in the first phase of his career Sejanus did not attempt to do more than carry out the duties assigned to him. It was only after Drusus died (September 23) - by a natural death, which was only much later alleged to have been murder - that a new situation arose. Tacitus exaggerated Sejanus' role in the treason trials of 23-26, '[u]m seine Fiktion von einem planvollen Vorgehen Sejans aufrechterhalten zu können'. After 23 the increasing hostility between Agrippina and Tiberius, which peaked in 26, meant that Sejanus could begin to see himself as future regent for the child Tiberius Gemellus, his model being Agrippa. After Tiberius' withdrawal from Rome Sejanus began to attack, although Agrippina and her eldest son, and even more so Tiberius himself, were responsible for the developments which led to their exile in 29. Thereafter Sejanus began to be honoured more and more - until the sudden crash in October 31. Hennig is unwilling to believe the 'official version', that Sejanus had conspired against Tiberius. Persons in Tiberius' entourage on Capri must have caused Tiberius to change his mind: he points to Macro, married to a presumed granddaughter of the court astrologer Thrasyllus, and argues that the decision to destroy Sejanus was not taken until May in the year 31 at the earliest.[47]

A year after Hennig's book there followed another monograph on Tiberius, by Levick, in many respects with similar conclusions. But she attributes the initiative to someone else: 'the very success of Sejanus in ruining the family of Germanicus provided them with a protagonist as cunning as Sejanus himself, who matched his will to power, and whose family connexions made him the ideal leader for a counter-move:

---

[45] Seager 1972, esp. 214-217. For the second edition (of 2005) see further below, at n. 55.

[46] R. Syme, 'History or biography: the case of Tiberius Caesar', *Historia* 23 (1974) 481-496 = Syme 1979-91, III 937-952, at 488=943 f.

[47] See Hennig 1975, *passim*, esp. his 'Zusammenfassung', 157-9, and the preceding chapter XI, 'Das Konsulat Sejans und sein Sturz im Jahre 31', 139-156.

Gaius Caligula... Gaius knew that if Tiberius' place were ever taken by Sejanus, his own life was not worth a farthing. On the positive side his pre-emptive action might give him direct access to the Principate: his elder brothers and the mother who favoured Nero were already disgraced, and as far as they were concerned the way was clear for himself. Gaius, like his brothers, found himself assailed by agents of Sejanus - and duly reported the fact to his grandmother [Antonia], who passed it on to Capri. The information may have been genuine... But there were others at court who benefited from the downfall of Sejanus... Macro, formerly Praefectus Vigilum, who executed the coup against Sejanus, benefited through the promotion he won to the post that Sejanus left vacant; his collaborator P. Graecinius Laco, the incumbent Praefectus Vigilum, was also honoured. Ti. Claudius Thrasyllus, the astrologer resident on Capri, benefited: his granddaughter Ennia Thrasylla was married to the new Prefect of the Guard; and she was said to have become Gaius' mistress.' She repeated this solution briefly in her biography of Claudius: '[The fall of Sejanus] was probably brought about by Gaius Caesar, the future emperor, and a small group of courtiers who benefited from it, one by promotion to Sejanus' post, others by enhanced influence with Tiberius'.[48]

A posthumously published *jeu d'esprit* by Syme deserves mention in passing. In what was pretended to be a fragment from a lost book of Tacitus' *Histories*, composed by Syme himself, he includes a remark about the grandfather of the future emperor Nerva, the only senator to accompany Tiberius to Capri (Tac. *Ann*.6.20.1): '14: *avus legum peritia ceteros id temporis praeminebat. Tiberio hic in Campaniam Capreasque secedenti individuus et fide inmota. credidere plerique ope Nervae senem usum quo Seiani dolos et incepta retegeret.*' He added in a commentary: 'That this master of legal science, "divini humanique iuris sciens", lent help in devising the plot that demolished Seianus appears a natural inference, although not indispensable.'[49]

In a biography of Caligula Barrett offers the view that '[w]hile it seems implausible that Sejanus would have planned any coup against Tiberius, it is not unlikely that he was plotting some move against Caligula.' He adds that the death of Nero Caesar in 31 'may have confirmed suspicions about Sejanus that Tiberius already felt, since the death was said to have occurred when he was already under a cloud'.[50] In the new edition of the *Cambridge Ancient History*, Wiedemann (combining the story in Josephus with that in Suetonius, *Tib*. 61.1) suggested that '[i]t was Antonia... who warned Tiberius... that Sejanus' consolidation of his power was not just aimed against Agrippina and her children, but beginning to threaten Tiberius' own chances of political survival.' He concludes: 'Had Sejanus managed to remove all the offspring of Germanicus, he might have been a real threat to Tiberius. As it was, the conspirator was not Sejanus, but Tiberius.'[51]

According to Tiberius' most recent biographer, Yavetz, Antonia's letter, of which he does not doubt the authenticity, is no proof that Sejanus really had plotted against

---

[48] Levick 1976, 170 ff.; ead., *Claudius* (London 1990) 25.

[49] R. Syme, '*Titus et Berenice*: A Tacitean fragment', Syme 1979-91, VII 647-652, with commentary, 652-662, at 649 and 654. Syme told me that he had entered the piece for a neo-Latin composition (won by someone else: he was *proxime accessit*). Timothy Barnes passed on to me the information that Syme originally wrote it for the *Oxford Magazine* in 1937, as a satire on the problems about the contemporary monarch and a modern Berenice (Mrs Simpson).

[50] A.A. Barrett, *Caligula. The Corruption of Power* (London 1989) 26 f. It is odd that he puts Caligula's summons to Capri '[at] some point after his nineteenth birthday (August 30, 31)' - Suetonius (*Cal*. 10.1) says this happened 'in his nineteenth year', i.e. after his *eighteenth* birthday. Even odder, J.P.V.D. Balsdon, *The Emperor Gaius* (Oxford 1934) 15, says that he went to Capri in AD 32.

[51] T.E.J. Wiedemann, *CAH* X[2] (1996) 213-219.

Tiberius - such evidence would not stand up in court. However, it is pointless to insist that Sejanus had no motive to plot against Tiberius: 'Insofern ist es sinnlos zu behaupten, daß der beste Beweis gegen die These einer Verschwörung Sejans das Fehlen jeglicher Motive für ein solches Komplott sei. Danach hätte Sejan sein Ziel - das heißt die Thronfolge - auch ohne Verschwörung gegen Tiberius erreichen können. Die Vermutung an sich entbehrt zwar nicht die Logik, garantiert aber noch lange nicht, daß Sejan von derselben Ratio geleitet wurde. In der Geschichte kommt es vor, daß Leute unklug handeln, und die Affäre Sejans ist möglicherweise ein Beispiel dafür, auch wenn es keine eindeutigen Beweise gibt.' He conjectures that Tiberius heeded Antonia's warning because he had begun to wonder why Sejanus wanted the tribunician power.[52]

Caligula's latest biographer, Winterling, evidently believes that Sejanus could not, in the end, resist the temptation to seize power: 'Zuviel Mißtrauen gegen alle, zuviel Vertrauen in einen, so läßt sich Tiberius' Verhalten charakterisieren. Er überforderte damit offensichtlich die Loyaliät Sejans. Angesichts der noch ungeklärten Nachfolgefrage scheint die Versuchung für ihn zu groß gewesen zu sein, aus der kaisergleichen Position heraus die Position des Kaisers anzustreben.'[53]

Most recent of all, Seager has re-issued his *Tiberius*, with thoughtful comment on over thirty years' further work. He continues to believe that Sejanus did not really conspire against Tiberius and treats with some reserve both the theory of Hennig, that it was Macro who instigated Tiberius to turn against Sejanus, and that of Levick, who makes Caligula the prime mover.[54]

Some reconsiderations

By the beginning of 31 Sejanus had reached astonishing heights: he was *consul ordinarius* with Tiberius as colleague, the latter for the fifth time. His statues were everywhere and it was voted that the two should hold office together every five years (Dio 58.4.3-4). He and his elder son received priesthoods; he was given *imperium proconsulare* and the senate 'voted that future consuls should emulate him in the conduct of their office' (Dio 58.7.4). The fact that Tiberius and Sejanus gave way to suffect consuls on 8 May should not be over-interpreted (although, to be sure, it is hard to explain why this precise day was chosen). Tiberius had resigned his last two consulships even earlier in the year, his third, in 18, with Germanicus, at the end of January, his fourth, in 21, with Drusus, at the end of March. The suffects who replaced Tiberius and Sejanus on 9 May, Faustus Sulla and Sex. Teidius Valerius Catullus, had conceivably been intended as the *ordinarii* until it was decided that Tiberius and the great minister should serve.[55] Marriage to the widow of Drusus Caesar, Livia Julia, may actually have followed, in late summer 31 (see below). Not much else was lacking to make him in effect the obvious successor to Tiberius - he was expecting to be given the *tribunicia potestas*, the *summi fastigii vocabulum*, as Tacitus calls it, reporting the grant to Drusus in 22 (*Ann.* 3.56.2); and he was still sole prefect of the guard. Quite

---

[52] Yavetz 1999, 144 ff.

[53] A. Winterling, *Caligula. Eine Biographie* (Munich 2003) 32.

[54] The new edition of Seager 1972 (Oxford 2005: I am grateful to Tony Woodman for drawing my attention to it) has *addenda* on Sejanus at pp. 227-230.

[55] For Faustus Sulla see Syme 1986, 164, 172, 174, 181, 267, 311, and stemma XVI. He was married to Domitia Lepida (one of the emperor Nero's aunts). Note also Syme 1986, 279 on Faustus' brother Sulla Felix, *cos. ord.* 33—later briefly married to the younger Agrippina after her first husband Domitius Ahenobarbus died in 40. For the consul Catullus see Syme 1979--91, VII 492-6 ('Verona's first consul').

when Tiberius began to call him *socius laborum*, not to mention other labels, is perhaps immaterial - not necessarily as early as 23 (as Tac. *Ann.* 4.2.3), but at all events in the 20s. Towards the end, in 31, Tiberius omitted titles and endearments for Sejanus when writing to the senate about the death of Nero Caesar (Dio 58.8.4). Whether this really meant, as was later supposed, that Sejanus was already suspect (Suet. *Tib.* 61.1) and that Tiberius was already planning the minister's downfall, may be doubted. At the time, on 18 October, the *verbosa et grandis epistula* came as a shock to all but a few.

The Claudii, Tiberius and the *gens Julia*

A question still requiring discussion is: why did Tiberius favour this man so much? The answer surely lies in the character and background of Tiberius. As shown by Woodman, Tacitus' account of the senate meeting on 17 September 14 (*Ann.* 1.11 ff.) and of Tiberius' actions before then (1.7) has been misunderstood: Tiberius was not portrayed as a hypocrite. The sentence at 1.7.5, 'he sent a letter to the armies as though the principate were acquired - in no respect reluctant except when he spoke in the senate', *litteras ad exercitus tamquam adepto principatu misit, nusquam cunctabundus nisi cum in senatu loqueretur*, should be understood as referring to a previous meeting, perhaps on 4 September, and after *cunctabundus* the sense is 'in no sense reluctant <concerning the acquisition of the principate> except when he spoke in the senate'. When he announced on 17 September that the burden Augustus had had was too great for one man (1.11.1), the senators were genuinely afraid (1.11.3); their 'one dread was that they semed to understand' - that he would decline the succession and retire. At the previous meeting he had not said anything on the subject. At 1.7.6-7, Tiberius is said to have been reluctant - and therefore not to have raised the issue - because he was afraid of Germanicus; because he wished to be seen to have been summoned (not just imposed by the influence of his mother and his adoption by the aging Augustus); and because he wanted to test the reaction of the aristocracy. After his attempt to decline had aroused shocked dissent, he offered a compromise, that he should share power with others; this too did not work (1.12.3- 13.5). But 'although his compromise proposal had seemed abandoned, he immediately adopted it in practice by taking on his sons Germanicus and Drusus as his helpers... It is a perfect - and perfectly Tacitean irony - that Tiberius would eventually find himself at the mercy of the last of his helpers, Sejanus, one of whose successes had been to persuade him to undertake the complete withdrawal for which he had expressed such desire, albeit in obscure language, during the accession debate in the autumn of AD 14.'[56] Woodman has also shown that the obituary notice at *Ann.* 6.51.1-3 must be reinterpreted: the last seven words, referring to the final phase, after the fall of Sejanus, *remoto pudore et metu suo tantum ingenio utebatur*, must be translated as 'with his shame and dread removed, he had only himself to rely on' - from 31- -37 he had no *adiutores*.[57]

Reliance on Sejanus fitted Claudian tradition. As Syme pointed out: 'Roman noble houses, decadent or threatened by rivals in power and dignity, enlisted the vigour of *novi homines*, helping them by influence to the consulate and claiming their support in requital. From of old the Claudii were great exponents of this policy...' Further, Tiberius surely greatly respected his father-in-law Agrippa, the *novus homo* who was

---

[56] Woodman 1998, ch. 4, 'Tacitus on Tiberius' accession', 40-69; the quotation is from p. 69. See now Woodman 2004, 5-11.
[57] A.J. Woodman, 'Tacitus' obituary of Tiberius', *CQ* 39 (1989) 197-205, repr. in Woodman 1998, 155-167; see also Woodman 2004, 193 f.

colleague of Augustus - and probably shared his feelings: 'For Agrippa, his subordination was burdensome [comparing Plin. *NH* 7.46, *praegrave servitium*, and Suet. *Tib.* 24.2 *miseram et onerosam iniungi servitutem*]. Like Tiberius after him, he was constrained to stifle his sentiments. What they thought of their common taskmaster was never recorded. The *novus homo* of the revolutionary age and the heir of the Claudian house were perhaps not so far apart in this matter - and in others. Though the patrician Claudii were held to be arrogant, they were the very reverse of exclusive, recalling with pride their alien origin. In politics the Claudii, far from being narrowly traditional, were noted as innovators, reformers and even as revolutionaries. In Tiberius there was the tradition, though not the blood, of M. Livius Drusus as well. Like other Romans of ancient aristocratic stock, Tiberius could rise above class and recognize merit when he saw it. In Agrippa there was a republican virtue and an ideal of service akin to his own. There was another bond. Tiberius was betrothed, perhaps already married, to Agrippa's daughter Vipsania. The match had been contrived long ago by Livia.' Finally, on Tiberius: 'Tiberius Caesar hated the monarchy - it meant the ruin of Rome and Republican virtue. The Principate was not a monarchy in name. That made it all the worse. The duty of rule was a grievous servitude: to the burden was added the discomfort of a false role. It broke Tiberius and the Principate as well.'[58]

Velleius' reference to Agrippa (2.127.1) can be interpreted reasonably enough as at least the expectation, if not the hope, that Sejanus was shortly to achieve a similar status alongside Tiberius as Agrippa had had under Augustus, son-in-law and colleague, with the tribunician power as well as *imperium*. Hence, incidentally, the case that commemorative Asses of Agrippa were first issued in the 20s, during Sejanus' predominance, is attractive.[59]

Tiberius was surely repelled by the notion that the *gens Julia* possessed *caelestis sanguis*, as supposedly reiterated in 26 to his face by Agrippina (Tac. *Ann.* 4.52.2), eldest daughter of the woman he had been forced to marry, and loathed, Augustus' only child Julia. Schmitzer has offered an interesting interpretation of the earliest part of Velleius' work: the stories about Hercules and Orestes there (1.12) reflect 'Alternativen zum iulischen Geschichtsbild'. Velleius deviates from 'dem spätestens in augusteischer Zeit allgemein akzeptierten Bild der römischen Vor- und Früh-geschichte'. He ignores Aeneas and the Trojan ancestry, institutionalised by Augustus. He suggests that Velleius 'mit diesem Verfahren Tiberius einen Platz am Beginn des Werkes, wenn schon nicht im Proömium, eingeräumt [hat].' This rewriting of pre-history would have been welcomed by Sejanus, for whom Hercules, the hero of *labor*, was an ideal model. Schmitzer also points out that Tiberius, and the Claudii, preferred Odysseus to Aeneas and Iulus as their forebears, Greeks, not Trojans.[60] One may also note Tiberius' sarcastic reply to the *legati Ilienses*, who had been commiserating him on the death of Drusus: he offered them in turn his condolences 'for the loss of their excellent

---

[58] Syme 1939, 24, cf. 285; 344 ff.; 484. See also the still instructive discussion by J.H. Thiel, *Kaiser Tiberius. Ein Beitrag zum Verständnis seiner Persönlichkeit* (Darmstadt 1970, conveniently reprinting three articles in *Mnemosyne*, 2 [1935] 245-270, 3 [1936] 177-218, 4 [1936] 17-42). Levick 1976, 173, while accepting that Agrippa's position was the precedent for that of Sejanus, nonetheless writes: 'there is no evidence that he [Tiberius] liked the man [Agrippa]; and politically they were far apart' One can only beg to differ. On Agrippa's powers as colleague of Augustus see now e.g. W. Ameling, 'Augustus und Agrippa. Bemerkungen zu PKöln VI 249', *Chiron* 24 (1994) 1-28; Eck et al. 1996, 158 ff.

[59] Thus e.g. S. Jameson, 'The date of the Asses of M. Agrippa', *NC*, 7th ser., 6 (1966) 95-124. It is true that her dating has been questioned, e.g. by G.F. Carter and W.E. Metcalf, 'The dating of the M. Agrippa Asses', *NC* 148 (1988) 145-7, assigning a small group tested metallurgically to the reign of Caligula. One may accept that these coins were still, or again, issued after the fall of Sejanus: disproof of Jameson's thesis that the issues began *c.* 23 is another matter.

[60] Schmitzer 2000, esp. 43-60.

fellow-citizen Hector' (Suet. *Tib*. 52.2). Further - just after recounting Agrip-pina's appeal to the *caelestis sanguis* - Tacitus reported the contest between eleven cities of Asia to build a temple for Tiberius and his mother: Troy did not win (*Ann*. 4.54-5, cf. 4.15.3). Soon after came the incident at the imperial villa in the cave called *Spelunca*: Sejanus saved Tiberius' life when the roof collapsed, providing 'grounds why he should place more trust in the friendship and steadfastness of Sejanus' (Tac. *Ann*. 4.59.1-2). Excavations at the presumed site have revealed that the villa was decorated with reliefs of Odysseus.[61] •Tiberius was on his way to Campania, never to return to Rome, and from 27 to establish himself on Capri. Tacitus had doubts about the view 'of the majority of authors', that it was Sejanus who urged Tiberius to leave Rome, noting other possible motives: shame at his own appearance, his face disfigured by the *mentagra*, and 'the unruliness of his mother, whom he spurned as his partner in despotism but could not dislodge' (*Ann*. 4.57.1-3). One may add that he must have been sick of Agrippina and her family and of senate meetings. In any case, Campania was an attractive retreat for the elite, and he was often on the mainland. But Capri was an unassailable refuge; and he had reason to be nervous.[62]

The altar of friendship

In 28 Sejanus' position reached a new peak: the senate, Tacitus writes, instead of reacting to a disaster on the distant frontier, the massacre of Roman troops by the Frisians, was pre-occupied by anxiety about affairs at home, *pavor internus occupaverat animos*. To assuage this they turned to flattery, *cui remedium adulatione quaerebatur. ita quamquam diversis super rebus consulerentur, aram clementiae, aram amicitiae effigiesque circum Caesaris ac Seiani censuere* (Tac. *Ann*. 4.74). A striking case has been made for the 'Grand Camée de France', the largest surviving item of its kind, having been carved precisely to commemorate the *amicitia* of Tiberius and his minister. There is general agreement that it depicts Tiberius as emperor, seated in the centre, with his mother next to him on his left; the deified Augustus is above, in heaven, with younger men on either side of him. Identification of the other figures has varied widely. In 1974 Jeppesen proposed that the standing male figure facing Tiberius, who extends his right hand towards him, is Sejanus, and that the wreathed female figure behind and between the two is the personified *Amicitia*. His treatise, published in Denmark, was largely ignored, and he produced a revised version nearly twenty years later. He argues that the deified Augustus is flanked by Drusus, on his right, and Germanicus, on his left, both also in heaven. Left of Sejanus, the boy is Tiberius Gemellus, Drusus' surviving twin son, with a deity, perhaps Apollo, standing behind him. At the right, behind the dowager empress, are Claudius, gesturing towards the figures in heaven, and sitting beside him, his sister Livia Julia, Drusus' widow, with a figure of Attis, suitably in mourning, head bowed, sitting facing these two. Below are smaller figures representing conquered peoples from the north and

---

[61] See A.F. Stewart, 'How to entertain an emperor? Sperlonga, Laokoon and Tiberius at the dinner-table', *JRS* 67 (1977) 76-90; B. Andreae et al., *Odysseus. Mythos und Erinnerung* (catalogue of an exhibition at Munich, 1999-2000; Mainz 2000); and now K. Vössing, *Mensa Regia. Das Bankett beim hellenistischen König und beim römischen Kaiser* (Munich-Leipzig 2004) 330 ff., with further references to the numerous publications on the subject at 331 n. 2. Vössing is himself slightly hesitant about the Tiberian dating of the Odysseus reliefs.

[62] On the *mentagra* as explanation for Tiberius' *ulcerosa facies* (*Ann*. 4.57.2), see R. Syme, 'Governors dying in Syria', *ZPE* 41 (1981) 125-44=Syme 1979-91, III 1376-1392, at 125f.=1376f., citing Pliny, *NH* 26.2ff. and Suet. *Tib*. 34.2. On Tiberius' retreat see the valuable paper by G.W. Houston, 'Tiberius on Capri', *G&R* 32 (1985) 179-196, with further references.

east.[63] This interpretation, surely the most convincing yet offered, has hardly been noticed in recent scholarship.[64] However this may be, the publicly proclaimed *amicitia* between Tiberius and Sejanus was vital: Valerius Maximus would denounce its breach, *amicitiae fide exstincta* (9.11., *ext.* 4).

The Aventine election

The consulship in 31 was of course preceded by designation and 'election' in the previous year. A fragmentary inscription from Rome supplies a curious statement: 'But(?) now, because the criminal incitement(?) of Sejanus has destroyed the peace(?) of sixty years and that shameless assembly has taken place on the Aventine at which Sejanus was made consul, and I, a weak companion of a useless walking-stick, so that I, to become a suppliant, ask you now, with all my might(?), good fellow-tribes-men, if I have ever seemed to you a good and useful member of the tribe, if I have never been unmindful(?) of my duty, nor...'.:

```
         .......
         [at?n]unc•quoniam•r[upit pacem?
         a]nnorum•LX•Seiani•sce[lerata
 4       inc]itatio•et•inprobae•comitiae
         [ill]ae•fuerunt•in•Aventino•ubi
         [Sei]anus•cos• factus•est•et•ego
         [de]bilis•inutilis•baculi•comes
 8       [..]ut•supplex•fierem omni•nunc <vi?>
         [v]os rogo•boni•contri
         [bu]les•si•semper•apparui
         [v]obis•bonus•et•utilis•tri
12       [bul]is•si nunquam offic[ii mei
         immemor f]ui•nec•rei[...
         ...]m•coi[...
         ...] rif[...]
```

(*CIL* VI 10213=*ILS* 6044; here slightly emended; the lettering in line 9 was larger than in the other lines.)

The author was a member of one of the thirty-five tribes, who, in the 'election' had presumably had some official role, for which he felt the need to ask forgiveness from

---

[63] K.K. Jeppesen, *Neues zum Rätsel des Grand Camée de France* (*Acta Jutlandica* 44.1, 1974) [*non vidi*]; id., 'Grand Camée de France. Sejanus reconsidered and confirmed', *MDAI (R)* 100 (1993) 141-175.

[64] Not mentioned by Levick, in the bibliographical addendum to the 1999 reprint of Levick 1976, xiii ff., but cited by Schmitzer 2000, 276 n. 70, and, evidently with approval, 282 n. 105. The same approximate dating was also put forward by B. Andreae, *Die Römische Kunst* (originally published in 1973; Freiburg-Basel-Vienna ²1999) 132ff. But at 133 he offers a baffling identification of the man taken by Jeppesen to be Sejanus: 'Eigentlich kann nur die Siegerehrung des ältesten Germanicussohnes, Nero Caesar (6 v.Chr.-31 n.Chr.), gemeint sein, der 26 von einem Feldzug gegen Barbaren auf dem Balkan nach Rom zurückkehrte.' There is no evidence for Nero Caesar leading an expedition against the barbarians, in the Balkans or anywhere else. Andreae does provide a plausible identification of the oriental-looking figure immediately below Divus Augustus, about which Jeppesen felt unable to pronounce, viz. Aion.

his *contribules*. His identity is unknown.[65] The key fact is that the meeting of the *comitia*, to 'rubber stamp' the consular election for 31, was held on the Aventine hill, not on the Campus Martius. Syme spelled out the symbolism. Tiberius had transferred the real choice of magistrates to the senate in 14, but 'there still remained vestigial ceremonies of the ritual to be gone through on the Campus.' Sejanus, he argued, chose the Aventine as 'the place of extraneous cults, and of secessions: Diana of the Latins had her temple there, built by injunction of Servius Tullius, and the Aventine was the stronghold of C. Gracchus.' He noted the Etruscan Sejanus' attachment to Servius Tullius and Fortuna: he possessed an image of the goddess once owned by the king (Dio 58.7.2). He compares also the stress laid on *novi homines* by the 'loyal and obsequious Velleius Paterculus, introducing his panegyric of the indispensable minister' (see further below).[66]

It is worth registering Velleius' verdict on Gaius Gracchus: 'with complete calmness of mind he could have been *princeps civitatis*', *cum summa quiete animi civitatis princeps esse posset* (2.6.2); he adds that at his death the tribune 'was leaving behind him nothing tranquil, nothing calm, in fact nothing in the same state', *nihil tranquillum, nihil quietum, nihil denique in eodem statu relinquebat* (2.6.4). His description of Sejanus, *vultu vitaque tranquillum* (2.127.4), will be recalled. *Quies* and *tranquillitas* were clearly qualities appropriate for a *princeps*, in the eyes of Velleius - and no doubt of Tiberius - as shown by the rapturous description of the rejoicing inspired by Tiberius' adoption in the year 4 (2.103-3-5), ending with the words 'then shone forth again the hope... for all mankind of safety, calm, peace, tranquillity', *tum refulsit certa spes... omnibus hominibus salutis, quietis, pacis, tranquillitatis.*[67] *Quies* is also associated favourably with the excellent M. Lepidus (2.125.2), already lavishly praised (2.114.5, 115.2-3). (By contrast, M. Caelius Rufus, who came to a bad end, is labelled *vir inquies et ultra fortem temerarius*). Tacitus happens to use both *tranquillitas* and *quies* when reporting Tiberius' response to Sejanus' bid for the hand of Livia Julia in 25 (referring to C. Proculeius, *Ann.* 4.41.6); and Sejanus recommended that Tiberius leave Rome, *extollens laudibus quietem et solitudinem* (4.41.3). More significant is an official document from the year 20: the *SC de Cn. Pisone patre* opens with the senate and people of Rome thanking the immortal gods that the evildoer had been unable to

---

[65] Levick 1976, 119 f. supplies a text, improving that in *ILS*; the version above differs in a few details. She conjectures that the 'suppliant' was none other than Tiberius himself (an idea which I recall being offered in a tutorial by the late C.E. Stevens in 1959) and that *inutilis baculi comes* means 'the companion' of Sejanus, who is the 'useless (or harmful) staff'. This ingenious notion is hard to accept, not only because of the solecism *comitiae* instead of *comitia* (which Levick has to attribute to the stone-cutter; other items are also rather odd). It seems much more likely that the 'suppliant' had played some symbolic role in the pseudo-electoral assembly, e.g. casting the first vote for the first tribe.

[66] Syme 1956=Syme 1979-91, I 305-314 restored *sce[lerata]* or *sce[lesta]* rather than *sce[elerati]*, also *[efflag]itatio* or *[flag]itatio* instead of *[inc]itatio* and *[qu]ae* rather than *[ill]ae*. Hennig 1975, 73 ff., cf. 140 ff., plays down the significance of the Aventine ceremony.

[67] It is true that the ill-fated Quinctilius Varus is also called *quietus*, but the term is modified by the other items: *inlustri magis quam nobili ortus familia, vir ingenio mitis, moribus quietus, ut corpore, ita animo immobilior*, etc. (2.117.2; he adds further criticisms, of course). The contrast with Sejanus' *sufficiente etiam vigori animi compage corporis* (2.127.3) is clear enough. Varus had been Tiberius' consular colleague back in 13 BC, when both were sons-in-law of Agrippa: see Syme 1986, ch. XXIII, 313-328, and *PIR²* Q 30, citing Augustus' funeral oration on Agrippa, partly preserved on papyrus. Varus' then wife (his second, Syme argues) was probably a half-sister of Tiberius' Vipsania; he later married Claudia Pulchra, grand-niece of Augustus. It is not improbable that Tiberius had quite liked the man; again, Velleius has the further comment on Varus: *sane gravem et bonae voluntatis virum*, lacking only *imperatoris consilio* (2.120.5).

disturb *tranquillitatem praesentis status r(ei) p(ublicae), quo melior optari non pote et quo beneficio principis nostri frui contigit.*[68]

Velleius takes care to recall the man who bravely defended Gaius Gracchus to the last, like Horatius Cocles, when the consul L. Opimius attacked, then took his own life, the knight Pomponius: *quo die singularis Pomponii equitis Romani in Gracchum fides fuit, qui more Coclitis sustentatis in ponte hostibus eius, gladio se transfixit.* (2.6.6). This was no doubt the M. Pomponius to whom Gaius Gracchus had addressed a pamphlet (Cic. *Div.* 14.16), surely an ancestor of the poet Pomponius Secundus, who, his biographer the Elder Pliny recalled, possessed manuscripts of both Tiberius and Gaius Gracchus, in their own hand (Plin. *NH* 13.83: Pliny had seen them, *Tiberi Gaique Gracchorum manus apud Pomponium Secundum vatem civemque clarissimum vidi annos post fere ducentos).*[69] After recounting the end of Gaius Gracchus and the later prosecution of Opimius, Velleius apologises for 'inserting an item of little direct relevance. This is the Opimius from whose consulship the very famous Opimian wine was named - the fact that there is by now none left can be inferred from the lapse of time, since it is now 150 years from his consulship to yours, Marcus Vinicius' (2.7.4-5). Velleius was misinformed: ten years later, in 40, the emperor Caligula was offered some Opimian wine, by now tasting like bitter honey, at a banquet - given by Pomponius Secundus. Pliny says that he had learned this when writing the biography of Pomponius (*NH* 14.55-56).

Pomponius was an adherent of Sejanus, arrested in 31 and kept in detention for years. He owed his life not least to his brother's protection (see below). The brother, Q. Pomponius Secundus, was consul when Caligula was murdered in 41 - he had been kissing the emperor's feet shortly before (Dio 59.29.5).[70] Velleius fails to mention something else about Opimius: that he dedicated a temple to Concordia, in due course renewed by Tiberius, who was commissioned to undertake the task by Augustus in 7 BC. For various reasons, not least his withdrawal in Rhodes the next year and, after his return to public life in AD 4, his military duties, he did not complete the task until 10. The temple and everything that it stood for were very important to Tiberius. Dedications were made there after the detection of the conspiracy of Libo Drusus in 16, and again later, for Tiberius' *salus.*[71] It was in that temple, too, that the senate met for the second time on 18 October, to condemn Sejanus to death (Dio 58.11.4).

Whether Sejanus or others, such as Velleius, saw something significant in the fact that the year of Sejanus' election to the consulship was the 150th anniversary of the death of C. Gracchus on the Aventine is hard to tell. Pomponius Secundus may even have encouraged Sejanus to remind the people of the great tribune. Later, Pomponius clearly changed his tune: bringing out the Opimian wine may have been a kind of

---

[68] Eck et al. 1996, 38, lines 13-15, cf. 57f. for their reading *pote et* for *pote ut*, keeping *pote* as an archaic form.

[69] F. Münzer, *RE* 2A.2 (1923) 1375 f.

[70] For sources on the two Pomponii, *PIR²* P 754, 757.

[71] See T. Pekáry, 'Tiberius und der Tempel der Concordia in Rom', *MDAI (R)* 73/74 (1966/67) 105-133. (I cannot agree with all his conclusions.) One of the dedicators (*CIL* VI 93) can be identified as L. Fulcinius Trio, at the time legate of Lusitania and consul designate. He was to take office on 1 July 31. A bronze tablet from his province names him as governor on 21 January 31, and gives the ordinary consuls, *Ti. Caesare V L. Aelio Seiano*—this is one of only two pieces of documentary evidence for Sejanus' consulship; the other is on local coins from Bilbilis, see Hennig 1975, 139 n.1, and even these display signs of attempted deletion. The Fasti for 31 omit him. As it happens, a small place on the Campanian coast near Sorrento, opposite Capri, perpetuates the name: *Seiano* (but I am unable to say when or why it was called this). Even Valerius Maximus does not name the man, *efferatae barbariae immanitate truculentior*, whom he denounces (9.11, *ext.*4).

gesture to this effect. Velleius, at least, was careful to stress that the younger Gracchus had ruined everything through his lack of *quies*.

Marriage to a princess

Sejanus was referred to after his death as Tiberius' son-law, *gener* (Tac. *Ann.* 5.6.2; 6.8.3). Zonaras, in a passage no doubt deriving from Dio, says that 'Tiberius, after raising Sejanus to great glory and making him a kinsman by alliance with Julia, daughter of Drusus, later killed him' (11.2=Dio 58.3.9). Suetonius refers only to the '*hope* of kinship and of the tribunician power', *spe affinitatis ac tribuniciae potestatis*, with which Tiberius deceived Sejanus, after the joint consulship (*Tib.* 65.1). In spite of Dio-Zonaras, Livia Julia, or Livilla, is a more plausible bride than her daughter. Sejanus had supposedly sought Livilla's hand six years before, to be gently rebuffed for the time being, 'but', Tiberius is said to have concluded, 'I shall not oppose either your designs or Livia's' and indicated intentions 'to make you and me inseparable' (*Ann.* 4.40). Perhaps the marriage did actually take place, in summer 31. It has been pointed out by Bellemore that the restoration of the name of Sejanus' wife, whose suicide is registered in the *Fasti Ostienses* for 26 October 31, as Apicata, conflicts with the literary evidence. Apicata is said to have taken her own life *after* the execution of her younger children, which happened several weeks later than 26 October (see below). Besides, as Bellemore further argues, why should the death of Apicata, divorced by Sejanus years before, be so recorded? She therefore restores *[Livia] Seiani se occidi[t...]*. The case seems very plausible. Perhaps the marriage was rushed through against Tiberius' wishes or even without his knowledge. Whether or not this triggered Tiberius' change of mind about his favourite, at all events, Livilla paid dearly, with her life.[72] One may also register here the fragment of Johannes Antiochenus, which describes how Tiberius was calling Sejanus 'son and successor', παῖδα καὶ διάδοχον, before having him killed (*FHG* IV 79, *Exc. de Virt.*, p.801, 8).

The aftermath

The treatment of Sejanus was spectacular enough. The even more horrific fate of the two younger children is recorded by the literary sources. Tacitus tells how 'there were transported to prison his son, intuiting the inevitable, and a girl so unaware that she asked frequently for what felony and to what place she was being dragged off: she would not do it again, she said, and could be admonished by a child's beating. Authors of the time transmit that, because it was unheard of for a virgin to have the triumviral reprisal inflicted on her, she was violated by the executioner alongside the noose; then, their throats crushed, their bodies despite their tender ages were thrown onto the Gemonians' (*Ann.* 5.9.1-2; cf., briefer, Dio 58.11.5). The *Fasti Ostienses* (Vidman 1972) supply the date and also register the elder brother's previous execution. The entry for the year 31 may be quoted:

---

[72] J. Bellemore, 'The wife of Sejanus', *ZPE* 109 (1995) 255-266. This contribution is not mentioned by Levick 1976 or Seager 1972 in the *addenda* to their second editions, of 1999 and 2005 respectively. But both prefer to see Livilla, not her daughter, as the bride of Sejanus.

Ti. Caesar A[ug]ustus V
            Faustus C[or]nel(ius) Sul[la]
   VII id. Mai.   9 May
               Sex. Tedius [Cat]ullu[s]
   k. Iul. L. Fulcinius [Tr]i[o]   1 July
   k. Oct. P. Memmius R[egulus]   1 October
        XV k. Nov. Seianus s[trang(ulatus),]   18 October
        VIIII k. Nov. Strabo [Seiani]   24 October
        f. strang(ulatus), VII k. No[v. Livia?]   26 October
        Seiani se occidi[t ....   ]
        Dec. Capito Aelia[nus et]   between 14 November
        Iunilla Seiani f. [in Gem(oniis)]   and 12 December
        iacuerunt.

The elder son was strangled six days after his father; the bodies of the younger son and the daughter were exposed on the Gemonian Steps a few weeks later (depending on whether a date before the Kalends, the Nones, or the Ides of December is missing).[73] As Dessau commented, it was a horrible business, cruelty on a scale previously unknown: 'eine Grausamkeit, die in der Geschichte der römischen Partei-kämpfe, geschweige denn in der der römischen Justiz, keinen Vorgang gehabt zu haben scheint.[74] *Sippenhaft*, one might call it, something Dessau, happily, did not live to see practised in his own country. Valerius Maximus, clearly aware of the children's fate, exulted: 'Moreover, he who attempted to subvert these things [*pax, leges*, etc.], violating the bonds of friendship, has been liquidated, with all his offspring, by the forces of the Roman People and even among the lower world, if indeed he is received into it, is paying the penalty', *qui autem haec violatis amicitiae foederibus temptavit subvertere, omni cum stirpe sua populi Romani viribus obtritus etiam apud inferos, si tamen illuc receptus est, quae meretur supplicia pendit* (9.11.*ext*.4, *ad fin*.). An inscription from Interamna set up in 32 registers the official reaction to Sejanus' end. A *sevir Augustalis* dedicated to the appropriate personifications, because of 'the removal of a most pernicious enemy of the Roman People':

   Salúti perpetuae Augustae   *Genio múnicipi anno post*
       libertatique publicae   *Interamnam conditam*
          populi Romani   *DCCIIII ad Cn. Domitium*
                                          Ahenobarbum ///////
                                          /////////////// *cos.*
   Providentiae Ti. Caesaris Augusti náti ad áeternitatem
     Románi nominis, sublato hoste perniciosissimo p.R.
     Faustus Titius Liberalis VIvir Aug. iter
              p.s.f.c

(*ILS* 157; the name of the second consul, Camillus Scribonianus, was deleted after his failed uprising against Claudius in 42; cf. also 158, from Gortyn, Crete, a dedication by the proconsul to the Numen and Providentia of Tiberius and of the Senate, 'in memory of that day, which was the 15th before the Kalends of November).'

Had Sejanus really been plotting against Tiberius? One may accept that he had had a contingency plan - but one that was only to be implemented if the news were suddenly to arrive that Tiberius had died, before his own position was cast-iron. This

---

[73] Vidman 1972, 42. For this interpretation of *Dec.* (not *Dec(imus)* as *praenomen* for Capito Aelianus) see also above, at n. 25.
[74] Dessau 1926, 78.

is enough to explain why he had secured access to the funds needed for a donative, with the co-operation of one of the prefects of the *aerarium militare*, who was among the first to be charged after the denouement, probably in November 31.[75] The prefect was the former *comes* of Germanicus in the east, who had earlier been one of the prosecutors of Cn. Piso, P. Vitellius: *illum indices arguebant claustra aerarii, cui praefectus erat, et militarem pecuniam rebus novis obtulisse* (*Ann.* 5.8.1). P. Vitellius was put in the custody of one of his brothers, but after frequent postponements of his trial, took his own life (*Ann.* 5.8.2; Suet. *Vit.* 2.3, not specifying the charge: *inter Seiani conscios arreptus et in custodiam fratri datus scalpro librario venas sibi incidit*). The brother was no doubt not Quintus: he had been expelled from the senate many years before (in 17, *Ann.* 2.48.3). The other two remained in high favour. Aulus was to be consul suffect the next year, 32, as colleague of the future emperor Nero's father (but died in office, Suet. *Vit.* 2.2). Lucius became *ordinarius* in 34, going on to govern Syria and to hold two more consulships under Claudius, as the emperor's colleague, even to hold the censorship with him.[76]

If Sejanus had indeed married Livilla in summer or early autumn 31, he had perhaps reckoned that, as stepfather of Tiberius Gemellus, then at most eleven years old, he would be accepted after the old emperor's death as interim *princeps*. He surely also needed - and intended - to get rid of Caligula. This was certainly claimed by Tiberius in 32, in a letter provoked by a senate meeting. 'At the start of the year, as if Livia's outrages were only recently known and not previously punished either, frightening proposals were voiced also against her likenesses and memory; and Sejanus' property was to be carried from the treasury to the *fiscus* (as if it made a difference)' (*Ann.* 6.2.1). Then the obscure Togonius Gallus urged that a bodyguard of twenty armed senators, chosen by lot, should protect Tiberius whenever he entered the *curia* - Tiberius was already on the mainland and skirting Campania, as if intending to come to Rome (6.1.1). Finally, Junius Gallio proposed a privilege for veteran Praetorian Guardsmen: at the theatre they should be allowed to sit in the Fourteen Rows reserved for the equestrian order. Tiberius rejected Togonius' suggestion in moderate, if slightly sarcastic terms, but reacted furiously to that of Gallio, labelled a 'satellite of Sejanus' seeking to corrupt the soldiery. Gallio was expelled from the senate and exiled, then recalled and placed under arrest (6.2.3-3.3). A further item in Tiberius' letter was greeted with great joy: he attacked the ex-praetor Sextius Paconianus, 'a bold malefactor, probing everyone's secrets, and chosen by Sejanus as the man to help his guileful preparations against C. Caesar', *audacem, maleficum, omnium secreta rimantem, delectumque a Seiano cuius ope dolus Gaio Caesari paratur* (*Ann.* 6.3.4). Paconianus was on the brink of being sentenced to death, but saved his skin by turning informer - against the hated *delator* Lucanius Latiaris, the man who had trapped Titius Sabinus four years earlier (*Ann.* 6.4.1, cf. 4.68.2, 4.71.1). Paconianus remained in prison: there he composed *carmina in principem*, for which he was executed in 35 (4.39.1).

One can only guess what kind of *dolus* had been planned against Caligula. Paconianus had presumably been commissioned by Sejanus to produce evidence of behaviour or statements by Caligula which would justify his arrest or death. As the charge against Paconianus was not made until over two months after Sejanus' fall, Tiberius may initially have treated the matter as subsidiary - perhaps until Caligula and his allies in the imperial entourage pressed him? It is at least very plausible that Sejanus

---

[75] Tacitus places the accusation of P. Vitellius (and of P. Pomponius Secundus, on whom see above) immediately before the execution of Sejanus' younger children (6.4.1: *placitum posthac ut in reliquos Seiani liberos adverteretur*, etc.), datable by the *Fasti Ostienses*, cited above, to late November or early December 31.

[76] See e.g. Syme 1979-91, VII, ch. 51, 'Ministers of the Caesars', 521-540, at 521 ff.

had set some steps against Caligula in train. Suetonius records how Tiberius, 'in the memoir that he composed in a brief and summary fashion about his own life, dared to write that he had punished Sejanus because he had found out that he was raging against the sons of his own son Germanicus - one of whom he himself killed when Sejanus was already under suspicion, the other when Sejanus was already suppressed!' *etsi commentario, quem de vita sua summatim breviterque composuit, ausus est scribere Seianum se punisse, quod comperisset furere adversus filios Germanici filii sui; quorum ipse alterum suspecto iam, alterum oppresso demum Seiano interemit* (*Tib.* 61.1). Suetonius waxes sarcastic, evidently assuming that Tiberius blamed Sejanus for the death of Drusus in 33 as well as that of Nero in summer 31. This can hardly be the case. But he might have blamed Sejanus for the death of Nero and for planning to dispose of Caligula.[77]

Tacitus quotes another letter of Tiberius to the senate from the year 32: 'The start of that letter of Caesar's was regarded as distinctive, for he opened with these words: "If I know what to write to you, conscript fathers, or how to write or what not to write at all at this time, may the gods and goddesses destroy me worse than the daily death I feel"'. *quid scribam vobis, patres conscripti, aut quo modo scribam, aut quid omnino non scribam hoc tempore, dii me deaeque peius perdant quam perire me cotidie sentio, si scio* (*Ann.* 6.6.1). It is also cited, in almost the same words by Suetonius (*Tib.* 67.1). Suetonius dates the letter considerably later, *postremo*, after citing an insulting letter to Tiberius from the Parthian king Artabanus, who advised him to commit suicide, rather than in 32, as in Tacitus. But both authors interpret the words as showing despair.[78] This fits what Dio relates, under the year 33: Tiberius was obliged to make Caligula his successor, though sure that he would murder Tiberius Gemellus, knowing his character only too well, but resigned himself, 'often quoting the old saying "When I die let the world be consumed by fire"' (58.23.2-4). This is all consistent with the view that the 'discovery', of which someone had convinced him, that his closest friend was untrue and had to be removed, plunged him into the depths of gloom, increased, no doubt, by the apparent proof, offered by Apicata before her suicide, that Sejanus had actually poisoned Drusus eight years before.

But if Sejanus had not really been plotting to overthrow Tiberius, who convinced Tiberius that he was - and how? Certainly, Caligula and Macro were the two persons who gained directly from destroying Sejanus. Caligula saved his own life and secured the succession to Tiberius, Macro gained Sejanus' post as Guard Prefect and (so he no

---

[77] Neither Drusus' death nor that of Agrippina, also in 33, on the second anniversary of Sejanus' execution, could be blamed on Sejanus. See on Tacitus' account of this (and much else) the illuminating comments by A.J. Woodman, *Tiberius and the Taste of Power. The Year 33 in Tacitus* (The Seventh Syme Memorial Lecture, Victoria University of Wellington, 2002), esp. 14. Levick 1976, 173 stresses that '[t]he tense of the verb in the sentence from Tiberius' autobiography is worth noting. It implies that Sejanus was still acting against the children at the time of his fall', i.e. against Caligula. Perhaps he meant Nero too. Suetonius says at one point that 'they think Nero was compelled to take his own life' (*Tib.* 54.2), later just that Tiberius killed him when 'Sejanus was already suspected', i.e. in summer 31 (Suet. *Tib.* 61.1, quoted above), whereas Dio (58.8.4) simply registers Tiberius writing to the senate about his death. Conceivably Tiberius wished to deny responsibility in this case.

[78] Levick 1976, 201 f., citing Tac. *Ann.* 6.2.5 f., *ludibria seriis permiscere solitus*, argues that Tiberius was teasing, since the expression about the gods and goddesses recalls the comic poets, who often use the phrase *di (deaeque omnes) te perduint*. She repeats this view at length in 'A cry from the heart from Tiberius Caesar?', *Historia* 22 (1978) 95-101. I am not convinced. Nor is Seager: 'By engaging in an elaborately artificial and superficially frivolous intellectual exercise of this kind, a mind like that of Tiberius, quirky and pedantic, may erect a barrier, however, between it and the abyss on the brink of which it stands' (in the second edition of Seager 1972, 2005, 230 f.).

doubt thought) the opportunity to control Caligula when he became emperor. Caligula and Macro's wife Ennia were certainly lovers. There are several different versions of when the relationship began and who initiated it. The earliest witness is Philo, who portrays Macro as a cuckold. First, he stresses at length that Macro repeatedly spoke up for Caligula and assuaged Tiberius' doubts about him (*Leg. ad Gaium* 32-8):

> 'Most people say that the reason why he did this', Philo goes on, 'was not merely because Gaius for his part courted the favour of Macro, as the one who had a dominant or even all-powerful position in the government. It was also because Macro's wife every day urged her husband on, and hammered it into him, that he should not let up in his enthusiasm and support for the young man. For great is the power that a wife has to paralyse and seduce her husband's judgement - particularly if she is wanton, because her guilty conscience makes her flatter him the more: the husband, unaware of the destruction of his marriage and his household, and thinking that her flattery is pure affection, is deceived, and does not realise that through her artifices he is taking his worst enemies to be his best friends' (ibid. 39-40).

After describing in detail how Caligula grew tired of Macro's attempts to keep him under control once he was emperor, and forced him to suicide, Philo adds: 'his wife met the same fate, although she was supposed once to have been Gaius' mistress' (ibid. 61).

Tacitus places Caligula's marriage to Junia in 33, 'at about the same time' as the execution of the remaining *Seianiani* (*Ann.* 6.19.2-3, 20.1), which the *Fasti Ostienses* show took place in the second half of July or the first half of August of that year: [... A]ug. coniur(atio) Seian[i exstincta e]t compl[ures in s]calis [Gemoniis iacuer(unt)].[79] He only mentions Ennia's relationship with Caligula, which he interprets quite differently, at the beginning of his account of the year 37:

> '...power [was] already being exercised excessively by Macro, who from day to day was fostering ever more keenly the good will - which in fact he never neglected - of Gaius Caesar. After the death of Claudia, whose wedding to the latter I recorded, Macro had driven his own wife, Ennia, to entice the young man into a feigned love affair and then, by a matrimonial agreement, to bind him fast, since he would not refuse anything provided he could achieve mastery: for, though he was temperamentally volatile, the falseness of hypocrisy had nevertheless been a lesson well learned in his grandfather's lap'.

> *...nimia iam potentia Macronis, qui gratiam Gai Caesaris numquam sibi neglectam acrius in dies fovebat impuleratque post mortem Claudiae, quam nuptam ei rettuli, uxorem suam Enniam imitando amorem iuvenem inlicere pactoque matrimonii vincire, nihil abnuentem, dum dominationis apisceretur; nam etsi commotus ingenio simulationum tamen falsa in sinu avi perdidicerat.* (*Ann.* 6.45.3).

According to Suetonius, Caligula was summoned to Capri 'in his nineteenth year', that is, between 30 August 30 and 29 August 31 (*Cal.* 10.1). He appears to put Caligula's marriage to Junia Claudilla before the fall of Sejanus:

---

[79] Vidman 1972, 42.

'Thus, not much later, he took as his wife Junia Claudilla, daughter of the most noble Marcus Silanus. Then, having been designated as augur in place of his brother Drusus, before he was enrolled he was transferred to a pontificate as an outstanding example of family loyalty and character, when, with the court being laid waste and deprived of remaining supports, with Sejanus being... suspected and soon oppressed, he was gradually being moved to hope for the succession.'

non ita multo post Iuniam Claudillam M. Silani nobilissimi viri f(iliam) duxit uxorem. deinde augur in locum fratris sui Drusi destinatus, prius quam inauguraretur ad pontificatum traductus est insigni testimonio pietatis atque indolis, cum deserta desolataque reliquis subsidiis aula, Seiano +vete suspecto mox et oppresso, ad spem successionis paulatim admoveretur (12.1).

Then, Suetonius goes on:

'to confirm [his hope] the more, having lost Junia in childbirth, he sollicited Ennia, already the wife of Naevius Macro, who was then commanding the praetorian cohorts, to adultery, even promising marriage to himself if he should gain the imperial power... Through her he enveigled Macro and attacked Tiberius with poison, as some think...'

quam quo magis confirmaret, amissa Iunia ex partu, Enniam Naevi <i>am[80] *Macronis uxorem, qui tum praetorianis cohortibus praeerat, sollicitavit ad stuprum, pollicitus et matrimonium suum, si potitus imperio fuisset... per hanc insinuatus Macroni veneno Tiberium adgressus est, ut quidam opinanture...* (12.2).

Cassius Dio evidently follows the same source as Tacitus. After describing how Caligula hastened the death of Tiberius by smothering him with blankets, he adds that

'he was aided to some extent by Macro. For, as Tiberius was now very ill, he was cultivating the young man, especially as he had previously led him to have sexual relations with his own wife, Ennia Thrasylla. And Tiberius, suspecting this, once said: "You do well to abandon the setting and hasten to the rising sun"' (58.28.4).

It is surely possible that Ennia and Caligula had already started their relationship - probably with Macro's blessing - well before Caligula lost his wife in childbirth, indeed, before the destruction of Sejanus. Ben Jonson, as it happens, took this to be the case:

Laco.   But, how comes Macro
        So in trust and favour with Caligula?
Pomponius. O, sir, he has a wife, and the young prince
        An appetite: he can look up, and spy
        Flies in the roof when there are fleas i'bed;
        And hath a learned nose to assure his sleeps.
        Who, to be favour'd of the rising sun,

---

[80] This seems a reasonable emendation for the MS *Enniam Naeviam*, which would mean that Ennia had the same name as her husband; rather, 'Ennia, already the wife of Naevius Macro'.

> Would not lend a little of his waning moon?
> 'Tis the saf'st ambition.

(*Sejanus His Fall*, Act. IV, scene v, 514-522).

Cichorius produced the plausible conjecture, which has been generally accepted, that Macro's wife Ennia Thrasylla was the granddaughter of the astrologer Thrasyllus, suggesting as her father the Roman knight L. Ennius, whose prosecution for *maiestas* in 22 was stopped by Tiberius (Tac. *Ann.* 3.70.1).[81] As already mentioned, Hennig argued that it was Macro who got Tiberius to change his mind about Sejanus; Levick suggested that it was Caligula who took the lead, while Macro, Laco and Thrasyllus also benefited. It may be noted, incidentally, that Macro may have been holding office as prefect of the *vigiles* up till the moment when he brought his letter of appointment to the Guard from Capri to Rome on 17 October; equally, that Laco was only appointed to take over the *vigiles* at the same time.

The question still arises: *how* could anyone persuade Tiberius to change his mind - if Sejanus had not, in fact, been conspiring against the *princeps*? Given that everyone else who has discussed the question has either accepted the sources' version of Sejanus' uninterrupted villainy, or produced a conjecture, another one may be offered: Macro and Caligula could have got Ennia Thrasylla to persuade her grandfather to construct a prediction for Tiberius. The learned astrologer, who was also a philosopher, had been Tiberius' constant companion for over thirty years, since he won the trust of his naturally suspicious patron on Rhodes. Suetonius registers a conversation of Augustus on Capri, in summer 14, not long before his death, with Thrasyllus, *Tiberi comitem* (Suet. *Aug.* 99.4). Under the year 16 Dio records that Tiberius 'was always in the company of Thrasyllus and used some kind of divination every day' (57.15.7). That Thrasyllus was capable of inventing a prediction - which convinced Tiberius - happens to be registered by Suetonius and Dio: before his own death, in 36, which he had correctly forecast to the day and hour, 'he falsely told [Tiberius] that he would live for ten more years'. This saved the lives of some who had been accused by Macro (Dio 58.27.1-3). Suetonius is briefer, but adds that Tiberius, had it not been for this prediction, 'is believed not to have been going to spare even his remaining grandsons, since he held Gaius to be suspect and despised Tiberius [Gemellus] as born of adultery', *ne reliquis quidem nepotibus parsurus creditur, cum et Gaium suspectum haberet et Tiberium ut ex adulterio conceptum aspernaretur* (Suet. *Tib.* 62.3).[82]

Thrasyllus was no ordinary astrologer, of the kind scornfully referred to by Juvenal, when he asks who would wish, like Sejanus, 'to be regarded as the protector of the *princeps* sitting on the narrow rock of Capreae with his Chaldaean flock?', *tutor*

---

[81] Cichorius 1922, 'IX. Historische Persönlichkeiten und historische Dokumente aus dem Jahrhundert nach Augustus. 2. Der Astrologe Thrasyllus und sein Haus', 390-398.

[82] A long treatment of Thrasyllus, with some very fanciful conjectures, was offered by Cramer 1954, 92-110: '[not] to be trusted, as a rule', in the view of M. Kaplan, *Greeks and the Imperial Court, from Tiberius to Nero* (London-New York 1990), 387 n. 1; see Kaplan's own discussion, esp. 43-49, accepting Cichorius on Ennia, at 49. There he also points out that Thrasyllus' supposed wife, a Commagenian princess called 'Aka', is a non-existent person, based on a misreading of a few letters in one of the poems by Julia Balbilla (his great-granddaughter), carved on the Colossus of Memnon in 130 (see also his n. 31, p. 390). Detailed discussion of Thrasyllus' son, the astrologer Ti. Claudius Balbillus, prefect of Egypt under Claudius, may here be waived. See Kaplan 49-62, prepared to accept that the various Balbilli of the period are one and the same man, a view also taken (without knowledge of Kaplan) in A.R. Birley, *Hadrian the Restless Emperor* (London 1997) 228, with n. 37, where an item in favour of this view, not mentioned by Kaplan, is cited, R. Merkelbach, 'Ephesische Parerga 21. Ein Zeugnis für Ti. Claudius Balbillus aus Smyrna', *ZPE* 31 (1978) 186-7.

haberi/ principis angusta Caprearum in rupe sedentis/ cum grege Chaldaeo? (10. 92-4). He was revered by later practitioners of astrology, but became better known to posterity as a philosopher, or, if one prefers, a philologist, devoted to editing Plato.[83] If one accepts, as many do, the premise that Tiberius really trusted Sejanus totally almost to the last, one needs an explanation for his change of mind. The intervention by Antonia (referred to above) would hardly have achieved this. Caligula, or Macro, surely could not have persuaded him even by manufactured evidence - but Thrasyllus might have done the trick for them. To be sure, such speculation may belong rather to a historical novel.[84]

The view has been implied here that Tiberius intended Sejanus to be his successor (some have suggested that he was to be 'Regent' - but it is not clear what that would mean: a proto-Stilicho?). Hence it still seems plausible that Velleius was thinking of Sejanus when he prayed, at the end of his work, for *successores quam serissimos* for Tiberius, 'whose shoulders may be as capable of sustaining bravely the empire of the world as we have felt his to be', *quorum cervices tam fortiter sustinendo terrarum orbis imperio sufficient, quam huius suffecisse sensimus* (2.131.2).[85] An authority on the Praetorian Guard took the view that its most famous commander would have made rather a good emperor. 'Si l'on admet qu'entre les flatteries d'un Velleius avant la chute et la partialité de l'historiographie après la chute la verité tient le milieu, Sejan eût été un prince non sans talent, dont l'adoption par Tibère eût pu éviter au peuple romain de tristes jours et avancer d'un siècle la prosperité antonine.'[86]

To be sure, Sejanus would probably have been a more competent ruler than Caligula, Claudius and Nero. But he can hardly be compared to Antoninus Pius or Marcus Aurelius. He was surely feared by many senators, and about his morals one may be a little sceptical too. Perhaps the stories of youthful self-prostitution to Gavius Apicius and multiple seductions of married women in his prime need to be treated with scepticism. But a neglected passage in the Elder Pliny should give pause for thought. As an example of a vast sum paid for unworthy persons, he refers to the purchase of 'one of Sejanus' eunuchs, Paezon' (i.e. Παίζων, meaning presumably 'playful' or perhaps 'dancing'), for 50 million sesterces, the price of 'lust, not beauty', *libidinis, non formae*. The buyer was one Sutorius Priscus, and he got away with it unchallenged, because 'during a time of national grief no one had the leisure to criticise him', *quam quidem iniuriam lucri fecit ille mercatus in luctu civitatis, quoniam arguere nulli vacabat* (*NH* 7.129). The MSS reading of the buyer's name is *Sutorio Prisco*: editors have emended to *Clutorio*. But Clutorius Priscus, a Roman knight, who had been rewarded in 19 or 20 for a poem on Germanicus' dying moments, had met his end in 21, condemned for a premature similar poem about Drusus - who recovered

---

[83] Some references are given by Cramer 1954, 92 ff. See further the extended investigation by H. Tarrant, *Thrasyllan Platonism* (Ithaca 1993). Unfortunately he scarcely discusses Thrasyllus' relations with Tiberius, referring only, p. 7, to Cramer. Thrasyllus is not mentioned at all by Yavetz 1999 and only once by Seager 1972.

[84] J. Henderson, *Telling Tales on Caesar. Roman Stories from Phaedrus* (Oxford 2004), who discusses at length, 65 ff., Phaedrus' claim to be a victim of Sejanus (3. *Prol.* 41 f.), quotes, at 68 f., 83, passages from a novel by D. Wishart, *Sejanus* (London 1998): *non vidi*.

[85] *Pace* Woodman 1977, 245-8, who emphatically rejects this view (held e.g. by Syme 1958, 367 f.): 'Nothing could be further from the truth'. Cf. Syme's later comment, Syme 1986, 436, cited above, n. 31. Preferable is the view of Schmitzer 2000, 283, who argues that (whatever his real feelings) Velleius could at least be understood by his readers as referring to Sejanus as the (still far off) successor who was strong enough to carry the burden of empire: '[d]abei ist es von untergeordneter Relevanz, ob dieser Wunsch bei Velleius vom Herzen kommt oder doch eher distanziert vorgebracht wird.'

[86] M. Durry, *Les Cohortes prétoriennes* (Paris 1938) 156.

(Tac. *Ann.* 3.49.1-2). Sutorius Priscus may well have been a freedman of Sutorius Macro, who was also a nasty piece of work.

Bibliography.

P. J. Ayres, *Ben Jonson. Sejanus His Fall* (1990 Manchester).

J. Bellemore, 'The wife of Sejanus' *ZPE* 109 (1995) 255-266.

H.W. Bird, 'L. Aelius Seianus and his political influence [or: significance]' *Latomus* 28 (1969) 61-98.

C. Cichorius, *Römische Studien* (Lepizig–Berlin 1922).

F.H. Cramer, *Astrology in Roman Law and Politics* (Philadelphia 1954).

H. Dessau, *Geschichte der römischen Kaiserzeit* II 1 (Berlin 1926).

W. Eck et al., *Das Senatum Consultum de Cn. Pisone patre* (Munich 1996).

D. Hennig, *L. Aelius Seianus. Untersuchungen zur Regierung des Tiberius* (Munich 1975).

E. Koestermann, 'Der Sturz Sejans' *Hermes* 83 91955) 350-373.

B. Levick, *Tiberius the Politician* (London 1976).

R. Seager, *Tiberius* (London 1972).

U. Schmitzer, *Velleius Paterculus und das Interesse an der Geschichte im Zeitalter des Tiberius* (Heidelberg 2000).

G.V. Sumner, 'The family connections of L. Aelius Seianus' *Phoenix* 19 (1965) 134-145.

R. Syme, *The Roman Revolution* (Oxford 1939).

R. Syme, 'Seianus on the Aventine' *Hermes* 84 (1956) 257-266.

R. Syme, 'Roman historians and renaissance politics' *Society and History in the Renaissance* (1960) 3-12.

R. Syme, *Tacitus* (Oxford 1958).

R. Syme, *Roman Papers* (I-II 1979, III 1984, IV-V 1988, VI-VII 1991, Oxford 1979-91).

R. Syme, *The Augustan Aristocracy* (Oxford 1986).

L. Vidman, ed., *Fasti Ostienses* (2nd ed., Prague 1972).

A.J. Woodman, *Velleius Paterculus. The Tiberian Narrative (2.94-131)* (Cambridge 1977).

A.J. Woodman, *Tacitus Reviewed* (Oxford 1998).

A.J. Woodman, *Tacitus. The Annals* (Indianapolis/Cambridge 2004).

Z. Yavetz, *Tiberius. Der traurige Kaiser* (Munich 1999).

PAUL HOLDER

OBSERVATIONS ON THE INNER FACES
OF AUXILIARY DIPLOMAS FROM THE REIGN OF ANTONINUS PIUS

Introduction

The diptych which today is called a military diploma is a typical double document which was necessary for validity in Roman law.[1] Each one was a certified copy of the text of the complete constitution published at Rome. The text engraved across the two inner faces was the guarantee of legality because the two tablets were wired together and sealed to preclude tampering. On the outer face of the first tablet was a duplicate copy which resembled the layout of the original bronze constitution (Weiß 2004, 250-251). On the outer face of the second were the names of the witnesses who certified the authenticity of the copy. A diploma for an auxiliary soldier from the Roman army was laid out according to the following framework:[2]

Imperial titles
equitibus et peditibus formula
Unit list
Name of province and of governor
Years of service and discharge where applicable
Details of the grant of citizenship and right of Roman marriage.
Day date and consuls
Recipient, his unit, his commander, his wife and family where applicable
descriptum et recognitum formula

For many years after the introduction of these documents by Claudius there was no abbreviation of the contents of either face. However from the reign of Vespasian part of the *descriptum et recognitum* formula began to be omitted from the inside. Rather than describing the exact location where the original constitution had been set up as on the outside the text on the inner face would finish with the words *in Capitolio* prior to about 90. Thereafter the formula would finish at *fixa est Romae* (TABLE 1). This *descriptum et recognitum* formula certified the diploma had been copied from the original constitution engraved on bronze and set up in Rome. For this omission to have been condoned it must have been decided that this formula had no bearing on the legality of the copy as a whole. Indeed from about 120 this formula was left out altogether until reinstated about 154 (TABLE 2). From about 114 the legal formulae on the inner faces of a diploma began to be abbreviated and from about 133 they could be fitted onto the inside of the first tablet leaving the second to contain the date and the details of the recipient (TABLE 2). From about 135 only the *cognomen* of each consul was engraved on the inner face rather than their full names. Early in the reign of Anto-

---

[1] There are two principal collections of diplomas. *Corpus Inscriptionum Latinarum* (*CIL*) XVI published 1936 and 1955; and *Roman Military Diplomas* (*RMD*) of which five volumes have been published between 1978 and 2006.

[2] Diplomas were also issued to the fleets and to the troops at Rome. These were slightly different according to the privileges being awarded or to the length of service. See Lambert and Scheuerbrandt 2002.

ninus Pius the day, date and the name of the consuls might be omitted. From the reign of Trajan abbreviations began to be used on the outer face of the first tablet. Generally they were not as severe.

Early in 138 part of the text recording the privileges awarded by the grant was changed. Again late in 139 further changes to the wording of this section of a diploma were carried out and from 140 children were no longer automatically included in the grant. These changes caused some confusion in the copying out of inner faces with parts of the old formula mixed with the new (Eck 2007). Omissions from the text as a whole are also known at this time. There are three examples of auxiliary diplomas where the phrase *divi Nervae pronepos* has been missed out from the titulature of Antoninus Pius.[3] The impression gained is that less care was taken by the copyists who engraved the inner faces of diplomas. They may even have been working from memory in engraving formulaic parts of the text (Roxan-Holder 2004, 272 and note 12). Thus, at about the same time, differences in the text of the unit list become noticeable between the faces of an auxiliary diploma.

Inner Faces 138-142.

At the beginning of the reign of Antoninus Pius the unit list on each face of an auxiliary diploma might look like that engraved on the one for Dacia inferior of 13 December 140 (*RMD* I 39):

intus
EQ ET PED Q MIL IN AL●III ET NVM EQ ILLYR ET
COH VIIII Q APP I ASTVR ET HISP ET I CL GAL
CAP ET I FL COM ET IBRACAVG ET I TYR SAG
III GAL ET I AVG PAC BRIT ∞ I HISP VET
II FL NVM II FL BES II GAL ET SVNT IN

extrinsecus
EQVITIB ET PED QVI MIL IN ALIS III ET NVM EQ
i]LLYR ET COH VIIII QVAE APP I ASTVR ET HISP
ET I CLAVD GALL CAPIT ET I FL COMM ET I
BRACAVG ET I TYRIOR SAG ET III GAL ET I
AVG NERV PAC BRITT ∞ ET I HISP VET ET II
FL NVM ET II FL BESS ET II GALL ET SVNT IN

Less care was taken by the copyist with the text on the inner face. A number of ETs were omitted as well as *Nerv(iana)* from the titles of *cohors I Aug(usta) Nerv(iana) Pac(ensis) Britt(onum) (milliaria)*. Otherwise the units have the same names and epithets although they were more abbreviated on the inner face. It is interesting to compare the layout of the lists here with that on the diploma of 22 November 139 for Syria Palaestina (*CIL* XVI 87):

intus
EQ ET PED Q MIL IN●AL III ET COH XII Q AP
GAL ET ANT ET VII PHR ET I THR ET I SEB ET I
DAM ET I MON ET I FL CR ET I ET II GAL ET
III ET IIII BR ET IIII ET VI PET ET V GEM CR

extrinsecus
EQVIT ET PEDIT QVI MILIT IN ALIS III ET COH XII
QVAE APPELL GALL ET THR ET ANT GALL ET VII
PHRY ET I THR ∞ ET I SEB ∞ ET I DAM ET I MONT
RT I FL CR ET I ET II GALA ET III ET IIII BRAC ET IIII
ET VI PETR ET V GEM CR ET SVNT IN SYRIA PALAE

Obviously more abbreviation was used. There are also divergences in the names of the units with significant omissions on the inner face. The first ala was named as *ala Gall(orum) et Thr(acum)* on the outer face but only *ala Gal(lorum)* on the inner. Its full name is given on the diploma of 15 January 142 below. The second ala was called *ala Antiana Gallorum et Thracum* which was shortened to *Ant(iana) Gall(orum)* on the outer face and *Ant(iana)* on the inner. It is also significant that the symbol ∞ denoting a mil-

---

[3] The diplomas are: Syria Palaestina, 22 November 139 (*CIL* XVI 87); Pannonia inferior, 7 August 143 (*RMD* IV 266); Dacia superior, 23 February 144 (*CIL* XVI 90). A fourth example occurs in a diploma for the Ravenna fleet of 1 August 142 (*RMD* V 392).

liary unit was omitted from the intus. Comparison with the diploma for Syria Palaestina of 15 January 142 (*RGZM* 29, published Pferdehirt 2004) shows that its unit list often records a more complete name for a unit albeit in an abbreviated form:

intus

EQ ET PED Q M [in   ●] COH XI Q A GAL ET ANT
gal et t]HR ET V[ii phry et i s]EB ET I DAM ET I MON
et i f]L ET I E[t ii gala et iii] ET IV CAL ET IV ET VI
pet et] V GEM [cr et sunt in s]YR PAL SVB[

extrinsecus

EQVIT ET PED[it qui milit in al]IS III ET COH
XI QVAE APPEL GALL ET THR CONST ET ANT
GALL ET THR ET VII PHRYG ET I SEB ∞ ET I
DAM ARM SAG ET I MONT CR ET [i] FL CR ET
I ET II VLP [galat e]T [iii et iv ca]LL BRAC
AVG ET IV [et vi ulp petr et v g]EMEL CR

It can be seen that the outer face generally has a more complete version of a unit name. How the names were engraved on the intus varies. *ala Antiana Gallorum et Thracum* appears in full on both faces, but *ala Gallorum et Thracum Constantium* is called only *ala Gal(lorum)* on the inner. On the intus there is *cohors I Dam(ascenorum)* but on the outer it is called *cohors I Dam(ascenorum) Arm(eniaca) sag(ittaria)*.[4] More intriguingly, on the outer face are two cohorts called *[Ca]ll(aecorum) Brac(araugustanorum)* which are named simply as *Cal(laecorum)* on the inner. In 139 they are called *III et IV Brac(araugustanorum)* on both faces.[5] The inner face consistently lacks the epithet *Ulpia* and, as in 139, the symbol ∞. The list on the inner face is thereby reduced in length and less time was needed to engrave it.

Inner Faces 143-153.

A diploma of 7 August 143 for Pannonia inferior (*RMD* IV 266) has a different inner face with the names of the units omitted altogether:

intus

EQ ET PED QVI MILIT●IN ALIS V ET COH XIII
ET SVNT IN PANN INFER SVB PONTIO

extrinsecus

EQVIT ET PEDIT QVI MILIT IN ALIS V ET COH XIII
QVAE APPEL I FL AVG BRIT ∞ ET I THR VETER
ET I CR ET I PRAET CR ET I AVG ITVR ET I ALPIN
ET I THR CR ET I NORIC ET I LVSIT ET I MONT ET
I CAMP ET I THR CR ET I ALPIN PEDIT ET II ASTV
ET II AVG THR ET III BATAV ∞ ET III LVSIT ET VII
BREVCOR ET SVNT IN PANNON INFER SVB PON

This pattern became the norm until 153 (TABLE 3). There were a few exceptions. For Britain, while the diploma of 1/3-146 (*RMD* II 97) had an abbreviated inner face, the diploma of 10 December 145/9 December 146 (*CIL* XVI 93) reads:

---

[4] It is recorded on a diploma of 90 for Iudaea as *cohors I Damascena Armeniaca* (*RMD* V 332) and on an unpublished diploma for the same province of 87. The names also appear on a diploma for Syria Palaestina of 160 (*RGZM* 41), see below.

[5] The double ethnic name of *cohors III Callaecorum Bracaraugustanorum* is recorded earlier on a diploma for Iudaea of 90 (*RMD* V 332) and on an unpublished example of 87 for the same province. The double ethnic name of *cohors IIII Callaecorum Bracaraugustanorum* can be restored on a diploma for Syria of 91 (*RMD* IV 214 = *RGZM* 6).

intus
EQ ET PED Q [
GAL PROC ET I [pann sab et i hisp ast et i
CLLT ET I HISP ET [i ael dac et i ael class
ET I FID ET II GAL E[t ii et vi nerv et iii
BRAC ET IIII LING [et iiii gal et sunt in
BRITTAN SVB PAPIR[io aeliano

extrinsecus
equit et p]EDIT QVI MILITAVER IN ALIS III
et coh xi qu]AE APPELL AVG GALL PROCVL ET I
pann sabin] ET I HISP ASTVR ET I CELTIB
et i hispan et] I AETIA DACOR ET I AELIA
CLASSICA [et i fid v]ARD ET II GALLOR ET II ET
VI NERV E[t iii bra]C ET IIII LING ET IIII GALL
ET SVNT IN B[ritta]NNIA SVB PAPIRIO AELI

The names of the units of the inner face are shortened more than those on the outer with *[I fid(a) V]ard(ullorum)* abbreviated to *I fid(a)* on the intus. Additionally *cohors I Celtib(erorum)* was mistakenly engraved as *I Cllt(iberorum)*.

For Moesia inferior the diploma of 1 January/9 December 146 (*RMD* IV 270) has a full unit list on both faces. However, the known copy of the constitution of 7 April 145 for this province exhibits a variant inner face (*RMD* V 399/165). The copyist seems to have decided to shorten the unit titles consistently either by abbreviating single word names as much as possible or by omitting the second part of a name:

intus
EQ ET PED Q M IN AL V●ET COH XI Q A I [gall
ET I CALL ET I VESP ET I FL ET II HISP [et i brac et
II MATTEAT II FL ET CLETICLAVD ET I CAL [et i cil
ET I THR ET I GERM ET II BRAC ET I LVSIT [et ii fl et
sunt i]N MOETIA INFERIORE XXV IT[em class

extrinsecus
EQVIT ET PEDIT QVI [milit
QVAE APPELL I GALLOR [et pa]NN ET I [gallor atect
ET I VESPAS DARDAN et I FL GAETVL ET II HISP A[ra
VAC ET I BRACAR CR ET II MATTIAC ET I FL NVM[id
ET I CLAVD SVGAMBR VET ET I CALCH SAG ET I CI
LIC SAG ET I THR SYR ET I GERMAN ET II BRACAR
AVGVST ET I LVSIT CYR ET II FL BRITTON ET SVNT

On the inner face the alae are called: *[I Gall(orum)]*; *I Call(orum)*; *I Vesp(asiana)*; *I Fl(avia)*; and *II Hisp(anorum)* instead of *I Gallor(um) et Pann(oniorum)*; *I [Gallor(um) Atect(origiana)*; *I Vespas(iana) Dardan)orum*; *I Fl(avia) Gaetul(orum)*; and *II Hisp(anorum) A[ra]vac(orum)* as on the outer face. How the copyist tried to shorten cohort names is confused because the text is difficult to decipher. It is best to look at the units individually with each name as preserved on the outer face first:

(1) *cohors I Bracar(orum) c(ivium) R(omanorum)*; not extant on the inner face.
(2) *cohors II Mattiac(orum)*; inner face II MATTEAT. It seems the copyist cut II MATTIA and then decided to abbreviate the name to II MATT. Then he altered IA to ET as best he could. The E is more heavily cut as is the top of the *T*. Read *II Matt(iacorum) e{a}t*.
(3) *cohors I ⌈F⌉l(avia) Num[id(arum)]*; inner face II FL originally read as II BL. This seems to be what is visible rather than II BL because the B is not fully formed. The numeral is incorrect. Read *{I}I Fl(avia Numidarum)*.
(4) *cohors I Claud(ia) Sugambr(orum) vet(erana)*; inner face ETCLETICLAVD. It seems that the copyist cut ET CLA and then realised that he had omitted the numeral. He changed A to E and added a cramped T. Then he cut I CLAVD and put a long horizontal on the numeral because there was no other way to rectify the error. Read *{etcl} et I Claud(ia Sugambrorum veterana)*.
(5) *cohors <I>I C<h>alc{h}(idenorum) sag(ittariorum)*; inner face ETICAL. Here the copyist perhaps thought he had cut the numeral II since he joined the top of the T to the top of the following letter like a bar over a numeral. Read *et I<I> C<h>al(cidenorum sagittariorum)*.
(6) *cohors I Cilic(um) sag(ittariorum)*; not extant on the inner face.
(7) *cohors I Thr(acum) Syr(iaca)*; inner face I THR.
(8) *cohors I German(orum)*; inner face I GERM.
(9) *cohors II Braca[r]august(anorum)*; inner face II BRAC.

(10) *cohors I Lusit(anorum) Cyr(enaica)*; inner face I LVSIT for *I Lusit(anorum Cyrenaica)*.

(11) *cohors II Fl(avia) Britton(um)*; not extant on the inner face.

Comparison with the list of cohorts on the inner face of the diploma issued in 146 indicates that the units were the same. Therefore the copyist here seems to have decided to save time by using this method of abbreviating unit names. This might also help to explain the carelessness because of the errors of transcription which include the omission of the governor's name. But he obviously thought that this was not too important and that the document would meet with official approval. The intus can therefore be transcribed as:

> eq(uitibus) et ped(itibus) q(ui) m(ilitaverunt) in al(is) V et coh(ortibus) XI q(uae) a(ppellantur)
> I [Gall(orum et Pannoniorum)] et I Call(orum Atectorigiana) et I Vesp(asiana Dardanorum)
> et I Fl(avia Gaetulorum) et II Hisp(anorum et Aravacorum) [et I Brac(arorum civium
> Romanorum) et] II Matt(iacorum) e{a}t {I}I Fl(avia Numidarum) {etcl} et I Claud(ia)
> Sugambrorum veterana) et <I>I C<h>al(cidenorum sag(ittariorum) [et I
> Cil(icum sagittariorum)] et I Thr(acum Syriaca) et I Germ(anorum) et
> II Brac(araugustanorum) et I Lusit(anorum Cyrenaica) [et II Fl(avia Brittonum)
> et sunt i]n Moe ⌈s⌉ ia inferiore <sub Claudio Saturnino> XXV it[em class(icis) ...

A variant of the abbreviated inner face is shown by the diploma of 23 February 144 for Dacia superior (*CIL* XVI 90). The names of two alae and eight cohorts are preserved from a unit list of three alae and ten cohorts as follows:

intus	extrinsecus
eq et ped] QVI MIL IN AL III ET COH X QVAE APP	[---]
i batav e]T I HISP ET I GALL ET II GALL PANN	I TVR ET I VIND ∞ ET I T[hrac sag
et sunt in] DACIA SVPER SVB MVSTIO PRISC	IIII HISP ET I VBIOR ET V[iii raet
	ET I ALPIN ET SVNT IN D[acia

The missing unit names can be supplemented from the inner face of the fragmentary diploma for the province of 13 December 156 (*CIL* XVI 107) which contained the same number of alae and cohorts but not in the same order. Alae by now were listed separately from cohorts (TABLE 4):

intus		extrinsecus
equit et pedit qui m]ILIT IN ALIS III QVAE		not preserved
app I batav ∞ et I hi]SPANOR CAMPAGON ET I		
gallor et bosporanor] ET COH X I VINDELICOR		
∞ et	et ii fl] COMMAGENOR ET I	
	et i] VLBIOR ET I THRAC SAG	
	et ii] GALLOR DACIC ET I AVG	
itur et	et ped]IT SINGVL BRITTANNIC	

It can be seen that on the inner face of the diploma of 144 the second part of the surviving ala names has been omitted. They are called simply *I Hisp(anorum)* and *I Gall(orum)* instead of *ala I Hispanorum Campagonum* and *ala I Gallorum et Bosporanorum*. The same occurred on the diploma for Moesia inferior of 7 April 145 described above. Here the cohorts are treated differently. Only the name of the unit of the recipient is given; the others are omitted altogether. Nor is this cohort name shortened by omitting the epithet *Pannonica*. Because the first part of the list of cohorts is missing on the outer face, *cohors II Gallorum Pannonica* could have been in first, second, or third place. Therefore it would seem the copyist chose just to list the recipient's cohort on the inner face after the shortened ala names. It then follows that if he had made another copy of this constitution for a soldier from a different unit it would have appeared on the inner face rather than *cohors II Gallorum Pannonica*.

A copy of the constitution of 22 December 144 for Mauretania Tingitana (*RMD* V 398) seems to have a modification of this type:

intus	extrinsecus
eq et ped qui m]IL IN ALIS V ET COH XI QVAE	not preserved
appel v delm]AT CR ET SVNT IN MAVR TINC	

Usually the latter part of the *equitibus et peditibus* formula on the inner face of a diploma with an abbreviated unit list was engraved as an abbreviated version of *militaverunt in alis et cohortibus et sunt in* (TABLE 4). Here a phrase has been inserted between COH XI and ET SVNT IN. It most likely reads *quae / [appel(lantur) V Delm]at(arum) c(ivium) R(omanorum)* (Holder 2004, 278). This cohort is the unit of the recipient of this copy of the constitution. Again the implication is that a different unit would be named at this point on other copies where the recipients had not served in *cohors V Dalmatarum civium Romanorum*.

It is possible that there was something similar in a constitution for Germania inferior of 5 September 152. A complete copy has been published but the inner faces are not available for study because the binding wires are still intact (Eck-Pangerl 2004, 262-268). The outer face reads:

intus	extrinsecus
not available	EQVITIB ET PEDIT EXERC GERM PII FID QVI
	MIL IN AL IV ET COH XV QVAE APPELL NORIC
	ET SVLPIC CR ET AFROR VET ET I THR ET I FL HISP
	ET I LATOBIG ET VARC ET VI INGEN ET I PANN
	ET DALM ET II CR ET I RAET ET VI RAET ET VI BRITT
	ET II ASTVR ET I CLASS ET II HISP ET I LVCENS
	ET XV VOL CR ET II VARC ET IV THR ET SVNT

There is a second, fragmentary copy (*RMD* V 408), where unit information is preserved as follows:

intus	extrinsecus
eq et ped qui mil i]N AL IIII ET COH XV	not preserved
et s]VNT IN GERM INFER	

From the space available it would seem that no abbreviated version of the phrase *exercitus Germanici pii fidelis* was engraved on the inner face. This is paralleled on the inner face of another diploma for Germania inferior which is preserved in Mainz (*RGZM* 35). The relevant section reads:

intus	extrinsecus
EQ ET PED QVI M[il in al	EQVITIB ET PEDIT EXER[c germ pii fid qui mil
QVAE APP NOR [	IN AL IIII ET COH XV Q[uae appell noric
]++IO IV[	ET SVLPIC CR ET AFRO[r vet et i thr et i fl hisp
	ET LATOBIC ET VARC ET [et vi ingen et i pann
	ET DALM ET II CR ET I RA[et et vi raet et vi britt
	ET II ASTVR ET I CLASS E[t ii hisp et i lucens
	ET XV VOL CR ET II VAR[c et iv thr et sunt

This fragment is dateable only from its layout, content and lettering. In all respects the outer face is very similar to that on the complete copy of 5 September 152 above. This would suggest they were contemporary. However, the first ala of the unit list, *ala Noricorum*, is named on the inner face apparently at the start of the list of the units. The few letter traces on the following line of the inner face do not, though, seem to be part of the unit list. They most likely represent SALV]IO IV[LIANO which is the name of the governor. Thus the Mainz fragment would be an example of an abbreviated inner face where the presumed unit of the recipient was named.[6] It would then follow that the other fragment was similarly laid out and that *cohors XV voluntariorum civium Romanorum* should be restored in the space between COH XV / --- ET S]VNT IN. This is because the cohort was the unit of the recipient. However, due to the unavailability of the inner face of the complete copy, also awarded to a veteran of the cohort, this restoration is not verifiable.

Inner Faces 154-161.

On present evidence, by the end of 153 unit lists had been restored to the inner faces of auxiliary diplomas (TABLE 3). There is only one exception. This is an issue of 2 July 158 for Dacia superior (*CIL* XVI 108) where the unit list reads:

intus
EQ ET PED Q M IN AL I[ii] E[t] CO[h i]I[i] ET VEX Q
SVNT CVM MAVR GENT IN DACIA SVPER
ET SVNT SVB STATIO PRISCO LEG XXV STIP

extrinsecus
EQVIT ET PEDIT QVI MILIT IN ALIS III
QVAE APPEL I BATAV ∞ ET I HISP CAMPAG
ET I GALL ET BOSPOR ET COH I THRAC SAG
ET IV HISP ET I AVG ITVR ET VEXIL AFRIC
ET MAV[r] ET CAES QVI SVNT CVM MAVRIS
GENTILIBVS IN DACIA SVPER ET SVNT
SVB STATIO PRISCO LEG QVINQ ET VI

The incongruity of the abbreviated unit list on the inner face compared with the new style list on the outer where alae are named separately from cohorts is obvious. This list is short, but complex, with three alae, three cohorts, *vexillarii*, and *Mauri gentiles*. It would have fitted easily onto the inner face but the copyist seems to have decided to save time by omitting it just as he would have done a few years earlier. On the outer face the copyist omitted the numeral III after COH. While changes had been made in work practices by the return to engraving the unit list on the inner face of a diploma, these faces became much less carefully engraved and hence much less legible. This can result in the unit list being unintelligible. Restoration of the names of units and of the *descriptum et recognitum* formula on the intus coincided with the reduction to their smallest size of the tablets on which the text was engraved (TABLE 5).

One such example is the diploma of 28 December 154 for Mauretania Tingitana (*RMD* I 48). The outer face preserves the ends of 14 lines of text on its outer face below a gap in the text where traces of the right hand binding hole can be made out above and between the M and the second I of DIMISS in line 1. This means that the lines of text on the inner face have lost half of their length. Nine lines have survived of which the first two record the names of units:

---

[6] Dr. B. Pferdehirt has carried out a further study of this fragment on my behalf and has confirmed the reading. Only the very tops of the letters before IO have survived and are therefore difficult to interpret.

intus   extrinsecus

    ] ET III GAL ET IV IVRGR   not preserved
    ]+FIT+M+++ ∞ SAC ET II
    ] MAVRET TINGIT SVB

Unfortunately the letters are poorly formed throughout this side and it is very difficult to decipher. The first surviving line can be read as *[---] et III Gal(lorum) et IV* ⌐T¬u⌐n¬ *gr(orum)*. On the constitution of 26 October 153 for the province *cohors III Gallorum felix* and *cohors IV Tungrorum vexillatio* are in ninth and eleventh place in a numerical list of cohorts:[7]

intus   extrinsecus
EQ ET PED Q M IN AL V ● ET COH XI Q A I AVG GALL   EQVITIB ET PEDITIB QVI MILIT IN ALIS V ET
ET GEMEL CR ET I TAVR VICTR CR ET III AST PF CR ET I   COH XI QVAE APPELL I AVG GALLOR ET GEMELLIAN
ITVR CR ET I HAM SYR SAG ET V DALM ET II HISP CR   CR ET I TAVRIAN VICTRIX CR ET III ASTVR PF CR
ET I AST ET CALL CR ET II SYR SAG ∞ ET III AST CR ET II   ET I HAMIOR SYROR SAG ET I ITVRAEOR CR ET V
HISP CR ET LEMAV CR ET III GALL FELIX ET IV GALL CR   DALMATAR ET II HISPANOR CR ET I ASTVR ET CALLAE
ET IV TVNGR VEXIL ET SVNT IN MAVRET TINGIT   COR CR ET II SYROR SAG ∞ ET IIIASTVR CR ET II HIS
                                                            PAN CR ET LEMAVOR CR ET III GALLOR FELIX ET IV
                                                            GALLOR CR ET IV TVNGROR VEXIL ET SVNT IN

A few years later in a diploma issued for the province between 10 December 156 and early 157 they are the last two cohorts in a non-numerical list (see below). It might therefore be expected they would have been near the end of the list of the diploma of 28 December 154 but the second surviving line also has unit names. But only the last few letters can be interpreted as ∞ SAG ET II. On the Mainz copy of the constitution of 26 October 153 *cohors II Syrorum sagittaria (milliaria)* is in fifth place among the cohorts followed *by cohors III Asturum civium Romanorum*. On the diploma for the province discussed below *cohors II Syrorum sagit(taria)* is in sixth again followed by *cohors III Asturum civium Romanorum*. However, the ethnic name of this archer unit does not seem to fit with the unclear surviving traces on the fragment under discussion. These have been read as [---] FL COMM ∞ SAG ET II which would indicate a completely different unit of archers.[8] The mysterious lettering has also been read as [---]FL I +MM+ ∞ +A+ ET II with no identification of the unit name.[9] One other solution has been to suggest that the copyist missed a line and inserted it at the end over an erased line giving the impression of a new name.[10] The fact that *cohors IV Tungrorum* follows *cohors III Gallorum* directly on the diploma of 28 December 154 suggests the unit list was non-numerical as later. If so *cohors IIII Gallorum* would probably have been in fourth place. It is then possible that, after engraving the abbreviation for *cohors II Hispanorum (Vasconum) civium Romanorum*, his eye strayed to *cohors III Gallorum felix*.[11] The copyist only realised his error after he had copied out his abbreviation for *cohors IV Tungrorum vexillatio*. He could have then copied out the names of the cohorts he had omitted:

---

[7] There are five published copies of which *RGZM* 34 in Mainz is complete. The others, not so complete, are *RMD* V 409, 410, 411, and Eck-Pangerl 2005a, 197-200.

[8] Rebuffat 1992, 475-480. He here suggested identification with *cohors I Flavia Commagenorum sagittaria* because it was not attested in Dacia Inferior after 140 (*RMD* I 39). It is now recorded in that province in 146 (*RMD* IV 269). But it is nowhere called milliary and there is now a constitution of 26 October 153 for the province (*RGZM* 34) which *lists cohors II Syrorum sagittaria milliaria.*

[9] M.Euzennat in a letter to M. Roxan (*RMD* III p.246 49*†48).

[10] Spaul 2000, 405.

[11] For some reason, perhaps carelessness, he omitted the epithet *felix*. It is present in 153 (*RGZM* 34, *RMD* V 409, 410, 411), 156/157 (*CIL* XVI 181, 182), 161 (*RMD* II 107) and probably 162/203 (*RMD* III 186).

```
                    ] ET III GALL ET IV IVRGR
        vexil et iv gall et i ast et call cr et
        ii syr ∞ sag et iii ast cr et ii hisp cr
        et lem cr et sunt in] MAVRET TINGIT SVB
```

For some reason the copyist seems merely to have chosen some letters from the unit names to make it look as if all had been listed. What seems clear is that no unit names can be identified in this line.

Another diploma for Mauretania Tingitana, which dates between 10 December 156 and early 157 (*CIL* XVI 181) shows how carelessly an inner face might be engraved.[12] Approximately one half of the Tabella I of this diploma issue has survived. This represents the top part of the outer face and the left side of the inner. Whereas the text on the former can be clearly read much less trouble was taken by the copyist on the inside:

intus
EQ..D QVI MILIT IN AL[is v quae app i aug
GALLOR ET GEMELC ●R [et
ET COH XI I ETVR CR ET [v dalm cr et ii hisp
VASCON ET IIII GALLOR [et
FELIX ET IIII TVNGR VE[xil
EF SVNT IN MAVRETA[n tingit
SVB VARIO PRISCO ●PR[oc quinque et
VIGINTI STIPENDIS [emeritis dimissis hon
SV+IV+R ////////[
+N+OR+++N+ ////[
CV+++++A++//[

extrinsecus
EQVIT ET PEDIT QVI MILIT IN ALIS VQVAE
APPEL I AVG GALL ET GEMEL CR ET TAVRI
AN VICTR ET III ASTVR ET I HAMIOR SVROR
SAG ET COH XI I ITVR CR ET V DALMAT CR
ET II HISP VASCON ET IIII GALLOR ET I ASTVR
et] CALLAEC ET II SVROR SAGGIT ET III ASTVRVM
et] II HISPAN CR ET I LEMAVOR ET III GALL
f]ELIX ET IV TVNGR VEXIL ET SVNT IN MAV
ret] TINGIT SVB VARIO PRISCO PROC QVIN
que] ET VIGINTI STIPENDIS EMER[itis

The surviving text on the inner face has a number of scribal errors:
First line: EQ..DQVI. There is only space for two letters after EQ but this is badly corroded. It therefore may be that EQPED was cut rather than EQETPED.
Third line: ETVR for ITVR.
Fifth line: FELIX. it looks as if FEX was cut and corrected to FEL.
Sixth line: EFSVNT. The S has been corrected.
More importantly the last three lines have not been engraved properly. The occasional letter can be made out but cannot be fitted into an abbreviated version of the expected text so that a restoration can be printed. Further anomalies are apparent in the unit list. A fully restored version of the list on the intus would read:

```
        EQ [pe]D QVI MILIT IN AL [is v quae app i aug
        GALLOR ET GEMEL C●R [et i taur victr et iii ast et i ham syr sag
        ET COH XI I ETVR CR ET [ v dalm cr et ii hisp
        VASCON ET IIII GALLOR [et i ast et call et ii sur sag et iii ast et ii hisp cr et  i lem et iii gall
        FELIX ET IIII TVNGR VE[xil
        ET SVNT IN MAVRETA[n tingit
```

---

[12] The diploma was issued during the twentieth year of tribunician power of Antoninus Pius which was from 10 December 156 until 9 December 157 when Varius Priscus was procurator. There is another diploma for the province issued when Pius held TRIB POT XX but with a different procurator. He has been identified as (Q. Claudius Ferox) Aeronius Montanus attested in 158 (Spaul 1993). With no obvious overlap of the two men Priscus would probably have left early in 157.

This clearly was not what was engraved because the second and fourth lines would not have fitted into the space available unless something was omitted. On the fourth line it is possible that the copyist's eye strayed to the *felix* of *cohors III Gallorum* after naming *cohors IIII Gallorum*. It is also clear the last two lines have too few letters unless blank spaces were left. Overall it appears that the copyist of the inner face of this diploma felt he did not have to be accurate as long as there was an impression of the interior text of the constitution.

Late in the reign of Pius there are examples of diplomas where the text on both faces has little abbreviation. This is best exemplified by the more complete copy of a constitution for Syria Palaestina of 7 March 160 (*RGZM* 41):[13]

intus	extrinsecus
EQVITIBVS ET PEDITIBVS QVI MILITAVERVNT IN A	EQVITIBVS ET PEDITIBVS QVI MILITAVE
LIS TRIBVS QVAE APPELLANTVR GALLORVM ET THRA	RVNT IN ALIS TRIBVS QVAE APPELLANTVR
CVM CONST ET ANTIAN G●ALLORVM ET THRACVM	GALLORVM ET THRACVM CONST ET ANTIAN
SAG ET VII PHRYGVM ET COHORTIBVS XII V GEMEL	GALLORVM ET THRACVM SAG ET VII PHRY
LA ET I THRACVM ∞ ET I SEBASTENORVM ∞ ET I DA	GVM ET COHORTIBVS DECEM ET DVABVS
MASCEN ARMENIAC SAG ET I MONTANORVM ET I FLA	V GEMELLA ET I THRACVM ∞ ET I SEBAS
VIA CR ET I ET II VLPIA GALATARVM ET III ET IV CALLAE	TENORVM ∞ ET I DAMASCEN ARMENIAC
COR BRACARAVGVSTAN ET IV ET VI VLPIAE PETREOR	SAG ET I MONTANORVM ET I FLAVIA CR ET
ET SVNT IN SYRIA PALA ● ESTINA SVB MAXIMO	I ET II VLPIA GALATAR ET III ET IV CALLAECOR
	BRACARAVGVSTANOR ET IV ET VI VLPIAE
	PETREOR ET SVNT IN SYRIA PALAESTINA

The earliest example of a more complete inner face is found on one copy of the constitution of 28 September 157 for Raetia (*RGZM* 38).[14] But it is also worth noting that more abbreviation was used on the other known copies of this constitution (TABLE 4). This shows that the conscientiousness of individual copyists was an important factor. From 160 less abbreviation became more general and this coincided with a small increase in the size of the tablets of a diploma. This enlargement is more obvious from 164 (TABLE 5).

Conclusion

In addition to the alterations to the awards to auxiliary soldiers which are recorded on diplomas from the reign of Antoninus Pius (Eck 2006) there are physical changes to the size of the tablets and to other aspects of the engraved text. Whether the introduction of new formulae to record the alterations to these awards precipitated attempts to save time in the engraving of the text on the - not visible - inside of a diploma is unknowable. However, it is clear these new formulae must have caused severe disruption to the accustomed working practices of the office at Rome where diplomas were produced because of the potential number of these documents to be engraved each year. There were about 370 auxiliary units in existence in the reign of Pius of which about 35 were milliary in strength (Holder 2003, 119-120). It has been estimated that a quingenary auxiliary unit would have, on average, ten men eligible for a diploma each year (Holder 2007). Potentially, therefore, the office at Rome would need to produce a maximum of about 4000 auxiliary diplomas each year plus copies of constitutions for the fleets and urban troops. This helps to explain the hints of preengraving of the formulaic parts of the text prior to the official publication of the constitution on which the copies were based. It is thus possible that the changes to some of the for-

---

[13] For another complete tabella I, see Eck-Pangerl 2005b, 101-106.
[14] There is a fragmentary diploma for the same province of 153/157 which starts *equitibus et peditibu[s]* on the inner face but the formula is not complete (*CIL* XVI 117).

mulae coupled with a reduction in the size of the tablets (TABLE 5) encouraged copyists to try to save time by employing more abbreviations on inner faces.

Apparently no checks were made in the workshop to verify what was engraved on auxiliary diplomas; the process was dependent on the conscientiousness of the copyists.[15] Therefore the amount of abbreviation increased until the entire unit list came to be omitted from the inner face in about 143. At this point diplomas were no longer accurate double copies of the original constitution and therefore were not legal or valid according to Roman law. Nothing happened until late 153 when unit lists were re-instated followed shortly afterwards by the separation of the names of alae and cohorts in the list and by the restoration of the *descriptum et recognitum* formula to the inner face. In Roman law diplomas were once more legal. However, the tablets on which this text was engraved reached their smallest size at this time (TABLE 5). It is also from this point that texts on the inside become increasingly less legible. Again, in spite of the recent problems in the production of diplomas, it would appear no checks were made on finished examples. Late in the reign of Pius the size of diplomas was increased making it easier to engrave a fuller copy of the constitution on both faces. While the text on the outer remained clear that on the inner did not always improve in quality after this date. Thus the inner text, the guarantee of legality, still was not necessarily an exact copy of the original constitution. Theoretically such diplomas were not legal but, in practice, it had become accepted that as long as the text on the outer face was an accurate copy of the original the document would be valid (Eck 2007). Indeed, from 178, the name of the recipient and of his unit was engraved in larger letters on the extrinsecus making it look even more like a miniature version of the original bronze constitution at Rome (Weiß 2005, 250-252).

---

[15] A praetorian diploma of 1 March 152 (*RGZM* 33) has however been corrected. On the inner face of tabella II MARCIA was engraved. A line was scored through it and PHIL was engraved. The latter is known to have been the correct home of the recipient because PHILIPP has been written in ink (*RGZM* Farbtafel III). The name of the recipient's tribe has also been corrected. In this instance the recipient would have been based in Rome and the witnesses were his fellow soldiers. It is therefore possible the tablets were only sealed after personal inspection. This option was not available to auxiliaries in the provinces.

Bibliography

W. Eck, 'Die Veränderungen in Konstitutionen und Diplomen unter Antoninus Pius'; in: *Neue Forschungsbeiträge zu den römischen Militärdipomen: eine Bestandsaufnahme.* Ed. M. A. Speidel (Mavors Bd. 14, 2007 forthcoming).

W. Eck & A. Pangerl, 'Neue Diplome für die Heere von Germania superior und Germania inferior' *Zeitschrift für Papyrologie und Epigraphik* 148 (2004) 259-268.

W. Eck & A. Pangerl, 'Neue Militärdiplome für die Truppen der mauretanischen Provinzen' *Zeitschrift für Papyrologie und Epigraphik* 153 (2005) 187-206.

W. Eck & A. Pangerl, 'Neue Militärdiplome für die Provinzen Syria und Iudaea/Syria Palaestina' *Scripta Classica Israelica* 24 (2005) 101-118.

P.A. Holder, 'Auxiliary deployment in the reign of Hadrian'; in: J. J. Wilkes (ed), *Documenting the Roman army: essays in honour of Margaret Roxan.* (Bulletin of the Institute of Classical Studies Supplement 81, London 2003) 101-145.

P.A. Holder, 'A diploma for Mauretania Tingitana of 22 December 144' *Zeitschrift für Papyrologie und Epigraphik* 149 (2004) 275-281.

P.A. Holder, 'Observations on multiple copies of auxiliary diplomas' in ed. M. A. Speidel, *Neue Forschungsbeiträge zu den römischen Militärdiplomen: eine Bestandsaufnahme* (Mavors Bd. 14, 2007 forthcoming).

N. Lambert und J. Scheuerbrandt, *Das Militärdiplom: Quelle zur römischen Armee und zum Urkundenwesen* (Stuttgart 2002).

B. Pferdehirt, *Römische Militärdiplome und Entlassungsurkunden in der Sammlung des Römisch-Germanischen Zentralmuseums* (= Kataloge vor- und frühgeschichtlicher Altertümer, Bd. 37, Mainz 2004).

R. Rebuffat, 'Complements au recueil des Inscriptions Antiques du Maroc' in ed. A.Mastino, *L'Africa romana: atti del IX convegno di studio, Nuoro, 13-15 dicembre 1991* (Sassarri 1992) 439-501.

M.M. Roxan & P.A. Holder, 'A diploma of the Ravenna Fleet: 1 August 142' *Zeitschrift für Papyrologie und Epigraphik* 149 (2004) 267-274.

J. Spaul, 'A note on IAM 809 - CIL XVI 182' *Zeitschrift für Papyrologie und Epigraphik* 96 (1993) 109-110.

J. Spaul, *Cohors²* (BAR International Series 841, Oxford 2000).

P. Weiß, 'Neue Fragmente von Flottendiplomen des 2. Jahrhunderts n. Chr.: mit einem Beitrag zum Urkundenwert des Außentexts bei den Militärdiplomen' *Zeitschrift für Papyrologie und Epigraphik* 150 (2004) 243-252.

TABLE 1: INNER FACE OF TABELLA II: Place of Publication, 74-120

Diploma	Date	Province/Type	Place of Publication
CIL XVI 20	21-5-74	Germania	QVAE FIXA EST ROMAE IN CAPITOLIO
RMD I 2	28-4-75	Moesia	QVAE FIXA EST ROMAE IN CAPITOLIO
RMD IV 206	75?	Aux/Clas	[QVAE FIXA EST ROM]AE IN CAPITOLIO
CIL XVI 22	7-2-78	Moesia	QVAE FIXA EST ROMAE IN CAPITOLIO
CIL XVI 23	15-4-78	Germania	QVAE FIXA EST ROMAE IN CAPITOLIO
CIL XVI 24	8-9-79	Classis	QVAE FIXA EST ROMAE IN CAPITOLIO
ZPE 146, 239	8-9-79	Noricum	QVAE FIXA EST ROMAE IN CAPITOLIO
CIL XVI 26	13-6-80	Pannonia	QVAE FIXA EST ROMAE IN CAPITOLIO
CIL XVI 28	20-9-82	Germania	QVAE FIXA EST ROMAE IN CAPITOLIO
CIL XVI 29	9-6-83	Aegyptus	[QVAE FIXA EST] ROMAE IN CAPITOLIO
CIL XVI 30	3-9-84	Pannonia	QVAE FIXA EST ROMAE IN CAPITOLIO
CIL XVI 18	30-5-85	Urban	QVAE FIXA EST ROMAE IN CAPITOLIO
CIL XVI 31	5-9-85	Pannonia	QVAE FIXA EST ROMAE IN CAPITOLIO
CIL XVI 32	17-2-86	Classis	QVAE FIXA EST ROMAE IN CAPITOLIO
CIL XVI 33	13-5-86	Iudaea	QVAE FIXA EST ROMAE IN CAPITOLIO
CIL XVI 159	9-1-88	MaurTing	QVAE FIXA EST ROMAE IN CAPITOLIO
CIL XVI 35	7-11-88	Syria	QVAE FIXA EST ROMAE IN CAPITOLIO
RMD I 3	7-11-88	Syria	QVAE FIXA EST ROMAE IN CAPITOLIO
CIL XVI 36	27-10-90	Germ sup	QVAE FIXA EST ROMAE
RMD I 5	12-5-91	Syria	QVAE FIXA E[ST ROMAE]
Chiron 2006	12-5-91	Syria	QVAE FIXA EST ROMAE
ZPE 148, 269	14-6-92	Moes inf	QVAE FIXA EST ROMAE
CIL XVI 38	13-7-94	Dalmatia	QVAE FIXA EST ROMAE
CIL XVI 39	16-9-94	Moes sup	QVAE FIXA EST ROMAE
RMD I 6	12-7-96	Moes sup	QV[AE FI]XA EST ROMAE
ZPE 151, 185	9-9-97	Moes inf	[QVAE F]IXA EST ROMAE
CIL XVI 42	20-2-98	Pannonia	omitted
RMD I 7	14-8-99	Moes sup	QVAE F[IX]A EST ROM[AE]
Dacia 2006	14-8-99	Moes inf	QVAE FIXA EST R[OMAE]
CIL XVI 46	8-5-100	Moes sup	QVAE FIXA EST ROMAE
RMD III 142	12-6-100	Classis	QVAE FIXA EST ROMAE
RMD III 143	15-4/15-6-101	Moes sup	QVAE FIXA EST ROMAE
CIL XVI 48	19-1-103	Britannia	QVAE FIXA EST ROMAE
CIL XVI 49	12-1-105	Moes sup	QVAE FIXA EST ROMAE
CIL XVI 50	13-5-105	Moes inf	omitted
RGZM 10	13-5-105	Moes inf	QVAE FIXA EST ROMAE
RGZM 11	13-5-105	Moes inf	QVAE FIXA [EST ROMAE]
RMD I 8	1-5/15-7-105	Britannia	QVAE FIXA EST R[OMAE]
RMD I 9	24-9-105	Aegyptus	QVAE FIXA EST ROMAE
CIL XVI 55	30-6-107	Raetia	QVAE FIXA EST ROMAE
CIL XVI 56	24-11-107	MaurCaes	QVAE FIXA EST ROMAE
RGZM 14	9/12-107	Moes inf	QVAE FI[XA EST ROMAE]
REMA 1, 103	27-7-108	Moes sup	QVAE FIXA EST ROMAE
RMD III 148	14-10-109	Dacia	QVAE FIXA EST ROMAE
CIL XVI 163	2-7-110	Dacia	QVAE FIXA EST ROM[AE]
CIL XVI 164	2-7-110	Dacia	QVAE FIXA [EST RO]MAE
RMD IV 222	25-9-111	Moes inf	QVA[E] FIXA EST ROMAE
AES 5, 247	29-1/29-3-112	Moes inf	omitted
RMD V 344	29-1/29-3-112?	Moes inf	QVAE FIX[A EST ROMAE]
RMD IV 223	3-5-112	Pann sup	QVAE FIXA EST ROMAE
RMD II 86	16-12-113	Pann sup	[QVAE FIXA EST RO]MAE
RMD IV 226	3/4-5-114	Dacia	omitted
RMD IV 227/141	19-7-114	Thracia	omitted
CIL XVI 61	1-9-114	Pann inf	[QVAE] FIXA EST ROMAE
RMD V 345/152 +228	1-9-114	Pann inf	QVAE FIXA EST ROMAE
CIL XVI 166	28-3-118	MaurTing	QVAE [FIXA EST ROMA]E IN MVRO POST TEMPLVM [DIVI AVG] AD MINERVAM
ArchBulg 9, 39	25-12-119	Classis	omitted
RMD I 18	114/120	MaurTing	QVA[E FIXA EST ROMAE IN MVRO POST TE]MPL DIVI AVG AD [MINERVAM]

TABLE 2: INNER FACE OF TABELLA II: First line, 88-161

Diploma	Date	Province/Type	First Line	Descript. Formula
CIL XVI 159	9-1-88	MaurTing	QVILLO QVI QVINA ET VICENA PLVRAVE	D
CIL XVI 35	7-11-88	Syria	NIORVM MVSVLAMIORVM ET SVNT IN	D
RMD I 3	7-11-88	Syria	IPSIS LIBERIS POSTERISQVE EORVM CIVITA	D
CIL XVI 36	27-10-90	Germ sup	QVORVM NOMINA SVBSCRIPTA SVNT IPSIS LIBE	D
RMD V 334	74/90	Auxilia	[...]	D
RMD I 5	12-5-91	Syria	IPSIS LIBERIS POSTERISQ[VE EORVM CIVITA]	D
Chiron 2006	12-5-91	Syria	SVBSCRIPTA SVNT [IP]SIS LIBERIS POS-TERIS[QVE]	D
ZPE 148, 269	14-6-92	Moes inf	DIMISSIS HONESTA MISSIONE QVORVM	D
ZPE 153, 207	14-6-92	Moes inf	[...]	D
CIL XVI 38	13-7-94	Dalmatia	DEDIT ET CONVBIVM CVM VXORIBVS	D
CIL XVI 39	16-9-94	Moes sup	AVT PLVRA MERVERVNT ITEM DIMISSIS	D
RMD V 335	16-9-94	Moes sup	AVT PLVRA MERVER[V]NT ITEM DIMIS	D
RMD I 6	12-7-96	Moes sup	SVBSCRIPTA SVNT IPSIS LIBERIS POSTERIS	D
CIL XVI 41	1-97	Auxilia	[...]E SVB IVLIO MAR	?
ZPE 151, 185	9-9-97	Moes inf	[...]BSCRIPTA SVNT IPSIS LIBERIS [...]	D
RMD III 140	9-9-97	Moes inf	[PENDIIS EMERITIS A OCTAVIO] FRONTONE	?
CIL XVI 42	20-2-98	Pannonia	RISQVE EORVM CIVITATEM DEDIT ET	No
RMD I 7	14-8-99	Moes sup	[I]PSIS LIBERIS POSTE[RISQVE EORVM CIVI]	D
Dacia 2006	14-8-99	Moes inf	TEM DEDIT ET CONVBIVM CVM VXORIBVS	D
RMD III 141	14/30-9-99	Auxilia	[... POSTERI]SQVE EORVM CIVITATEM	?
CIL XVI 46	8-5-100	Moes sup	ITEM DIMISSIS HONESTA MISSIONE QVI QV	D
RMD III 142	12-6-100	Classis	CIVITAS IIS DATA AVT SIQVI CAELI	D
RMD III 143	15-4/6-101	Moes sup	CVM EST CIVITAS IIS DATA AVT [SIQVI C]AE	D
CIL XVI 48	19-3-103	Britannia	SCRIPTA SVNT IPSIS LIBERIS POSTE	D
CIL XVI 49	12-1-105	Moes sup	VM CVM VXORIBVS QVAS TVNC HABVIS-SENT CVM EST	D
RMD V 339	12-1?-105	Moes sup	[...]	D
CIL XVI 50	13-5-105	Moes inf	TEM DEDIT ET CONVBIVM CVM VXORIBVS	No
RGZM 10	13-5-105	Moes inf	NOMINA SVBSCRIPTA SVNT IPSIS LIBERIS	D
RGZM 11	13-5-105	Moes inf	CONV[BIV]M CVM VX[ORIBVS ...]	D
RMD I 8	1-5/13-7-105	Britannia	[CVM EST] CIVITAS IS DATA A[VT SIQVI CAELIBES]	D
CIL XVI 51	1-5/13-7-105	Britannia	[... DEDIT ET CO]NVBIVM [CVM VXORIBVS ...]	?
RMD I 9	24-9-105	Aegyptus	SVNT IPSIS LIBERIS POSTERISQVE EO	D
RMD V 342	92/105	Aux/Clas	ITEM D[IMISSIS HONESTA MISSIONE QVO]	?
CIL XVI 55	30-6-107	Raetia	NVBIVM CVM VXORIBVS QVAS TVNC HA	D
CIL XVI 56	24-11-107	MaurCaes	CVM EST CIV[IT]AS [II]S DATA AVT SI QVI	D
RGZM 14	9/12-107	Moes inf	IVM CVM VXORIBV[S QVAS TVNC]	D
RMD III 146	1/5-108	Britannia?	[DATA A]VT SIQVI C[AELIBES ...]	?
REMA 1, 103	27-7-108	Moes sup	[QVA]S TVNC HABVISSENT CVM EST CIV[ITAS]	D
RMD III 148	14-9-109	Dacia	NOMINA SVBSCRIPTA SVNT IPSIS LIBE	D
CIL XVI 161	14-10-109	MaurTing	EORVM CIVITATEM D[EDIT ET CONVBIVM CVM VXO]	?
RMD I 12	99/110	MaurTing	[... CO]NVBIVM	?
RMD I 13	105/110	MaurTing	[... CIVITAT]EM DEDIT ET	?
RMD IV 220	17-2?-110	Dacia	[CONVBIVM CVM VXOR]IBVS QVAS TVNC	?
CIL XVI 163	2-7-110	Dacia	RVM NOMINA SVBSCRIPTA SVNT IPSIS LIBERIS POSTE	D
CIL XVI 164	2-7-110	Pann inf	[TEM DEDIT ET C]ONVBIVM CVM VXORIBVS QVAS	D
RMD IV 222	25-9-111	Moes inf	TEM DEDIT ET CONVBIVM CVM VXO	D
AES 5, 247	29-1/29-3-112	Moes inf	[...]	No
RMD V 344	29-1/29-3-112?	Moes inf	[...]	D
RMD IV 223	3-5-112	Pann sup	EORVM CIVITATEM DEDIT ET CONV	D
RMD III 149	82/112	Auxilia	[... QVORVM NO]MINA SVB	?

Diploma	Date	Province/Type	First Line	Descript. Formula
RMD II 86	16-12-113	Pann sup	[QVAS TVNC H]ABVISSENT CVM EST CIVI-TAS	D
RMD IV 226	3/4-5-114	Dacia	DATA AVT SIQVI [CA]ELIBES ESSEN[T CVM IS QVAS]	No
RMD IV 227/14	19-7-114	Thracia	ESSENT CVM IIS QV[AS] POSTEA [D]VXI[SSENT]	No
CIL XVI 61	1-9-114	Pann inf	[PO]ST DVXISS DVM TAXAT	D
RMD V 345/152 +228	1-9-114	Pann inf	[... AV]T SIQ CAE[LIB] ESS CVM IS QVAS]	D
RMD V 346/154	1-9-114	Pann inf	DVXI[SS DVMT]AX SINGVLI SI[NGVLAS]	?
ZPE 152, 234	1-5/31-8-115	Auxilia	MISSIONE QVORV[M NOMINA SVBSCRIPTA SVNT]	?
CIL XVI 65	98/117?	Auxilia	[...]QVE EORVM C[IVITATEM ...]	?
CIL XVI 166	28-3-118	MaurTing	[... CV]M EST CIVITAS IIS DATA AVT	D
AMN 39-40, 25	3/4-119	Pann inf	[... AV]T SI[QVI CAELIBES ...]	?
RMD V 349	118/119	Moes inf	TEA DVXISSENT [DVMTAXAT SINGVLI SIN]	?
ArchBulg 9, 39	25-12-119	Classis	QVAS TVNC HABVISSENT CVM	No
RMD V 352	25-12?-119	Classis	CVM IIS Q[VAS POSTEA DVXISSENT DVM]	?
ZPE 152, 237	14/31-12-119	Aux/Clas	[... SINGVLI SINGVL[AS]	?
RMD IV 232	16-5/13-6-120	Auxilia	[... DV]XISSENT DVMTAX	?
RMD V 356	19-10-120	Moes inf	[CVM VXORIBVS QVAS TV]NC HABVISSENT CVM EST	?
RMD I 18	114/120	MaurTing	[...]	D
CIL XVI 168	13-1/3-121	Classis	CIVIT DEDIT [ET CONVB CVM VXORIB QVAS TVNC]	?
RMD V 359	19-3-122	Auxilia	[... POSTEA DVXISS]ENT DVMTAXAT [...]	
CIL XVI 69	17-7-122	Britannia	NOMINA SVBSCRIPTA SVNT IPSIS LIBERIS POSTERISQV	
REMA 1, 64	17-7-122	Britannia	[POMPEI]VM FAICONEM Q[VORVM ...]	
RMD I 20	118/122	Auxilia	[...]	No
RMD V 362	118/122	Aux/Clas	[...]	No
RMD IV 233	10-8-123	DaciaPor?	CAELIBES ESSENT C[VM IIS QVAS POSTEA]	
ZPE 152, 238	17-10-123	Auxilia	[... QVAS PO]STEA DVXISSE[NT]	
RMD V 363	4/6-124	Auxilia	[CAELIBES ESSEN]T CVM IIS QVAS POSTEA	
ZPE 152, 242	7-126	Auxilia	[...] SINGVL[I SINGVLAS]	
CIL XVI 71	ante 127	?	[...] ET CONVBIVM [CVM ...]	
RMD I 30	14/30-4-127	Auxilia	[...] K MAI	
RGZM 23	20-8-127	Moes inf	A D XIII K SEPTEMBRES	
CIL XVI 74	18-2-129	Classis	DVMTAXAT SINGVLI SINGVLAS	
CIL XVI 75	22-3-129	Dacia inf	SING SINGVLAS [A] D XI K APR	
RMD I 34	30-4-129	Pann inf	PR K MAI	
RMD IV 245	114/129?	Auxilia	[...]	
RMD V 375	125/129?	Moes inf	DATA AVT SIQVI [CAELIBES ESSENT CVM IIS]	
CIL XVI 76	2-7-133	Pann sup	[A D] VI NON IVL	
RMD III 159	9/12-132/133	Germ sup	SING SINGVL [A D ...]	
CIL XVI 78	2-4-134	Moes inf	A D IIII NON APR	
CIL XVI 79	15-9-134	Classis	A D XVII K OC	
CIL XVI 105	129/134	Raetia	[...]	
RMD IV 251	19-5-135	Pann inf	XIIII K IVN	
RMD I 36	135?	Auxilia	A D I[...]	
CIL XVI 83	28-2-138	Moes inf	PR K [FEBR]	
RMD V 385/260	10-10-138	Thracia	[...]	
RMD IV 255	117/138	Aux/Clas	[...]	
RMD I 38	13-2-139	Classis	IDIB FEBR	
RMD V 386	30-10-139	Raetia	A D [III K NOV]	
CIL XVI 87	22-11-139	Syria Pal	A D X K DEC	
CIL XVI 177	26-11-139	Classis	A D VI ⌐K⌐ DEC	

TABLE 2: INNER FACE OF TABELLA II: First line, 88-161 (cont.)

Diploma	Date	Province/Type	First Line	Descript. Formula
RMD I 39	13-12-140	Dacia inf	EX NVMER EQ ILLYRIC	
AMN 39-40, 46	133/140	Dacia Por	[...]	
RGZM 29	15-1-142	Syria Pal	A D XIIX [K FEBR]	
RMD IV 264	1-8-142	Classis	K AVG	
RMD V 392	1-8-142	Classis	K AVG	
RMD V 396	9/10-142	Auxilia	[...]	
RMD I 40	138/142	Dacia Por	[COH II] AUG NERV BRIT [∞ CVI PRAEST]	
RMD IV 266	7-8-143	Pann inf	A D VII ID AVG	
RMD V 398	22-12-144	MaurTing	COH V DEL[MAT C R CVI PRAEST]	
RMD I 44	26-10-145	Classis	A D VII K NOV	
CIL XVI 178	19-7-146	Pann sup	A D XIV K AVG	
RMD V 402	144/146	Auxilia	ALAE CALL [... CVI PRAEST]	
CIL XVI 95	29-2-148	Praetorian	PR K MART	
CIL XVI 96	9-10-148	Pann sup	COH I VLP PANN CVI PRAEST	
CIL XVI 179	9-10-148	Pann inf	A D VII ID OCT	
CIL XVI 180	9-10-148	Pann inf	A D VII ID OCT	
RMD II 99	140/148	Noricum	[...]	
CIL XVI 97	5-7-149	Pann sup	COH V CALL LVCENS CVI PRAEST	
CIL XVI 99	1-8-150	PS/PI	K AVG	
RGZM 31	20-1-151	Moes sup	COH III BRITTONVM CVI PRAEST	
RMD V 404	24-9-151	Dacia Por	COH I VLP BR ∞ CVI PR[A]EST	
RGZM 33	1-3-152	Praetorian	K MAR	
RMD V 406	4/6-152	Pann sup	[...]	
CIL XVI 100	5-9-152	Classis	NON SEPT	
RGZM 34	26-10-153	MaurTing	ALAE I AVG GALLOR CR CVI PRAEST	
ZPE 153, 197	26-10-153	MaurTing	[ALAE I AVG GALL]OR CR CVI PRAEST	
RMD V 412	148/153	Moes inf	COH I CILIC SAG CVI PRAEFVIT	
ZPE 146, 247	27-9-154	Pann inf	[QVAS POSTE]A DVXISS DVMTAXAT SINGVLIS	D
CIL XVI 110/RMD I 47	27-9-154	Dacia Por	[COH I] VLP BRITT ∞ [CVI PRAEST]	D
CIL XVI 104	3-11-154	Pann sup	A D III NON NOV	D
RMD II 102	8-2-157	Pann inf	COH I THR GERM CVI PRAEST	No
RMD II 103	8-2-157	Pann inf	A D VI ID F[EBR]	D
RGZM 37	23-4-157	Moes sup	A D IX K MAI	D
CIL XVI 107	13-12?-157	Dacia sup	[ID DEC]	D
RMD V 420	27-2-158	Britannia	[...]	D
CIL XVI 108	8-7-158	Dacia sup	A D VIII ID IVL	No
ZPE 152, 256	7-158	Aux/Clas	A D X [...]	?
RMD V 424	21-6-159	Pann sup	A D [XI K IVL]	D
RMD II 105	7-2-160	Classis	A D VII ID FEBR	D
RMD IV 277	7-2-160	Classis	A D VII ID FEB	D
RGZM 39	7-2-160	Classis	A D VII [ID FEBR]	D
RMD V 427	7-2-160	Classis	A D VII ID FEBR	D
RGZM 41	7-3-160	Syria Pal	NON MART	D
RMD IV 278	18-12-160	Raetia	A D XV K [IAN]	D
RMD V 429	148/160	Auxilia	[A] D III [...]	?
RMD V 430	8-2-161	Pann sup	A D VI ID FE[B]	D
RMD IV 283	154/161	Aux/Clas	[...]	D

TABLE 3: INNER FACE OF TABELLA I: Abbreviated Unit Lists, 140-159

Diploma	Date	Province	Inner Face
RMD II 95/58	3/11-140	Raetia	complete
RMD V 387	11/12-140	Raetia	complete
RMD I 39	13-12-140	Dacia inferior	complete
RMD V 391	7/9-141	Pannonia superior	complete
ZPE 150, 253	10-12-141/31-7-142	Arabia	complete
RMD IV 268	141/142	Pannonia inferior	complete
RGZM 29	15-1-142	Syria Palaestina	complete
RMD IV 266	7-8-143	Pannonia inferior	abbreviated
CIL XVI 90	23-2-144	Dacia superior	unit named
RMD V 397	7-9-144	Pannonia inferior	abbreviated
RMD V 398	22-12-144	Mauretania Tingitana	unit named
RMD V 399/165	7-4-145	Moesia inferior	complete
CIL XVI 91	9/10-145	Pannonia inferior	?abbreviated
REMA 1, 75	143/145	Pannonia superior	?abbreviated
RMD II 97	1/3-146	Britannia	abbreviated
CIL XVI 178	19-7-146	Pannonia superior	abbreviated
RMD IV 269	19-7-146	Dacia inferior	not available
RMD V 401	11-8-146	Pannonia inferior	abbreviated
CIL XVI 93	10-12-145/9-12-146	Britannia	complete
RMD IV 270	1-1/9-12-146	Moesia inferior	complete
CIL XVI 94	1-1/9-12-147	Raetia	abbreviated
CIL XVI 179	9-10-148	Pannonia inferior	abbreviated
CIL XVI 180	9-10-148	Pannonia inferior	abbreviated
CIL XVI 96	9-10-148	Pannonia superior	abbreviated
CIL XVI 97	5-7-149	Pannonia superior	abbreviated
CIL XVI 99	1-8-150	Pannoniae utr.	abbreviated
RGZM 31	20-1-151	Moesia superior	abbreviated
RGZM 32	24-9-151	Pannonia superior + Noricum	ink inner face
RMD V 404	24-9-151	Dacia Porolissensis	abbreviated
ZPE 148, 262	5-9-152	Germania inferior	not available
RMD V 408	5-9-152	Germania inferior	?unit named
RGZM 35	5-9-152?	Germania inferior	unit named
RMD III 167	9/10-152	Pannonia inferior	?abbreviated
CIL XVI 101	1/2-153	Raetia	abbreviated
RMD IV 274	5-3-153	Germania superior	abbreviated
RGZM 34	26-10-153	Mauretania Tingitana	complete
RMD V 409	26-10-153	Mauretania Tingitana	complete
RMD V 410	26-10-153	Mauretania Tingitana	complete
RMD V 411	26-10-153	Mauretania Tingitana	complete
RMD I 46	10/12-153	Raetia	abbreviated
Chiron 2006	10/12-153	Syria	complete
CIL XVI 110/RMD I 47	27-9-154	Dacia Porolissensis	complete
ZPE 146, 247	27-9-154	Pannonia inferior	complete
CIL XVI 104	3-11-154	Pannonia superior	complete
RMD I 48	28-12-154	Mauretania Tingitana	mistake
REMA 1, 91	10-3-155	Thracia	complete
RMD V 414	c.155	Moesia inferior	complete
CIL XVI 107	13-12-156	Dacia superior	complete
RMD V 415	154/156	Pannonia inferior	complete
RMD V 416	155/156	Pannonia superior	complete
RMD II 102	8-2-157	Pannonia inferior	complete
RMD II 103	8-2-157	Pannonia inferior	complete
RMD V 417	23-4-157	Thracia	complete
RGZM 37	23-4-157	Moesia superior	complete

TABLE 3: INNER FACE OF TABELLA I: Abbreviated Unit Lists, 140-159 (cont.)

Diploma	Date	Province	Inner Face
RMD V 418	23-4-157	Moesia superior	complete
CIL XVI 181	10-12-156/early 157	Mauretania Tingitana	complete
RGZM 38	28-9-157	Raetia	complete
RMD III 170	28-9-157	Raetia	complete
RMD II 104/51	28-9-157	Raetia	complete
RMD IV 275	28-9-157	Raetia	complete
CIL XVI 106	28-9?-157	Syria	complete
CIL XVI 182	early/9-12-157	Mauretania Tingitana	complete
RMD I 50	c.157	Moesia inferior	complete
CIL XVI 183	10-12-156/9-12-157	Raetia	complete
RMD V 420	27-2-158	Britannia	complete
CIL XVI 108	8-7-158	Dacia superior	abbreviated
RMD I 52	7-158	Germania inferior	complete
CIL XVI 112	27-12-157 or 158	Pannonia inferior	complete
RMD I 53	9/12-157 or 158	Mauretania Tingitana	complete
REMA 1, 96	1-1/9-12-158	Thracia	complete
RMD V 421	10-12-157/9-12-158	Syria Palaestina	complete
RMD V 422	21-6-159	Pannonia superior	complete
RMD V 423	21-6-159	Pannonia superior	complete
REMA 1, 80	21-6-159	Pannonia superior	complete
REMA 1, 83	21-6-159	Pannonia superior	complete

After W. Eck – P. Weiß ZPE 135, 198

TABLE 4: INNER FACE OF TABELLA I: equitibus et peditibus Formula, 127-161

Diploma	Date	Province	equitibus et peditibus Formula
RMD IV 239	20-8-127	German inf	equit et pedit exerc pf qui milit in alis et coh quae app
RMD IV 240	20-8-127	Britannia	[ ]mil in al et coh qu app
RMD V 368	10/12-127	Africa	[ ] quae app
ZPE 152, 243	10/12-127	Africa	[ ] quae app
CIL XVI 75	22-3-129	Dacia inf	eq et pe⌐d¬ qui mil in al et coh quae app
RMD V 371	22-3-129	Syria	[ ] coh quae app[
Chiron 2006	22-3-129	Syria	eq et pedit qui mil in al et coh quae a[pp
Chiron 2006	22-3-129	Syria	[ ] et coh [
RMD V 373	128/4-129	Africa	[ ] et ped qui mil in a[
RMD IV 243	5/12-129	Raetia	[q]ui m in a[l et co]h qu [app]
RMD V 376	1-1/9-12-130	Dacia inf	equ et pe[d] coho[
RMD II 90	129/130	German sup	eq et ped qui mil in [ ] ap
ZPE 153, 188	131	Maur Caes	pe[dit] qu[i m i]n coh I Fl Mus
RMD V 377	128/131	Maur Caes	[pe]d qui m in [
RMD V 378	130/131	Dacia Porol	iquitib et peditib [ ] quae appell
ZPE 156, 245	130/131	Britannia	equit et ped qui mil[
RMD IV 247	9-9-132/133	Moesia sup	[ ] al et coh quae app
CIL XVI 174	9/12-132/133	Noricum	[ ] alis et coh [
CIL XVI 173	18-8-129/132	Maur Ting	[i]n alis et coh quae [
CIL XVI 76	2-7-133	Pannon sup	equit et p[edit] qui milit in alis et coh quae appell
RMD I 35	2-7-133	Dacia Porol	eq et ped qui mil in al et coh quae app
CIL XVI 78	2-4-134	Moesia inf	equ et ped qui mil in alis et [c]oh quae app
CIL XVI 80	16-10-134	German sup	equ et ped qui mil in al et coh [
RMD IV 250	16-10/13-11-134	Pannon sup	eq et ped qui mil in al et ⌐c¬oh qu[a]e app
SCI 24, 114	132/134	Syria	[ped] et eq q m[
CIL XVI 82	14-4-135	Britannia	[ ] quae app
RMD IV 251	19-5-135	Pannon inf	equ et ped qui mil in al et coh qu app
RMD V 382	31-12-135	Maur Ting	[c]oh quae appellantur
CIL XVI 103	127/136	Syria	[et c]oh q a

Diploma	Date	Province	equitibus et peditibus Formula
RMD III 160	136/137	Syria Palaest	[　　　　al]is et coh q[
CIL XVI 83	28-2-138	Moesia inf	[　　　　a]l et coh q app
CIL XVI 84	16-6-138	Pannon sup	[　　　] in al et coh q app
RMD III 161	1-3/10-7-138	Lycia Pamph	pedit et equit qui [
RMD V 384	136/10-7-138	Dacia sup	eq et ped q m [　　　　] q ap
RMD V 385/260	10-10-138	Thracia	[pe]dit et [e]quit qui militav in coh qua[e a]pp
RMD II 94	10-7/12-138	Raetia	[eq] et ped qui mil in [
CIL XVI 175	3/8-139	Pannon inf	[　　　　　] et coh q ap
RMD V 386	30-10-139	Raetia	[　　pe]d qui mil in alis [et c]oh q app
CIL XVI 87	22-11-139	Syria Palaest	eq et ped q mil in al et coh q ap
RMD I 39	13-12-140	Dacia inf	eq et ped q mil in al et coh q app
RMD V 387	11/12-140	Raetia	[　　　]m in al [e]t coh [
RGZM 29	15-1-142	Syria Palaest	eq et ped qu[i　　　　co]h q a
ZPE 150, 253	10-12-141/31-7-142	Arabia	eq et ped q mi[l in
RMD IV 266	7-8-143	Pannon inf	eq et ped qui milit in alis et coh et sunt
CIL XVI 90	23-2-144	Dacia sup	[　　　] qui mil in al et coh quae app
RMD V 397	7-9-144	Pannon inf	[　　q]ui mil in alis [e]t coh [e]t sunt
RMD V 398	22-12-144	Maur Ting	[　　m]il in alis et coh quae [
RMD V 399/165	7-4-145	Moesia inf	eq et ped q m in al et coh q a
CIL XVI 178	19-7-146	Pannon sup	eq et ped q m in al et coh et sunt
RMD IV 270	1/12-146	Moesia inf	eq et ped qui mil in al [
CIL XVI 93	10-12-145/9-12-146	Britannia	eq et ped q[　　]
CIL XVI 94	1-1/9-12-147	Raetia	[　　　　] m in al et [
CIL XVI 96	9-10-148	Pannon sup	eq et ped q m in al et coh et sunt
CIL XVI 179	9-10-148	Pannon inf	eq et ped q m in al et coh et sunt
CIL XVI 180	9-10-148	Pannon inf	[eq et p]ed q m in al et coh et sunt
CIL XVI 97	5-7-149	Pannon sup	eq et ped q m in al et coh et sunt
CIL XVI 99	1-8-150	Pannon utr	equit qui milit in al quae sunt
RGZM 31	20-1-151	Moesia sup	eq et ped q m in al et coh et sunt
RMD V 404	24-9-151	Dacia Porol	eq [e]t [p]ed q m in al et coh [et] sunt
RMD V 407	4/6-152	Moesia sup	[　　q]ui mili[t
RMD V 408	5-9-152	German inf	[　　　　i]n al et coh [
RGZM 35	5-9-152?	German inf	eq et ped qui m[il　　　] quae app
RMD I 46	1/3-153	Raetia	[　　　　i]n al et [coh et s]unt
CIL XVI 101	10/12-153	Raetia	[　　　　] in al et coh [et
RGZM 34	26-10-153	Maur Ting	eq et ped q m in al et coh q a
RMD V 409	26-10-153	Maur Ting	eq et ped q m in a[l et
RMD V 410	26-10-153	Maur Ting	eq et ped q m in al [et
RMD V 411	26-10-153	Maur Ting	[　　　　] coh q a
ZPE 146, 247	27-9-154	Pannon inf	equit et pedit qui milit in alis quae appel
CIL XVI 110	27-9-154	Dacia Porol	[　　　] qui mil in alis quae [
CIL XVI 104	3-11-154	Pannon sup	eq et ped q m in alis q a
REMA 1, 91	10-3-155	Thracia	ped et equit qui mil in coh q[ua]e app
RMD V 415	154/156	Pannon inf	[　　　　　] q a
RMD V 416	155/156	Pannon sup	[eq et] ped q[m in] al q a
CIL XVI 107	13-12-156	Dacia sup	[　　　　m]ilit in alis quae [
RMD II 102	8-2-157	Pannon inf	equit et pedit qui mil in al quae ap
RMD II 103	8-2-157	Pannon inf	equit et pedit qui mil in al quae app
RGZM 37	23-4-157	Moesia sup	equit et pedit qui mil in al quae appel
CIL XVI 181	10-12-156/early 157	Maur Ting	eq ..d qui milit in al[
RGZM 38	28-9-157	Raetia	equitib et peditib qui militaver in alis qua[e] appellantur
RMD III 170	28-9-157	Raetia	equit et pedit qui milit in al [quae
RMD II 104/51	28-9-157	Raetia	equitib et peditib qui milit in al [quae] appel
RMD IV 275	28-9-157	Raetia	[　　　　　mili]t in alis quae appel
CIL XVI 106	28-9?-157	Syria	[　　pe]d q m in alis q appe[l
CIL XVI 182	early/9-12-157	Maur Ting	[eq et] ped qui mil[
RMD I 56	138/142 or 153/157	Maur Ting	eq et pe[d
CIL XVI 117	153/157	Raetia	equitibus et peditibu[s
RMD V 420	27-2-158	Britannia	[　　　q]ui mil in al quae ap
CIL XVI 108	8-7-158	Dacia sup	eq et ped q m in al et co[h] et [v]ex q sunt cum Maur gent in
RMD I 52	7-158	German inf	[　　　　i]n al quae app

TABLE 4: INNER FACE OF TABELLA I: equitibus et peditibus Formula, 127-161 (cont.)

Diploma	Date	Province	equitibus et peditibus Formula
REMA 1, 96	1-1/9-12-158	Thracia	peditib et equit q[
CIL XVI 112	27-12-157 or 158	Pannon inf	[mil]it {in}in al quae app
RMD I 53	9/12-157 or 158	Maur Ting	[in ali]s q a
RGZM 40	1/2-160	Moesia sup	[in a]l q ⌐a⌐
CIL XVI 111	1/2-160	Moesia sup	equit et ped qui mil in [al
RGZM 41	7-3-160	Syria Palaest	equitibus et peditibus qui militaverunt in alis quae appellantur
SCI 24, 101	7-3-160	Syria Palaest	equitibus et peditibus qui militaverunt in alis quae appellantur
RMD III 173	7-3-160	Syria Palaest	[ ] peditibus qui militaverunt in alis [quae appella]ntur
RGZM 42	156/160	Pannon sup	eq et ped q m in [
RMD V 430	8-2-161	Pannon sup	equit et pedit qui milit in a[li]s q a
RMD I 55	8-2-161	Moesia sup	equitib et pedit qui milit in al quae appell
RMD II 107	1/3-161	Maur Ting	[mi]lit in [a]l q app
RMD I 60	154/161	Syria Palaest	[ ] pedit [
RMD III 175	154/161	Raetia	equitib [et
RMD IV 284	154/161	Pannon inf	[ ] milit in al [
RMD III 174	154/161	Pannon sup	eq et pe[d
RMD I 57	138/161	Maur Ting	eq et ped [

TABLE 5: SIZE OF AUXILIARY DIPLOMAS, 127-179

Diploma	Date	Size in cms	Comments
RMD IV 239	20-8-127	14.8 x 12.1	tab I
RMD IV 240	20-8-127	x 12.3	tab I
RMD IV 241	20-8-127	14.5/14/6 x 12.4/12.5	tab I + II combined
RGZM 23	20-8-127	14.9 x 12.4	tab II
CIL XVI 75	22-3-129	15.7 x 12.2	tab I + II combined
RMD I 34	30-4-129	14.8 x 13.0	tab II
ZPE 153, 188	131	15.0 x 12.3	tab I
RMD IV 247	9-9-132/133	x 11.4	tab I
CIL XVI 76	2-7-133	14.75 x 11.8	tab I only, tab II i
RMD I 35	2-7-133	14.7 x 11.7	tab I
CIL XVI 78	2-4-134		tab I + II; measurements not given
CIL XVI 80	16-10-134	15.3 x 12.4	tab I; height restored
RMD IV 250	16-10/13-11-134	15.9 x 12.4	tab I
CIL XVI 82	14-4-135	15.4 x 12.7	tab I; height restored
RMD IV 251	19-5-135	15.6 x 12.1	tab I
		15.5 x 12.0	tab II
RMD V 382	31-12-135	x 12.0	tab I
CIL XVI 83	28-2-138	14.0 x 12.0	tab I + II combined; height restored
RMD III 161	1-3/10-7-138	14.0 x 11.0	tab I
RMD V 386	30-10-139	13.0 x 12.0	tab I + II combined
CIL XVI 87	22-11-139	13.0 x 11.8	tab I + II combined
RMD I 39	13-12-140	14.3 x 11.5	tab I + II combined
RGZM 29	15-1-142	14.3 x 11.1	tab I
		14.3 x 11.2	tab II
RMD I 40	138/142	x 10.6	tab II
ZPE 150, 253	10-12-141/9-12-142	x 12.0	tab I
RMD IV 266	7-8-143	14.5 x 11.6	tab I
		14.5 x 11.5	tab II
RMD V 398	22-12-144	13.4 x 11.1	tab I; height restored
		13.2 x 10.9	tab II; height restored
RMD V 399/165	7-4-145	x 11.1	tab I
CIL XVI 178	19-7-146	14.0 x 10.8	tab I + II combined
RMD IV 269	19-7-146	13.7 x 10.5	tab I + II combined
RMD IV 270	1-1/9-12-146	13.0 x 11.3	tab I; height restored

Diploma	Date	Size in cms	Comments
CIL XVI 93	10-12-145/9-12-146	x 10.8	tab I
RMD V 402	144/146	x 9.5	tab II
CIL XVI 95	29-2-148	12.4 x 10.3	tab I + II combined
CIL XVI 96	9-10-148	12.6 x 10.6	tab I + II combined
CIL XVI 179	9-10-148	14.0 x 10.5	tab I + II combined
CIL XVI 180	9-10-148	14.2 x 10.5	tab I + II combined
RMD II 100	1-9/9-12-148	14.4 x 11.1	tab I
CIL XVI 97	5-7-149	13.0 x 10.5	tab I + II combined
CIL XVI 99	1-8-150	14.0 x 10.8	tab I + II combined
RGZM 31	20-1-151	13.2 x	tab I
		10.4/10.6	tab II
		13.1 x 10.5	
RGZM 32	24-9-151	13.0 x 10.2	tab I
		x 10.2	tab II
RMD V 404	24-9-151	13.0 x 10.8	tab I + II combined
RMD V 406	4/6-152	x 11.0	tab II
ZPE 148, 262	5-9-152	13.2 x 10.4	tab I + II combined
RGZM 34	26-10-153	12.9/13.2 x 10.4	tab I + II combined
Chiron 2006	10/12-153	13.2 x 10.5	tab I; height restored
RMD V 412	148/153	13.6 x 10.7	tab II
CIL XVI 110/RMD I 47	27-9-154	12.0 x 9.5	tab I; height restored
ZPE 146, 247	27-9-154	12.8 x 9.3	tab I
		12.9 x 9.5	tab II
CIL XVI 104	3-11-154	11.8 x 9.8	tab I + II combined
REMA 1, 91	10-3-155	13.3 x 10.5	tab I
CIL XVI 107	13-12-156	x 10.2	tab I + II combined
RMD II 102	8-2-157	13.1 x 10.0	tab I
		13.1 x 9.9	tab II
RMD II 103	8-2-157	12.8 x 9.6	tab I
		13.0 x 9.5	tab II
RGZM 37	23-4-157	12.7 x 9.8	tab I + II combined
RGZM 38	28-9-157	12.2 x 9.7	tab I
RMD III 170	28-9-157	12.8 x 10.0	tab I; height restored
RMD IV 275	28-9-157	x 9.5	tab I
CIL XVI 106	28-9?-157	x 9.7	tab I
CIL XVI 181	10-12-156/early 157	x 10.0	tab I
RMD V 420	27-2-158	12.6 x 9.6	tab I + II combined; height restored
CIL XVI 108	8-7-158	12.0 x 9.5	tab I + II combined
RMD V 422	21-6-159	x 9.0	tab I
RMD V 424	21-6-159	x 9.5	tab II
CIL XVI 112	27-12-157 or 158	x 9.0	tab I
CIL XVI 111	1/2-160	x 9.6	tab I
RGZM 41	7-3-160	12.9 x 10.0	tab I
		13.1 x 10.0	tab II
SCI 24, 101	7-3-160	13.2 x 10.0	tab I
RMD III 173	7-3-160	12.8 x 10.0	tab I; height restored
RMD IV 278	18-12-160	13.1 x 9.9	tab I + II combined; height restored
RMD I 55	8-2-161	13.2 x 10.1	tab I
RMD V 430	8-2-161	14.0 x 10.2	tab I + II combined
CIL XVI 185	21-7-164	13.6 x 11.0	tab I
RMD I 64	21-7-164	14.0 x 10.0	tab I
		14.2 x 10.2	tab II
CIL XVI 120	18-2-165		tab II; measurements not given
CIL XVI 121	3/4-166	15.0 x 12.0	tab I + II combined
RMD II 120	23/28-3/7-161/167	14.2 x 11.2	tab II
CIL XVI 128	23-3-178	13.0 x 11.5	tab I + II combined
RMD III 184	23-3-178	14.5 x 11.3	tab I + II combined
RMD IV 293	23-3-178	14.2 x 11.2	tab I + II combined
RMD IV 294	23-3-178	14.5 x 11.5	tab I
RMD III 185	23-3-179	14.5 x 11.2	tab I
RMD II 123	1-4-179	14.3 x 11.5	tab I + II combined

ROBIN SEAGER

NOTES ON AMMIANUS MARCELLINUS XVIII

I am grateful for discussion of some of the problems treated here to David Levenson, the members of my graduate class at Florida State University, and the members of the Classics and Ancient History Research Seminar at the University of Liverpool.

> 2.12
> et collecti nocte prouecta impositique omnes, quos lusoriae naues quadra-
> ginta, quae tunc aderant solae, ceperunt, decurrere iubentur per flumen adeo
> taciti, ut etiam remi suspenderentur, ne barbaros sonitus excitaret undarum,
> atque mentis agilitate et corporum, dum hostes nostrorum ignes obseruant,
> aduersas perrumpere milites ripas.

The reading of V is *perrumpere milites*. Rolfe and Pighi (*Aevum* 11, 1937, 376) retain this, with *perrumpere*, like *decurrere*, dependent on *iubentur*, which is, as Seyfarth points out (n.27 *ad loc.*), impossible, given the change from *omnes*, the subject of *iubentur*, to *milites*. Sabbah also keeps *perrumpere milites*, but punctuates with a semi-colon instead of a comma after *undarum*. His translation indicates that he regards *perrumpere* as a historic infinitive. The historic infinitive is very rare in Ammianus, but should not on that account be emended to extinction (cf. *CR* 51, 2001, 57 on Sabbah's text of 29.6.1). But the retention of both *perrumpere* and *milites* together here is possible only with Sabbah's punctuation, and this, as is argued below, is unacceptable. There are two other possible solutions: to read *perrupere* (E) instead of *perrumpere* and retain *milites* as its subject (thus Clark, Seyfarth and De Jonge, who offers no comment), or to keep *perrumpere* as dependent on *iubentur* and delete *milites* (as Eyssenhardt, Novák).

It may be possible to choose between these options. *Pace* Seyfarth (*loc. cit.*), *atque...ripas* should constitute part of the order given to *omnes*. It would be odd if they were instructed to proceed downstream in total silence without also being told what they were supposed to do when they had gone a sufficient distance to escape the notice of the enemy. (It is possible, though not certain, that the clause *dum... obseruant* should be regarded as an authorial insertion, as might be suggested by the use of *nostrorum*.)

It may also be fairly claimed that *atque* reads far more naturally if it is taken as linking the two infinitives *decurrere* and *perrumpere*, both dependent on *iubentur*, than if it is assumed to introduce a new main clause, in which case it is extremely feeble.

It might be claimed in favour of *perrupere* that without it there is no plain statement that the Roman forces succeeded in their objective of crossing the river unobserved. The narrative of the mission is interrupted by the episode of Hortarius' banquet (13) before Ammianus returns to it (14) in the words *cognito denique transitu Romanorum*. But in fact this is a strong argument in favour of *perrumpere*. For Ammianus first to describe Julian's plan, then to reduce its execution to an ablative absolute recording not the execution itself but its eventual discovery by the Germans is a brilliantly economic and powerful way of indicating that its success was inevitable and could therefore be taken for granted.

If these arguments hold good, both the substitution of *perrupere* for *perrumpere* and Sabbah's punctuation are ruled out, and only the deletion of *milites* produces an acceptable text.

6.5-6

ibique principis scripta suscepimus iubentia omni causatione posthabita reuerti Mesopotamiam sine apparitione ulla expeditionem curaturi periculosam ad alium omni potestate translata. (6) quod ideo per molestos formatores imperii struebatur ut, si Persae frustra habiti redissent ad sua, ducis noui uirtuti facinus assignaretur egregium, si fortuna sequior ingruisset, Vrsicinus reus proditor rei publicae deferretur.

Commentators and translators perhaps attach too broad a sense to the phrase *formatores imperii*. Thus Rolfe: 'the mischievous moulders of the empire'; Sabbah: 'maîtres du pouvoir'; Seyfarth: 'die widerwärtigen Lenker des Reichs'; Hamilton: 'those who moulded the policy of the government'.

Sabbah observes (n.186 *ad loc.*) that *formator* can mean either 'creator' or 'preceptor', and prefers the latter here as appropriate to Eusebius and company, the manipulators of Constantius. In 26.2.7 (cited by De Jonge), the only other occurrence of *formator* in Ammianus, *imperii formatore* undoubtedly refers to an Augustus. De Jonge therefore takes the phrase sarcastically: the courtiers wield the power that should in fact belong to Constantius.

This is by far the most attractive interpretation if *imperii* = 'of the empire', but it is at least worth considering that *formatores imperii* might mean 'authors of the order', i.e. the letter of Constantius ordering Ursicinus to return to the East; cf. *ex imperio* in 18.6.5, referring to the emperor's original letter summoning Ursicinus to court, which this second letter countermanded. The only other instance of *formator* = 'author' recorded in *TLL* is Ennod.*Opusc.*5.6: *ut essem clarorum uersuum seruata lege formator*. But the use of the verb *formare* in this sense is of course common; see *OLD* sense 8 and add Suet. *Dom.*20.

The implication that the emperor was being manipulated by his courtiers or had surrendered his power to them is even more clearly present on this assumption. The choice of a phrase that might at first sight seem appropriate only to an emperor, the use of *imperium* to describe the letter and the plural *formatores* should all be seen as ironic in the light of what should and would have happened if Constantius had been in control.

6.8

... Nisibin propere uenimus utilia paraturi, ne dissimulantes obsidium Persae ciuitati superuenirent incautae.

The sense of the striking phrase *dissimulantes obsidium* is almost universally agreed to be that the Persians desired to besiege Nisibis but pretended that they did not in order to secure the advantage of surprise. Thus, in various formulations, Rolfe, Seyfarth and Hamilton. (Sabbah keeps V's *ni* instead of *ne*, which is preferred by all other recent editors. He translates: 'des dispositions qui auraient été salutaires, si les Perses, en camouflant leur attaque, n'étaient pas tombés sur la cité à l'improviste'. But this would surely require *superuenissent*, even if *obsidium* could mean merely 'attack' rather than 'siege'.)

This interpretation presents two problems, one of sense, one of consistency within Ammianus' account. It is difficult to conceive what might be meant by 'they concealed their intention of besieging the city in order that the eventual siege might come as a surprise'. The preparations for a major siege are surely such that they can hardly be undertaken unbeknownst to the potential victims. Moreover, Ammianus elsewhere consistently suggests that on this campaign the Persians wished to avoid time-consuming sieges. In 18.6.3f. he claims that in the previous autumn the defector Antoninus had persuaded the Persians to change their strategy and give up their customary practice of besieging cities in favour of an attempt to overrun the whole Roman East in a *Blitzkrieg*. Consistently with this decision, the main Persian force did not on this occasion besiege

Nisibis (18.7.8). Similarly at 19.1.3, 6 and 2.1 it is made clear that Sapor had originally had no intention of besieging Amida. There is nothing in 18.6.3f. to suggest that this Persian change of plan was not already known to Ursicinus at the time of his arrival at Nisibis, reported in 18.6.8. How then could Ammianus write that the Persians wanted to besiege Nisibis but tried to conceal this purpose, when he knew perfectly well that they had no such intention?

These considerations combine to suggest that *dissimulantes obsidium* should be differently understood. Whatever the precise meaning of the phrase, the fundamental antithesis in Ammianus' mind here appears to be between a siege and a surprise attack, the perceived danger of which explains the need for haste (*propere uenimus*). Two possible senses for *dissimulantes obsidium* might follow from this: (i) 'refraining from a siege (in favour of a surprise attack)'; (ii) 'pretending they intended a siege (when in fact they did not but planned a surprise attack)'.

The weight of Ammianus' usage favours (i). By far the most common meaning of *dissimulare* in his work is 'ignore / neglect' (20.4.4; 21.3.2; 22.9.10, 14.2; 28.1.24). At 20.4.8 textual problems preclude certainty, but the most likely sense is again 'neglect', as is the case with the two instances of *dissimulatio* at 28.4.5 and 31.5.1. The meaning 'conceal', required by the standard interpretation of *dissimulantes obsidium*, though common in classical Latin, occurs in Ammianus only at 30.1.4.

There is on the other hand no instance of *dissimulare* with a direct object = 'feign'. However, two uses with infinitive are revealing. At 14.7.14 Gallus describes Montius as *contumacem praefectum, quid rerum ordo postulat, ignorare dissimulantem*. In 30.8.8 comes Ammianus' famous description of Valens as *dissimulans scire, quod sunt aliqua, quae fieri non oportet, etiam si licet*. The fundamental point is the same in each case: both men knew the proper way to behave but acted as if they did not. But in 30.8.8 *dissimulans scire* must mean 'ignoring / neglecting the fact that he knew', whereas in 14.7.14 *ignorare dissimulantem* can only mean 'pretending that he did not know'. Thus 14.7.14 offers some support for the view that *dissimulantes obsidium* could mean 'pretending (they intended) a siege'.

A further practical argument militates in favour of this interpretation: the point of the Persian tactic described by *circumuallato murorum ambitu* (18.6.10). This circumvallation, whatever it was, was obviously ineffective, as Ammianus' own comings and goings make clear. It might, however, be consistent with a halfhearted pretence at a siege, designed to lull the defenders into the belief that they had plenty of time to organize their resistance and so make them vulnerable to a sudden attack.

6.12

When Ursicinus and his party left Nisibis en route for Amida, Ammianus was ordered to take back to the city a young refugee found abandoned on the road some two miles from the city (10). The historian, who would clearly have preferred to leave the boy to his fate, dumped his burden with unceremonious haste and set out to rejoin his comrades. On the way he was, so he claims, nearly captured (11). By way of explanation he offers the following anecdote:

nam cum Abdigildum quendam tribunum fugientem cum calone ala sequeretur hostilis lapsoque per fugam domino seruum deprehensum, cum ego rapido ictu transirem, interrogassent, quisnam prouectus sit iudex, audissentque Ursicinum paulo ante urbem ingressum montem Izalam petere, occiso indice in unum quaesiti complures nos irrequietis cursibus sectabantur.

Doubts about the historicity of this tale were raised by Dillemann (*Syria* 38, 1961, 102) and shared by Seyfarth (n.107 *ad loc.*). The precise temporal reference of *cum ego... transirem* is unclear; it could be taken with *deprehensum*, the moment of the slave's capture, or with *interrogassent*, the moment of (the completion of) his interrogation. In either case it is obvious that Ammianus himself would not have had time to overhear what went on, even if the exchanges were audible above the din of galloping hoofs. Hence, of course, Dillemann's objection to the story.

However, Sabbah (n.189 *ad loc.*), followed by De Jonge (*ad loc.*), attempted to defend Ammianus by suggesting that Abdigildus himself, who is not mentioned elsewhere, might have been his source.

Where then and when did Ammianus make his acquaintance? There would seem to be three possibilities. (1) In Nisibis, during the period covered by 18.6.9. (2) At Amudis (cf. 13), if Abdigildus succeeded in making his way there, or later at Amida. (3) Through a fortuitous meeting on the actual flight to Amudis: it might even be argued that the change to the plural at the end of 12 is significant and that *nos* means 'Abdigildus and me'. (This may be what Sabbah assumes, since he is the only translator to render *nos* as 'nous' rather than 'me' or 'mich'.) It would, however, be difficult to reconcile this with the series of first person singulars in 13; one might expect at least *praegressi* and *inuenissemus*. At all events, if Abdigildus is to figure as Ammianus' source, he and Ammianus must have been together either at Amudis or subsequently elsewhere, regardless of whether they had already met at Nisibis.

But there is another more important question to be asked: not 'How and when did Ammianus get his information from Abdigildus?' but 'What information could Abdigildus have had to impart?' For in fact Abdigildus could not have been a witness to the details of the slave's interrogation any more than Ammianus. *Lapso* and *deprehensum* must refer to more or less the same moment, at which the slave was captured while his master made his escape. It must surely follow that the master was well out of earshot before the interrogation of the slave took place, even if the enemy wasted no time in fruitless pursuit of Abdigildus before questioning their captive. Ammianus' credit cannot be saved by appeal to Abdigildus.

It remains, however, to consider how much of Ammianus' story must be rejected. One might of course dismiss the whole episode, including the very existence of Abdigildus, but this is hardly necessary. It would not be unreasonable to accept that Ammianus and Abdigildus met in one of the ways indicated above and exchanged accounts of their respective adventures. It would then have been instantly apparent that the group Ammianus had passed had almost certainly been Abdigildus' slave and his captors. That he would have been interrogated could have safely been assumed. Only the questions asked and answers given need be relegated to the realm of invention or, to put it more charitably, (not implausible) conjecture.

6.22

Grumbates, Chionitarum rex nobis quidem aetate media rugosisque membris,
sed mente quadam grandifica multisque uictoriarum insignibus nobilis.

Thus V. The most common solution is to read *nobilis, aetate quidem media*, though *notabilis* has also been mooted. In either case it must be assumed that the adjective stands apart from the following ablatives, since one cannot rationally be described as *nobilis* or even *notabilis* for being middle-aged and arthritic. But neither reading is at all attractive in the light of the occurrence of *nobilis* so soon afterwards.

Any acceptable solution must respect the antithesis Ammianus is clearly drawing between Grumbates' present physical decrepitude on the one hand and his continuing loftiness of mind and the proofs of his past successes on the other. If one supposes, as all editors do, that *quidem* belongs immediately before *media*, two possibilities suggest themselves.

The first is palaeographically more attractive, namely that *nobis aetate* conceals *mobilitate*. The statement that Grumbates was now only moderately mobile would accord well with the allusion to his shrivelled limbs. However, it must be conceded that *TLL* records no instance of *mobilitas* = 'physical mobility' qualified by *media* or any other adjective of degree. If this be deemed an insuperable objection, a palaeographically more adventurous suggestion may be canvassed.

This involves the assumption that beneath *nobis aetate* there lies buried a noun in the ablative which must meet the following criteria: (a) it ends in *-tate* (b) it makes sense when combined with *media* (c) it stands in meaningful contrast with *mente quadam grandifica*. The obvious candidate would be *proceritate*. A contrast between Grumbates' middling physical stature and the lofty aspirations of his mind would give admirable sense.

The phrase *proceritate media* creates no problems. The noun occurs with numerous adjectives of degree, ranging from *enormis* (Suet.*Vit.*17.2) and *uasta et ardua* (Gell. 9.11.15, Amm. 25.10.14) by way of *eximia* (Flor. 1.38.10) and *magna* (Plin., *HN* 16.174) to *exigua* (Rufin., *Greg.Naz.* 3.10.3) and *pedalis* (Chalc., *Comm.* 284). Most relevant to the present passage is *proceritate perquam modica* at Plin., *NH* 16.65. It may also be noted that *media statura* is found at Liv. 7.10.7, *media magnitudo* at Plin., *NH* 10.8, 21.19, *D.*34.2.31 (Labeo).

Bibliography:

The following are referred to by author's name only:-

P. De Jonge, *Philological and Historical Commentary on Ammianus Marcellinus XVIII* (1980).

W. Hamilton, *Ammianus Marcellinus, The later Roman Empire (A.D.354-378)* (1986).

J. C. Rolfe, *Ammianus Marcellinus I* (1935).

G. Sabbah, *Ammien Marcellin, Histoire II* (1970).

W. Seyfarth, *Ammianus Marcellinus, Römische Geschichte II* (1968).

NICK HIGHAM

ARTHUR, JOSHUA AND THE ISRAELITES: HISTORY AND ITS PURPOSES IN EARLY NINTH-CENTURY NORTH WALES

As a history undergraduate in the early 1970s at the Victoria University of Manchester, I had the considerable good fortune to be taught Ancient History by Cosmo Rodewald, and so benefit from his exceptional gifts as a dedicated teacher. He was also a most generous tutor in other respects, both in the assistance he provided to anyone genuinely interested in his subject and also as regards the warmth of his hospitality, throwing his home open on numerous occasions to entertain students and colleagues alike. The following essay on a rather later Latin text than those to which he introduced me is offered in his memory in appreciation of a great teacher and an open-hearted human being.

In the fourth regnal year of Merfyn ap Gwriad of Gwynedd (*c.*829/30), a writer working at, or at least for, his court in North West Wales set about writing a *sermo* now long known as the *Historia Brittonum*. This proved a very popular work during the Middle Ages, with numerous variant copies produced, and we are seriously disadvantaged by not having a particularly early recension (Faral 1929 offers the earliest: BL Harley MS 3859, of *c.*1100).

This problem of a highly complex textual history has been the source of numerous difficulties of interpretation, not least of which are issues of authorship and historical reliability. All those who have accepted the late attribution to 'Nennius' (more properly *Ninnius*: see most recently Field 1996), have also accepted the preface which is found only in the handful of texts derived from the Corpus Christi College, Cambridge, MS. 139, written in 1164. Both attribution and preface are, perforce, absent from all other, and earlier manuscripts, and this must weigh against their claim to be part of the original text of *c.* 829-30, as has been recognised for at least three quarters of a century (Chadwick & Chadwick 1932, 153; more recently, Dumville 1972-4). That said, David Howlett (1998, 103) has latterly offered a rather different defence of the originality of this preface, suggesting that it was composed in the same Cambro-Latin style as the main ninth-century text, which might imply that it was not so far distant from the original as Dumville had supposed. Be that as may be, this preface, which is published in detail but without translation by Dumville (1975-6), famously claims, *inter alia*, that I:

> 'have heaped up everything that I have found, as much from the annals of the Romans as from the chronicles of the holy fathers (that is, of Jerome, Eusebius, Isidore [and] Prosper), and from the annals of the Scots [Irish] and Saxons [English], and what many learned men and scribes have tried to write down from the traditions of our ancient [?times]. For what reason I am unaware, whether because of very frequent plagues or disasters of warfare, they have left it rather intractable.'

This notion of a 'heaping up' has encouraged many historians in the twentieth century to imagine that the text contains comparatively unaltered and much earlier source materials (the classic statement is that of Myres in Collingwood and Myres 1936, 329-30, but see also Hanning 1966, 91). It is David Dumville's great achievement that he has demonstrated the weakness of this approach, and begun the process of redefining the style of this work as a 'synchronising history' of a type common in Ireland at this date (Dumville 1986). This may be too narrow a label, however, and Thomas Charles-Edwards proposed (1991) that we should also think of this as a 'synchronistic history', which exhibits characteristics of both *historia gentis* (the history of a people) and *historia ecclesiastica* (Christian history). Latterly, the *Historia* has been reviewed once more and interpreted as a full, national pseudo-history (Coe & Young 1995), albeit with considerable debts to a wider Cambro-Irish intellectual community (Dumville 1994). It has additionally been heralded as a particularly fine example of the sophisticated 'biblical style' of Welsh Latin text (Howlett 1998, 74-83), within which the authenticity of specific sections as original to the text – including those on Patrick and Arthur – may be capable of being demonstrated stylistically.

What became clearer during the course of the nineteen-nineties was the extent to which we should see this as an authored text, and not just a collection of pre-existing source materials lumped crudely together by a poorly qualified copyist and editor.

Although it is not clear from internal evidence what title, if any, the author intended his work should bear, we should be in no doubt that it was written as a history, within the context in which that term was understood at the time. Certainly it has all of a moral purpose, motivation, causation and consequence. It is a story which focuses on one ethnically defined community within Britain and which is constructed in part at least against other communities. More particularly, it offers a unique but complex, political and ideological position of immediate relevance to the court of King Merfyn, and in that respect it must be viewed as a text written for pressing and current, political purposes. Like the works of Gildas and Bede, this is a providential work, which develops its story via exposition of the relationship between God and His people as modelled on the Testaments. It is therefore, a story about both retribution and redemption, and one which seeks to place the Britons, as a people, in the present, the past and the future, in an honourable and valued position within salvation history. As such, this is a text which seeks to develop a nationalistic agenda and which has been worked up by a member of the local establishment, primarily for consumption within that same establishment but also, to a lesser extent, by some at least of its competitors.

The actual name of the author is of relatively little significance. We know of a clerical author named *Ninnius* in the early ninth century and he may have been the author of this work, but our information about him is so slight that there is little difference between an ascription to this named author and the far safer assumption which is followed here: the work is presently best considered anonymous.

The *Historia* has traditionally been used by scholars for a variety of purposes, chief among which has been as a source of information to be mined for facts concerning the fifth and sixth centuries, and particularly Arthur's role therein. However, many of the source materials used seem only to date to the late eighth or early ninth centuries, so to the generation of its author or perhaps of his parents (Dumville 1986). Take, for example, the list of *civitates* (66), which it is usually assumed was original to the *Historia* and written by the same author, although it follows the *Annales* and genealogies in the Harleian text. While the total of 28 towns presumably derives from Gildas (*DEB* iii, 2, in Winterbottom 1978), the actual sites chosen are clearly not consistent with a date much earlier than 800, even if some of the unidentified names have not been made up by the author (a possibility mooted in Jackson 1938). Most obviously, the English genealogical material incorporated in chapters 57 to 61 includes Offa's son Ecgfrith, so is unlikely to predate his consecration in 787 and may indeed belong to the sole year in which he actually reigned (796). This English-derived material was therefore not quite up-to-date when incorporated in the *Historia c.*829-

30, but it was only one generation adrift. It is highly retrospective as regards its earlier figures and cannot be relied upon without independent verification as evidence for a much earlier epoch, despite the reservations recently argued by Charles-Edwards (1991).

We should focus, therefore, on what this work can tell us about the thought world of its author and his political and ideological objectives in writing it (as Hanning 1966; Dumville 1986, 1994). It was, after all, as far as we know, the first work of its kind to be written by a British scholar since Gildas's historical introduction to his polemical attack on the rulers and clerical elite of his own day, in the late fifth or early- to mid-sixth century. It is only in this context that we can begin to understand his references to Arthur and the other putative figures of history alongside whom he makes a brief appearance.

To recapitulate to this point, therefore, the *Historia Brittonum* is a history which offers a vision across time from a particular British (or Welsh) perspective, and which has obvious (and less obvious) debts as regards its specifics to a variety of other sources. It is, however, not a simple amalgam of other existing pieces. It should be read as a highly original piece. Indeed, it must be stressed that its originality has to date generally been underestimated. Like much other early- to central-medieval history, it is important to realise that this is an ideological and rhetorical tract, which has been written both for, and against, particular ideas and specific groups.

At a detailed level, this is a work which has been written very much with Merfyn and his patronage in mind, and to a significant extent against other rulers, both within Wales and without. There is sufficient internal evidence for us to be confident that it was written in an area under Merfyn's control and quite possibly at his court, for the king himself. That is the social logic of the text. It is in that context a work of dynastic propaganda, the function of which was to validate and sustain Merfyn's kingship. This does not mean that it was necessarily written by a north Welshman: Asser's *vita* of Alfred, for example, provides a significant parallel, where an outsider under royal patronage and protection was the author of a highly supportive, personal history. In fact, the few internal clues available suggest that the author had a particular knowledge of, and interest in, the central or southern marches, and he even reveals to us that he has been, in the past, in Gwent (72) and the upper valley of the Wye (73). His knowledge of Old Welsh, Latin, Old English and perhaps some Old Irish (Dumville 1986, although there may be some doubt of his competence in Old Welsh as a written language: Coates & Breeze 2000, 37) points to a multi-cultural background which was unlikely to fit particularly well with what little we know of Gwynedd. Rather, such suggests the more cosmopolitan interface between southern Wales and England, perhaps in a Welsh monastery or minster-type community in an area of Irish influence such as Builth or Brycheiniog, or Gwent to the south. He seems also to have ingested current ideas about Old Testament comparisons for local events and individuals, which were, by the 790s, beginning to circulate via works composed in Carolingian France (Garrison 2000). This suggests that the author was close to continental scholarship, with access to several recent Carolingian texts. He was perhaps attracted to Gwynedd by a patron who was in need of the diversity of his intellectual skills and talents, in much the same way that Alcuin left York for Charlemagne's court a generation earlier, and Asser departed St David's two later to join Alfred's circle. These parallels would suggest a figure whose learning was well-known even outside his immediate environment. Once in Gwynedd, however, the author seems to have been keen to present himself as more *Guenedotian* than the *Guenedotians* (the people of Gwynedd), and there should be little doubt that his text was written expressly for Merfyn and his circle.

Other than the little which can be surmised from the text itself, we know virtually nothing regarding the context of this work or the purposes of its author. However, among other objectives, this work seems to have been written to attempt two things which are far from compatible one with the other. In the first place it tries to engage with, to explain and to an extent chronicle the transition of Britain from British to Saxon control. In the second, it attempts to defend the providential status of the Britons as a favoured people of the Lord, to write them into a venerable position within insular history and make connections between the Britons and the origin stories of other ancient peoples, including the Romans.

This combination was problematic within the system of historical causation then in circulation, which found it far easier to associate divine approval with long-term military and political success than with failure. The very obvious facts of political life at this date must be remembered: Anglo-Saxon England was long- established, however its origins and early development should be viewed. To these facts we will return.

Our author clearly found his two pre-existing narratives of redemption, by Gildas and Bede, somewhat at odds with his perception of his own mission. Gildas had assumed that his British countrymen should be equated with the Israelites but at the same time indicted them as both wicked and cowardly. These themes were taken up and exploited by Bede in turn, who reversed the characterization he found in Gildas and claimed, albeit implicitly, for his own 'English or Saxon' people the status of God's chosen race within Britain at least from the conversion era onwards, relegating the Britons to a marginal position excluded from divine approval. In the early ninth century, faced both by these well-established narratives and by the very fact of Anglo-Saxon England and its undoubted successes, it required all sorts of rhetorical stratagems, selected omissions, imaginative additions and wholesale manipulations of received text, to contest the pre-existing vision of the Britons and Saxons and claim that the Britons of the present were both courageous and beloved by the Lord.

Central to these processes of re-envisioning the past for contemporary purposes is Chapter 56, the chapter in which Arthur is portrayed as if an 'historical' figure and a 'real' player in the events of the late fifth to early sixth centuries. This is one the most commonly read pieces of medieval text, and on it is constructed pretty well the whole matter of the 'historical' Arthur, from the *Annales Cambriae* and *Historia Regum Britanniae* onwards. I will suggest here that this Arthur is rhetorically constructed to serve particular and very immediate purposes within the text, and that the author was knowingly constructing an historical mythology for his own 'British' people, and more particularly for King Merfyn (see further Higham 2002, 98-169). The 'truth' of this history lay not primarily in the past but in the present, when it served transparently political, factional and nationalistic causes, and it should be approached not literally but metaphorically and typologically.

This is not, of course, the only occurrence of Arthur in the *Historia Brittonum*, for he is introduced as a character in two of the *mirabilia* which constitute chapters 67-75 of the Harleian text. Arthur is, in both, part of folk etymologies attached to what were probably in both instances burial mounds of prehistoric date in the upper Wye Valley. Oliver Padel has argued persuasively (1994) for the 'historical' Arthur of chapter 56 to have derived from the folkloric Arthur of chapter 73, but this is far too big an issue to be dealt with here. Suffice it to note, therefore, that stories which featured Arthur had already by the early ninth century come to be used within vernacular folk etymologies of two local names which were apparently already known to the author when he came to write the *Historia*. Indeed, one was a place which he claimed to have visited. In default of any other option, this may well have been where he found the name which he then deployed in the 'historical' passage. These occurrences require that Arthur was then already a significant figure within Brittonic folklore. It should be stressed that our author does not seem to have invented the name himself. Nor does the form of the name, which consistently has Arthur as opposed to Artguir/Arthwyr in Medieval Welsh, allow us to argue that it derives solely from the vernacular idiom 'Bear-man'. Rather, direct descent of the name from Latin Artorius underlies these stories and this author's own use of the name.

Let us focus on the 'historical' passage itself. Chapter 56 is, in Latin, only 245 words in length. Arthur is not introduced until after the first two sentences (of 32 words), which deal with the numerical growth of the Saxons in Britain and how authority passed from Hengist to his son. Nor does he have any part to play either in the last two sentences, totalling a further 47 words, which revert to the same theme and the arrival with reinforcements of barbarian kings from Germany. The 'Arthurian' passage is strictly, therefore, only 186 words long. It is inserted between two sets of remarks about the Saxons, which derive primarily from Bede's *Historia Ecclesiastica* (Colgrave and Mynors 1991), whose various references to Hengist (i,15), Octa, Oeric (ii,5), Ida (v,24) and the influx of immigrants from Germany (i,15) they loosely paraphrase, albeit with additional, but probably imaginative, details added in.

The 'Arthurian' filling of this Saxon sandwich seems entirely original to the text, and the construction should be read as this author's, and not a result of his merely copying some pre-existing source. There is a clear logic to the ordering of these three blocks. The first 'Saxon' section establishes the threat. The 'Arthurian' text then proclaims British successes against the Saxons under God's protection, which spells out very clearly just where this episode and the participants within it belong in providential history. Then the second 'Saxon' passage describes the response of the defeated English, who brought in overwhelming forces from Germany along with their kings. In very general terms, therefore, it was the Britons who won all the victories mentioned within this text, who fought heroically, and who enjoyed the support of both Christ and the Virgin Mary on the battle field. That they finally lost is acknowledged only by default and is to be understood only against the moral juxta- positioning of the two sides. Like Bede writing of Rædwald (*HE* ii, 12), for example, this author felt that it was acceptable to acknowledge the victory of the 'baddies' provided they had overwhelming numerical superiority. Therefore mass migration by the English was an essential part of the explanation of the loss of Britain from a British perspective. One can almost hear the shouts of "unfair" and "cheat", and heart-rendering appeals to the great referee in the sky.

The 'Arthurian' passage consists of a single, introductory sentence, which contextualises Arthur and positions him within the author's vision of contemporary 'British' society, then a group of eight interconnected sentences detailing eleven of his glorious victories. There is a brief concluding sentence, which describes Arthur's fantastic achievements at Badon, then provides a separate and concluding phrase of just six words which sums up and emphasises his achievements. The theme of the conclusion, that he was 'victorious in all his campaigns', connects neatly with the introductory sentence, in which 'Arthur fought against them [the Saxons] in those days, together with the kings of the British; but he was their leader in battle'. This is one of several indications that the text as we have it is unchanged from the original, as David Howlett has recently argued on very different grounds.

There are several features which spring immediately to our attention. One is the sense in which, excluding chapter 73, Arthur is entirely contained within this specific context, and has no part to play in this text other than as an iconic, Christian, British war-leader against the Saxons in this rhetorical interlude inserted between two references to Saxon immigration and the growth of Anglo-Saxon power inside Britain. His exploits are used here to break up the otherwise depressing story of Germanic occupation, for powerful ideological and rhetorical purposes, within the context of an author who himself identified cogently with the Britons and expected his primary audience to react in the same way. Arthur provides a very necessary 'feel-good' factor at this point in the tale.

Secondly, Arthur is positioned exceptionally loosely in terms of the internal dating of the narrative. That might not be a matter of much concern in some other early medieval texts, but this author was as interested in the passage of time as was Bede and was careful to make sure he located such figures as Vortigern and Patrick with some precision. Arthur is, by contrast, located only by the phrase *In illo tempore* with which the author began his initial remarks about the Saxons, then the *Tunc* with which he began the Arthurian passage proper. Thereafter, Ida and other unnamed Anglo-Saxon kings were introduced as a consequence of an appeal to Germany '*dum* they were defeated in all their battles'. This appeal carries resonances of the two British appeals to Rome against the Picts and Scots, as described first by Gildas and then by Bede, and then, of course, of the subsequent appeal to Germany for mercenaries, which again Bede distilled in essence from Gildas. Our author knew both and his *auxilium a Germania petebant* perhaps owes something to Bede's *de transmarinis partibus in auxilium uocarent* (i,14). But that is to digress. The point I am seeking to make is that Arthur's chronology in this text is far less clearly marked than that of other early figures whose putative deeds the author described. There is no attempt to even denote the number of years across which he won his great battles, so his years of service, to compare with the regnal years which occur throughout the following sections of his work. His presence lacks any clear positioning within the wider framework of the author's vision of British history.

Thirdly, this passage is infused with biblical number. This is only to be expected, perhaps, since so too is the previous section dealing with Patrick, but the fact does little to inspire confidence in the detail. So, for example, Arthur's name occurs three times and he won 12 battles. This emphasises the rhetorical construction of the text. If we look in a little more detail at the points in this story at which his name actually appears, the first reference introduces Arthur as the overall military leader, leading the warriors of the British kings; the second stresses his achieving victory while bearing the emblems of the Virgin and slaughtering the *pagani* under the protection of both Mary and Christ, and the third positions him as the superhuman hero who killed 960 men in a single charge at Badon. The 12 battles imply that Arthur should be equated with the Saviour, so confirming and reinforcing the connections made in the second reference to 'Our Lord Jesus Christ'.

We have, therefore, an Arthur portrayed as the paramount military leader of the Britons, an invariably successful Christian soldier and a great warrior who personally achieved heroic deeds. He is constructed against the numerous but pagan Saxons, who were invariably defeated in battle and whose death and destruction God encompassed via the heroic Arthur as an agent of divine will. Arthur is, therefore, a saviour figure and a warrior type of the messiah for his people.

To develop our understanding of this Arthur figure, it is helpful to explore his role in the wider narrative which our author was developing. Arthur's comparatively brief appearance follows lengthy passages devoted to the careers of both Vortigern and St. Patrick, the former of nineteen chapters and the latter of five. Vortigern's reign was characterised by the arrival of the Saxons, which the author viewed as the great national disaster of the sub-Roman period, and for which he held Vortigern, and Vortigern alone, wholly responsible. He attempted, however, to mitigate the moral consequences of that disaster, by introducing several virtuous figures who contested variously with the satanic Vortigern or with the Saxons. So St. Germanus preached at Vortigern and sought to convert him, to mitigate his evil and to provide for the son he had putatively sired incestuously on his own daughter. The boy, Emrys, whom the author revealed as the great Ambrosius Aurelianus of Gildas's text, interpreted the prophesy provided by the magical contest between the red and white worms, to which we shall return. So too did Vortigern's putative son Vortimer defeat the Saxons in four highly contrived battles which were constructed in part at least on the basis of Bede's *Historia*, and are most unlikely to be factual. The author's historical method relied heavily on the construction of paired characters, either in harness (as St. Germanus and Vortimer, for example) or in opposition (as Vortimer and Hengist), and this is a form of construction which influenced his portrayal of Arthur as well.

Having read Bede, our author was aware that the earlier writer had presented the whole British people as sinful and in rebellion against God, which was a theme which had then been substantially developed to his own rhetorical advantage from Gildas. The purpose here was to contest this positioning of the Britons as a race, and argue instead that they had a special place in providential history. He therefore separated out Vortigern, as a uniquely wicked type of anti-Christ, from the wider British people, and so insulated the race from the viciousness and sinfulness of this one ruler, so as to protect the status of the Britons as a people of the Lord in the present.

Gildas had referred (*DEB* xxiii, 2) to the council advising the *superbus tyrannus* (whom Bede later called Vortigern) to call in the Saxons as: "'the silly princes of Zoan", as has been said, "giving foolish advice to Pharaoh"'. However, he thereafter abandoned this analogy with the history of the Israelites in Egypt and turned to the deeds of the Assyrians (xxiv, 2), and ultimately the sack of Jerusalem by the Babylonians (i, 4,5) as the principal biblical metaphors by which to inject meaning into his account of the Saxon revolt, the killing or enslavement of his people and the destruction of Britain's towns. The author of the *Historia Brittonum*, however, seems to have been particularly attracted by the comparison between Vortigern and Pharaoh, and developed the analogy for his own purposes. His St. Patrick was, therefore, explicitly compared with Moses, and constructed as a prophet-figure for the Britons whose role it was to lead them from a metaphorical Egypt, under the inimicable Vortigern, to the Promised Land. Patrick begins as a captive among the Irish in the time of Vortigern, much as the Israelites were captives in Pharaoh's Egypt. Thereafter he preached the Gospel for forty years, achieved many miracles and (54): 'fasted for forty days and forty nights on the summit of a Eile hill...; and on that hill that reached to the skies, he gently asked three petitions for those of the Irish who had received the faith... On that hill he blessed the peoples of Ireland, and he climbed it in order to pray for them and to see the fruits of his labour'.

The positioning of Patrick as a Moses figure is to this point implicit, although far from difficult to decipher. Thereafter, in chapter 55, the connection is made explicit, for 'In four ways Patrick is like Moses: in talking with an angel in the burning bush; secondly he fasted on a mountain for 40 days and 40 nights; thirdly, both alike were 120 years old; fourthly no man knows his tomb... The matter demands that more should be said of St. Patrick, but nevertheless I must be brief, to shorten my sermon'.

Our author took this material from Irish hagiographical texts (primarily Tirechan's *Memorandum*), but he was biblically literate and presumably knew that the later passages derive verbatim from the last chapter of the Book of Deuteronomy. In verse nine thereof, reference is made to Joshua: 'And Joshua the son of Nun was full of the spirit of wisdom; for Moses had laid his hands upon him: and the children of Israel hearkened unto him, and did as the Lord commanded Moses'. There follows the Book of Joshua. Joshua is presented in the Bible as the universally victorious martial leader of his people, under God's guidance, who led the twelve tribes of the Israelites across the Jordan, picking up twelve stones as they crossed from the river bed. During the first twelve chapters of this Book, he won battle after battle against the Canaanites under divine guidance and took control of the land.

As the great prophet Moses was succeeded by the war leader Joshua, therefore, so too was the British Moses-figure, St. Patrick, followed in this text by the British Joshua-figure of Arthur. The twelve tribes of Israel, the twelve stones and the twelve chapters of the Book of Joshua which detail his victories are paralleled by Arthur's twelve victories over the Saxons (Higham 2002, 141-4).

The connection is entirely implicit, but the author made it relatively simple to unravel for those of his audience who knew the Bible. At the start of Judges, the book which follows Joshua, we find:

'After the death of Joshua the children of Israel consulted the LORD, saying, Who shall go up before us against the Canaanites, to be the leader in battle?'

The phrase used of Joshua's role is *dux bellum*, a somewhat tautological phrase meaning 'war-leader of war', or 'general in war'. The author of the *Historia Brittonum* used almost the same phrase of Arthur, who *ipse dux erat bellorum*. Since there immediately follows the list of twelve battles, the author perhaps substituted the plural in recognition of these numerous individual engagements. This is the only occurrence of these two words in combination in the Bible, and there can be little doubt that our author derived it from this passage. This would seem to confirm that his implicit portrayal of the British Arthur as a metaphorical Joshua of the Israelites was entirely intentional.

That said, the phrase *dux bellum* does occur in three other works written after Jerome wrote the Vulgate but before the *Historia*. It was used by Sulpicius Severus in a very similar context in his *Chronicle*, almost certainly derived from the same source. It was also used by Bede, in both of his two chronicles, of St. Germanus as commander of the Britons in the Halleluia Victory, perhaps under the same stimulus, but he reverted to the language of his immediate source (Constantius's *Vita Germani*) for the account of this event in his *Historia Ecclesiastica*. Our author certainly had access to the latter but there is no particularly good reason to think that he had read any of these three Chronicles, and plentiful reason to assume that he will have followed the sign-posting in his Irish materials on Patrick to the end of the Book of Deuteronomy, the Book of Joshua and the opening remarks in Judges.

Arthur was, therefore, implicitly being constructed as a Joshua figure, to sustain the metaphorical vision of the Britons as the latter day Israelites, so the Saxons as the Canaanites. This construct should be put alongside that already established of Arthur as a Christ-figure and type of warrior Christ to provide a package of biblical influences on the ways in which he was developed in this text. Joshua and Jesus were, of course, identical names in Hebrew, and the connection between the two seems to have been commonplace in the Early Middle Ages. It seems very likely that it was both the Book of Joshua and the numbering of the apostles which encouraged the author to provide Arthur with twelve battles, particularly seeing as he struggled to reach this total. He appropriated battles from all sorts of existing narratives, none of which seem to have had anything previously to do with an Arthur, Badon included, and even placed four (nos. 2-5) at a single site, which suggests that even his imagination was unequal to the task of assembling twelve strong candidates.

Arthur was, therefore, constructed in defence of the positioning of the Britons within the history of salvation, and to contest divine approval of Anglo-Saxon domination of Britain in the present, which resulted from overwhelming military supremacy rather than right. His connections with both Joshua and Christ were intended to parallel the positioning of Patrick as a type of British Moses, making a complimentary doublet of God-beloved, British characters, and proclaim that even following the *adventus Saxonum* the Britons remained God's chosen people in a British context. By contrast, the Saxons were represented as pagans, implicitly as Canaanites, whom God did not favour and whose land ultimately would be re-conquered by the Israelites.

Such a message had obvious political value in North Wales in 829/30. It may be helpful to look for a moment at the immediate political context. The Britons of Wales had suffered savage Mercian raids, tribute-taking and territorial expansionism over the previous two generations. The construction of Offa's Dyke and a series of forays deep into western Wales underwrote Mercian power under King Offa himself, although we know far less about these events than we might wish. Thereafter the process climaxed in the first two decades of the ninth century, so up to just a decade before this text was written, with what looks like a concerted attempt to conquer both Powys and Gwynedd. This period of expansion had ended in the 820s, as a consequence of an ongoing crisis in Mercia. The conquest of Wales had initially faltered at the death of Cœnwulf I at Basingwerk in 821, and was then halted by the deposition of his brother Ceolwulf I only two years later. His fall initiated a period of dynastic conflict during which the Mercian leadership progressively failed to maintain its wider hegemony across southern Britain. Beornwulf, who supplanted Ceolwulf, was defeated by Ecgberht of the West Saxons when he invaded Wessex, then killed by the East Angles. This disaster and the chaotic state into which Mercia was falling presumably offered cause for renewed hope in Wales that the tide of history was indeed turning at last against the Saxons, or at least against the Mercians, who, after all, constituted their recent experience of the Saxons. Our author betrayed a considerable interest in this text in directly comparable events. So, for example, he noted with some pleasure the collapse of Northumbrian expansionism back in 685, when King Ecgfrith was killed by the Picts. He seems to have sensed that a new cusp moment was now upon his people. He seems even to have been preparing the Welsh to ally themselves with Mercia's English rivals, for he made a number of links between the Britons and Northumbrians and was even prepared to recognise the sanctity of various Northumbrian and East Anglian figures, including Oswald, Cuthbert and Anna. Not so the Mercians, whose kingship was personified above all else by the pagan Penda, who 'was himself the victor through devilish art. He was not baptized and never believed in God'. The failure of his contemporary successors in Mercia may well have seemed in some quarters to be the opportunity for which the Welsh had been waiting.

There is, however, a more particular message to be found here than this general defence of 'Britishness' would imply, which pertains to Merfyn himself. To return to Merfyn, therefore, the king of Gwynedd of the day was the founder of the second dynasty of Gwynedd, who only attained the throne c.825 at the death of his maternal great-uncle and dynastic rival. His reign coincided with the troubles in Mercia and his seizure of the throne may well have been much easier than it otherwise might have been as a consequence of that crisis, following which Mercian war bands had been pulled out of northern Wales. Merfyn arguably came from the Isle of Man, and was certainly not a king's son, so his dynastic position was contestable in the early years of his reign, supposing that there were other faction-leaders around with their own claims to the throne of Gwynedd (see Kirby 1976). The *Historia Brittonum* was clearly written by a supporter, whom internal evidence suggests had come originally from another part of Wales. The *Historia* reads as a text composed to please his royal patron, so to gain some reward, by constructing a polemical text in Merfyn's interest. One purpose of the work was necessarily obfuscation of the sensitive hereditary situation by constructing an historical mythology uniquely supportive of Merfyn's kingship.

The key lies in the contest of the two worms of prophesy (42) as explained through the mouth of the boy Emrys, who is developed from Gildas's Ambrosius. The red worm represents the British dragon and the white the Saxons, and their struggle is a metaphor for the contest for Britain. They fought together three times, 'then the red worm was seen to be weaker, and then was stronger than the white, and drove him beyond the edge of the cloth'. The key stages of this rather complex prophesy were developed within the historical narrative. The author provided a series of British war leaders who had enjoyed successes against foreigners and made implicit connections between each and Merfyn himself. Following the *adventus Saxonum* there were three British generals introduced, each of whom won victories over the Saxons and almost drove them out. The first was Vortimer, Vortigern's son, who putatively won four victories and expelled the Saxons from Thanet for a while (43, 44), the second was Arthur (56), and the third was Urien who led a British alliance in the north which besieged the Saxons on Lindisfarne (63). Thereafter, for a time, the Saxons (42) 'will reach almost from sea to sea', which is a phrase the author found in Gildas's description (*DEB*, xxiv, 1) of the great raid in which the Saxon revolt began. That said, it is a fair summary of the situation in Merfyn's reign, with English kings and aristocracies in secure control of all southern Britain except the Welsh heartlands and Cornwall. The prophesy looked, however, to the resurgence of the Britons thereafter, driving the English *viriliter* right out of Britain: 'but later our people will arise, and will valiantly throw the English people across the sea.'

When looking at the map of Britain at this date from the perspective of Gwynedd, one might well be reminded of the map of Gaul with which all the Asterix books open, with his one free village on the western coast and the rest of the country overrun by the Roman legions. Prophesies which look towards the expulsion of the English provide a common theme in Welsh literature, of course, but its introduction in this text is very early within the history of nationalist works. The form adopted suggests that it was intended for immediate consumption. Emrys's interpretation of the contest of the two worms had been fulfilled, point by point, within the text, up to the red worm being weaker, which aptly described very recent experience. Its revival thereafter, and the final expulsion of the white worm was, therefore, being conceived as an imminent event. What is more, the vision of a red dragon chasing the white out into the seas beyond Britain arguably had a particular meaning at Merfyn's court. The king of Gwynedd was known in the vernacular as Merfyn Frych, 'Merfyn the freckled'. If his highly freckled complexion was accompanied by red or reddish hair, as is commonplace, then the red dragon of prophesy which finally expelled the white from Britain was arguably to be understood as a metaphor for Merfyn himself, who was destined to achieve this marvellous feat in reality.

This is not the only instance of a historical metaphor developed by the author to sustain the image of King Merfyn in the present. In some senses, all of Vortimer, Arthur and Urien should be viewed in this context. So too should Cunedda, the legendary founder-figure of Gwynedd, who had, in chapter 62, come from the northern *Manau Gododdin* and (in chapter 14) expelled the foreigners (the Irish) from 'all the British regions' in the distant past. Merfyn, from the northern *Eu[b]onia*, also called *Manaw* (*HB*8), was being established as a new national hero-figure, who could be expected to do likewise. So too was Patrick putatively called *Mann* or *Maun* prior to his consecration. These wittily conceived connections between Merfyn, the dragon, Cunedda and Patrick should probably be interpreted as subtle panegyric by the author, intended to compliment his patron. Such touches were presumably designed to ensure that his text received as welcoming a reception as possible among its prime audience, which we should conceive as the royal court of Gwynedd gathered around Merfyn's own household.

To conclude, therefore, the *Historia Brittonum* should be conceived as a highly political text written for very specific purposes to do with the political and dynastic situation at the date of composition. These pertained both to the quest for patronage by its immigrant British author, and a desire to achieve this by writing in support of the particular political establishment of the day in North-West Wales. The central meanings of the text relate not to the distant past but to the immediate present, and that is where its truths should be conceived. The treatment of Arthur in this, the earliest securely 'Arthurian' text now surviving, should be read within this contemporary agenda. Arthur's role is a complex one. He is developed as a means of mitigating the rhetorical impact of Saxon conquest in Britain, so of claiming for the Britons their due status as a people of the Lord. To this purpose, the 'Arthurian' passage is inserted within a description of the rising tide of the Saxon presence, and assertions regarding the weight of numbers which eventually led to the loss of Britain. Over and against the pagan Saxons, is Arthur's implicit depiction as a British-type of Joshua and the more explicit connections with Christ and Mary. So too is Arthur the hero-figure par excellence, not just a great leader but a warrior as well. Just as the Lord had 'magnified Joshua in the sight of all Israel' (Joshua iv, 14), so too were Arthur's exploits magnified out of all proportion. That there is a witty allusion to this capacity of Arthur to pile up the bodies of his slain enemies in a text of the Early Welsh poem, *Y Gododdin*, does suggest that this magnification of Arthur as the supreme warrior struck a chord among the audience to which the *Historia Brittonum* was directed (for the text, see Jarman 1988, 64-5).

The key message which this will arguably have imparted to an early ninth-century audience in Gwynedd is that the time was right for the Lord to give back Britain, the birthright of the British people, to its true owners; the prophesy of Emrys was coming to fruition and should now be fulfilled. What Vortimer, Arthur and Urien had each attempted in the past could now be fulfilled under Merfyn's leadership. What sort of reception the *Historia Brittonum* received is unfortunately unknown, but it was eagerly copied and widely distributed over the following century or so, so it was apparently welcomed in elite circles. The author of *Armes Pryddein* probably knew it around a century later and the *Annales Cambriae* was certainly constructed with an excellent knowledge of this the Arthurian section (Higham 2002, 201-2). We do not, regrettably, know whether or not its author was rewarded with lands or ecclesiastical preferment, but one or both seem highly likely. If we take note of the obvious parallel of Asser writing for King Alfred just two generations later, the omens at least look good.

Did Merfyn take any notice of the messages embedded in the rhetoric of the text? He did not launch a crusade against the English, so in that sense the answer must be an emphatic 'no'. Instead, he was presumably one of the Welsh kings who were reputed by the *Anglo-Saxon Chronicle* to have accepted the 'overkingship' of Ecgberht of the West Saxons in 830. Indeed, the rather obvious omission of Wessex and its dynasty from the *Historia* may well be connected with the development of this relationship and the arrival of West Saxon emissaries at Merfyn's court at just about the same time as our author was composing his *magnum opus*. Merfyn did not, therefore, take up the baton of attempting to throw out the English from Britain but seems to have restricted his activities far closer to home.

That said, Merfyn's son and grandsons did establish themselves as the rulers of almost all Wales, and some at least adopted a hostile position towards the English. It may well be that the *Historia*, with its claims on behalf of Merfyn as the leader of the entire British race against their enemies, privileged his successors vis-à-vis other Welsh dynasties and assisted them in rather more local political ambitions than its author seems to have sought to expound. Certainly, he eroded the status and authority of other lineages, deriving that of Powys, for example, from a slave ancestor and those of the central marches from the terrible Vortigern himself. The briefest comparison of his text with the inscription on the approximately contemporary Pillar of Eliseg (Nash-Williams 1950, 123) demonstrates just how factional was his portrayal of the past.

Where contemporary reality ended, and panegyric began, is unclear now and was perhaps even unclear at the time. Certainly, it would be a great mistake to imagine that anyone took the *Historia Brittonum* seriously. Merfyn and his courtiers presumably enjoyed this 'sermon', and it provided useful political messages of immediate relevance within the household of a king whom many must have viewed at the time as a usurper. We can be reasonably confident that the Arthur figure of the *Historia* would have been understood in 829/30 primarily by virtue of his capacity to bolster the career of Merfyn in the present, and will have been read and heard as such. His great victories, his connections with Mary and Christ, his leadership of all the forces of the British kings, and his implicit role as a latter-day Joshua figure leading his people into a land promised by God, all had valuable meanings in the context of Merfyn's court. He was being constructed as an historical figure at a moment when the Mercian superpower seemed at last to have stumbled, and these must have seemed heady days in North Wales, with all to play for. It was surely these contemporary meanings, not some poorly formed attempt to recover what actually occurred in the distant past, which conditioned the appearance of Arthur in this text. If Arthur was the invincible beloved of Mary, Christ and Joshua, all rolled into one, so too was Merfyn Frych, who was now being invited to position himself in the role of a king capable of completing what Arthur, like Vortimer and Urien, had left incomplete. Now he should take upon himself the role of the red dragon itself, highjack the nationalist agenda and emulate in the present the deeds of Cunedda, Gwynedd's legendary founder in the distant past, who had gloriously expelled the foreigner. This is a potent piece of polemic, particularly given its power to shift attention away from Merfyn's weak hereditary title to the throne onto a highly supportive, but highly contrived, re-configuration of British national mythology. It surely pleased the king and offered him ways to market his kingship to a wider audience, but he was not apparently so naïve as to imagine that the *Historia* offered him a realistic or deliverable policy of ethnic cleansing. There is a great deal of difference between political posturing and the practical steps needed to actually launch a war from Wales against England.

The *Historia* re-worked the past quite imaginatively, therefore, to accord with the needs of a particular political faction in the present. Like others, the 'Arthurian' passage should be read very much in that context. This is not an attempt to recover the past as it occurred, even in the broadest outline, and however badly it was achieved. History was providential, after all, and its purposes lay in the carriage of far greater truths concerning the relationship between God and man than mere chronology and past event. In this context, our author was exercised about the relationship between the Welsh or Britons and the Christian God, and more particularly between King Merfyn and the Lord above. With this established as his goal, it is easy to savour the wit and subtlety of his work and appreciate his success in writing a 'sermon' for his king.

Where does all this leave Arthur? Not well-placed as an historical figure of the fifth to sixth century I fear. I have already suggested (in 1994) that the vision of a great British victory in the 'war of the Saxon federates', which is a common reading of Gildas's *De Excidio*, is seriously misplaced and probably mistaken. There is very little evidence to be had from archaeology which supports the vision of British domination of the lowlands in the late fifth and early sixth centuries, to sustain such readings (despite Dark 2000). Taken together, there seems no contemporary evidence capable of supporting the notion of an 'Age of Arthur'. Nor does the historicity of Arthur himself stand up to scrutiny. His appearance in the *Historia* seems to have been constructed for highly rhetorical purposes, within a framework which was the author's own and not culled from any much older text. We can detect powerful biblical parallels in Arthur's positioning as military commander and as the *victor* in twelve battles. The literary context suggests that he was developed for purposes of mitigation, inserted into an otherwise hopeless narrative to detract from the awfulness of Anglo-Saxon immigration and settlement across so much of Britain, which was a story developed from the author's reading of Bede as much as his understanding of the present. Arthur's characterisation is, therefore, subservient to an over-riding authorial agenda, which is primarily to construct the Britons at the time of writing as a martial people of the Lord. There is no space herein for a pre-existing battle-list, as has so often been suggested (since Chadwick and Chadwick 1932). Nor is there a meaningful title to be construed from *dux bellorum*, derivative perhaps of Late Roman army commanders, for this derives from problems surrounding Joshua's death as portrayed in the Book of Judges. That does not mean that Arthur is entirely fictional, for the name-trail leads backwards, presumably to some such figure as the second-century Dalmatian army officer, Lucius Artorius Castus, whom the philologist K. Malone suggested as long ago as 1925 might underlie the later legend. But there is no real possibility that this Artorius, who led Roman forces from Britain to put down a revolt in Armorica, was anything but a legend in ninth-century Wales, whose name had been 'borrowed' and reworked into indigenous folklore to construct a type of British folk hero. We can be reasonably sure that the Arthur whom the author of the *Historia* positioned with such care within his narrative of redemption carries little with him of Malone's Artorius – or any other of history - beyond the name and a general sense of martial prowess, for his immediate source was apparently folkloric. We know far more about the original than did this author, assuming that is that we have identified the right man, and that is far from certain. The 'historical' Arthur is, therefore, reborn in this text as if a phoenix rising from the ashes, probably in a different time and with a different face to the original. His subsequent rise to great fame originated primarily here, and has no obvious roots in the earlier insular past. One must suspect that no one would have been more surprised at the meteoric rise of this Arthur to great fame than our author, who surely knew better than anyone just how highly contrived a vision of the past he had developed in order to sustain a story focused tightly on present truths. And these were not any truths but particular political and ideological ones pertinent to the kingship of Merfyn ap Gwriad, also known as Merfyn Frych, whom the author rather cleverly connected, metaphorically at least, with the red dragon of the British race. Like Arthur, Merfyn was being presented as a messiah figure, therefore, who was destined to restore to the Britons their island home. But unlike Arthur, Merfyn was flesh and blood at the moment of composition, he was arguably the author's patron and certainly the focal figure in his audience.

Bibliography:

H.M. Chadwick & N.K. Chadwick, *The Growth of Literature* I (Cambridge 1932).

T.M. Charles-Edwards, 'The Arthur of History' in edd. R. Bromwich et al., *The Arthur of the Welsh* (Cardiff 1991) 15-32.

J.B. Coe & S. Young, *The Celtic Sources for the Arthurian Legend* (Llanerch 1995).

R. Coates & A. Breeze, *Celtic Voices English Places: Studies of the Celtic Impact on Place-Names in England* (Stamford 2000).

B. Colgrave & R.A.B. Mynors (ed. and trans.) *Bede: Ecclesiastical History of the English People* (Oxford rev. ed. 1991).

R.G. Collingwood & J.N.L. Myres, *Roman Britain and the English Settlements* (Oxford 1936).

K.R. Dark, *Britain and the End of the Roman Empire* (Stroud 2000).

D.N. Dumville, 'The Corpus Christi "Nennius"', *Bulletin of the Board for Celtic Studies* 25 (1972-4) 369-80

D.N. Dumville, '"Nennius" and the *Historia Brittonum*', *Studia Celtica* 10-11 (1975-6) 78-95.

D.N. Dumville, 'The Historical Value of the *Historia* Brittonum' *Arthurian Literature* 6 (1986) 1-26.

D.N. Dumville, '*Historia Brittonum*: an Insular History from the Carolingian Age' in A. Scharer & G. Scheibelreiter (eds), *Historiographie im frühen Mittelalter* (Wien & Munchen 1994).

E. Faral, *La légende arthurienne: Études et documents, les plus anciens textes* 3 vols (Paris 1929).

P.J.C. Field, 'Nennius and his History' *Studia Celtica* 30 (1996) 159-65.

M. Garrison, 'The Franks as the New Israel' in edd. Y. Hen & M. Innes (eds) *The Use of the Past in the Early Middle Ages* (Cambridge 2000) 114-61.

R.W. Hanning, *The Vision of History in Early Britain* (New York & London 1966).

N.J. Higham, *The English Conquest: Gildas and Britain in the Fifth Century* (Manchester 1994).

N.J. Higham, *King Arthur: Myth-making and History* (London 2002).

D. Howlett, *Cambro-Latin Compositions: Their Competence and Craftsmanship* (Dublin 1998).

K.H. Jackson, 'Nennius and the twenty-eight Cities of Britain' *Antiquity* 12 (1938) 44-55.

A.O.H. Jarman (ed.& trans.), *Aneirin. Y Gododdin* (Llandysul 1988).

D.P. Kirby, 'British Dynastic History in the Pre-Viking Period' *Bulletin of the Board of Celtic Studies* 27 (1976) 81-114.

K. Malone, 'Artorius' *Modern Philology* 22 (1925) 367-74.

V.E. Nash-Williams, *The Early Christian Monuments of Wales* (Cardiff 1950).

O. Padel, 'The Nature of Arthur' *Cambrian Medieval Celtic Studies* 27 (1994) 1-31.

M. Winterbottom, Gildas: The Ruin of Britain and other documents (London and Chichester 1978).